THEOLOGY OF THE NEW TESTAMENT

VOLUME ONE

THEOLOGY
OF THE
NEW TESTAMENT

RUDOLF BULTMANN

VOLUME ONE

SCM PRESS LTD

Translated by Kendrick Grobel from the German
Theologie des Neuen Testaments
published 1948 by
J. C. B. Mohr (Paul Seibeck), Tübingen

334 01622 3

First British edition 1952
published by SCM Press Ltd
26 30 Tottenham Road, London N1 4BZ
Tenth impression 1983

Printed in Great Britain by
Richard Clay (The Chaucer Press) Ltd,
Bungay, Suffolk

ILLUSTRISSIMAE
ST. ANDREAE APUD SCOTOS UNIVERSITATI
OB SUMMUM IN S.S. THEOLOGIA HONOREM SIBI OBLATUM
HUNC LIBRUM
GRATUS VENERABUNDUS
D. D. D.
RUDOLFUS BULTMANN

Contents

PART I

Presuppositions and Motifs of New Testament Theology 1

CONTENTS

PART II

The Theology of Paul 185

CONTENTS

PART ONE

PRESUPPOSITIONS AND MOTIFS
OF
NEW TESTAMENT THEOLOGY

CHAPTER I

The Message of Jesus

1. *The message of Jesus* is a presupposition for the theology of the New Testament rather than a part of that theology itself. For New Testament theology consists in the unfolding of those ideas by means of which Christian faith makes sure of its own object, basis, and consequences. But Christian faith did not exist until there was a Christian kerygma; i.e., a kerygma proclaiming Jesus·Christ—specifically Jesus Christ the Crucified and Risen One—to be God's eschatological act of salvation. He was first so proclaimed in the kerygma of the earliest Church, not in the message of the historical Jesus, even though that Church frequently introduced into its account of Jesus' message, motifs of its own proclamation. Thus, theological thinking—the theology of the New Testament—begins with the *kerygma* of the earliest Church and not before. But the fact that Jesus had appeared and the message which he had proclaimed were, of course, among its historical presuppositions; and for this reason Jesus' message cannot be omitted from the delineation of New Testament theology.

2. The synoptic gospels are the *source for Jesus' message.* Their use as history is governed by the so-called two source theory: i.e. Mark (which we know, however, only in a later redaction) is one source of Matthew and Luke; the other is a collection of Jesus' sayings (Q). Furthermore, throughout the synoptics three strands must be distinguished: old tradition, ideas produced in and by the Church, and editorial work of the evangelists. The critical analysis of these strands cannot be presented here; it is available in my book, *Die Geschichte der synoptischen Tradition,* 2nd ed. (1931). Throughout this book, passages from Mark are cited without the addition of "par." wherever the Matthew and Luke parallels offer no independ-

[3]

ent tradition; "par." is added to a passage from Matthew or Luke wherever a tradition taken from Q is involved. That is what "par." is intended to indicate.*

§ 1. The Eschatological Message

1. The dominant concept of Jesus' message is the *Reign of God.* Jesus proclaims its immediately impending irruption, now already making itself felt. Reign of God is an eschatological concept. It means the regime of God which will destroy the present course of the world, wipe out all the contra-divine, Satanic power under which the present world groans—and thereby, terminating all pain and sorrow, bring in salvation for the People of God which awaits the fulfilment of the prophets' promises. The coming of God's Reign is a miraculous event, which will be brought about by God alone without the help of men.

With such a message, Jesus stands *in the historical context of Jewish expectations about the end of the world and God's new future.* And it is clear that his thought is not determined by the *national* hope then still alive in certain circles of the Jewish people, in which the time of salvation to be brought in by God was thought of as the restitution of the idealized ancient kingdom of David. No saying of Jesus mentions the Messiah-king who is to crush the enemies of the People, nor the lordship of Israel over the earth, nor the gathering of the twelve tribes, nor the joy that will be in the bounteous peace-blessed Land. Rather, Jesus' message is connected with the hope of other circles which is primarily documented by the *apocalyptic* literature, a hope which awaits salvation not from a miraculous change in historical (i.e. political and social) conditions, but from a cosmic catastrophe which will do away with all conditions of the present world as it is. The presupposition of this hope is the pessimistic-

---

* Quotations from the New Testament are given according to the Revised Standard Version (1946), with the kind permission of the copyright owner, Division of Christian Education, National Council of the Churches of Christ in the U.S.A., unless there is an indication to the contrary. "Blt." (= Bultmann's version) means that the author himself translated the passage into German, for which an English equivalent is here offered; "tr." (= translator's version) means that the author quoted only the Greek text, which the translator of this book felt compelled to translate anew in the sense implied by the author's context. Rarely King James or a modern private translation is quoted, and always by name.

dualistic view of the Satanic corruption of the total world-complex, which is expressed in the special doctrine of the *two aeons* into which the world's career is divided: The old aeon is approaching its end, and the new aeon will dawn with terror and tribulation. The old world with its periods has an end determined by God, and when the day He has determined is here, the judgment of the world will be held by Him or by His representative, the Son of Man, who will come on the clouds of heaven; the dead will arise, and men's deeds, good or bad, will receive their reward. But the salvation of the faithful will consist not in national prosperity and splendor, but in the glory of paradise. In the context of these expectations stands the message of Jesus. However, it is free from all the learned and fanciful speculation of the apocalyptic writers. Jesus does not look back as they did upon past periods, casting up calculations when the end is coming; he does not bid men to peer after signs in nature and the affairs of nations by which they might recognize the nearness of the end. And he completely refrains from painting in the details of the judgment, the resurrection, and the glory to come. Everything is swallowed up in the single thought that then God will rule; and only very few details of the apocalyptic picture of the future recur in his words.

The contrast between this aeon and that is barely mentioned. The passages which speak of the "sons of this age" (Lk. 16:8; 20:34f.) and of the reward in the age to come for having followed him (Mk. 10:30) are secondary. The expression "close of the age" (Mt. 13:49) may be genuine tradition, though it is secondary in the parable interpretations (Mt. 13:39f. and 24:3). "The present time," Καιρὸς οὗτος, meaning the remnant of time before the eschatological end, at Lk. 12:56 is probably original, but at Mk. 10:30, as the opposite of "the age to come," is secondary.

But it is evident that Jesus has this conviction: This age has run out. The summary of his preaching in the saying, "The time is fulfilled, and the Reign of God is at hand" (Mk. 1:15), is appropriate. Jesus is convinced that the world's present course is under the sway of Satan and his demons, whose time is now expired (Lk. 10:18). He expects the coming of the "Son of Man" as judge and savior (Mk. 8:38; Mt. 24:27 par. 37 par. 44 par.; [Mt. 10:23; 19:28];

Lk. 12:8f.; [Mt. 10:32f.]; Lk. 17:30).* He expects the resurrection of the dead (Mk. 12:18–27) and the judgment (Lk. 11:31f. par., etc.). He shares the idea of a fiery Hell into which the damned are to be cast (Mk. 9:43–48; Mt. 10:28). For the blessedness of the righteous he uses the simple term "Life" Ζωή (Mk. 9:43, 45, etc.). While he can indeed speak of the heavenly banquet at which they will recline at table with Abraham, Isaac, and Jacob (Mt. 8:11) and also of his hope of drinking wine anew in the Reign of God (Mk. 14:25), he nevertheless also says, "When they rise from the dead, they neither marry nor are given in marriage, but are like angels in heaven" (Mk. 12:25).

2. Thus Jesus does take over the apocalyptic picture of the future, but he does so with significant reduction of detail. What is new and really his own about it all is the certainty with which he says, *"Now the time is come! God's Reign is breaking in! The end is here!"* That is what the following words mean:

"Blessed are the eyes which see what you see!
For I tell you:
Many prophets and kings desired to see what you see and did not see it,
And to hear what you hear, and did not hear it!"
   (Lk. 10:23f. par.)

Now is no time to mourn and fast; this is a time of joy like that of a wedding (Mk. 2:18f.). So he now cries his "Blessed are you!" to the waiting, expectant ones:

"Blessed are you poor, for yours is the Reign of God!
Blessed are you that hunger now, for you shall be satisfied!
Blessed are you that weep now, for you shall laugh!" (Lk. 6:20f. Blt.)

Satan's reign is now collapsing, for "I saw Satan fall like lightning from heaven" (Lk. 10:18).

Signs of the time there are, indeed; but not such as those after which apocalyptic fantasy peers. For "God's Reign comes not so that it can be calculated; and none can say, 'Lo here or there!' For lo, God's Reign is (all at once) in your midst!" (Lk. 17:21 Blt.).

---

* Formulations presumably due to the Church, or words edited by the evangelists are placed in brackets. Lk. 17:30 is perhaps original.

"And if you are told: lo here! lo there! do not go, do not follow them. For as the lightning flashes and lights up the sky from one side to the other, so will it be with the Son of Man in his day" (Lk. 17:23f. Blt.).

The people, it is true, are blind to the true signs of the time; they can well enough interpret the signs of the heavens (clouds and wind) and know when it is going to rain or be hot—why can they not discern the signs of the present? (Lk. 12:54–56). When the fig tree sprouts and gets green men know summer is near; so from the signs of the time they should know that the End is at hand (Mk. 13:28f.).

But what are the signs of the time? He himself! *His presence, his deeds, his message!*

"The blind see, and the lame walk,
   Lepers are cleansed and the deaf hear,
   The dead arise and the poor have the message of salvation pro-
      claimed to them" (Mt. 11:5 par. Blt.).

It can be asked whether these words only express the certainty that the prophetic predictions of salvation (Is. 35:5f.; 29:18f.; 61:1) will presently be fulfilled, or whether Jesus means that their fulfilment is already beginning in his own miracles. Probably the latter. For though he refuses the demand made of him to legitimate himself by a "sign from heaven" (Mk. 8:11f.), he nevertheless sees God's Reign already breaking in in the fact that by the divine power that fills him he is already beginning to drive out the demons, to whom he, like his contemporaries, attributes many diseases: "If I by the finger of God drive out demons, then God's Reign has come upon you!" (Lk. 11:20 par. Blt.). "No one can enter a strong man's house and plunder his goods, unless he first binds the strong man" (Mk. 3:27), hence, since he is robbing Satan of his plunder, it is apparent that Satan has been attacked by one stronger than himself.

All that does not mean that God's Reign is already here; but it does mean that it is dawning. Man cannot hasten the divinely determined course of events, either by strict observance of the commandments and by penance—as the Pharisees supposed—or by driving out the Romans by force of arms—as the Zealots fancied. For "with the Reign of God it is as if a man should scatter seed upon the ground and should sleep and rise night and day, and the seed should sprout and grow, he knows not how. The earth produces

[7]

of itself, first the blade, then the ear, then the full grain in the ear. But when the grain is ripe, at once he sends the harvesters, because the harvest has come" (Mk. 4:26–29 Blt.).

From this *parable of the seed growing of itself*, in which "of itself" is the point, one must not draw the conclusion that God's Reign (or Kingdom) is an entity growing in history; rather it assumes that its coming is a miracle independent of every human act—as miraculous as the growth and ripening of seed, which proceeds without human help or comprehension. It is far from Jesus and the world he moved in to regard the growth of seed as a natural process of development. The meaning of the parable can be clarified by placing beside it a similar one, handed down to us in I Clem. 23, which is intended to picture how certainly the judgment of God will come: "O fools, compare yourselves with a tree, for instance a grapevine! First it casts off its old leaves, then young shoots arise, then leaves, then blossoms, then the tiny clusters, then the full bunch is there. You see how quickly fruit gets ripe. Verily, quickly and suddenly shall God's decree be accomplished. . . ."

Neither do the *parables of the mustard-seed and of the leaven* (Mk. 4:30–32 or Mt. 13:31f. par.) tell of a gradual development of the "Kingdom of God" in history. Their point is the contrast between the minuteness of its beginning and the magnitude of its completion; they do not intend to give instruction about the process which leads from beginning to completion. Both beginning and completion of God's Reign are miraculous, and miraculous is the happening which brings its fulfilment. Then Jesus' presence and activity are understood to be its beginning—that is, if these parables really have for their subject the beginning and completion of God's Reign. That is admittedly uncertain; the related parables in the Shepherd of Hermas (Mand. V 1, 5f.; XI 20f.) about the drop of wormwood which makes a whole jug of honey bitter, and about the hailstone which can cause great pain, have an entirely different meaning. The former intends to illustrate how practice in patience is brought to nought by an attack of wrath; the latter illustrates the power of the Holy Spirit. So it might be that the parables of the mustard-seed and of the leaven originally dealt with the individual and were intended to instruct him, either as a warning or as a consolation, how great a result may grow out of small beginnings.

The introductory formula, "The Kingdom is like" (ὁμοία

ἐστίν) or "is likened" (ὁμοιώθη) in these parables and in Matthew's so-called *Kingdom-of-Heaven parables* (Mt. 13:44, 45; 18:23; 20:1; 22:2; 25:1) does not mean that what is named in the parable is to be directly compared with the Reign of God, but does mean that the parable teaches a truth that in some way applies to the Reign of God—for example, that God's Reign requires sacrifice of men; for when it is said (Mt. 13:45), "The Reign of God is like a merchant," it is clear that the merchant is not a portrait of God's Reign, but that his conduct portrays the attitude required by it. Besides, the introductory formula, frequently at least, is due to the editing of the evangelist; it is missing in the Lucan parallel (14:16) to Mt. 22:2 as well as in all the parables peculiar to Luke. On the interpretation of the parables in general *cf.* Ad. Jülicher, *Die Gleichnisreden Jesus* I 2nd ed. (1899), II 2nd ed. (1910); R. Bultmann, *Gesch. d. synopt. Trad.*, 2nd ed. (1931), 179–222 (where further references are given).

3. All that man can do in the face of the Reign of God now breaking in is this: Keep ready or get ready for it. Now is the *time of decision*, and Jesus' call is the *call to decision*. The "Queen of the South" once came to hear the wisdom of Solomon; the Ninevites repented at the preaching of Jonah—"behold, something greater than Solomon is here! behold, something greater than Jonah is here!" (Lk. 11:31f. par.). "Blessed is he who takes no offense at me!" (Mt. 11:6 par.).

Basically, therefore, *he in his own person is the "sign of the time."* Yet the historical Jesus of the synoptics does not, like the Johannine Jesus, summon men to acknowledge or "believe in" his person. He does not proclaim himself as the Messiah, i.e. the king of the time of salvation, but he points ahead to the Son of Man as another than himself. *He in his own person signifies the demand for decision,* insofar as his cry, as God's last word before the End, calls men to decision. Now is the last hour; now it can be only: either—or! Now the question is whether a man really desires God and His Reign or the world and its goods; and the decision must be drastically made. "No one who puts his hand to the plow and looks back is fit for the Reign of God!" (Lk. 9:62 Blt.). "Follow me, and leave the dead to bury their own dead!" (Mt. 8:22 par.). "Whoever comes to me and does not hate his father and mother, wife and children, brothers and sisters, yes, and even himself, he cannot be my disciple" (Lk. 14:26

par. Blt.). "Whoever does not bear his own cross and follow me, he cannot be my disciple" (Lk. 14:27 par. Blt. or Mk. 8:34).

He himself renounced his relatives; "whoever does God's will, he is brother and sister and mother to me" (Mk. 3:35 Blt.). And evidently he also uprooted by his word a band of men out of their homes and occupations to accompany him in his wandering life as his "disciples"—i.e. his pupils (Mk. 1:16–20; 2:14). Still he did not found an order or a sect, far less a "Church," nor did he expect that everyone should or could forsake house and family.

The saying about the building of the "Church" (ἐκκλησία) Mt. 16:18 is, like the whole of Mt. 16:17–19, a later product of the Church; cf. *Gesch. d. synopt. Trad.*, 2nd ed., 147–150, 277f.; *Theol. Bl.* 20 (1941), 265–279. An excellent account of the discussion of this problem is given by O. Linton, *Das Problem der Urkirche in der neueren Forschung* (1932). For more recent literature, cf. R. N. Flew, *Jesus and his Church* (1938). J. B. Bernardin, "The Church in the N.T." [*Anglican Theol. Rev.* 21 (1939), 153–170]. F. C. Grant, "The Nature of the Church" (*ibid.* 190–204). B. S. Easton, "The Church in the N.T." [*ibid.* 22 (1940), 157–168]. F. J. Leenhardt, *Études sur l'Église dans le N.T.* (1940). Especially: N. A. Dahl, *Das Volk Gottes* (1941); W. G. Kümmel, *Kirchenbegriff und Geschichtsbewusstsein in der Urgemeinde und bei Jesus* (*Symb. Bibl. Upsal.* I) (1943); E. Fascher in the article, "Petrus" in Pauly-Wissowa-Kroll: *Realenzykl. der Klass. Altertumswiss.* XIX, 1353–1361.

But everyone is confronted with deciding what he will set his heart upon—on God or on worldly goods. "Do not lay up for yourselves treasures on earth. . . . For where your treasure is, there will your heart be also!" (Mt. 6:19–21 par.). "No one can serve two masters!" (Mt. 6:24 par.). How dangerous wealth is! "It is easier for a camel to go through the eye of a needle than for a rich man to enter the Reign of God!" (Mk. 10:25 Blt.). Most men cling to earthly goods and cares; and when the time for decision comes, they fail—as the parable of the banquet shows (Lk. 14:15–24 par.). A man must make up his mind what he wants, what degree of effort he is capable of, just as the means for building a tower or waging a war must first be estimated (Lk. 14:28–32). But for the Reign of God one must be ready for any sacrifice—like the farmer who finds a treasure and gives all he has to get possession of it, or like the merchant who sells everything in order to acquire the one precious pearl (Mt. 13:44–46).

"If your hand causes you to sin, cut it off! It is better for you to enter life maimed than with two hands to go to hell. . . . "

"If your eye causes you to sin, pluck it out! It is better for you to enter the Reign of God with one eye, than with two eyes to be thrown into hell" (Mk. 9:43, 47 Blt. or Mt. 5:29f.).

But this renunciation toward the world, this "unworldliness," is not to be thought of as asceticism, but as simple readiness for God's demand. For the positive thing that corresponds to this renunciation, the thing, that is, which constitutes readiness for God's Reign, is the fulfilment of God's will, as Jesus makes evident in combatting Jewish legalism.

§ 2. Jesus' Interpretation of the Demand of God

1. As interpretation of the will, the demand, of God, Jesus' message is a great *protest against Jewish legalism*—i.e. against a form of piety which regards the will of God as expressed in the written Law and in the Tradition which interprets it, a piety which endeavors to win God's favor by the toil of minutely fulfilling the Law's stipulations. Here there is no differentiation between religion and morality, nor are laws about worship and ethics separated from statutes of everyday law. This state of affairs is typified by the fact that the "scribes" are theologians, teachers, and lawyers all at the same time. What religion and morality require is prescribed by the Law, but civil and criminal law are also regarded as divine Law. The result is not merely that a mass of ordinances which have lost the meaning they once had under earlier conditions remain in force and so have to be twisted by artificial interpretation into relevance for today; not merely that regulations appropriate to the present have to be wrung out of the ancient Law by artificial deduction to meet new conditions of life. Nor is the result merely that a plethora of cultic and ritual laws are regarded as God's demand, or as ethical demand, and thus frequently overshadow the really ethical demands. The real result is that motivation to ethical conduct is vitiated. That is the result not only in the wide extent to which the idea of reward and punishment becomes the motivation, but also—and this is the characteristic thing for Judaism—that the obedience man owes to God and to His demand for good is understood as a purely formal

one; i.e. as an obedience which fulfills the letter of the law, obeying a law simply because it is commanded without asking the reason, the meaning, of its demand. And though many a scribe protests against the prevalence of reward and punishment as the motive for obedience, demanding instead an obedience from the heart which would fulfill the commandment not out of fear but out of love to God, nevertheless obedience cannot be radical, genuine obedience so long as man obeys only because it is commanded—so long, that is, as he would do something else if something else were commanded, or, rather, would not do the thing in question if it did not stand in the commandment. Radical obedience is only possible where a man understands the demand and affirms it from within himself. And only of such obedience is it meaningful to say that in fulfilling the ethical demand it fulfills God's demand, for God requires radical obedience. The error of Jewish legalism reveals itself finally in the following. A statute, unlike an ethical demand, can never embrace every specific situation of life; instead there inevitably remain many cases unprovided for, cases for which there is no command or prohibition; that leaves room not only for every desire and passion that may arise but also—and that again is characteristic of Judaism—for works of supererogation. In principle, when a man's duties are conceived of as the committing or omitting of specific acts under legal requirement, he can completely discharge them and have room left over for extra deeds of merit. So there developed in Judaism the notion of "good works" that go beyond the required fulfilment of the Law (such as almsgiving, various acts of charity, voluntary fasting, and the like), establishing literal merits and hence also capable of atoning for transgressions of the Law. This indicates that here the idea of obedience is not taken radically.

2. Seen against this background *Jesus' proclamation of the will of God appears as a great protest*. In it the protest of the great prophets of the Old Testament against the cultic worship of God in their time is renewed under altered circumstances. Whereas they had upheld justice and uprightness as God's demand in opposition to the cultic piety of the people, Jesus demanded radical obedience in opposition to that merely formal obedience which to a large extent regarded the fulfilment of the ritual prescriptions as the essential thing. He does not, as the prophets did, raise the demand for justice and right; for the preaching of these things, once decisive

for Israelitic national life, has lost its meaning now that there is
scarcely any national life left. What Judaism has left as the product
of the prophets' work is codified law, which now, however, no longer
serves primarily to regulate national life but governs the relation of
the individual to God. And that is just what Jesus protests against—
that man's relation to God is regarded as a legal one. God requires
radical obedience. He claims man whole—and wholly. Within this
insight Jesus takes for granted that God requires of man the doing
of the good and that ethical demands are the demands of God; to
that extent religion and ethics constitute a unity for him, too. But
excluded from the demands of God are all cultic and ritual regulations, so that along with ethics Jesus sets free the purely religious
relation to God in which man stands only as one who asks and
receives, hopes and trusts.

The antitheses (Mt. 5:21–48) *in the Sermon on the Mount* throw
legalism and the will of God into sharp contrast: "You have heard
that it was said to the men of old . . ., But I say to you . . .!" The
meaning is this: God does not lay claim to man only so far as conduct can be determined by formulated laws (the only way open to
legalism), leaving man's own will free from that point on. What
God forbids is not simply the overt acts of murder, adultery, and
perjury, with which law can deal, but their antecedents: anger and
name-calling, evil desire and insincerity (Mt. 5:21f., 27f., 33–37).
What counts before God is not simply the substantial, verifiable
deed that is done, but how a man is disposed, what his intent is.
As the laws concerning murder, adultery and perjury are thus radicalized, so others which were once meant to restrict arbitrary action
but now are conceived as concessions defining an area of leeway for
permissive acts, are from the point of view of God's intention altogether abolished: the provision for divorce, the law of retaliation,
the limitation of the duty of love to one's neighbor alone (Mt. 5:31f.,
38–41, 43–48). *God demands the whole will of man* and knows no
abatement in His demand.

> Are grapes gathered from thorns,
>   or figs from thistles?
> Each tree is known by its own fruit;
>   a good tree cannot bear evil fruit.
>   (Mt. 7:16, 18 combined with Lk. 6:43f. Blt.)

> The eye is the lamp of the body.
> So, if your eye is sound,
> Your whole body will be full of light.
> But if your eye is not sound,
> Your whole body will be full of darkness.
> (Mt. 6:22f. par.)

Man, upon whose whole self God's demand is made, has no freedom toward God; he is accountable for his life as a whole—as the parable of the talents teaches (Mt. 25:14–30 par.). *He may not, must not, cannot raise any claim before God,* but is like the slave who only has his duty to do and can do no more (Lk. 17:7–10).

This parable is paralleled in the saying of a pre-Christian rabbi, Antigonus of Socho: "Be not like servants who serve their lord on condition of receiving reward; but rather be like servants who serve their lord under no condition of receiving reward" (Pirqe Aboth 1, 3). In demanding unconditional obedience Jesus and the rabbi agree. That the idea of obedience is taken radically by Jesus follows from the whole context of his ethical utterances.

Man must become like a child, who, knowing no such thing as appeal to any rights or merits of his own, is willing simply to be given a gift (Mk. 10:15). Those who proudly brag of their merits are an abomination to God (Lk. 16:15), and the virtue-proud Pharisee has to take a lower place than the guilt-conscious publican (Lk. 18:9–14). So Jesus rejects all this counting up of merit and reward: The worker who went to work in the last hour of the day is rewarded just as much as the one who had worked all day long (Mt. 20:1–15). And Jesus also refuses to regard the misfortune that befalls individuals as punishment for their special sins; no man is better than another (Lk. 13:1–5).

One must, of course, admit that for Jesus it is certain that God does reward faithful obedience; back of the demand stands the promise; and in view of his battle against the motive of retribution his position must be so described: He promises reward precisely to those who obey not for the sake of reward. Even so, his words are not without self-contradiction, since he does occasionally use the *idea of recompense* as motivation for a demand—either by referring to heavenly reward (Mt. 6:19f. par. Mk. 10:21 and elsewhere) or

[14]

by threatening with hell-fire (Mt. 10:28 par. Mk. 9:43, 47 and elsewhere). Still the contradiction can probably be resolved in this way: The motive of reward is only a primitive expression for the idea that in what a man does his own real being is at stake—that self which he not already is, but is to become. To achieve that self is the legitimate motive of his ethical dealing and of his true obedience, in which he becomes aware of the paradoxical truth that in order to arrive at himself he must surrender to the demand of God—or, in other words, that in such surrender he wins himself. This paradoxical truth is taught in the following saying:

> "Whoever seeks to gain his life will lose it,
> But whoever loses his life will preserve it." (Lk. 17:33)

Both Mark and Q hand down this saying. At Mk. 8:35 "whoever loses it" has the addition: "for my sake and the gospel's." The parallels to this passage, Mt. 16:25 and Lk. 9:24, read only "for my sake," and that is probably all they had found in their Marcan text. To accord with it Mt. 10:39 also added "for my sake" in the Q-parallel to Lk. 17:33. John also knew the saying, and knew it without the addition, so that he corroborates the form of Lk. 17:33 as the original one when he says, "He who loves his life loses it, and he who hates his life in this world will keep it for eternal life" (12:25), though he, on his part, has added "in this world" and "for eternal life."

3. From the standpoint of this radical attitude of Jesus toward the will of God, what is to be said of *his position toward the Old Testament?* Without contesting its authority he makes critical distinctions among the demands of the Old Testament. Yes, Moses did permit divorce, but only "in consideration of your hard-heartedness." By no means is that the actual intention of God; rather He intends marriage to be inseparable (Mk. 10:2–9).

"Woe to you, scribes and Pharisees, hypocrites! For you tithe mint and dill and cummin, and have neglected the weightiest in the Law: justice and mercy and good faith; these things ought to be done and the others not neglected. You blind guides, straining out a gnat and swallowing a camel!" (Mt. 23:23f. Blt.). If the words "These things ought to be done and the others not neglected" are really an original component of this "woe" (they are missing in the Luke-parallel 11:42 in Codex D), they indicate that a reformer's polemic against the Old Testament legislation is far from Jesus' intention. In any case these verses indicate a sovereign attitude assumed by Jesus toward the Old Testament, an attitude which critically distinguishes the important from the unimportant, the essential from the indifferent. This is in harmony with the rest of Jesus' words concerning the Old Testament.

God did indeed declare His will in the Old Testament. Whoever inquires about the will of God is referred to the ethical demands of the Old Testament—for instance, the rich man with his question: "What must I do to inherit eternal life?" or the "lawyer"-scribe with his query about the highest commandment (Mk. 10:17–19, 12:28–34). But the rich man straightway has to accept the accusation that his previous fulfilment of the commandments has been an illusion, since he is incapable of giving up everything—he cannot radically obey.

That Jesus did not polemically contest the authority of the Old Testament is proven by the course later taken by his Church; it clung faithfully to the Old Testament Law and thereby came into conflict with Paul. The Church formulated its standpoint—no matter whether against Paul or against other Hellenistic missionaries—in the words placed on Jesus' lips about the imperishability of even the tiniest letter in the Law and expressly declaring that Jesus did not come to abolish the Law, but to fulfill it (Mt. 5:17–19)—a saying that in view of other sayings of Jesus and of his actual practice cannot possibly be genuine; rather it is a product of the Church coming out of the later period of conflict over the Law. Yet clearly this conservative attitude of the Church would not have been possible if Jesus had called into question the validity of the Old Testament. Its authority stands just as fast for him as for the scribes, and he feels himself in opposition to them only in the way he understands and applies the Old Testament. Neither did he oppose *the pious practices of Judaism*—almsgiving, prayer, and fasting—though he did protest against their being put into the service of personal vanity and so becoming a lie (Mt. 6:1–4, 5–8, 16–18).

His answer to the question about fasting, Mk. 2:19, does not reject fasting on principle, but means that in the dawning of messianic joy the mourning custom of fasting (which in itself is not opposed) does not make sense. The original meaning of the sayings about the new patch on an old garment and new wine in old skins (Mk. 2:21f.) is no longer clearly discernible. It may have intended some such meaning as this, that in the messianic period the old mourning customs have become meaningless.

Polemic against the temple cult is completely absent from the words of Jesus. As a matter of fact it, too, had essentially lost its original meaning in his time; for Judaism was no longer a cultic religion, but had become a religion of observance. The temple cult was faithfully carried out, and at the great festivals really cultic piety probably revived. But in general the temple cult with its sacrifices was carried out as an act of obedience— for was it not commanded in the Law? The synagogue with its interpretation of the regulation of daily life by the Law had pushed the temple service into the background; for the people, the scribes had replaced the priests as the seat of authority. So Judaism, borne up by the synagogue and the scribes, survived the fall of the temple without disaster. In Mt. 5:23f. participation in the temple cult is taken for granted without misgiving. It may well be a genuine saying of Jesus, whereas Mt. 17:24–27 is a later legend, but one that proves, nevertheless, that the Christian Church paid the temple tax. In the same way accounts contained in Acts also show that the Church held gatherings within the temple area.

Actually the Old Testament legislation, so far as it consists of cultic and ritual prescriptions, has been lifted off its hinges by Jesus. As he rises above the Sabbath law, so he attacks *legalistic ritualism* which strives for an external correctness which can go hand in hand with an impure will. Thus he quotes the prophet (Is. 29:13):

"This people honors me with their lips
But their heart is far from me.
In vain do they worship me,
Teaching as doctrines the precepts of men." (Mk. 7:6f.)
"Woe to you, scribes and Pharisees, hypocrites!
For you cleanse the outside of the cup and of the plate,
But inside you (*cf*. Lk. 11:39) are full of extortion and rapacity!" . . .
"Woe to you, scribes and Pharisees, hypocrites!
For you are like whitewashed tombs, which outwardly appear beautiful,
But within they are full of dead men's bones and all uncleanness.

So you also outwardly appear righteous to men,
But within you are full of hypocrisy and iniquity." (Mt. 23:25–
28 par. Blt.)

How alms, prayer, and fasting can be misused to impress others
(Mt. 6:1–4, 5f., 16–18)! Unless fasting expresses real grief, it has no
meaning (Mk. 2:18f.). How God's command to honor one's parents
can be set aside by declaring a cultic command to be more important (Mk. 7:9–13)! The laws of cleanliness are meaningless, for
"there is nothing outside a man which by going into him can defile
him; but the things which come out of a man are what defile him"
(Mk. 7:15). "The sabbath was made for man, not man for the
sabbath" (Mk. 2:27). And though it is true that the same insight
flashes up now and then among the scribes, still Jesus is the first to
draw the consequence of it with his question:

"Is it lawful on the sabbath to do good or to do harm,
To save a life or to kill?" (Mk. 3:4 Blt.)

that is, there is no third choice, no holy indolence. To do nothing
where an act of love is required would be to do evil. So Jesus is
"a friend of publicans and sinners" (Mt. 11:19 par., Mk. 2:15–17);
he cannot avoid being slandered as "glutton and drunkard" (Mt.
11:19), and he can actually use a Samaritan as a good example (Lk.
10:30–36).

4. What, positively, is the will of God? *The demand for love.*
"You shall love your neighbor as yourself!" as the second greatest
commandment belongs together with the first: "You shall love the
Lord your God with all your heart and with all your soul and with
all your mind and with all your strength" (Mk. 12:28–34). There
is no obedience to God which does not have to prove itself in the
concrete situation of meeting one's neighbor, as Luke (10:29–37),
probably unhistorically but with the right of correct understanding
of the subject-matter, makes clear by combining the illustrative narrative of the Good Samaritan with Jesus' discussion of the greatest
commandment.

The demand for love surpasses every legal demand; it knows no
boundary or limit; it holds even in regard to one's enemy (Mt. 5:43–
48). The question, "How often must I forgive my brother when he

sins against me? Is seven times enough?" is answered: "I tell you: not seven times, but seventy times seven" (Mt. 18:21f. par. Blt.).

The demand for love needs no formulated stipulations; the example of the merciful Samaritan shows that a man can know and must know what he has to do when he sees his neighbor in need of his help. The little words "as yourself" in the love-commandment pre-indicate both the boundlessness and the direction of loving conduct.

Jesus completely refrained from making the love-commandment concrete in specific prescriptions. That fact shows that his proclamation of the will of God is not an ethic of world-reform. Rather, it must be described as an eschatological ethic. For it does not envisage a future to be molded within this world by plans and sketches for the ordering of human life. It only directs man into the Now of his meeting with his neighbor. It is an ethic that, by demanding more than the law that regulates human society does and requiring of the individual the waiver of his own rights, makes the individual immediately responsible to God.

5. At this point it begins to be clear how *Jesus' eschatological message and his ethical message constitute a unity*—in other words, how the same Jesus can be both the prophet who proclaims the irruption of God's Reign and the rabbi who expounds God's Law.

There is such a unity, but it is a false unity if it is reached by conceiving God's Reign as the triumph of the Demand for Good either in the human mind or in historical human affairs. This misconception may say: God's Reign is a reigning of God in the mind which occurs when the divine Demand prevails there and takes shape in ethical character. Or it may say; It is a reigning of God in human affairs which occurs when the divine Demand prevails there and takes shape in an ethical social order. Both forms not only distort the concept Reign of God but also misunderstand the intent of God's demand—it aims neither at the formation of "character" nor at the molding of human society.

Neither is it feasible, recognizing the rivalry between the eschatological and the ethical message of Jesus, to deny one of the two to belong to the historical Jesus and pronounce it a later product of the Church. It cannot be maintained that Jesus was only a teacher of ethics who taught a "superior righteousness" and that it was the Church that first put into his mouth the eschatological message of the irruption of God's Reign. For we can readily see that the origin of the Church lies in the certainty of that imminent End, but not that that certainty itself could have been a later community product. The tradition shows, on the contrary, that alarmed anxiety arose in the Church at the delay of the expected Reign of God. This alarm is expressed in words put into the mouth of Jesus (Lk. 12:35–38, Mk. 13:31, 33–37). But above all, the movement which Jesus evoked among the people and his crucifixion by the Roman procurator show that it was in the role of a messianic prophet that he appeared. On the other hand, it is just as impossible to regard only his eschatological message as historically genuine and his ethical preaching as a secondary product of the Church. For, aside from the fact that it would not be intelligible how the Church should have come to make a rabbi of him whom they regarded as Messiah, the scrupulous observance of the Law by the earliest Church indicates that the radical sayings about the Law and its observance cannot have originated in it.

The unity of the eschatological and the ethical message of Jesus may be so stated: Fulfilment of God's will is the condition for participation in the salvation of His Reign. Only "condition" in that statement must not be taken in the external sense of an arbitrarily set task, in place of which some other could have been set—a condition, that is, without inner relation to the gift for whose receipt it constitutes the presupposition—as it is taken to mean, for instance, when Jesus' interpretation of the divine demand is held to be no more than an "interim ethic" and its imperatives are therefore regarded as exceptional commands which only held for the last short interval until the end of the world. Rather, these imperatives are clearly meant radically as absolute demand with a validity independent of the temporal situation. Neither the demands of the Sermon on the Mount nor Jesus' attacks against legalistic morality are motivated by reference to the impending end of the world. But precisely Jesus' knowledge of the absolute validity of the divine demand is the basis of his radical verdict over "this evil and adulterous generation" ripe for divine judgment (Mt. 12:39 par., Mk. 8:38)—the same verdict, that is, that comes to expression in the eschatological proclamation. Then this is clear: The fulfilment of God's will is the condition for participation in the salvation of God's Reign in *this* sense, that it means nothing else but true readiness for it, genuine and earnest desire for it. The Reign of God, demanding of man decision for God against every earthly tie, is the salvation to come. Hence, only he is ready for this salvation who in the concrete moment decides for that demand of God which confronts him in the person of his neighbor. They who, conscious of their poverty, wait weeping and hungering for salvation, are identical with those who are merciful, pure of heart, and peace-makers (Mt. 5:3–9). Whoever has his will set upon God's Reign also wills to fulfill the commandment of love. It is not that he fulfills the commandment of love as an irksome requirement while his real will is directed at something else (viz. God's Reign), for the sake of which alone he obeys the commandment of God. Rather there is an inner connection: Both things, the eschatological proclamation and the ethical demand, direct man to the fact that he is thereby brought before God, that God stands before him; both direct him into his Now as the hour of decision for God.

6. Thus it happens that at the sight of the actual state of the leaders of the people and of the great mass of the people itself—at the sight of religion frozen into ritualism, at the sight of superficiality and love of self and the world—Jesus' message becomes *a cry of woe and repentance.*

"Woe to you, scribes and Pharisees! . . ."
(Mt. 23:1ff. par.; Mk. 12:38ff.)
"Woe to you that are rich, for you have received your consolation!
Woe to you that are full now, for you shall hunger!
Woe to you that laugh now, for you shall mourn and weep!"
(Lk. 6:24–26)

"The time is fulfilled, the Reign of God is at hand! Repent!" (Mk. 1:15)—this is the condensed summary of Jesus' cry. But this contemporary "generation" is "adulterous and sinful" (Mk. 8:38; Mt. 12:39). Men say "yes" to God's demand and then do not do what He requires (Mt. 21:28–31). They refuse to "repent," to turn about from their perverted way (Lk. 11:31f. par.), and so the judgment will break in upon sinners (Lk. 13:1–5), and all predictions of woe will come to pass (Mt. 23:34–36 par.), especially upon Jerusalem (Mt. 23:37–39 par.) and its temple: not a stone that will not be thrown down! (Mk. 13:2). Only in the despised—the publicans, sinners, and harlots—is there readiness to repent; to them and not to the "righteous," Jesus considers himself sent (Mk. 2:17); these who first said "no" repent (Mt. 21:28–31), and God has more joy over one sinner who repents than over ninety-nine "righteous" (Lk. 15:1–10). They who await God's Reign aright, hungering and sorrowing, knowing how poor they are—to them pertains the promise of salvation (Lk. 6:20f. or Mt. 5:3–6).

§ 3. Jesus' Idea of God

1. Once one has understood the unity of the eschatological and the ethical preaching of Jesus, one also has the answer to the real meaning of the eschatological message, namely: the answer to the question, what *idea of God* is at work in it. For, in view of the fact that the proclamation of the irruption of God's Reign was not fulfilled—that is, that Jesus' expectation of the near end of the world turned out to be an illusion—the question arises whether his idea of God was not also illusory. This question is frequently avoided, it is true, by the escape-reasoning that Jesus saw the presence of God's Reign in his own person and in the followers who gathered about him. But such a view cannot be substantiated by a single saying of Jesus,* and it contradicts the meaning of "God's Reign." On the contrary, Jesus clearly expected the irruption of God's Reign as a miraculous, world-transforming event—as Judaism, and later also his own Church, did. Nowhere to be found in his words is there polemic against this view, so taken for granted by his time, or any correction of it.

But it is a fact that *prophetic consciousness* always expects the judgment of God, and likewise the time of salvation to be brought in by God, in the immediate future, as may be clearly seen in the great prophets of the Old Testament. And the reason this is so is that to the prophetic consciousness the sovereignty of God, the absoluteness of His will, is so overpowering that before it the world sinks away and seems to be at its end. The consciousness that man's relation toward God decides his fate and that the hour of decision is of limited duration clothes itself in the consciousness that the hour of decision is here for the world, too. The word which the prophet

* Not by Lk. 17:21 either. On the meaning of this saying, see p. 6 above.

is conscious of having to speak by God's commission takes the form of the final word by which God summons men to definitive decision.

So also with Jesus. He is certain that he is acquainted with the unswerving will of God, who sternly demands the good from man and, through the message by which He is preached, thrusts man into the alternative of salvation or condemnation. It is this certainty which gives Jesus the consciousness of standing at the end of time. His message grows neither out of weariness with the world and longing for the world beyond nor out of fanciful speculation, but out of knowing the world's futility and man's corruption in God's eyes and out of knowing the will of God. The essential thing about the eschatological message is the idea of God that operates in it and the idea of human existence that it contains—not the belief that the end of the world is just ahead.

2. God, in keeping with Old Testament tradition, is, for Jesus, *the Creator* who governs the world with His care, feeds the beasts and adorns the flowers, without whose will not a sparrow falls dead to earth, and who has counted every hair of our heads (Mt. 6:25-34 par., 10:29f. par.). All anxious care, all haste to get goods to insure life, is therefore senseless—yes, wicked. Man is at the mercy of the Creator's will; he can neither add a cubit to his height nor make a single hair of his head white or black (Mt. 6:27 par., 5:36). If he imagines himself self-insured by the wealth he has amassed and able now to take his ease, he has forgotten that he still can die this very night (Lk. 12:16-20). Trust in God and consciousness of dependence are both alike demanded of man.

In the above, Jesus' idea of God does not essentially differ from that of the Old Testament and of Judaism, though it is true that in the common piety of Judaism faith in God the Creator had weakened even while it was strictly preserved in its official theology and confession. God had retreated far off into the distance as the transcendent heavenly King, and His sway over the present could barely still be made out. For Jesus, God again became *a God at hand.* He is the power, here and now, who as Lord and Father enfolds every man—limiting and commanding him. This contrast finds expression in the respective forms of address used in prayer. Compare the ornate, emotional, often liturgically beautiful, but often over-loaded, forms of address in Jewish prayer with the stark simplicity of "Father"! The "Prayer of Eighteen Petitions," for instance, which the devout Jew is expected to say three times daily, begins, "Lord God of Abraham, God of Isaac, God of Jacob! God Most High, Creator of heaven and earth! Our Shield and the Shield of our fathers!" ° † The "Lord's Prayer" stands out above Jewish prayers not only in its simple address but in its direct simplicity throughout (Mt. 6:9–13, or Lk. 11:2–4). God is near; He hears and understands the requests which come thronging to Him, as a father understands the requests of his own child (Mt. 7:7–11 par.; *cf.* Lk. 11:5–8; 18:1–5).

But God has also come near as the "Demand-er" whose will need not wait to be found in the letter of the Law or its scribal exegesis. The remoteness interposed by Law and Tradition between God and man is closed up, and man's uncertain searching for what is forbidden and what allowed is over. A man learns what God wants of him immediately out of his own situation in the encounter with his neighbor. And so God also stands before every man as the Judge to whom he owes accounting. "I tell you, on the day of judgment men will render account for every careless word they utter" (Mt. 12:36). "Do not fear those who kill the body but cannot kill the soul! Rather fear him who can destroy both soul and body in hell!" (Mt. 10:28 par.).

But the demanding God of judgment is also the merciful *God of forgiveness*; and whoever turns back to Him in repentance can be certain of His forgiving kindness. The scribes shut the Kingdom of Heaven in men's faces with their legalism (Mt. 23:13 par.); Jesus' very call to repentance opens the way to it and they have no need of the long penitential prayers that are characteristic of Judaism. The publican who dares not raise his eyes to Heaven, but strikes his breast and says, "God be merciful to me, a sinner!" is accounted righteous (Lk. 18:9–14). The "prodigal son" says only, "Father, I have sinned against Heaven and before you; I am no longer worthy to be called your son"—and then fatherly kindness embraces him (Lk. 15:11–32). The proud and self-righteous are an abomination to God (Lk. 16:15; 18:9–14); but over the sinner who contritely repents, God rejoices (Lk. 15:1–10). But forgiveness has been truly received only when it makes the heart forgiving, as the parable of the wicked servant teaches (Mt. 18:23–35; *cf.* Lk. 7:47), and only

° Palestinian recension, Dalman's emendations, *Die Worte Jesu*, appendix.
† *Cf.* espec. IV Esdras 8:20ff.

he who is willing to forgive can honestly ask for God's forgiveness (Mt. 6:12, 14f.). God's forgiveness makes a man new; and whoever is willing to become new receives it.

3. Jesus no longer speaks, as the ancient prophets did, of the revelations of God in the history of the Nation and the nations. And when he refers to the coming judgment of God, unlike them he is no more thinking of catastrophes in the affairs of nations than he expects God's Reign to be fulfilled in the erection of a mighty and glorious Israelitic kingdom. Unlike the prophets' preaching, his preaching is directed not primarily to the people as a whole, but *to individuals*. The judgment is coming not on nations but on individuals who must give account of themselves before God; and it is individuals whom coming salvation will bless. Judgment and salvation are eschatological events in the strict sense; i.e. events in which the present world and all history cease to be.

Thus, *Jesus in his thought of God*—and of man in the light of this thought—"de-historized" God and man; that is, released the relation between God and man from its previous ties to history (history considered as the affairs of nations). While this was already more or less the case in Judaism (but not in the religion of the Old Testament prophets), Jesus' thought, in contrast to that of Judaism, also *radically "historized"* God in a different sense of "history." In Judaism God is de-historized by having become a distant God enthroned in heaven; His governance of the world is carried out by angels, and His relation to man is mediated by the book of the Law. And man in Judaism is de-historized by being marked off from the world by ritual and by finding his security within the ritually pure congregation. The Jewish congregation artificially accomplishes its de-secularization (*Entweltlichung*) by means of its legalism. For Jesus, however, man is de-secularized by God's direct pronouncement to him, which tears him out of all security of any kind and places him at the brink of the End. And God is "de-secularized" by understanding His dealing eschatologically: He lifts man out of his worldly ties and places him directly before His own eyes. Hence, the "de-historization" or "desecularization" both of God and of man is to be understood as a paradox (*dialektisch*): precisely that God, who stands aloof from the history of nations, meets each man in his own little history, his everyday life with its daily gift and demand; de-historized man (i.e. naked of his supposed security within his historical group) is guided into his concrete encounter with his neighbor, in which he finds his true history.

§ 4. The Question of the Messianic Consciousness of Jesus

1. The Church of Jesus' disciples understood his claim that men's destiny is determined by their attitude to him in such a way that they regarded Jesus himself as the Messiah they had been expecting, or else still awaited Jesus himself as the coming Son of Man. The common opinion is that this belief of the earliest Church rests upon the self-consciousness of Jesus; i.e. that he actually did consider himself to be the Messiah, or the Son of Man. But this opinion is burdened with serious difficulties. It does agree with the evangelists' point of view, but the question is whether they themselves have not superimposed upon the traditional material their own belief in the messiahship of Jesus. In discussing this question it is important to bear in mind that if the fact should be established that Jesus was conscious of being the Messiah, or the Son of Man, that would only establish a historical fact, not prove an article of faith. Rather, the acknowledgment of Jesus as the one in whom God's word decisively encounters man, whatever title be given him—"Messiah (Christ)," "Son of Man," "Lord"—is a pure act of faith independent of the answer to the historical question whether or not Jesus considered himself the Messiah. Only the historian can answer this question—as far as it can be answered at all—and faith, being personal decision, cannot be dependent upon a historian's labor.

Some advance the following reasoning as an argument from history: The Church's belief in the messiahship of Jesus * is comprehensible only if Jesus was conscious of being the Messiah and actually represents himself as such—at least to the "disciples." But is this argument valid? For it is just as possible that belief in the messiahship of Jesus arose with and out of belief in his resurrection. The scene of *Peter's Confession* (Mk. 8:27–30) is no counter-evidence—on the contrary! For it is an Easter-story projected backward into Jesus' life-time, just like the story of the Transfiguration (Mk. 9:2–8). The account of Jesus' baptism (Mk. 1:9–11) is legend, certain though it is that the legend started from the historical fact of Jesus' baptism by John. It is told in the interest not of biography but of

* Disregarding the distinction between Messiah and Son of Man; after all, both mean the eschatological bringer of salvation.

faith, and it reports Jesus' consecration as Messiah. It originated in the time when Jesus' life was already regarded as having been messianic, whereas the transfiguration story, originally a resurrection-account, dates his messiahship from the resurrection onward. The Temptation story (Mk. 1:12f. or Mt. 4:1–11 par.), which involves reflection about what kind of messiah Jesus was or what kind of messiah the Christian believes in, is legend. The story of Jesus' entry into Jerusalem has been colored by legend, and the passion-narrative is also to a considerable degree overspread with legend; for to the Church that venerated the Crucified as the Messiah it was soon perfectly certain that it was as Messiah that he had been crucified.

Moreover the synoptic tradition leaves no doubt about it that *Jesus' life and work* measured by traditional messianic ideas *was not messianic.* And Paul, like others, also did not understand it as messianic, as the Christ-hymn quoted by him at Phil. 2:6–11 indicates. It conceives Jesus' life as that of a mere man, without messianic glory. Likewise Acts 2:36 and Rom. 1:4, where Paul is evidently using a traditional formulation, show that in the earliest Church, Jesus' messiahship was dated from the resurrection. Actually, "Messiah" was the term for the eschatological ruler; the word means "the Anointed" and came to mean simply "king."* But it was not as a king, but as a prophet and a rabbi that Jesus appeared—and, one may add, as an exorcist. Nothing of the might and glory, which according to Jewish supposition would characterize the Messiah, was realized in Jesus' life—not in his exorcisms, for example, nor in his other mighty works. For though miracles were indeed a characteristic of the messianic period in Jewish belief, still the Messiah himself was not thought of as a miracle-worker. And even if it be said, in view of Jesus' words about the Son of Man, that Jesus thought of the Messiah not so much, or not at all, as the Davidic king, but rather as that other figure, the heavenly judge and salvation-bringer (viz. the apocalyptic Son of Man), that does not change the situation, for it was not as judge of the world and supernatural bringer of salvation that Jesus appeared.

---

* *Cf.* the substitution of the word "king" Βασιλεύς Mk. 15: 2, 9, 18, 26, 32; Jn. 1:49; Ps. Sol. 17:23, etc. See P. Volz, *Die Eschatologie der jüdischen Gemeinde im neutestamentl. Zeitalter* (1934), 173f.; W. Staerk, *Soter* I (1933), 48ff.

2. Well, then, it has often been asked, did Jesus *reinterpret the traditional Messiah-concept?* Did he "spiritualize" it by exercising his sovereign office through the effect of his word? Only the tradition could inform us as to that. But where in it is such a thing indicated? Where, in the words of Jesus, is there polemic against the conventional Messiah-concept? It is no more to be found than is any criticism of the Jewish conception of the Reign of God!

At the most, the question about the Son of David (Mk. 12:35–37) might be cited; it seems to contain a criticism of the conception of the Messiah as the Son of David: The Messiah is not a descendant of David since David himself called him his lord. In any case, that does not constitute a re-interpretation of the Messiah-concept of such sort that a prophet-and-teacher's life and activity are to be regarded as messianic, and there is no thought here of "spiritualization." What it does say is that when the Messiah is called Son of David, his rank and dignity are given too humble a name. What, then, is the implied but unexpressed Messiah-concept out of which the title "Son of David" is criticized? It could be the apocalyptic concept of the heavenly Son of Man, and it is not impossible that criticism of this sort might go back to Jesus or to the Church. In that case, however, it would be hard to understand how the view came to prevail in the Church that Jesus was a Son of David (*cf.* the lineages of Jesus—Mt. 1:1ff.; Lk. 3:23ff.; Rom. 1:3, and the unretouched report that Jesus was addressed as Son of David—Mk. 10:47; Mt. 9:27, etc.). Or is the title "Son of God" implied as the counter-concept? * If so, this could only be meant as Hellenistic Christianity meant it: as a term for supernatural origin; for in Jewish-Christian use, this term, like Messiah, is only a designation of the king (*cf.* W. Staerk, *Soter* I:89 and e.g. Mk. 14:61; Lk. 1:32, 4:41, etc.). But in that case the passage had its origin in the Hellenistic Church. But if the meaning of Mk. 12:35–37 is held to be that the Messiah is both Son of David and Son of Man (Schniewind's view), then this passage is all the more meaningless for deciding whether Jesus' life had messianic character.

3. Since alleged re-interpretation and spiritualization of the Messiah-concept to mean anything but the king of the time of salvation

---

* So understood by Barn. 12:10f.; see W. Wrede, *Vorträge und Studien* (1907), 171ff.

has now been ruled out, there remains only the frequently chosen escape of saying that Jesus was conscious of being the one *destined to be the future Messiah,* that his idea of the Messiah was "futuristic." Nothing could be cited in favor of this idea except those words of Jesus in which he speaks of the coming Son of Man (Mk. 8:38 or Lk. 12:8f. par.; Mt. 24:27, 37, 44 par.; Lk. 11:30). But it must be admitted that in them he speaks of the Son of Man in the third person without identifying himself with him. There is no question but that the evangelists—and likewise the Church which had handed down these sayings—make this identification; but can that be asserted of Jesus himself?

At any rate, the synoptic tradition contains no sayings in which Jesus says he will sometime (or soon) return. (Neither was the word παρουσία, which denotes the "coming" of the Son of Man, ever understood in the earliest period of Christianity as "return," but correctly as "arrival, advent." The apologete Justin in the second century was the first to speak of the "first" πρώτη and "second coming" δευτέρα παρουσία (Dial. 14:8, 40:4) and of the "coming back πάλιν παρουσία (Dial. 118:2). And how would Jesus have conceived *the relation of his return as Son of Man to his present historical activity?* He would have had to count upon being removed from the earth and raised to heaven before the final End, the irruption of God's Reign, in order to come from there on the clouds of heaven to perform his real office. But how would he have conceived his removal from the earth? As a miraculous translation? Among his sayings there is no trace of any such fantastic idea. As departure by natural death, then? Of that, too, his words say nothing. By a violent death, then? But if so, could he count on that as an absolute certainty— as the consciousness of being raised to the dignity of the coming Son of Man would presuppose? To be sure, *the predictions of the passion* (Mk. 8:31, 9:31, 10:33f.; *cf.* Mk. 10:45, 14:21, 41) foretell his execution as divinely foreordained. But can there be any doubt that they are all *vaticinia ex eventu?* Besides, they do not speak of his parousia! And the predictions of the parousia (Mk. 8:38, 13:26f., 14:62; Mt. 24:27, 37, 39, 44 par.) on their part, do not speak of the death and resurrection of the Son of Man. Clearly the predictions of the parousia originally had nothing to do with the predictions of death and resurrection; i.e. in the sayings that speak of the coming of the Son of Man there is no idea that this Son of Man is already

[29]

here in person and must first be removed by death before he can return from heaven.

Observe in what unassimilated fashion the prediction of the parousia Mk. 8:38 follows upon the prediction of the passion and resurrection 8:31. In Mk. 9:1, 11–13 only the parousia is assumed (v 12b is an interpolation modeled after Mt. 17:12b), while the transfiguration 9:2–10, which the evangelist inserted between these originally connected verses, contains only the idea of resurrection. Later Mt. 17:12b connects the motif of the suffering Son of Man with the sayings that involve reflection about the parousia, and Lk. 17:23–25 likewise combines the passion-motif with prediction of the parousia (*cf.* Lk. 17:23–25 with Mt. 24:26–27)—an altogether secondary combination.

Furthermore, it is not to be doubted that the predictions of the parousia are older than those of the passion and resurrection; Q knows only the former and not yet the latter. The latter are probably later products of the Hellenistic Church, in which the title "Son of Man" was no longer understood in its original sense, while the predictions of the parousia are old and are probably original words of Jesus.

The synoptic Son-of-Man sayings fall into three groups, which speak of the Son of Man (1) as coming, (2) as suffering death and rising again, and (3) as now at work. This third group (Mk. 2:10, 28; Mt. 8:20 par., 11:19 par., 12:32 par.) owes its origin to a mere misunderstanding of the translation into Greek. In Aramaic, the son of man in these sayings was not a messianic title at all, but meant "man" or "I." So this group drops out of the present discussion. The second group contains the *vaticinia ex eventu* which are not yet present in Q; the first group alone contains very old tradition. The sayings belonging to it speak of the Son of Man in the third person. —The secondary material peculiar to Matthew or Luke does not need to be taken into account here; it is significant that for these later evangelists the original meaning of the title is lost and Son of Man has become so completely a self-designation of Jesus that Matthew can substitute either "I" for a traditional Son of Man (Mt. 10:32f. against Lk. 12:8f; *cf.* Mk. 8:38; *cf.* Mt. 16:21 with Mk. 9:31; Mt. 5:11 with Lk. 6:22), or, vice versa, Son of Man for an "I" (Mt. 16:13 against Mk. 8:27).

Now it is true that in the predictions of the passion the Jewish concept Messiah-Son-of-Man is re-interpreted—or better, singularly enriched—insofar as the idea of a suffering, dying, rising Messiah or Son of Man was unknown to Judaism. But this re-interpretation of the concept was done not by Jesus himself but by the Church *ex eventu*. Of course, the attempt is made to carry the idea of the suffering Son of Man back into Jesus' own outlook by assuming that Jesus regarded himself as Deutero-Isaiah's Servant of God who suffers and dies for the sinner, and fused together the two ideas Son of Man and Servant of God into the single figure of the suffering, dying, and rising Son of Man. At the very outset, the misgivings which must be raised as to the historicity of the predictions of the passion speak against this attempt. In addition, the tradition of Jesus' sayings reveals no trace of a consciousness on his part of being the Servant of God of Is. 53. [*]

The messianic interpretation of Is. 53 was discovered in the Christian Church, and even in it evidently not immediately. The passion story, whose telling is colored by proof of predictions, reveals the influence especially of Ps. 21 (22) and 68 (69), but not before Lk. 22:37 is there any influence from Is. 53; and in Mt. 8:17, even Is. 53:4, so easily applied to vicarious suffering, serves as a prediction not of the suffering, but of the healing Messiah. The earliest passages in which the Suffering Servant of God of Is. 53 clearly and certainly appears in the *interpretatio christiana* are: Acts 8:32f., I Pet. 2:22-25, Heb. 9:28; such interpretation may be older than Paul and perhaps is behind Rom. 4:25, probably a saying quoted by Paul. Whether Is. 53 is thought of in "according to the scriptures," I Cor. 15:3, cannot be said. It is significant that Paul himself nowhere adduces the figure of the Servant of God. The synoptic predictions of the passion obviously do not have Is. 53 in mind; otherwise why is it nowhere referred to? Only later do such specific references as I Clem. 16:3-14 and Barn. 5:2 come along. So far as it understood Is. 53 messianically, the synagogue applied precisely the suffering and death of the Servant not to the Messiah, but to the People (or to something else); *cf.* Str.-B. II 284; P. Seidelin, ZNW 35 (1936), 194-231.

---

[*] Hans Walter Wolff attempts to prove the opposite in his Halle dissertation: *Jesaja 53 im Urchristentum* (1942). The attempt is scarcely successful.

4. It was soon no longer conceivable that Jesus' life was unmessianic—at least in the circles of Hellenistic Christianity in which the synoptics took form. That Jesus Christ, the Son of God, should have legitimated himself as such even in his earthly activity seemed self-evident, and so the gospel account of his ministry was cast in the light of messianic faith. The contradiction between this point of view and the traditional material finds expression in the theory of the Messiah-secret, which gives the Gospel of Mark its peculiar character: Jesus functioned as the Messiah, but his messiah-ship was to remain hidden until the resurrection (Mk. 9:9). The demons, who recognize him, are commanded to be quiet; silence is also commanded after Peter's Confession (8:30), after the Transfiguration (9:9), and after some of the miracles. The motif of the disciples' incomprehension likewise serves the secrecy-theory: Though the disciples receive secret revelation, they fail to understand it. Of course, this secrecy-theory, whose existence and importance W. Wrede pointed out, was incapable of being consistently carried through; hence the Gospel of Mark has been rightly characterized by the paradoxical term, book of "secret epiphanies" (Dibelius).

The attempt to understand the Messiah-secret not as a theory of the evangelist but as historical fact (Schniewind), falls to pieces against the fact that its literary location is in the editorial sentences of the evangelist, not in the body of the traditional units. This understanding would further assume that Jesus had on the one hand spiritualized the conception of the Messiah's activity (for this was the case if his activity on earth was to be regarded as already secretly messianic) and on the other hand that Jesus regarded himself as the Son of Man whose secret would someday come out at his return. But against this assumption arise the already named difficulties of attributing to Jesus the supposition that he was himself the future Son of Man.

CHAPTER II

The Kerygma of the Earliest Church

PRELIMINARY REMARK

Since Acts offers only an incomplete and legend-tinted picture of the earliest Church, an historical picture of it, so far as one is possible at all, can be won only by the route of reconstruction. The following serve as sources: 1. The tradition utilized by the author of Acts, so far as it can be ascertained by critical analysis; 2. data occurring in the Pauline letters; 3. the synoptic tradition; its collection, first of all, and its selection, too, of course, and, in part, its shaping all took place in the earliest Church, and hence the tendencies that were operative in the earliest Church cannot but appear in that tradition.

§ 5. The Problem of Relationship between the Message of the Earliest Church and the Message of Jesus

1. As the synoptic tradition shows, the earliest Church resumed the message of Jesus and through its preaching passed it on. So far as it did only that, Jesus was to it a teacher and prophet. But Jesus was more than that to the Church: He was also the Messiah; hence that Church also proclaimed him, himself—and that is the essential thing to see. He who formerly had been the *bearer* of the message was drawn into it and became its essential *content*. *The proclaimer became the proclaimed*—but the central question is: In what sense?

It is clear in the first place that when Jesus was proclaimed as Messiah it was *as the coming Messiah,* in other words *as Son of Man.* Not his *return* as Messiah, but his *coming* as Messiah was expected. That is, his then past activity on earth was not yet considered messianic by the earliest Church (see § 4, 3 and 4).

But that means that *in itself the proclamation of Jesus as Mes-*

[33]

*siah or Son of Man keeps quite within the frame of Jewish eschata-
logical expectation.* Of course, if God has raised from the dead Jesus
of Nazareth, the teacher and prophet crucified by the Romans, and
made him Messiah, exalted him to be the Son of Man who is to come
on the clouds of heaven to hold judgment and to bring in the salvation of God's Reign, then the indefinite mythical figure, Messiah, has
become concrete and visible. The myth has been transferred to a
concrete historical man, and the consequence will be that trust in it
will have been immeasurably strengthened. But neither the picture
of the future is thereby basically remolded as yet, nor is man's relation to God understood anew. For the latter is obviously not yet
founded upon one's relation to the person of Jesus, but is merely
externally mediated, if he is nothing more than the Judge and Salvation-bringer whom Judaism also expected. If he were only that,
he would be merely the guarantor, so to speak, that the ancient
dreams would shortly be fulfilled.

2. But a limit was set to these dreams by the fact that Jesus had
been, and in the Church's preaching continued to be, *the proclaimer
of the radical demand of God.* For grasping what kind of Messiah
he was it could not be immaterial that the Messiah was *he* who, as
prophet and teacher, had also expounded the will of God with ines-
capable clarity. And inasmuch as the proclamation of salvation can
also be called "gospel," the bearing of that gospel upon the Law is
well founded in the fact that the prophet and teacher is also the
Messiah—a bearing which only gradually came to clear recognition.
But Jesus' messiah-ship does not *rest* upon the fact that he was
prophet and teacher. For, however much his preaching in its radicality is directed against Jewish legalism, still its content is nothing
else than true Old Testament-Jewish faith in God radicalized in the
direction of the great prophets' preaching. And though it surpasses
the latter in its individualization of man's relation to God, because it
places not the People but first of all the individual into the immediate presence of God, and because it views not the People's future
but God's Reign as eschatological salvation, still even in that it is
only the consummation of tendencies that underlie the preaching
of the great prophets. The concepts of God, world, and man, of Law
and grace, of repentance and forgiveness in the teaching of Jesus
are not new in comparison with those of the Old Testament and
Judaism, however radically they may be understood. And his criti-

cal interpretation of the Law, in spite of its radicality, likewise stands within the scribal discussion about it, just as his eschatological preaching does within Jewish apocalyptic. This is also the only way of understanding why the teaching of the historical Jesus plays no role, or practically none, in Paul and John, while, on the other hand, modern liberal Judaism can very well esteem Jesus as teacher.[*]

3. Neither does the messianic significance of Jesus rest in the eyes of the earliest Church upon regarding him as a great "personality" standing as impressive power behind his teaching. It was not as the one who was the living embodiment of the religion, the obedience, which he demanded nor as the one who filled those open to his influence with fascination and enthusiasm, kindling them to "imitation" of himself that he was esteemed. And so the earliest Church was also far from understanding his way to the cross as the deed of one who heroically sacrifices himself for his cause. Not the power of his "personality," however great it may factually have been, was what the Church beheld—nor was it *the mystery of his nature* as if the "numinous" had there taken form. True though it may be that as miracle-worker or exorcist he made an awesome, "numinous" impression—although the sentences that say or hint the like belong to the editorial work of the evangelists and are not old tradition—that plays no role in the kerygma of the Church. The Church proclaimed him as prophet and teacher and beyond that as the coming Son of Man, but not as the "divine man" θεῖος ἀνήρ of the Hellenistic world, who was a numinous figure. Not before the growth of legend on Hellenistic soil was the figure of Jesus assimilated to that of the "divine man." The Old Testament-Jewish world knew neither "heroes" in the Greek sense nor *homines religiosi* in the Hellenistic sense. And so it comes about that the personality of Jesus has no importance for the kerygma either of Paul or of John or for the New Testament in general. Indeed the tradition of the earliest Church did not even unconsciously preserve a picture of his personality. Every attempt to reconstruct one remains a play of subjective imagination.

4. It can be taken for granted that the earliest Church did not ponder over *the uniqueness of the place in history and the historical influence* of him whose "advent" as Son of Man would presently end all world history. Nor did their faith in him as Messiah rest upon

[*] *Cf.* Gösta Lindeskog, *Die Jesusfrage im neuzeitlichen Judentum*, 1938.

understanding the historical phenomenon of Jesus in the way the Old Testament and Judaism spoke of historical persons and events, calling them "mercies of God." His ministry was not understood as a decisive event for Israel's history like the call of Moses, the exodus from Egypt, the giving of the Law on Sinai, or God's raising up of kings and prophets.

It might appear that beginnings in this direction are present where, in keeping with the Jewish Messiah-theology, the Messiah Jesus and the "first redeemer" Moses are placed in parallel (Jn. 6:31f., 49f.; Acts 3:22), or where the situation of the Christian Church is compared with that of Israel in the desert (I Cor. 10:1–11; Heb. 3:7–4:11); also, for that matter, wherever the Messiah-Son-of-Man is regarded as the Son of David. But except for the last idea, these are theological reflections which scarcely go back to the earliest Church and are, at any rate, only later attested. But note, above all, that what is involved here is not a paralleling of historical persons and events, but an interpretation of Old Testament history as a foreshadowing of what would happen in the eschatological period.

These events and persons are important for their influence upon the history of the People; and they become meaningful—as acts of revelation or as mercies of God—to the individual through his membership in the People. Each thing that God did to the fathers, the People as a whole, He did to each individual, as it is expressly said in the Jewish Passover liturgy. But neither in the earliest Church nor anywhere in the New Testament is Jesus looked back upon as a deed of God by which—as by Abraham, Moses or David—He showed "mercy" upon the People. Of course not! For Jesus' importance as Messiah-Son-of-Man lies not at all in what he did in the past, but entirely in what is expected of him for the future. And once this expectation is fulfilled by the eschatological drama, that event will never become, like the crossing of the Red Sea, a past to which one could look back thankfully, drawing confidence from it, but it will be God's last deed of all, by which he puts history to an end.

5. Now it is clear that Jesus—that is to say, his coming, his cross, and his resurrection or exaltation—has for Paul, and still more radically for John, *the meaning of eschatological occurrence.* But how is it for the earliest Church, to which the meaning of messiah-ship is of course also eschatological, but to which the messiah-ship itself

is a thing still to come? If Jesus' significance to the earliest Church were exhausted in its expecting him as the coming Son of Man, it would still be only a Jewish sect and would not properly be called Christian Church. Nor would the additional fact that it proclaimed the Crucified as the Risen One, change matters. For so long, at least, as the resurrection means no more than proof of the exaltation of the Crucified to Son of Man, it is not yet understood as an event that breaks the frame of Jewish eschatology. And that the earliest Church was in danger of remaining a Jewish sect is shown by Paul's battle against its understanding of the situation created by Jesus' coming, dying, and rising. Nevertheless, however little the earliest Church explicitly developed an understanding of Jesus' person and fate as *the* eschatological occurrence in Paul's sense, it did implicitly understand him in this sense through the fact that it conceived of itself as the eschatological Congregation.

§ 6. The Earliest Church as the Eschatological Congregation

1. *That the earliest Church regarded itself as the Congregation of the end of days,* is attested both by Paul and the synoptic tradition. In the saying Mt. 16:18f. placed upon the lips of Jesus by the Church, Jesus' band of disciples is called the "Church" (Congregation) whose leader possesses the keys of the Kingdom of Heaven. This Congregation, therefore, is the vestibule, so to say, of God's Reign that is shortly to appear. Nor can it be overwhelmed by the powers of the underworld whose attack upon the Congregation of God is one of the predicted "woes" of the end of days. It is the "little flock" to whom God will give His Reign (Lk. 12:32). It is represented by "the Twelve," who, when God's Reign has appeared, will sit upon twelve thrones to rule the tribes of Israel (Mt. 19:28 or Lk. 22:29f.). The less likely it is that the twelve were called by Jesus himself, the more characteristic they are for the eschatological consciousness of the Church; for they are "the Twelve" not as apostles but as the eschatological regents.

2. Further testimony for eschatological consciousness is the fact that Jesus' disciples after the Easter experiences in Galilee soon betook themselves to *Jerusalem* as the focus of the coming Reign of God. Here the Congregation awaited the fulfilment of the promises. Further evidence is furnished especially by the designations of the

Church and its members that are attested by Paul. In understanding themselves as Congregation or Church the disciples appropriate to themselves the title of the Old Testament Congregation of God, the קְהַל־יְהֹוָה . On the one hand, this title designates Israel as the People of God, and on the other hand, it had already become an eschatological term; for Judaism expected of the end of days that it would bring the gathering together of now scattered Israel and the revealing of the now hidden Congregation. By designating itself Congregation—more exactly, Congregation of God—the earliest Church declared that it itself was the fulfilment of the hopes of the apocalyptists. Its members accordingly bear the eschatological titles "the chosen" or "the elect" and "the saints."

On the discussion about what Aramaic word lies behind the word "Church" ἐκκλησία of the Greek New Testament, cf. the literature given at § 1, 3; in addition especially Leonh. Rost, *Die Vorstufen von Kirche und Synagoge im AT* (1938). K. L. Schmidt, especially, has concerned himself with the lexicographic problem [*Festgabe für Ad. Deissmann* (1927), 258–319]; he would like to establish not קְהָלָא (Heb. קָהָל,), "Congregation, Gathering," but כְּנִשְׁתָּא (Heb. כְּנֶסֶת) "Gathering, Synagogue," as the Aramaic word—hardly rightly. In content "Church (of God)" ἐκκλησία (τοῦ Θεοῦ) corresponds at any rate with קהל (יהוה). For קהל, ἐκκλησία usually is found in the LXX (but significantly not where it would mean a heathen קהל!), and especially in Deut. (which was important because of the parallelism of the Christian Congregation with the Sinai-congregation) and in the Psalms which were so important for the self-consciousness of the Christian Congregation. In the LXX עֵדָה, "assembly of people" is never rendered ἐκκλησία; instead עדה in the great majority of cases, though not exclusively, is rendered συναγωγή, "Gathering, Synagogue," which occasionally also is the translation of קהל. In Ecclesiasticus, too, ἐκκλησία seems to stand only for קהל, never for עדה. In the Psalms of Solomon, ἐκκλησία as a term for Israel (as the People of God) and συναγωγή as a term for individual congregations (hence in the plural, while ἐκκλησία occurs only in the singular) are clearly distinguished. Philo uses only ἐκκλησία for the Sinai-assembly and for the קהל־יהוה Deut. 23:1ff., and uses συναγωγή only for the synagogue-building. On the titles "saints" ἅγιοι and "elect" ἐκλεκτοί, see especially Kümmel, *Kirchenbegriff*, etc. (§ 1, 3), 16ff. It is not impossible that the members of the earliest Church called themselves "the poor," a term which even in the Psalms is already synonymous with "pious, religious." In the Psalms of Solomon the pious who constitute the true Israel are also called "the poor." According to Origen c. Cels. 2:1 (I 126, 19) and Epiphanius 30, 17, 2 (I 356, 2), the Jewish Christians were likewise called אֶבְיוֹנִים (the poor). This title would also characterize the earliest Church as "Israel of God," and to that extent would also be eschatological. But it is uncertain whether this title was already in use in the earliest Church; anyway that cannot (as K. Holl, H. Lietzmann, E. Lohmeyer and others think it can) be deduced from Gal. 2:10: "only they would have us remember the poor"; for Rom. 15:26 speaks of "the poor among the saints" πτωχοὶ τῶν ἁγίων indicating that the "poor" πτωχοί are only a part of the Congregation and hence that πτωχός here is used in the sociological sense and not as a religious term.

3. Without doubt, *baptism* is to be understood in this sense. It can be regarded as certain that from the very beginning it was practiced in the earliest Church as the rite of initiation, for Paul assumes that all Christians are baptized (Rom. 6:3, I Cor. 12:13). But the meaning of baptism can hardly have been different from that of John's baptism, which Jesus and his first "disciples" had themselves received. That is, baptism in conjunction with repentance was a bath of purification (closely connected with repentance) for the coming Reign of God—in other words, an initiation rite of the eschatological Congregation similar to the Jewish proselyte baptism, which was a purifying bath that (in conjunction with circumcision) made the baptized a member of the Congregation of Israel. A difference between these baptisms is admittedly present in the fact that Christian baptism made the baptized a member of the eschatological Congregation; but probably the greatest difference is that proselyte baptism was considered to free a man from ritual defilement, whereas Christian baptism, like that of John—corresponding to the fact that both presuppose confession of sin and repentance—evidently promised purity from sin. For the phrase "for the forgiveness of sins," a characteristic of John's baptism according to Mk. 1:4, was likely true of Christian baptism from the very beginning

(*cf.* Acts 2:38). Inasmuch as such purification was regarded as brought about by an immersion, baptism in the earliest Church (like John's baptism) already had sacramental character and hence completely deserves to be described as an eschatological sacrament which made one a member of the holy Congregation of the end of days. How early the additional view arose that baptism brings the baptized into sacramental relation with the person of Jesus as Son of Man, making him the property of the latter and putting him under the protection of his "Name," can no longer be made out. When Paul presupposes that baptism was done "into (or in) the name of Christ" εἰς τὸ ὄνομα τοῦ Χριστοῦ (I Cor. 1:13), that probably goes back to the usage of the Hellenistic-Christian congregations. But perhaps very early exorcistic effect (by means of naming "the name of Jesus Christ" ὄνομα Ἰησοῦ Χριστοῦ?) was already attributed to baptism. Since when the positive effect of endowment with the "Spirit" was also attributed to it, is uncertain. It probably arose as a Hellenistic-Christian conception.

The analogy which exists between early Christian baptism and the Jewish baptism of proselytes does not signify that the former originated out of the latter; for if that were the case, one would expect it to have been performed on Gentiles only. Certain testimony to the practice of proselyte baptism is not found before the end of the first century A.D. It may have been older, but that cannot be proved. At any rate, Christian baptism did not originate in it, but in the baptism of John. The best orientation concerning these questions is given by Jos. Thomas, *Le mouvement baptiste en Palestine et Syrie* (1935), 356–391.

4. Likewise, *the common meals* (the "breaking of bread") receive their character from the eschatological consciousness of the Congregation. According to the obviously retouched tradition in Acts 2:42–47 there prevailed at these meals ἀγαλλίασις, "gladness," which probably means the mood of eschatological joy.* And it is permissible to form an idea of these celebrations from the table-prayers of which Did. 9 and 10 offer a tradition even though we have no way of knowing whether or to what extent these prayers go back to the earliest Church.† Since these are Jewish table-prayers with Christian editing and they therefore derive from Jewish-Chris-

* See *Th.* WB I 19f.
† See M. Dibelius, ZNW 37 (1938) 32–41.

tian tradition, they may be taken as characteristic of the prayers προσευχαί mentioned at Acts 2:42. They show that an eschatological mood filled the Congregation at these meals. Besides thanks for the gifts given in Jesus (in the formulation of these, specifically Hellenistic phraseology occurs), their chief content is the petition for eschatological fulfilment: "Remember, Lord, thy Church, to deliver it from all evil and to make it perfect in thy love, and gather it together in its holiness from the four winds to thy kingdom which thou hast prepared for it! . . . Let [the Lord °] come, and let this world pass away!" (Did. 10:5f., Lake's tr.).

5. As Jesus scented the irruption of the end of days in the flight of the demons before the spirit that worked in him (Mk. 3:28f.; Mt. 12:28f.; cf. Lk. 11:20), and as for Paul, the Spirit πνεῦμα at work in the Church was the firstfruit ἀπαρχή (Rom. 8:23) or the guarantee ἀρραβών (II Cor. 1:22; 5:5) of the imminent fulfilment, so the earliest Church knew that it had been given *the Spirit*, that gift of the end of days which, according to the Jewish view, had departed from Israel with the last of the prophets, but whose impartation was promised for the end of days. Driven by this Spirit, prophets arise once more, as Acts 11:28; 21:9, 10ff. testify; and Paul as well as the Didache takes the presence of prophets in the Church for granted. In the power of this Spirit miracles occur (Mt. 10:8; Mk. 6:13; Acts 11:28; 21:10f.), as Paul also takes for granted (I Cor. 12:9, 28f.). In times of persecution the Spirit gives the right word in court (Mt. 10:19f. or Mk. 13:11). Whether the manifestations of the Spirit in ecstasy and speaking in tongues (I Cor. 14), which later played so great a role in Hellenistic congregations, had already appeared in the earliest Church, is uncertain. An account of one such event appears to underlie the legendary pentecost story (Acts 2:1–13), as the last verse betrays.†

6. There is no doubt that in the earliest Church *the proving of Old Testament predictions* was practiced, sometimes for edification, sometimes for missionary purposes, but especially for apologetic reasons. However, the Old Testament prophecies were regarded as

° This, following the Coptic text, is probably the correct reading and not ἡ χάρις, "grace."

† It is not hard to conjecture that the last sentence, 4:31, of the account worked into the fourth chapter of Acts by its author originally ran in the source: καὶ ἐπλήσθησαν ἅπαντες τοῦ ἁγίου πνεύματος καὶ ἐλάλουν γλώσσαις—"and they were all filled with the Holy Spirit and spoke with tongues"; cf. 10:45f.

predictions of the time of the End; hence, the Church's certainty that they had been and were still being fulfilled presupposes once more its eschatological consciousness. In I Cor. 10:11 the principle that proof of prophecy is to be sought in "us," the Church, is clearly formulated (*cf.* "for our sake" δι' ἡμᾶς, I Cor. 9:10 and Rom. 15:4). Which statements out of the ever-increasing body of predictions regarded as fulfilled go clear back to the earliest Church, naturally can no longer be ascertained. The tradition παράδοσις cited at I Cor. 15:3ff. with its "according to the scriptures" κατὰ τὰς γραφάς—a phrase not otherwise occurring in Paul—establishes the Christian use of such proofs before Paul's time; and the synoptic tradition shows us that Christians early began to understand Jesus' person and his work, especially the passion, in the light of realized prediction.

7. Belief in the immediately impending End also governs *the missionary activity* of the earliest Church; that is reflected by the "charge to the apostles" placed into the mouth of Jesus. They must hasten through the land to call Israel to repentance (Mt. 10, especially verses 7 and 9ff.); they will not have finished with all the towns of Israel before the Son of Man comes (Mt. 10:23).

8. Q, finally, the collection of Jesus' sayings that goes back to the earliest Church, testifies to the same belief. It is prefaced by the eschatological preaching of John the Baptist; the beatitudes, full of eschatological consciousness, follow; the close is constituted by sayings dealing with the parousia.

§ 7. Jesus' Meaning to the Faith of the Earliest Church

1. Thus, when regarded from the history-of-religions point of view, the earliest Church presents itself as an eschatological sect within Judaism, distinguished from other sects and trends not only by the fact that it awaits the crucified Jesus of Nazareth as the Son of Man, but especially by the fact that it is conscious of being already the called and chosen Congregation of the end of days. When the Church proclaims Jesus as Messiah-Son-of-Man, that does not mean that it has thereby added an item to Old Testament tradition and Jesus' message. Rather, the kerygma of Jesus as Messiah is the basic and primary thing which gives everything else—the ancient tradition and Jesus' message—its special character. All that

went before appears in a new light—new since the *Easter faith in Jesus' resurrection* and founded upon this faith. But if Jesus' person and work appear to them in the light of Easter faith, that means that his significance lay neither in the content of what he had taught nor in some modification of the Messiah idea. It does mean, though, that *Jesus' having come was itself the decisive event* through which God called His Congregation (Church). It means that Jesus' coming itself was already eschatological occurrence. Indeed, that is the real content of the Easter faith: God has made the prophet and teacher Jesus of Nazareth Messiah!

2. *To what extent the earliest Church itself already explicitly recognized* that the fact that Jesus had come was the decisive eschatological occurrence is another question. Statements like those of Paul that when the fulness of time was come, God sent his son (Gal. 4:4) or that by virtue of Jesus' death the "old" had passed away and (all) had become new (II Cor. 5:17) are still foreign to the earliest Church along with their consequences—that now the epoch of the Law is past and the Law is abolished. And that the earliest Church was distinctly conscious that the new age had dawned (Kümmel's opinion), is probably an exaggeration. As the synoptic tradition shows, the expectation of the imminent dramatic End, the parousia of Jesus as Son of Man, controlled the consciousness of the Church, and Jesus' advent and ministry was not yet clearly recognized as eschatological occurrence. Only implicitly in the Church's eschatological understanding of itself was this recognition present, and only beginnings toward its development are manifest—beginnings that lay under certain restraints.

That this recognition was implicitly present is shown in the first place by the fact that for the Church, as for Jesus himself, the content of his message was not the decisive thing. In his lifetime he had demanded decision for his person as the bearer of the Word; the Church has now made this decision. Jesus' call to decision implies a christology. That call does not justify speculation about him as a heavenly being. Nor does it support the Messiah-consciousness attributed to him. But it does imply a christology which will unfold the implications of the positive answer to his demand for the decision, the obedient response which acknowledges God's revelation in Jesus. Such christology became explicit in the earliest Church to the extent that they understood Jesus as the one whom God by the resurrection has made Messiah, and that they awaited him as the coming Son of Man. For it is apparent that in that very fact they understood his sending as God's decisive act. In expecting him as the Coming One they understood themselves as the Congregation of the end of days called by him. For them factually—no matter to what degree it may have been clearly conscious—the old had passed away and the world had become new.

In the synoptic tradition a series of sayings shows that Jesus' work was conceived as decisive happening, especially such as speak of him as *having come* or *having been sent*. They are scarcely (at least in the majority of cases) original words of Jesus, but mostly products of the Church. And so far as they had already arisen in the earliest (i.e. the Palestinian) Church (which cannot in every case be clearly made out), they testify that this Church in retrospect conceived the phenomenon of Jesus together with its meaning as a unity: It was a divine "sending" by which the Church was called, its destiny determined, its problems decided. He "came" not to call the righteous, but sinners (Mk. 2:17). He "was sent" to the lost sheep of the house of Israel (Mt. 15:24). He "came" to cast fire on the earth (Lk. 12:49). His "coming" means not peace, but a sword (Mt. 10:34-36 par.), i.e. it means the eschatological hour of decision and division. Whoever receives him, receives Him who "sent" him (Mk. 9:37 or Mt. 10:40); whoever rejects him, rejects Him who "sent" him (Lk. 10:16). Other related sayings will be discussed in another context.* That his sending meant doom for Jerusalem is expressed by the saying Lk. 13:34f. par., probably in origin a Jewish prophecy concerning "Wisdom," perhaps once quoted by Jesus, but as we now have it, re-interpreted by the Church and put back into his mouth: It was he who had desired in vain to gather Jerusalem's "children" together, so that it now was forsaken.†

3. The decision which Jesus' disciples had once made to affirm and accept his sending by "following" him, had to be made anew and radically in consequence of his crucifixion. *The cross,* so to say, raised the question of decision once more. Little as it could throw into question the content of his message, all the more it could and did render questionable his legitimation, his claim to be God's mes-

---

* *Cf.* on the "I-sayings," *Gesch. d. synopt. Trad.*, 2nd edition, 161–176.
† *Cf. Gesch. d. synopt. Trad.*, 2nd edition, 120f.

senger bringing the last, decisive word. The Church had to surmount the scandal of the cross and did it in the Easter faith.

How this act of decision took place in detail, how the Easter faith arose in individual disciples, has been obscured in the tradition by legend and is not of basic importance. Mk. 14:28 and 16:7 indicate that after Jesus' arrest the disciples fled to Galilee and that there Peter was the first to behold the Risen One, as I Cor. 15:5 corroborates. A trace of this fact is also preserved in Lk. 24:34, and Lk. 22:31f. probably goes back to the same event (see *Gesch. d. synopt. Trad.*, 2nd edition, 387f.). This basic event is reflected in the narratives of Peter's confession [Mk. 8:27–29], the transfiguration [Mk. 9:2–8 (§ 4, 1)], and Peter's miraculous catch of fish [Lk. 5:1–11], as well as in the words about Peter, the Rock [Mt. 16:17–19 (§ 1, 3)]. The accounts of the empty grave, of which Paul still knows nothing, are legends. According to I Cor. 15:5–8, where Paul enumerates the appearances of the risen Lord as tradition offered them, the resurrection of Jesus meant simultaneously his exaltation; not until later was the resurrection interpreted as a temporary return to life on earth, and this idea then gave rise to the ascension story (Lk. 24:50–53, Acts 1:3–11). The appearances of the risen Lord probably were not confined to Galilee but also occurred at Jerusalem after the disciples had return there (Luke reports only such). How the appearances enumerated in I Cor. 15:5–8 are to be distributed between Galilee and Jerusalem cannot be known, and it is a mere supposition that the appearance to the five hundred brethren (I Cor. 15:6) is identical with the event of Pentecost. Concerning these matters see in recent literature: Lyder Brun, *Die Auferstehung Christi in der urchristl. Überlieferung* (1925); Selby Vernon McCasland, *The Resurrection of Jesus* (1932); Maurice Goguel, *La foi à la Résurrection de Jésus dans le Christianisme primitif* (1933); Kirsopp Lake in *The Beginnings of Christianity* V (1933), 7–16; Em. Hirsch, *Die Auferstehungsgeschichten und der christliche Glaube* (1940); W. Grundmann, ZNW 39 (1940), 110–121; Paul Althaus, *Die Wahrheit des kirchlichen Osterglaubens* 2 (1941).

The rise of the Easter faith made necessary *a way of understanding the cross* that would surmount, yes, transform, the scandal of the curse which in Jewish opinion had befallen the crucified Jesus (*cf.* Gal. 3:13); the cross had to make sense in the context of the salvation-process. How far such an understanding was worked out in the earliest Church cannot clearly be seen. Scripture proof explaining Jesus' suffering and death as divinely decreed in the manner of Lk. 24:26f. can be taken as characteristic of one stage of the earliest Church's reflection on the subject: "'Was it not necessary that the Christ should suffer these things and enter into his glory?' And beginning with Moses and all the prophets, he interpreted to them in all the scriptures the things concerning himself." If that was their understanding, one would have to admit that as yet the stumbling-block of the cross had only been negatively removed so so long as it was only placed under the divine "must" (δεῖ), and that its positive meaning had not yet become clear. Yet even so in this surmounting of the σκάνδαλον (stumbling-block, scandal) it would have come to light that in the cross of Christ Jewish standards of judgment and human notions of the splendor of the Messiah are shattered. Thus, the acknowledgment of the Crucified as Messiah implicitly contains a new understanding of man-before-God.

But probably something more may be said. In the tradition that had come down to Paul, do not both "according to the scriptures" κατὰ τὰς γραφάς and "for our sins" ὑπὲρ τῶν ἁμαρτιῶν ἡμῶν go back to the earliest Church? Then Jesus' death would already have been conceived as an expiatory sacrifice in the earliest Church! In favor of this view speak two other passages from Paul; in them he is visibly leaning on traditional formulations, perhaps even quoting them —at least in part. One of these sentences is Rom. 3:24f., in which one only needs to set off the specifically Pauline expressions with parentheses as his additions: ". . . justified (by his grace as a gift) through the redemption which is in Christ Jesus, whom God put forward as an expiation by his blood (to be received by faith); this was to show God's righteousness, because in his divine forbearance he had passed over former sins" (Blt.). The designation of Christ as the ἱλαστήριον (expiation, mercy-seat) occurs only here in Paul; nor is it Paul's habit elsewhere (except Rom. 5:9 and, again following tradition, in reference to the Lord's Supper, I Cor. 10:16; 11:25, 27) to speak of "the blood" of Christ, but of "the cross." Finally the idea found here of the divine righteousness demanding expiation for former sins is otherwise foreign to him. Hence, what we are here dealing with is evidently a traditional statement, which perhaps can be traced back to the earliest Church. It is the same with Rom. 4:25—a sentence which in form (synthetic parallelism of members) makes the impression of a quotation. Perhaps this statement was formulated in reminiscence of Is. 53; if so, that would make it probable that in Is. 53, too, a prophecy of Jesus' passion had already been found by the earliest Church, though this discovery did not take place in its very earliest period (see § 4, 3).

The interpretation of Jesus' death as an expiatory sacrifice for sins was, in itself, not unnatural to Jewish thinking. For in it the idea of the expiating power of the suffering of the righteous, especially of the martyr, had been developed. *Cf.* Str.-B. II 275-282; W. Bousset, *Die Religion des Judent.*, 3rd edition, 198f.; G. F. Moore, *Judaism* I 547-549; E. Sjöberg, *Gott und die Sünder im paläst. Judentum* (1939), 174f., 222. However, to the Judaism of Jesus' time the idea of a messiah suffering for sinners is entirely foreign; *cf.* G. Dalman, *Der leidende und der sterbende Messias der Synagoge* (1888); W. Staerk, *Soter* I (1933), 78-84; Str.-B. I 273-299; G. F. Moore, l.c. 551f. A different opinion in Joach. Jeremias, *Jesus als Weltvollender* (1930).

4. Through the fact that the Church awaits the prophet and teacher as Son of Man and in the light of Easter faith understands Jesus' earthly ministry anew, *a power to determine the present is also attributed to the figure of Jesus.* The future ruler and bringer of salvation already exercises his royal sway in a certain manner now from heaven, into which he has been exalted. When his words are collected that is done not simply because of their didactic content, but because they are his, the coming king's, words. According to rabbinic ideas the Messiah, when he comes, will also act as a teacher of Torah°—the Church already possesses Jesus' exegesis of the Law and in his "But I say unto you!" hears him speak as Messiah. In his words they already have the wisdom and knowledge which according to the belief of the apocalyptic writers the Messiah will someday bestow.† Out of such conviction new "words of the Lord" arise whose purpose is to decide moot questions; such are: "Think not that I have come to abolish the Law and the prophets! I have come not to abolish them but to fulfill them . . ." (Mt. 5:17,

° *Cf.* P. Seidelin, *ZNW* 35 (1936), 194ff.; P. Volz, *Die Eschatologie der jüd. Gemeinde* (1934), 218.
† *Cf.* P. Volz, *l.c.*

cf. 18–19). "I was sent only to the lost sheep of the house of Israel" (Mt. 15:24). There also arise sayings that testify that whatever fate one now experiences is understood as sent from him and whatever one conceives to be his task as commanded by him: "Do not believe that I have come to bring peace to the earth—but rather the sword! . . ." (Mt. 10:34 par. Blt., *cf.* 35–36 par.; see above, 2). "Fear not little flock, for the Father has decided to give you the Reign" (Lk. 12:32 Blt.). It is he who sends the messengers who are to carry the cry of the approach of God's Reign through the land (Mk. 6:7ff. or Mt. 9:37ff. par.). In his name the prophets speak: "Lo, I send you out as sheep into the midst of wolves" (Mt. 10:16 par. Blt.). "Behold, I have given you authority to tread upon serpents and scorpions; . . . and nothing shall hurt you" (Lk. 10:19);—just as we also find in Revelation examples of Christian prophets speaking in the name of the exalted Christ (*cf.* Rev. 3:20; 16:15). The invitation "come unto me," promising rest to those "that labor and are heavy laden" (Mt. 11:28f.) probably comes from some old "Wisdom" book; perhaps the earliest Church already put this saying into the mouth of Jesus. Certainly out of the earliest Church come the words in which the risen Lord, with royal bearing, delegates to Peter the direction of the Congregation—which he even calls "my Congregation" (Mt. 16:17–19); likewise his promise to the twelve that they shall someday be the regents of the tribes of Israel (Mt. 19:28 or Lk. 22:28–30). It is easily understandable that rules of Church discipline, which become necessary in the course of time, are regarded as his orders (Mt. 18:15–18). Indeed the earliest Church seems to have transformed a saying already current among the Jews which spoke of the presence of God with two men occupied with interpreting the Torah, into the saying: "Where two or three are gathered in my name, there am I in the midst of them" (Mt. 18:20). And it is not impossible that the name of Jesus in reminiscence of his own banning of demons was used as an effective means for exorcisms and other miraculous deeds. If Mk. 9:38–40 (though it probably was lacking in Mark as it originally was) should have come out of the tradition of the earliest Church, it would be a witness to such practice; likewise Acts 3:6.

5. The *titles* the Church conferred upon Jesus to indicate his significance and dignity were borrowed from the tradition of Jewish messianic faith, in which motifs of diverse origin were admittedly

united. All these titles, though their original meanings may have been various, agree in being designations for the eschatological salvation-bringer. Naturally Jesus was given the ancient title *"Messiah,"* i.e. anointed king, as the synoptic tradition testifies and Paul, too, clearly implies. This is the only reason that the double name Jesus Christ could then arise, as it did, in Hellenistic Christianity.

However, the predominant title in the earliest Church, by the testimony of the synoptic tradition, was "Son of Man," which comes out of the apocalyptic hope and means a supra-mundane, pre-existent being who at the end of time will come down from heaven to hold judgment and bring salvation (§ 1, 1); whereas the Messiah-title, coming out of the national hope, designates the king (of David's line), who is thought of as a mere man, no matter how much his arrival and his deeds may be guided and determined by God's supranatural intervention.

The title *Son of David* also comes out of the national tradition and is synonymous with Messiah. This title seems not to have played any great role in the earliest Church, since its occurrence is relatively rare in the synoptic tradition (not found in Q at all). On the other hand, Paul must have found it in current use before him. For though the title is of no importance to him, he refers to it in Rom. 1:3, a sentence which is evidently due to a handed-down formula; he desires thereby to accredit himself to the unknown Roman Church as an apostle who advocates right doctrine. Released from its Pauline syntax and freed of Pauline additions, the formula may be regarded as having run as follows:

"(Jesus Christ) the Son of God,
   Come from the seed of David,
   Designated Son of God in power by his resurrection from the
      dead." (Blt.) *

Whether or not the mutually divergent lineages (Mt. 1:1–17 and Lk. 3:23–38), which were intended to demonstrate the Davidic descent of Jesus, go back to the earliest Church, or to what extent they may do so, cannot be said. If Mk. 12:35–37 originated in the earliest Church, then criticism against transferring this title to Jesus had

* II Tim. 2:8 is also to be regarded as going back to an old formula; *cf.* H. Windisch, ZNW 34 (1935), 213–216.

possibly arisen in it (§ 4, 2). At any rate the title promptly established itself.

The messianic king is also meant by the title *Son of God*, which Rom. 1:3 likewise attests as already traditional before Paul. Whether Son of God was already current as a messianic title in Judaism, is uncertain and debated; it has not been proved to have been so used. Still it must be regarded as perfectly possible, since Ps. 2, in which by the use of the ancient oriental formula of adoption, the king is called Son of God, was already interpreted messianically in Judaism as it was in the Christian Church. But it is clear that neither in Judaism nor in the Christian Church could this title have the mythological meaning it later had in Hellenistic Christianity; that is, it did not designate the Messiah as a supernatural being begotten by God, but was simply a royal title. Though the synoptic passages in which Jesus is called Son of God are mostly either secondary and of Hellenistic-Christian origin, or else were formulated by the respective evangelist, still the transfiguration with "this is my beloved son" (Mk. 9:7) goes back to early tradition. If it was originally an Easter story (§ 4, 1), then it may be regarded along with Rom. 1, 3 as proving that the earliest Church called Jesus Son of God (messianic) because that was what the resurrection made him. However, unlike the later Hellenistic Church it did not regard the earthly Jesus as a Son of God (mythological); and the legend of Jesus' birth from the virgin is unknown to it as also to Paul.

In the apocalypses, IV Ezra and II Baruch, occurs the messianic title *"Servant of God"* which means nothing else than Messiah or Son of God. It comes from the Old Testament, in which favored men of piety, found worthy of a special mission by God, such as Abraham, Moses, and the prophets, are so called, and also kings, and the title clings especially to David of whom it became traditional; in this last sense it also occurs at Lk. 1:69, Acts 4:25, Did. 9:2 (in the last case used both of David and of Jesus). Hence, it is easily understandable that the Messiah as Son of David also was given this title. In the more detailed description of the messianic Servant of God Deutero-Isaiah may occasionally have played a part —though not the Servant of God of Is. 53 suffering vicariously for sinners, for this servant was interpreted by Jewish exegesis as the people of Israel; and the apocalyptic writers' Servant of God is not a suffering figure, but the messianic ruler and judge. Still influence from Is. 42:1ff. or 49:1ff. is possible, for the dignity of being the "Light of the Gentiles" conferred upon the servant of God in Is. 42:6; 49:6 is transferred to the Son of Man in I Enoch 48:4; i.e. it has become a messianic attribute. Early Christianity took over the title "Servant." Whether the earliest Church had already done so, we, of course, do not know, since it does not occur in the synoptic tradition; only Matthew introduced it (12:18ff.) in one of his reflective quotations (Is. 42:1ff.). It occurs later at Acts 3:13, 26; 4:27, 30, in the last two cases in a prayer of the Church, then in the table-prayers (Did. 9:2f.; 10:2f.) and in the prayer of the Roman congregation (I Clem. 59:2ff.); so it appears to have been early, at any rate, that it was taken into the liturgical vocabulary of the Church.°

The Pauline letters indicate that in the Hellenistic Church Jesus was called "*Lord*" Κύριος and was cultically worshiped. Since W. Bousset's book, *Kyrios Christos* (1913, 2nd edition, 1921), there has been debate whether this implies that the earliest Church had already entitled Jesus "Lord" and invoked him as such in prayer. Bousset, who vigorously denied it, is probably right. In any case, the earliest Church did not cultically worship Jesus, even if it should have called him Lord; the Kyrios-cult originated on Hellenistic soil.

Judaism, at any rate, never entitled the Messiah "Lord." At the very outset the un-modified expression "the Lord" is unthinkable in Jewish usage. "Lord" used of God is always given some modifier; we read: "the Lord of heaven and earth," "our Lord" and similar expressions. Used of Jesus, therefore, at least "*our* Lord" or something similar would be required. The oldest stratum of the synoptic tradition does not speak of Jesus as Lord; in Q the title never appears, in Mark only in the legendary story 11:3, while Luke, and he alone, frequently uses an absolute ὁ Κύριος (the Lord) in narrative. The vocative "Lord" Κύριε, which also occurs in the old tradition, proves nothing, for it is only a translation of the Aramaic title of address used by a pupil ("disciple") to his teacher ("master"): "my (or our) lord"; and Lord Κύριε and Rabbi ῥαββί (= my great one) alternate in Mark and Matthew as titles of address to Jesus. The eschatological prayer "Maranatha!" μαρὰν ἀθᾶ (מָרָנָא תָא = "Our

---

° *Cf.* besides Bousset, *Kyrios Chr.*, 2nd edition, 56f., and W. Staerk, *Soter* I 24ff., 77ff.: Ad. v. Harnack, *Die Bezeichnung Jesu als "Knecht Gottes" und ihre Geschichte in der alten Kirche* [Sitzungsber. d. Preuss. Akad. d. Wiss., Phil.-hist. Kl. (1926), 28]; P. Seidelin, ZNW 35 (1936), 230f.

Lord, come!") found at I Cor. 16:22 certainly comes out of the earliest Church, but it likewise is no proof that the earliest Church invoked Jesus as Lord; for it can originally have meant God, even if it was later taken to refer to Jesus (*cf.* Rev. 22:20). And though the phrase "those who call on the name of our Lord Jesus Christ" (I Cor. 1:2; *cf.* Acts 9:14, 21; 22:16; II Tim. 2:22) became a current designation for Christians in the Hellenistic Church, that proves nothing for the earliest Church. On this point, besides Bousset's *Kyrios Christos, cf.*: P. Wernle, *Jesus und Paulus* NKZ (1915), 439–457, 513–545; W. Heitmüller, *Jesus und Paulus* ZThK 25 (1915),156–179; W. Bousset, *Jesus der Herr* (1916); Werner Foerster, *Herr ist Jesus* (1924); E. Lohmeyer, *Kyrios Christos* (1928) (in which foreign literature is also tabulated); Wolf W. Graf Baudissin, *Kyrios als Gottesbezeichnung im Judentum und seine Stellung in der Religionsgeschichte* I–IV (1929); E. V. Dobschütz, Κύριος ʼΙησοῦς ZNW 30 (1931), 97–123.

In his book *Galiläa und Jerusalem* (1936), E. Lohmeyer developed the thesis, since carried out in other investigations and especially in his commentary on Mark, that there were really two "earliest Churches" on Palestinian soil, or at least two characteristically differing parties: the Galilean and that of Jerusalem. For the Galilean Church, or party, according to him, Jesus as Son of Man was characteristic; for Jerusalem, Jesus as Messiah—but the title "Lord" also comes from the Galilean Church. It is probably correct that there were various parties in the Palestinian Church—but scarcely from the very beginning; they probably developed only gradually. It is perhaps also right that Jesus' whole following in Galilee did not move from there to Jerusalem after the Easter experiences, and that a Galilean Church existed side by side with that at Jerusalem, though it scarcely had the importance that Lohmeyer attributes to it. Paul, at any rate, takes only the Jerusalem Church into account, where at first the twelve were at the head until James, the Lord's brother, won the leadership—all Galileans in origin and hence representatives of Galilean tradition. At any rate, it is evidently impossible to conceive the titles "Messiah" and "Son of Man" as expressions of two differing theological views about Jesus and hence as distinguishing marks of two differing Churches or parties. Both alike denote the eschatological salvation-bringer. The ancient title "Messiah," once expressing Israelitic national hope, was no longer confined to this narrower meaning but could just as well be transferred to the heavenly salvation-bringer awaited by the apocalyptists, as the salvation to be brought by the latter could, vice versa, take on nationalistic traits. In the parables of I Enoch, "Son of Man" and "Messiah" alternate as titles of the same figure; likewise in IV Ezra. In the latter the messianic title "Servant of God" also appears, and it is expressly given to the Son of Man (13:32, 37, 52), while in II Bar. 70:9 it is the Messiah who is designated Servant of God. Furthermore in II Baruch the Messiah is pictured in every respect as the supernatural salvation-bringer of apocalyptic expectation except that he does not bear the title "Son of Man." Neither does anything in the synoptic tradition indicate that the varying titles "Messiah" and "Son of Man" express varying conceptions of Jesus' person; moreover, Paul, who does not use the apocalyptic title "Son of Man," clearly does not use the term Christ (so far as that is a title for him, and not a personal name) in the sense of the nationalistic hope, but in that of apocalypticism.

§ 8. Beginnings toward Development of Ecclesiastical Forms

1. What consequences did the earliest Church draw from its eschatological consciousness for its practical everyday attitudes, particularly its conduct toward Judaism and its institutions and adherents? How far did it see the total reality of its life in the light of eschatological occurrence?

Naturally the eschatological Congregation does not regard itself as a new religion—i.e. a new historical phenomenon—*and does not draw a boundary between itself, as a new religion, and Judaism.* It remains loyal to the temple and the temple cult. According to Acts 2:46 it customarily gathers within the temple area; according to Mt. 5:23f. it did not give up the sacrificial practices of Judaism, as Jesus also had not polemized against the temple cult (§ 2, 3). And just as the legend (Mt. 17:24–27) testifies that the Christian Congregation paid the temple tax in spite of knowing its inner separation from the old Jewish congregation, so Mk. 13:9 or Mt. 10:17 testifies that it felt itself subject to synagogal jurisdiction. As the Congregation of the end of days it conceives of itself as that true Israel, which is the goal of Israel's salvation-history, and for which the promises of the Old Testament are now being fulfilled (§ 6, 6).

That is where the problem lies: how far is "true Israel" understood as a really eschatological thing and how far as only a selection out of the historical People? How far is "Israel"—the subject to whom salvation happens—understood as meaning an absolutely eschatological entity, as it is by Paul, and how far as just the empirical People of history? Will the earliest Church eliminate from the idea of the Chosen People whatever applies only to the historical People? In what sense will the Old Testament's consciousness of history be adopted?

2. The question becomes acute *over the validity of the Law.* Is the Old Testament Law binding upon the members of the eschatological Congregation? And is obedience to the Law, therefore, the condition for participation in eschatological salvation? At first, this question does not seem to have been clearly answered; in fact, it does not seem even to have been clearly asked at first. In practice, however, a relative liberty toward the cultic-ritual demands of the Law must have existed. For could men preserve Jesus' critical and polemic words against Jewish legalism without orienting themselves by them? Could a man pass on Jesus' words against counting up reward and against the pride of the legally correct and at the same time impose the condition of legal merit upon the sharing of salvation? It is freely granted that the antinomy uncovered by Paul—faith, or works of the Law—did not become explicit in the earliest Church. On the contrary, its attitude toward Hellenistic Christianity, especially toward Paul, indicates that it did not achieve freedom from the Law. Presumably a retrogression had taken place so that the old scruples and fidelity to the Law had gradually gained ground; such was completely the case later with Jewish-Christian sects. This is partly attributable to the personal influence of James, the Lord's brother, and is partly a reaction against the criticism of the Law and the temple-cult on the part of the Hellenistic Church. The conclusions drawn by the Hellenists were terrifying and thus originated the famous saying placed into Jesus' mouth, "Think not that I have come to abolish the law and the prophets; I have come not to abolish them but to fulfill them. For truly, I say to you, till heaven and earth pass away, not an iota, not a dot will pass from the law . . ." (Mt. 5:17f.). And if he who relaxes one of the least of the commandments is to be counted as least in God's Reign (Mt. 5:19), that is said with regard to the Hellenists, perhaps to Paul himself.

But this lack of certainty and clarity was probably heightened by the fact that another question mingled with the question of the Law as the way to salvation. For the Law was not merely the way to salvation, and its fulfilment had not merely the character of meritorious accomplishment. It was also the gift of God which gave the Chosen People its rank and dignity. The history of salvation was the history of the People of Israel, the eschatological Congregation was the true Israel. Hence, fulfilment of the Law was the condition for participation in salvation insofar as it was the condition for membership in the People of Israel. And it is now clear that the earliest Church clung to this condition. However much (at least in the beginning) it may (under the influence of Jesus' words) have had a critical attitude toward Jewish legalism, and however much it may have broken with the Jewish idea of merit, it clung to the Law as a characteristic of the Chosen People which it was conscious of embodying.

This is indicated, in the first place, by the fact that the *mission to the heathen* was not regarded as an obligation by the Jerusalem Church. Rather, the saying placed into Jesus' mouth, "Go nowhere among the Gentiles, and enter no town of the Samaritans, but go rather to the lost sheep of the house of Israel" (Mt. 10:5f.), shows that in the earliest Church there was at least a party which altogether rejected the mission to the Gentiles; the saying (Mt. 10:23) also assumes a message for Jews only. Perhaps there were various opinions on this subject; perhaps a development took place from one opinion to another. At any rate the legendary stories of the Centurion at Capernaum (Mt. 8:5-10 par.) and the Syrophoenician woman (Mk. 7:24-30), both variations on the same motif, inform us on the one hand that before long Gentiles, too, were received into the Congregation of salvation and on the other hand that that was only exceptionally and hesitantly done. And the tradition worked into Acts 10:1ff. about Cornelius the Centurion at Caesarea permits the same insight. But especially Galatians and the tradition on which Acts 15 is based indicate that it was required of Gentiles who wished to join the eschatological Congregation of salvation that they adopt the Law, especially circumcision. But that means: the condition for sharing in salvation is belonging to the Jewish People —the empirical People of history. This, then, is the point where the conflict breaks out, first within the Church in Jerusalem between the old followers of Jesus and the Hellenistic Jewish-Christians, then between the Jerusalem Church and Paul.

Hellenistic Jews who had returned to Jerusalem and had their own synagogues there (Acts 6:9) as a matter of course took a more liberal stand toward the Law. It is understandable that when such men joined the Christian Congregation, criticism of the Law and the temple cult made itself heard from their midst; such is testified (Acts 6:11, 13f.) of Stephen, one of their number. The conflict that had broken out in the Jerusalem Church apparently lurks behind the choice of the "seven men" (Acts 6:1ff.). For those seven were not "deacons," but were, as their Greek names (6:5) show, representatives of the *Hellenistic party*. What is told of Stephen, and later of Philip, also indicates that their office was by no means serving table, but that they were proclaimers of the word. These Hellenistic Christians occasioned among the Jews an uproar that evidently was not directed against the old Jewish-Christian Congregation, but against the Hellenists. Stephen was stoned and his fellow-partisans were driven out, and thereby the problem was for the time being beaten down both for the Jews and for the Jewish-Christian Church. But it soon arose again—and partly in direct consequence of the missionary activity of those driven out (Acts 8:4ff.; 11:19ff.)—when Gentile-Christian congregations arose for which adoption of the Law and especially circumcision no longer held as the condition for admission to the Congregation and for participation in messianic salvation.

In the dispute with Paul and Barnabas at the *"apostolic council"* reported in Gal. 2:1–10,* the Jerusalem Church acknowledged the right of Gentile Christianity to exist free from the Law. But Gentile Christians were evidently not regarded as having fully equal rights, as appears from the fact that in Antioch, and presumably elsewhere, new conflicts broke out over the question of table-fellowship in mixed congregations (Gal. 2:11ff.). To settle the dispute, regulations were released in Jerusalem which demanded certain concessions from Gentile Christians. These constitute the so-called "apostolic decree" (Acts 21:25).†

In his monograph *Apostel und Jünger* (1921), Rol. Schütz attempted to prove that Torah-free Hellenistic Christianity was the earlier stage, i.e. that it consisted of the congregations which grew up in Galilee, Samaria and the Decapolis out of Jesus'

---

* A parallel account is found in Acts 15; but the source on which it rests told about another meeting and decision—*viz.*, the one which resulted in the so-called "apostolic decree."

† See the foregoing note.

preaching, and that the Torah-loyal Church in Jerusalem was a later formation. This view, based upon a questionable literary analysis of Acts, cannot be maintained. On the basis of an unsuccessful source-analysis, W. Grundmann unconvincingly discusses *"das Problem des hellenist. Christentums innerhalb der Jerusalemer Urgemeinde"* ZNW 38 (1939), 45–73. Concerning the various parties and the position of Peter, James, and Paul within the conflict, *cf.* H. Lietzmann, *Zwei Notizen zu Paulus,* Sitzungsber. d. Preuss. Ak. d. Wiss., Phil.-Hist. Kl. (1930), VIII; Em. Hirsch, *Paulus und Petrus,* ZNW 29 (1930), 63–76; Gerh. Kittel, *Die Stellung des Jakobus zu Judentum und Heidenchristentum,* ZNW 30 (1931), 145–157; W. Grundmann, *Die Apostel zwischen Jerusalem und Antiochia,* ZNW 39 (1940), 110–137.

3. The development of the Church concept in the earliest Church was of course also hindered in other ways by its ties to the Jewish congregation. The Church as eschatological Congregation had not yet found appropriate expression in a cult of its own, since it had not cut itself loose from the temple cult. Only beginnings in that direction are present in the fact that the Church met not only in the temple area, but also in private houses (Acts 2:46)—whether as a whole or in separate groups (*cf.* Acts 12:12), information is lacking. But with the increase of the Church, especially after the acceptance of Hellenistic members, they can probably only have been group meetings. It can be taken for granted that they here sought edification together by interpretation of Scripture and that they called to mind words of Jesus. Nor is it impossible that the earliest Church set up its own synagogue service, since a number of synagogues are known to have existed in Jerusalem for the various groups of Judaism; but about that we know nothing.

Baptism (§ 6, 3), of course, was also a point of departure for the development of cultic forms of their own, and even more so *the common meals* (§ 6, 4), but they were no more than points of departure. For though these meals can indeed be called celebrations of the Congregation, still they are not actual cultic celebrations, much less the sacrament of the "Lord's Supper" as celebrated in the Pauline or Hellenistic congregations, whose liturgy we know from Mark and Paul. Rather, they are the main meal of the day, for nourishment, made into a solemn occasion. When this meal is called "the breaking of bread" (Acts 2:42, 46), that implies that they outwardly resembled Jewish meals which began with the act of breadbreaking and the accompanying blessing. That bread-breaking and blessing belong together, the Christian accounts also show (Mk. 6:41, 14:22; Lk. 24:30; Did. 9:3, 14:1). Wine might, of course, be drunk at such a meal, too, when it was available, but it had no cultic significance; otherwise the meal could not have been called simply "the breaking of bread." The origin of these meal-celebrations lies without doubt in the table-fellowship which once had united Jesus and his "disciples." No special reference to Jesus' last meal is in them. That comes only in the "Lord's Supper" of the Hellenistic congregations.

On the differentiation of the two forms of the Meal, the Palestinian form of the earliest Church and the Hellenistic-Pauline form, *cf.* H. Lietzmann, *Messe und Herrenmahl* (1926); O. Cullmann, *La signification de la Sainte-Cène dans le Christianisme primitif* (1936). E. Lohmeyer has dealt extensively and instructively with the questions involving the Lord's Supper and with the discussion of them in recent literature in *ThR*, NF 9 (1937), 168–227, 273–312; 10 (1938), 81–99. He also distinguishes the two types but believes he has found both in the earliest Church and thinks he can attribute them to the respective parties that he thought he had distinguished in it (§7, 5): the "breaking of bread," he thinks, was the "Galilean" tradition, while the Lord's Supper was characteristic of the "Jerusalem" party; the latter, he maintains, was regarded as instituted in Jesus' last meal, and its center was the memorial of Jesus' death. He also developed this idea in *JBL* LVI (1937), 217–252.

4. *The direction of the Church* was at first in the hands of "the twelve." Yet this was not really an office of the Church. Borne along by the expectation of the approaching End, they at first naturally did not think of setting up any such thing. "The twelve," as the future princes of the twelve tribes of Israel (§ 7, 4), are not so much an institution as a symbol of the eschatological Congregation as the true Israel. Their practical work was evidently as proclaimers of the word both within the Congregation and outside, and on missionary journeys they seem to have left Jerusalem either temporarily or (like Peter) permanently. The dominant authority was at first

Peter, as is testified by Mt. 16:17–19, Lk. 22:31f. and by the role that Peter played both in the synoptic tradition as a whole and in Paul. Besides him, John, the son of Zebedee, and James, the Lord's brother, must soon have won a leading position; Paul speaks of those three as the "pillars" (Gal. 2:9, *cf.* 1:18f.). Then, when Peter had left Jerusalem and John (presumably about 44 A.D.) had been executed with his brother James, the Lord's brother James remained the recognized authority (Acts 12:17, 21:18).

The *"elders"* constitute a real office of the Congregation. In accordance with Jewish precedent elders were evidently chosen at a relatively early period—when, we do not know. They are first encountered in the source behind Acts 11:30; and in 21:18, another passage with a source behind it, they are named with James. It may be due to editing by the author that in Acts 15 (as in 16:4) "the apostles and elders" appear as leaders of the Congregation. Presumably James was chairman of the council of elders.

The question that really matters is: *What office can be appropriately instituted* for the direction of the eschatological Congregation? Undoubtedly it can only be one *founded upon the proclamation of the word*: It was clear to Paul that at the same time that God instituted "reconciliation" he thereby instituted "the ministry of reconciliation" διακονία τῆς καταλλαγῆς, "the message of reconciliation" λόγος τῆς καταλλαγῆς (II Cor. 5:18f.). This "service," this "message," was at first and above all the concern of "the twelve" in the earliest Church —not, of course, as the future twelve princes of the salvation time, but because they were proclaimers of the word and guardians of the tradition. For since the Congregation is not founded by the persons it includes, as if it were a club or an association, but is conscious of having been founded by God's deed, it, like the Old Testament-Jewish congregation, needs *tradition*, in which the history which founded it is preserved and made present. Secondarily this tradition is the passing on of Jesus' message, but primarily it is the passing on of the specifically Christian kerygma—and is the former only within the frame of the latter. The legendary story of the election to re-complete the number of the twelve quite correctly expresses the substance of the matter: "So one of the men who have accompanied us during all the time that the Lord Jesus went in and out among us, beginning from the baptism of John until the day when he was taken up from us—one of these men must become with us a witness to his resurrection" (Acts 1:21f.). And I Cor. 15:3-7 as well as 11:23 shows that a kerygma is developing in which the tradition about the occurrence of salvation was fixed. The significant question for the future is whether the traditional message will be conceived as the factor which constitutes the Church—and if so, how.

Tradition requires continuity, i.e. *succession*, which need not be one mediated by an institution or sacraments. In Paul, too (*cf.* I Cor. 12:28), and even as late as Eph. 4:11f., the succession is a free one; i.e. not institutionally regulated but left to the free sway of the Spirit. The apostle is called in the first place by having seen the Lord—i.e. the Risen One (I Cor. 9:1); then he is legitimated by his missionary labor ἔργον (I Cor. 9:1); and that also means he is accredited by "all patience, with signs and wonders and mighty works" (II Cor. 12:12. *Cf.* I Thess. 1:5, I Cor. 2:4f., Rom. 15:19, Heb. 2:4). The idea of apostolic succession as an institution, the custom of ordination by the laying on of hands, appears for the first time in the pastoral epistles. The restriction of the concept "apostle" to the "twelve," which is an incipient tendency in this direction, can scarcely have taken place in the earliest Church. It is true that the apostle-concept is determined by the idea of tradition and hence also by that of divine commission and legitimation. But it is not yet narrowed down to a closed number; for Paul calls all missionaries "apostles" (I Cor. 9:5; Rom. 16:7; II Cor. 11:5, 13; 12:11f.) and the same usage is still found in Acts 14:4, 14 and Did. 11:4-6.

Karl Holl in his article, "Der Kirchenbegriff des Paulus in seinem Verhältnis zur Urgemeinde," [*] asserts that in the earliest Church the apostolate was a legal institution and restricted to the twelve. The opposite view is convincingly maintained by Wilh. Mundle, ZNW 22 (1923), 20-42, and W. G. Kümmel, *Kirchenbegriff*, etc., 6f. *Cf.* also Ferd. Kattenbusch, *Die Vorzugstellung des Petrus und der Charakter der Urgemeinde in Jerusalem*, Festgabe für Karl Müller (1922), 322-351.

However, the idea of tradition and succession finds characteristic expression in the fact that *Jerusalem is regarded as the center of the whole Church*—and obviously is so regarded not merely in the con-

---

[*] "Sitzungsb. d. Preuss. Akad. d. Wiss., Phil.-hist. Kl." (1921), 920-947; reprinted in Holl's collected essays: *Gesammelte Aufsätze zur Kirchengeschichte.*

sciousness of the Jerusalem Church. Paul and the author of Acts also bear witness to that fact. Paul finds it very important that the Gentile Congregations, to whom this idea in itself was necessarily strange, shall preserve connection with Jerusalem. Under this point of view the decision of the "apostolic council" that the Gentile congregations shall raise funds for the poor in Jerusalem (Gal. 2:10) is of special significance. I Cor. 16:1-4, II Cor. 8-9, Rom. 15:25-28 show how much Paul was concerned with this collection, for the collection has not just the meaning of a simple act of charity, but that of an act of faith, inasmuch as it documents their connection with the history of salvation. It is neither "a pious work toward the circle of charismatics and ascetics at Jerusalem" (Er. Peterson *RGG*, 2nd ed., III 464) nor a church tax (K. Holl, *l.c.*). When in Acts the legal right of supervision over all Christian congregations is ascribed to the Jerusalem congregation, that is certainly legendary. Barnabas, who according to Acts 11:22 was dispatched from Jerusalem to the Antioch congregation, was in the source-account underlying 11:19-26 evidently not a Jerusalem inspector, but belonged himself (as a Hellenistic Jewish Christian, *cf.* Acts 4:36) to those Hellenistic exiles from Jerusalem who had founded the congregation in Antioch.

Against Holl's assertion that the Jerusalem Congregation claimed a legal right of supervision and direction over the younger congregations, see Kümmel, *l.c.*, 9, 25, 53f. (footnote 85).

5. As time went on and membership increased, *life within the congregation* naturally needed a *certain regulation* which could not be left to the council of elders to decide from case to case; but the sources barely permit us a glimpse of that. Mt. 16:19 and 18:18 testify that the authority "to bind and to loose," i.e. a disciplinary power, lay first in the hands of Peter, then in those of the Congregation—and that probably means, in the hands of the elders; and Mt. 18:15-17 gives rules for settling quarrels in the congregation. The passage on Jesus' authority to forgive sins, Mk. 2:5b-10, which is inserted into the old miracle-story, 2:1-12, is to be regarded as having originated in the earliest Church, which proved its right to forgive sins by referring it back to Jesus; the Church's legitimation to forgive sins is its power of miraculous healing.*

* See *Gesch. d. synopt. Trad.*, 2nd edition, 12f.

The right of apostle-missionaries to support by the congregations (I Cor. 9:1ff.), which is expressly referred to in a saying of the Lord (I Cor. 9:14; Mt. 10:10 par.) cannot be regarded as a regulation of church law; it corresponds to Jewish custom and is not limited to apostles, as Gal. 6:6 shows.

It is self-evident that in an eschatological congregation awaiting the near end of this world no special economic system was set up. What is often called the community of property in the earliest Church on the basis of Acts 2:45; 4:34ff. is in reality a practical sharing of property on the basis of love. To call this actual communism is out of the question, for it lacks both a social program and organized production.

As there are only tendencies and beginnings in the direction of institutional forms that would give the eschatological Congregation a shape appropriate to its own nature in the historical world, so also the danger is still avoided of regarding the Church as an institution of salvation which mediates salvation by virtue of its offices and sacraments. As the eschatological Congregation, it is the fulfilment of the promises, that is true, but it is also the Congregation that awaits the future.

The *questions* which arise for the future are: How will the eschatological-transcendent character of the Congregation assert itself against its ties with the Jewish people without tearing its ties with the history of salvation? How will the idea of tradition and succession take form? Will the Word remain the constitutive factor? And what institutions will be created to give order to tradition and the life of the Congregation? How in all of this will the relation of the Congregation to the person of Jesus be conceived?

The first answer will be given by Paul's viewpoints: freedom from the Law, the ministry or the message of reconciliation, the body of Christ, and being in Christ, ἐν Χριστῷ.

CHAPTER III

The Kerygma of the Hellenistic Church Aside from Paul

PRELIMINARY REMARKS

1. The historical presupposition for Paul's theology is not the kerygma of the oldest Church but that of the Hellenistic Church; it was the latter that mediated the former to Paul. His theology presupposes a certain development of primitive Christianity which it had undergone after the Christian message had crossed the boundaries of Palestinian Judaism, and congregations of Hellenistic Christians, both Jewish and Gentile, had arisen. Our next task must, therefore, be to sketch a picture of this pre-Pauline Hellenistic Christianity.

But *pre-Pauline Hellenistic Christianity was by no means a unity*. It soon branched out according to whether influences of the synagogue were operative or those of Gentile religions (especially those of the Gnostic stream). Therefore, it is not in every one of its forms that it is pertinent as a presupposition for Paul's theology, and, therefore, also, its significance is not exhausted in its being a pre-stage for Paul. Side by side with Paul it lived on and developed partly along paths of its own, partly under Pauline influence. Its various types unfold and some are represented in such important developments as the Johannine theology—without Pauline influence—or Ignatius of Antioch—under the influence of Paul.

As complete a picture as possible is here to be given of Christianity before and during the time of Paul. At the same time the post-Pauline period will be taken into account wherever it is a matter of indicating theological tendencies which may be recorded only in sources of later date (this could be purely accidental) or which perhaps did not even take effect until after Paul's time, but which were potentially present in the situation itself: the entrance of Christianity into the Hellenistic world and the problems arising therefrom. We must make visible *the whole field of conditions and possibilities* in which independent and significant theological phenomena arise and out of which the theological and ecclesiastical forms of the early Church gradually grow.

2. *For the delineation of Hellenistic Christianity before and contemporary with Paul* there are scarcely any direct witnesses available. The so-called catholic epistles all come from a later time. Hence, it is essentially by reconstruction that the picture must be derived. What means can this task employ? At its disposal stand (1) some few data in *Acts* which are contained in the (Antiochene?) source used in chapters 6–8 and in 11:19–30. Next (2) it must depend upon *inferences from the Pauline letters.* Primary material, of course, is offered by what Paul himself designates as tradition, like I Cor. 11:23ff. and 15:1ff., of which it must be asked in each case how far back such tradition may go. But beyond that, such propositions and terms may be claimed to be tradition as Paul treats as self-evident—generally accepted—matters which he does not introduce as new and neither proves nor defends; this refers to such things as honorific titles of Christ, eschatological propositions, his use of the Old Testament and his method of exegesis, statements about the sacraments, and the like. Finally (3) *inferences from other sources of later date* are both permissible and necessary, especially sources which represent a non-Pauline type of Hellenistic Christianity, such as Hebrews, Barnabas, I Clement, James, and the Kerygma Petri. Here, too, formula-like expressions, statements of a generally accepted character, are the material to be considered. Where these agree with corresponding expressions and statements in Paul, they bear witness not only to other primitive Christian types existing before and by the side of Paul but also to a general Christian kerygma in which all forms agree. Additional corroboration is lent at times by the agreement of such statements with motifs of the Hellenistic-Jewish missionary propaganda; for the Christian mission not only competed with it but also to a large extent inherited it. To this I Clement and the Shepherd of Hermas, and also the Epistle of James, bear witness.

§ 9. The Preaching of God and His Judgment, of Jesus Christ, the Judge and Savior, and the Demand for Faith

1. *Christian missionary preaching in the Gentile world* could not be simply the christological kerygma; rather, it had to begin with *the proclamation of the one God.* For it was not just a prevalent Jewish and Jewish-Christian opinion that the one true God was unknown to the Gentile world and that Gentile religion was polytheism and idolatry, but it was actually true that the Christian mission first reached those classes in which polytheism was still a living force.

The Jewish mission had anticipated the Christian in the preaching of monotheism. In the later literature of the Old Testament polemic against heathen religions is already beginning, with criticism of the worship of many gods and the manner of that worship, especially of their representation in tangible form. This is shown by the redaction of the second half of Isaiah, by the book of Daniel, and by the story of Bel and the Dragon appended to it in the LXX, also by the apocryphal Epistle of Jeremiah and especially by the Wisdom of Solomon. This last document shows at the same time that Hellenistic Judaism in its criticism of paganism took over both the criticism of naive polytheism and its cults that had developed within the Hellenistic enlightenment itself and also positive ideas of Hellenistic philosophic religiosity: God's rule over the world through Wisdom is conceived in analogy to the Stoic view of the administration διοίκησις of the world by the spirit. When IV Macc. places its story of martyrdom under the theme: "whether the Reason is supreme over the passions," εἰ αὐτοκράτωρ ἐστὶν τῶν παθῶν ὁ λογισμός (1:13), it is using a Stoic theme. Especially in Philo is the whole tradition of Greek philosophy pressed into the service of Jewish propaganda.

In this process the Old Testament-Jewish *concept of God* is frequently modified or obscured by the concept of God from the Greek philosophical tradition, a concept determined by the idea of the law and order of the cosmos. The "natural theology" of the Stoa is taken over with its proofs of the existence of God, and along with it its demonstration of God's providence πρόνοια in nature, and its proof of theodicy. God's demand is presented as rational moral law; the concept of virtue (ἀρετή), foreign to the Old Testament, and the notion of a system of virtues take root and along with them the idea of education and methods of education.

All these tendencies are taken along by Christian-Hellenistic missionary preaching, though at first only in individual motifs and with characteristically Christian modifications.

2. In its basic features *Hellenistic-Christian missionary preaching* and its language, which gave the faith of the Church its stamp, can be characterized as follows:

The pagan world is held to be sunk in ignorance ἄγνοια and error πλάνη.

Paul, who takes up (I Thess. 4:5) the Old Testament description of the Gentiles as "heathen who do not know God" (τὰ ἔθνη) τὰ μὴ εἰδότα τὸν Θεόν (Jer. 10:25, Ps. 78:6 LXX), says to the Galatian Gentile-Christians (Gal. 4:8f.): "Formerly when you did not know God (οὐκ εἰδότες Θεόν) you were in bondage to beings that by nature are no gods; but now that you have come to know God (γνόντες Θεόν) ..." Acts 17:30 speaks of the pre-Christian period as the "times of ignorance" χρόνοι τῆς ἀγνοίας; and the Areopagus discourse takes the altar inscription "to an unknown god" ἀγνώστῳ Θεῷ (17:23) for its point of contact. Eph. 4:18 describes the Gentiles ἔθνη as "darkened in their understanding, alienated from the life of God because of the ignorance ἄγνοια that is in them"; and I Pt. 1:14 exhorts believers to conduct "not conformed to the passions of your former ignorance." The "Greeks" are described by Kerygma Petri 2 as "driven by ignorance and not knowing God" ἀγνοίᾳ φερόμενοι καὶ μὴ ἐπιστάμενοι τὸν Θεόν, and of their former sins it is said further on (3): "whatsoever sins one of you has done in ignorance not clearly knowing God" ὅσα ἐν ἀγνοίᾳ τις ὑμῶν ἐποίησεν μὴ εἰδὼς σαφῶς τὸν Θεόν. (Such utterances are not peculiar but typical and are handed down to later writers; for the apologetes, cf. Justin, Apol. I 12:11; Aristides 17:3, p. 27, 15 Geffcken; Athenagoras 28, p. 147, 10f. Geffcken; see also M. Dibelius on I Tim. 1:13 in Lietzmann's *Handbuch zum N.T.*) Similarly the "error" πλάνη of the Gentiles is spoken of in Rom. 1:27; II Pet. 2:18; II Clem. 1:7; Gentile Christians were once "led astray" πλανώμενοι Tit. 3:3 or "straying like sheep" ὡς πρόβατα πλανώμενοι I Pet. 2:25. Cf. Heb. 5:2—though perhaps the "ignorant and wayward" ἀγνοῦντες καὶ πλανώμενοι here named are not specifically the Gentiles but sinners of any kind.

Hence to accept the Christian faith is called "to know God" or "the truth."

"To know God" γινώσκειν (τὸν) Θεόν is used for conversion to the Christian faith by Paul (Gal. 4:9) and also, e.g., by I Clem. 59:3; II Clem. 17:1 (cf. 3:1) Herm. sim. IX 18, 1f. The compounds ἐπίγνωσις (full knowledge) and ἐπιγινώσκειν (fully know) are especially popular in this meaning; in such cases the object may be God (as in Herm. sim. IX 18, 1 and elsewhere), but more frequently is truth ἀλήθεια. To become a Christian means "to come to the knowledge of the truth" εἰς ἐπίγνωσιν ἀληθείας ἐλθεῖν (I Tim. 2:4) or "to receive the knowledge of the truth" λαβεῖν τὴν ἐπίγνωσιν τῆς ἀληθείας (Heb. 10:26) or to "know the truth" ἐπιγινώσκειν τὴν ἀλήθειαν. With this meaning ἐπιγινώσκειν or its noun also occurs at Col. 1:6; Tit. 1:1; II Pet. 1:3, 2:20f.; II Clem. 3:1; Kerygma Petri 3; Herm. sim. IX 18, 1. According to I Clem. 59:2, God called the Church "from ignorance to the full knowledge of the glory of His name" ἀπὸ ἀγνωσίας εἰς ἐπίγνωσιν δοξῆς ὀνόματος αὐτοῦ. That corresponds to the use of language in Hellenistic Judaism; cf. ThWB I 706, 22ff.

"Truth" ἀλήθεια in this context is right doctrine, right belief, in contrast to "ignorance" ἄγνοια and "error" πλάνη, so that Paul can characterize his apostolic activity as a "manifestation of the truth" φανέρωσις τῆς ἀληθείας (II Cor. 4:2) which is substantially synonymous with saying that God through him spreads "the fragrance of the knowledge of Him" ὀσμὴ τῆς γνώσεως αὐτοῦ (II Cor. 2:14). Christian faith is called "obedience to the truth" (I Pet. 1:22; cf. Gal. 5:7). The gospel itself can be called the "word of truth" λόγος τῆς ἀληθείας (II Cor. 6:7; Col. 1:5; Eph. 1:13 and often). This, too, corresponds to Hellenistic-Jewish language; cf. ThWB 244, 32ff.

I Thess. 1:9, where Paul reminds the Thessalonians "how you turned from idols to serve a living and true God," indicates that he began his missionary preaching with the proclamation of the one God; so does the reminder of having formerly worshiped "dumb idols" ἄφωνα εἴδωλα (I Cor. 12:2) or "beings that by nature are no gods" φύσει μὴ ὄντες θεοί (Gal. 4:8). I Cor. 8:4–6 shows how characteristic and rich in consequences monotheistic faith was for the whole congregation; the consciousness "that an idol has no real existence and that there is no God but one," leads the "strong" to a thoughtless attitude toward heathen cult-meals.

Such preaching of monotheism is of course not specifically characteristic of Paul. In it he is continuing the propaganda of Hellenistic Judaism, and from its writings some idea of primitive Christian
missionary preaching, for which we have no direct sources, can be
formed.

> *Cf.* Ps. Aristeas 132ff.: "For he (our Law-giver) proved first
> of all that there is only one God and that his power is manifested
> throughout the universe." It goes on to say that God, as the
> Judge, views all that happens on earth, and no one is hidden
> from Him. (Then follows a polemic against polytheism and a
> defense of the Law.) Philo closes his commentary on the
> creation-story with this summary: "Five things Moses teaches
> through the creation-story: 1. that the Deity is and has been
> from eternity. . . . 2. that God is one. . . . 3. that the world
> came into being. . . . 4. that the world is one. . . . 5. that God
> also exercises forethought on the world's behalf." (*On the Cre-
> ation* [*Opifex mundi*] 170–172 Whitaker tr.)

The other Christian missionaries contemporary with Paul and
later speak in the same way. Examples of this are the discourses
which the author of Acts has Paul deliver in Lystra and Athens
(Acts 14:15-17; 17:23-30). Among the basic elements of Christianity is "belief in God" πίστις ἐπὶ Θεόν according to Heb. 6:1 (*cf.* I Pet.
1:21).

> Correspondingly Herm. mand. 1 (where Jewish tradition
> has been re-worked): "First of all believe that God is one, who
> made all things and perfected them, and made all things to be
> out of that which was not and contains all things, and is him-
> self uncontained. Believe then in him and fear him . . ." (Lake).
> According to Kerygma Petri 3, Jesus sends out the apostles
> "to preach the gospel to men throughout the world that they
> should know that there is one God," and so the cry rings out
> (2): "Know ye then that there is one God who made the begin-
> ning of all things and hath power over the end." Further ex-
> amples are II Clem. 1:4ff.; Aristides Apol. 15, 3 p. 23, 20ff.
> Geffcken; Ps. Clem. hom. 15, 11 p. 150, 10ff. Lagarde. Texts on
> the doctrine of God are compiled in Alfr. Seeberg, *Die Didache
> des Judentums,* 11-23.
> Formula-like expressions, established locutions, are taken
> out of Old Testament-Jewish theology or out of the Hellenistic

enlightenment-theology, enter new combinations, or, in some cases, arise for the first time. Philo's teaching "that God is one" (see above) occurs, as in Herm. mand. 1 and Kerygma Petri 2f. (see above), also at Jas. 2:19, Ign. Mag. 8:2 and similarly at Rom. 3:30; I Cor. 8:6; Eph. 4:6; I Tim. 2:5; I Clem. 46:6. *Cf.* also Er. Peterson, Εἶς Θεός (1926); H. Lietzmann, ZNW 21 (1922), 6f. A standing attribute of God is "only" μόνος, already current in the Old Testament and Judaism, but also found in Greek antiquity (see Bultmann, *Das Johannes-Ev.* 204, 2); *cf.* I Tim. 1:17, 6:15f. and the doxologies Rom. 16:27, Jude 25. Combining it with "true" ἀληθινός is especially popular: Joh. 17:3; I Clem. 43:6 and elsewhere (see Bultmann, *Joh.-Ev.* 378, 2 and H. Lietzmann ZNW 21 [1922], 6f.). The latter term, which likewise comes from the Old Testament tradition אֱלֹהֵי

אֱמֶת or אָמֵן 'א) also occurs alone, of course, or in other combinations; *cf.* I Jn. 5:20, Rev. 6:10, etc. (see ThWB I 250, 14ff.). In I Thess. 1:9 it is combined with "living," which is likewise an Old Testament-Jewish attribute for God (אֵל חַי) and one also used by Paul, II Cor. 3:3, Rom. 9:26 (quoted); *cf.* further [II Cor. 6:16] I Tim. 3:15; Acts 14:15; Heb. 3:12, 9:14, 10:31, 12:22; Ign. Philad. 1:2, II Clem. 20:1, Herm. vis. II 3, 2; III 7, 2; sim. VI 2, 2; heathen gods, by contrast, are dead νεκροί, II Clem. 3:1; *cf.* Sap. 15:17.

God is described as essentially the *Creator*, often in expressions of the Old Testament or Judaism. The prayer in Acts 4:24 says in broad liturgical style "Sovereign Lord, who didst make the heaven and the earth and the sea and everything in them"; likewise in the speech Acts 14:15 after which v. 17 further describes God's creating. Rev. 10:6 and 14:7 are similar; still more ornate is Herm. vis. I 3, 4. Briefer: Rev. 4:11, Did. 10:3 and Eph. 3:9 (3rd person) "thou didst create all things" or "God who gives life to all things" I Tim. 6:13. Or God may be described with a stronger expression: "who gives life to the dead and calls into existence the things that do not exist" Rom. 4:17 (*cf.* Herm. mand. 1, quoted above and Herm. sim. V 5, 2; VI 4). This creation out of nothing which is in accord with Hellenistic-Jewish tradition is emphasized also in Herm. vis. I 1, 6; mand. I 1; II Clem. I, 8.

Cf. further the lengthy description of God's sway as creator in I Clem. 20, 59:3, 60:1. To the designation "creator," "father"

is often joined: I Clem. 19:2, 62:2 and "father" of course also occurs alone or in other combinations: I Cor. 8:6; Eph. 3:14f., 4:6; Did. 1:5; I Clem. 23:1, 29:1; II Clem. 14:1; Ign. Rom. pr., combined with δημιουργός, "Creator," I Clem. 35:3 (the latter without "father" also found I Clem. 20:11, 26:1, 33:2, 59:2). "Almighty" παντοκράτωρ is added to "Father," Mart. Pol. 19:2 (as later in the Roman and the Jerusalem creeds) or also to "God" (I Clem. pr., 2:3, 32:4, 62:2; Pol. Phil. pr.) or to "Sovereign" (δεσπότης) (Did. 10:3); it occurs as an attribute of the "Will" of God, I Clem. 8:5, of His "Name," I Clem. 60:4; Herm. vis. III 3, 5 and it stands by itself or in apposition to "God" at Rev. 1:8, 4:8, 11:17, etc. (9 times). Participial characterizations are also common, such as: ὁ κτίσας (the maker, see above), ὁ ποιήσας (the maker, Did. 1:2; I Clem. 7:3, 14:3; Barn. 16:1), ὁ πλάσας (the molder, I Clem. 38:3; Barn. 19:2). Since the Creator of the world is also the Ruler of the world, God is often called "Sovereign" ὁ δεσπότης in such contexts (Acts 4:24; Rev. 6:10), "Sovereign of all" (I Clem. 8:2; 33:2, 52:1; joined with "Demiurge" δημιουργός I Clem. 20:11, 33:2). In addition, other terms occur, e.g. "Sovereign" δυνάστης (I Tim. 6:15) "king of ages" I Tim. 1:17, "King of kings and Lord of lords" (I Tim. 6:15), "who rules (κυριεύων) over all the world" Barn. 21:5. Concerning these and other terms for God as Creator, see W. Bousset, *Kyrios Chr.*, 2nd edition, 291f.; H. Lietzmann ZNW 21 (1922), 6f. On the equivalent Jewish terms for God: W. Bousset, *Die Religion des Judentums*, 2nd edition, 1926, 359f., 375ff.

In addition to these terms, certain Hellenistic (Stoic) formulations serve to describe God's creatorhood and rulership of the world. God is praised because "from him and through him and to him are all things" (Rom. 11:36); it is He "from whom are all things and through whom we exist" (I Cor. 8:6), "for whom and by whom all things exist" (Heb. 2:10), "who is above all and through all and in all" (Eph. 4:6. Here, however, the originally cosmological formulation is probably intended to be understood of the Church). Another formulation intended to express both God's immanence and transcendence at the same time is that of Herm. mand. I, 1 (see above): "(He) contains all things, and is himself alone uncontained" or, Kerygma Petri 2: "the . . . Uncontained, who contains all things"; this expression with variations also occurs in Hellenistic Judaism.

The Hellenistic parallels may be found in Lietzmann's commentary on Rom. 11:36 and Dibelius' on Col. 1:16f., both in the *Handbuch zum N.T.*, and in Ed. Norden's *Agnostos Theos* (1914), 240–250; see further Dibelius on Herm. mand. I, 1 in the supplement to the same *Handbuch*.

The Stoa's *"natural theology"* with its proofs of the existence of God—human intelligence divines the invisible creator from the visible world, the master-workman from his works—is taken over by Paul Rom. 1:19f. and to a still greater extent by the author of Acts in the Areopagus-address which he places in Paul's mouth, Acts 17:22ff.: The order of the allotted periods and boundaries of the earth proves God's governance of the world. Still more according to Stoic pattern is the description (I Clem. 20) of God's government (διοίκησις) of the universe manifested in the law and order of natural phenomena. In a proof of the resurrection of the dead, I Clem. 24:5, occurs the concept of divine "providence" (πρόνοια) in nature which is still absent from the New Testament because its thought is not concerned with nature, but with history, and because, consequently, it is governed by the concept of divine pre-determination (foreknow προγινώσκειν, pre-destine προορίζειν, etc.; *cf.* Rom. 8:29, etc.), rather than that of "providence." But as Hellenistic Judaism had taken over the concept of providence in nature, so Christianity also soon took it over, and we have no way of knowing whether it had already been taken over before or during Paul's time. The first witness after I Clement is Herm. vis. I 3, 4 where "providence" is coupled with Old Testament concepts descriptive of God's rule over nature. At any rate, Paul himself already took over the concept "nature" along with the phrases "according to" or "contrary to" nature (Rom. 1:26, 11:24); these phrases document the Stoic understanding of man as a being fitted into the totality of the cosmos.

That others besides Paul did this is shown by Jas. 3:7, Ign. Eph. 1:1, Tr. 1:1 (with the antithesis "by habit"—"by nature"), Barn. 10:7, II Pet. 1:4 actually uses the expression "that . . . you may become partakers of divine nature" (θείας κοινωνοὶ φύσεως). Other anthropological concepts from the tradition of popular philosophy, which were still foreign to the Old Testament, were also already taken over by Paul: "conscience" (Rom. 2:15, I Cor. 8:7, etc.), "what is proper" (Rom. 1:28 tr.), and ἀρετή in the sense of "virtue" (Phil. 4:8); they also have Christian attestation outside of Paul. ("Conscience" in the rest of the New Testament: Pastorals, Heb., I Pet., Acts; outside of New Testament: I Clem., Ign., Did. 4:14, Barn. 19:12. "Virtue": II Clem. 10:1, Herm. mand. I:2 VI 2, 3 and frequently. "The proper" or "the improper": I Clem. 3:4, 41:3; "properly" I Clem. 1:3; likewise "what is fitting": Did. 16:2, I Clem. 35:5, 45:1, 62:1, Barn. 17:1). The Hellenistic manner of describing the nature of God by the *via negationis* (the way of negation) is quickly appropriated by Christian language in its use of adjectives formed with the alpha-privative prefix. Such are: "*in*visible" (Rom. 1:20, Col. 1:15f., I Tim. I:17, Heb. 11:27, Ign. Mg. 3:2, Herm. vis. I 3, 4; III 3, 5, II Clem. 20:5 and "*in*corruptible" (ἄφθαρτος, Rom. 1:23, I Tim. 1:17). Ign. Pol. 3, 2 piles up the negatives: "time*less*, *in*visible, *im*palpable, *im*passive" (all α-privatives) and in Kerygma Petri 2 occurs this detailed description of God's nature: "the Unseen who sees all things, the Uncontained who contains all things, the Un-needy whom all things need and by whom they exist—incomprehensible, unending, incorruptible, unmade, who made all things by his word of power." Its "uncontained" occurs in Herm. mand. I:1, while un-needy takes up a characteristic Greek-Hellenistic motif which appears with variations in Acts 17:25, I Clem. 52:1, and later in the works of the apologetes. In all of this, of course, Hellenistic Judaism had already gone before.

Finally, let it be recalled that the Hellenistic idea of man's relatedness to God is already taken up in the Areopagus-discourse, Acts 17:28f., where it is expressed by nothing less than a quotation from the Stoic poet Aratus; also that "blessed" (μακάριος), a Greek attribute for the divine, already occurs in I Tim. 1:11 and 6:15.

3. According to Jewish opinion, there is a *causal connection between heathen polytheism and idolatry and the heathen world's degradation in sin and vice.* Paul took over this idea, too; in Rom. 1:24–32 the vices of the Gentiles appear as the consequence of—or as divine penalty for—the basic sin of idolatry. Thus, early Christian opinion takes for granted that heathen living is sinful living. Christians described that way of life in vice-catalogues such as Hellenistic Judaism had already taken over from the ethical parenesis of general Hellenism (Rom. 1:29–31, I Cor. 6:9f., Gal. 5:19–21, Col. 3:5, 8, Eph. 4:31, 5:3f., I Tim. 1:9f., I Clem. 35:5, Pol. Phil. 2:2, 4:3, etc.). Just as Paul (Rom. 6:17f., I Cor. 6:9–11) contrasts the former and the present states of Gentile Christians as their time of

sin and of righteousness, respectively, there soon develops a stereotyped scheme of primitive Christian preaching, in which this contrast of then and now is presented in variations (Col. 1:21f., 3:5ff.,
Eph. 2:1ff., 11ff., Tit. 3:3ff., I Pet. 1:14ff., 2:25, II Clem. 1:6ff.).

Hence, the call to believe in the one true God is simultaneously a
call *to repentance*. According to Heb. 6:1, "repentance from dead
works" in conjunction with "belief in God" (see above, 2) stands at
the threshold of Christianity—i.e. repentance from or turning back
from sinful deeds. Accordingly, the author of Acts lets Paul before
Agrippa say, "I declared . . . that they should repent and turn to
God . . ." (26:20). Rev. 9:20f. also shows that "conversion" to God
and repentance constitute a unity (*cf.* 16:9, 11). The specifically
Christian close of the Areopagus discourse begins, "The times of
ignorance God overlooked, but now he commands all men everywhere to repent" (Acts 17:30) and the Paul of Acts, looking back
upon his missionary labors, describes himself as "testifying . . . of
repentance to God" (20:21). In Paul's own writing, the idea of
"repentance" plays only a negligible role (Rom. 2:4, II Cor. 12:21;
II Cor. 7:9f. means the repentance of men who are already Christian) for which an explanation will be given later. But otherwise
"repentance" is represented as the basic requirement for conversion. In addition to the passages already named, Ign. Eph. 10:1 and
especially Kerygma Petri 3 illustrate this: "Whatsoever sins one of
you has done in ignorance, not clearly knowing God, when he has
come to know (God) and has repented, shall be forgiven him" (tr.).
Finally two other facts support this assertion. First, that the repentance which opens the way to salvation can be called a gift of
God, as at Acts 11:18, "Then to the Gentiles also God has granted
(ἔδωκεν) repentance unto life" (*cf.* 5:31), or I Clem. 7:4, where of
the blood of Christ it is said, "it brought the grace of repentance to
all the world" (*cf.* 8:5) or Barn. 16:9, where it is said of God, "giving
repentance to us" (*cf.* Pol. Phil. 11:4, Herm. sim. VIII 6, 1f.). Second, the fact that very early the possibility of a second repentance
was already being discussed. Whereas this is declared impossible
by Heb. 6:4–6, the author of Hermas feels himself called by a revelation to preach repentance to the Christian Congregation once more
for the last time (Herm. mand. IV 3).

But the call to repentance has its basis in the fact that *God the
Creator is also the Judge*; moreover His judgment takes place not in

the private fate of the sinner (or at least not only and not primarily there)—an idea which is both current in Judaism and not unknown to the Gentile world—but will soon be held over the entire world. Hence, Christian preaching of the one true God is at the same time *eschatological proclamation*, preaching of the impending *judgment of the world*. While Christian preaching thus agrees with Jewish apocalyptic (this motif had receded in Hellenistic Judaism), its peculiarity consists first in the fact that it proclaims the judgment of the world as close at hand and then in the fact that it binds the accomplishment of the judgment, or deliverance from its damning verdict, to the person of Jesus.

Acts 17:31 shows that the preaching of monotheism, the call to repentance, and the proclamation of the eschatological judgment form a unity; here the reason given for the call to repentance (see above) following upon the proclamation of the one God, is: "because he has fixed a day on which he will judge the world in righteousness by a man whom he has appointed." Likewise I Thess. 1:9f. attests the inter-relatedness of monotheistic and eschatological preaching: ". . . how you turned to God from idols, to serve a living and true God, and to wait for his Son from heaven, whom he raised from the dead, Jesus who delivers us from the wrath to come." According to Heb. 6:2, "the elementary doctrines" of Christianity include in addition to "repentance" and "belief in God" (also baptism and the laying on of hands), the doctrines of "resurrection of the dead" and "eternal judgment." Heb. 11:6 also characteristically says, "whoever would draw near to God must believe that he exists and that he rewards those who seek him." And in Herm. mand. I when "first of all believe that God is one" (see above, 2) is followed by: "Believe then in him, and fear him, and in your fear be continent," that also contains reference to God as Judge.

It is unnecessary to itemize *how the proclamation of the impending judgment* pervades all the writings of the New Testament. Only in the Gospel and Epistles of John is there a peculiar situation in regard to it; but though the idea of the judgment has found a peculiar new interpretation in them, that only proves how solidly the idea belonged to the structure of Christian thought. Understood in the traditional way, i.e., as the tremendous eschatological drama of the imminent world-judgment, it occurs both in Paul and in the deutero-Pauline literature, both in Acts and in Hebrews and James, and appears dressed in powerful pictures in Revelation; it is defended against doubt in II Pet. It is noteworthy and indicative of the extent to which Paul keeps within the frame of general Christian preaching, that he does not hesitate, in at least seeming contradiction to his doctrine of justification by faith alone, to speak of judgment according to one's works (I Cor. 3:13–15, 5:4, II Cor. 5:10, Rom. 2:5ff., 14:10–Rom. 2:16, however, is a gloss). So, also, the exhortation to be ready, the warning not to become negligent, runs through the whole New Testament. For "the appointed time has grown very short" (I Cor. 7:29); i.e. there is only a little time left until the End. "The night is far spent, the day is at hand" (Rom. 13:12 KJ; cf. Heb. 10:25, Jas. 5:8). "The end of all things is at hand" (I Pet. 4:7). "The moment is near" (Rev. 1:3, 22:10; cf. Ign. Eph. 11:1). Everything depends upon being kept "to the end" ἑώς τέλους (I Cor. 1:8), to be faithful "until the end" (μέχρι or ἄχρι τέλους –Heb. 3:6 ℵ D, etc., 3:14, 6:11, Rev. 2:26)–"for the whole time of your faith shall not profit you except ye be found perfect at the last time" (Did. 16:2).

The same terminology in all strata, even in details, shows that these are general-Christian ideas. God is called "the Judge" (Jas. 4:12, 5:9), "the Judge, God of all" (κρίτης Θεὸς πάντων Heb. 12:23), "the righteous Judge" (Herm. sim. VI, ᛫ 3, 6). (On Christ as judge, see below.) His "judging" (κρινεῖν) is spoken of (Rom. 2:16, 3:6, Acts 17:31, Heb. 10:30, Barn. 4:12) or "being judged" (κρίνεσθαι) by Him (II Thess. 2:12, Jas. 2:12, 5:9, I Clem. 13:2, II Clem. 18:1); or the noun κρίσις (judgment) is used (II Thess. 1:5, I Tim. 5:24, Heb. 9:27, 10:27, Jas. 2:13, 5:12, Jd. 6, II Pet. 2:4, 9; 3:7, Rev. 14:7, 18:10, Ig. Sm. 6:1, Pol. Phil. 7:1, Barn. 1:6); or the participle "coming" (μέλλουσα or ἐρχομένη) is added to the preceding (II Clem. 18:2, Herm. vis. III 9, 5); the eschatological judgment is called κρίμα (Pet. 4:17) or "κρίμα of God" (Rom. 2:2f.) or "coming" (μέλλον) or "eternal" κρίμα (Acts 24:25, Heb. 6:2). Κρίμα is also used as the eschatological verdict or condemnation (Gal. 5:10, Jas. 3:1, Jd. 2, II Pet. 2:3, Rev. 17:1, 18:20, I Clem. 21:1, Ign. Eph. 11:1); the same meaning is in "the judgments to come" (μέλλοντα κρίματα I Clem. 28:1).

Adapting the Old Testament phrase, "Day of Jahweh," various expressions speak of the "Day" of judgment: It is "the day of wrath when God's righteous judgment will be revealed"

(Rom. 2:2; "of wrath" also Rev. 6:17) or the "day of judgment" ἡμέρα κρίσεως (II Pet. 2:9, 3:7, Barn. 19:10, 21:6, II Clem. 16:3, 17:6) or "the day in which God will judge" ἡμέρα ἐν ἧ κρινεῖ ὁ Θεός (Rom. 2:16), or, after Joel 3:4, simply "the day of God" (Acts 2:20, II Pet. 3:10, 12; or "the day of the Lord Jesus Christ," see below) or "the great day of God the Almighty" (Rev. 16:14) or "that day" ἐκείνη ἡ ἡμέρα (II Thess. 1:10, II Tim. 1:12, 18; 4:8), "the great day" ἡ μεγάλη ἡμέρα (Jd. 6; *cf.* Rev. 6:17, Barn. 6:4) and, altogether abbreviated, "the day" (I Cor. 3:13, I Thess. 5:4, Heb. 10:25, Barn. 7:9). Instead of "day," "*hour*" of judgment" (Rev. 14:7), or "the hour to reap" (Rev. 14:7), or "the last hour" (I Jn. 2:18).

As the eschatological judgment can be called "day of wrath" ἡμέρα ὀργῆς, it can also be called simply "wrath" ὀργή (Rom. 5:9, *cf.* 12:19), or "coming (ἐρχομένη and μέλλουσα) wrath" (I Thess. 1:10, Ign. Eph. 11:1) or "the wrath of God" (Col. 3:6, Eph. 5:6, Rev. 19:15; *cf.* Rev. 11:18, 14:10, 16:19).

In the exhortations to be ready, the following figurative expressions occur again and again: "keep awake" (γρηγορεῖν), I Thess. 5:6, I Cor. 16:13, Col. 4:2, I Pet. 5:8, Acts 20:31, Rev. 3:2f., 16:15, Did. 16:1, Ign. Pol. 1:3; *cf.* Barn. 4:13; "arise (from sleep)" ἐγερθῆναι (Rom. 13:11) or ἐγείρειν intransitive (Eph. 5:14); "be sober" (νήφειν I Thess. 5:6, 8, I Pet. 1:13, 4:7, 5:8, Ign. Pol. 2:3, Pol. Phil. 7:2, II Clem. 13:1); also the figure of the "thief" κλέπτης which pictures the unexpected coming of "the Day" (I Thess. 5:2, 4, Rev. 3:3, 16:15, II Pet. 3:10). In addition many a traditional expression out of the Old Testament hope or Jewish apocalyptic occurs. It is noteworthy that among them the expression "Reign of God" is only seldom used. Paul has it only at Rom. 14:17, I Cor. 4:20, 6:9f., 15:50, Gal. 5:21 (I Thess. 2:12); of these I Cor. 6:9f., 15:20, Gal. 5:21 are certainly traditional, more or less crystallized statements which Paul either quotes or paraphrases—perhaps also Rom. 14:17, I Cor. 4:20. Add to these the following cases from deutero-Pauline literature: II Thess. 1:5, Col. 4:11, Eph. 5:5; from the rest of the New Testament: Acts 1:3, 8:12, 14:22, 19:8, 20:25, 28:23, 31 (Jas. 2:5). On the reign of Christ which Eph. 5:5 combines with that of God, see below. Beyond the New Testament, *cf.* Did. 9:4, 10:5 (in table-prayers); also (frequently in quotations): I Clem. 42:3, II Clem. (5:5, 6:9), 9:6, 11:7, 12:1ff., Barn. 21:1, Ign. Eph. 16:1, Phld. 3:3, Pol. Phil. 2:3, 5:3, Herm. sim. IX 12, 3 ff.; 13, 2; 15, 2f.; 16, 2ff.; 20, 2f.; 29, 2. In the Hellenistic sphere this concept is pushed into the background by that of "life (eternal)" ζωή (αἰώνιος), alongside of which "incorruption" ἀφθαρσία is used: Rom. 2:7, I Cor. 15:42, 50, 53f., Eph. 6:24, II Tim. 1:10, Ign. Eph. 17:1, Mg. 6:2, Phld. 9:2, Pol. 2:3, II Clem. 14:5, 20:5.

The preaching of *resurrection from the dead* is inseparable from that of God's judgment, for the dead, too, are to be brought to account for their former deeds. Closely connected with "eternal judgment" is "resurrection from the dead" among the elementary doctrines of Christian faith according to Heb. 6:2. To deny the resurrection is to deny the judgment (Pol. Phil. 7:1, II Clem. 9:1). The author of Acts distinctly feels the shocking novelty of such preaching to Gentile ears when he relates that Paul's preaching at Athens occasioned the misunderstanding: "He seems to be a preacher of foreign divinities"—and specifically: "because he preached Jesus and Anastasis" (Resurrection, mistaken for a proper name, Acts 17:18). He feels it again when he later has the audience interrupt Paul's speech where it comes to the resurrection theme: "hearing 'resurrection of the dead,' some mocked; but others said, 'We will hear you again about this'" (17:32). The same conclusion can be reached from Paul's own writings. He takes for granted that "the resurrection of the dead" belongs to the very core of Christian faith—if there is no such thing, then kerygma and faith are null and void (I Cor. 15:12–34). But this message is so incredible to his Corinthian audience that he has to prove its right to be heard. But in the Thessalonian Church, also, this portion of his preaching, which he surely cannot have skipped in his mission at Thessalonica, has died away without effect, so that he has to reassure that Church of the resurrection (I Thess. 4:13–18). I Clem. 24–26 is a detailed proof of the reality of the resurrection, and the resurrection is presupposed wherever the judgment is dealt with, whether expressly mentioned or not.

4. Inasmuch as He is the Creator, God is the Judge of the world. This inner connection, which also is emphasized in Judaism (IV Ez. 5:56–6:6, etc.) is occasionally made explicit, as at Kerygma Petri 2: "Know therefore that there is one God who made the beginning of all things and has power over the End."

Cf. also Kerygma Petri 3: the apostles are to preach "that there is one God," proclaiming at the same time "the things that are to come so that they who have heard and believed may be saved, and that they who do not believe though they have heard must bear witness thereto without the excuse of saying, 'We have not heard'" (tr.). The Creator is at the same time the Judge, I Clem. 20–23 declares; and to this theme of the divine governance of the world and its accompanying exhortation is joined the eschatological theme of the resurrection of the dead followed by its appropriate exhortation, 24–28.

Accordingly, Paul names God as the Judge of the world at I Thess. 3:13, Rom. 3:5, 14:10; cf. outside of Paul: I Pet. 1:17, Jas. 4:12, 5:4, Rev. 11:17f., 20:11ff., etc. (cf. the passages indicated on p. 75). But at this point the christological motif enters the kerygma: At God's side or in place of God *Jesus Christ appears as Judge of the world*; he represents God, so to say, as His plenipotentiary. Acts 17:31 phrases it: "He has fixed a day on which he will judge the world in righteousness by a man whom he has appointed." In general, no thought is taken to reconcile the ideas. In Paul, statements about God's judgeship stand unreconciled beside others about Christ as Judge of the world (I Thess. 2:19, I Cor. 4:5); Paul can speak both of the "judgment seat of God" (Rom. 14:10) and of Christ (II Cor. 5:10). Christ, too, is called "the righteous judge" (II Tim. 4:8); Christ will judge (Barn. 5:7, 15:5) and instead of "God's Reign" "Christ's Reign" is spoken of (Col. 1:13, II Tim. 4:1, 18, II Pet. 1:11, I Clem. 50:3, Barn. 4:13, 7:11, 8:5f.; implied by Paul I Cor. 15:24). Here, also, there is no reflection about reconciling the ideas; Eph. 5:5 presents a simple combination of the two: "in the kingdom of Christ and of God." Gradually the idea of Christ's office as Judge of the world comes to predominate. Rom. 14:9 already says: "For to this end Christ died and lived again, that he might be Lord both of the dead and of the living"; out of this a formula develops: Christ is he "who is to judge the living and the dead" (II Tim. 4:1, Barn. 7:2), "who is ready to judge the living and the dead" (I Pet. 4:5), "the one ordained by God to be judge of the living and the dead" (Acts 10:42), "the judge of the living and the dead" (Pol. Phil. 2:1, II Clem. 1:1)—down to the sentence in the Symbolum Romanum: "whence he comes to judge the living and the dead" (ὅθεν ἔρχεται κρῖναι ζῶντας καὶ νεκρούς).

Thus, *Christ* belongs in the eschatological kerygma—nevertheless not only as the Judge but in that very fact also as the Savior for those who belong to the Congregation of the faithful. According to I Thess. 1:9f., the preaching of this fact belongs intimately with the proclamation of the one God; the Thessalonians "turned to . . . the living and true God" "to serve" Him (see above 2) "and to wait for his son from heaven, whom he raised from the dead, Jesus who delivers us from the wrath to come." And when Paul says (Phil. 3:20), "But our citizenship is in heaven from which also we eagerly await a Savior (σωτήρ), our Lord Jesus Christ," that is all the more certainly an appeal to a common-Christian statement the more clearly we recognize how singular a phraseology this is to find in Paul, who does not otherwise use the title "Savior" for Christ. And Paul expressly appeals to the tradition when he describes the eschatological appearing of Christ to save the faithful (I Thess. 4:15-18). The expectation of the parousia or the manifestation (ἐπιφάνεια) of the Savior Christ Jesus was so taken for granted as an item of the Christian hope (Tit. 2:13) that "Savior" became a title for Christ used in a formula-like manner.

Of course, other influences are also at work in the use of the title "Savior." They are: first, the Old Testament tradition, in which God is called Savior (still so used in the New Testament: the pastoral epistles, Lk. 1:47, Jd. 25) and second, the Hellenistic usage in which both mystery and salvation deities and divinely worshiped rulers bear the title. See W. Bousset, *Kyrios Christos*, 2nd ed., 240–246, where the abundant literature on this subject is also cited, and M. Dibelius, Excursus on II Tim. 1:10 (Lietzmann's *Handbuch zum NT* 13, 2nd ed. (1931), 60–63). In a meaning clearly or probably eschatological the title occurs at Phil. 3:20, Tit. 2:13, Acts 5:31, 13:23. The hope of the parousia of Christ is attested by I Cor. 15:23, I Thess. 2:19, 3:13, 4:15, 5:23; then II Thess. 2:1, 8, Jas. 5:7f. (where, however, originally the parousia of God was meant), II Pet. 1:16, 3:4. In the same sense his "manifestation" (ἐπιφάνεια) is mentioned at II Thess. 2:8 (here tautologically combined: "the manifestation of his parousia"), I Tim. 6:14, II Tim. 4:1, 8, Tit. 2:13, II Clem. 12:1, 17:4; but the appearing of the historical Jesus is meant by the "manifestation of the Savior" at II Tim. 1:10 and by his parousia in Ign. Phld. 9:2. Cf. also the designation of Christ as "our hope," I Tim. 1:1, on which see Dibelius, *op. cit.*

Though the figure of Christ as the eschatological Judge and Savior corresponds to the Son of Man figure in Jewish apocalyptic and in the earliest Palestinian Church (§ 5, 1), nevertheless the *title* "Son of Man" drops out of Hellenistic Christianity, and—except in John, where it has a special meaning—is found in the rest of the New Testament only in Acts 7:56 (it is not as a title that Rev. 1:13 and 14:14 use it). Thus it comes about that Son of Man (Barn. 12:10, Ign. Eph. 20:2) can be contrasted with the title "Son of God" to indicate the mere humanity of Jesus. *The title "the Christ"* (ὁ Χριστός) also gradually is lost and "Christ" becomes a proper name; later, accordingly, in Latin-speaking Christendom, Χριστός is no longer translated, but simply transliterated Christus. As a title, "the Christ" was not understandable to the Hellenistic world and any such paraphrase as "the King" (ὁ βασιλεύς), which would have corresponded in content, was out of the question, in the first place because "King" had no soteriological meaning; and also because it would have exposed the Christian message to the misconception that it was a political program.

The favorite combination in which the proper name Christ is used is "Jesus Christ." "Christ" as a title is still relatively frequent in Acts (side by side with "Jesus Christ"), likewise in Rev., Jn., and I, II Jn.; also in Eph. (and Col.), where, however, it is often hard to decide whether "Christ" is really meant as a title. Only rarely does Paul use it as a title. Peculiar to him is "Christ Jesus," in addition to which he less frequently uses "Jesus Christ." But in either order, "Christ" is a proper name, as his frequent expression "our Lord Jesus Christ" shows. For Paul, "Lord" and not "Christ" is Jesus' title. The Pauline "Christ Jesus" persists in the literature dependent upon Paul along with the usual "Jesus Christ" down to the Symbolum Romanum, which exhibits it.

But in contrast to the Son of Man of the apocalypses and in agreement with the Son of Man of the earliest Church, the eschatological Judge and Savior Jesus Christ is none other than the crucified Jesus of Nazareth whom God raised from the dead and appointed to his eschatological role. Hence, the message of the *raising* or the *resurrection of Jesus* is a basic constituent of the Hellenistic kerygma, as the "tradition" of I Cor. 15:1ff. expressly attests, no matter whether any or all of its formulation goes back to the earliest Church or not. Accordingly, when Paul speaks (I Thess. 1:9f., see above) of the expectation of Christ as the coming Savior he expressly describes him as him "whom [God] raised from the dead." According to Acts 17:31 God gave proof that He had appointed Christ Judge of the world by raising him from the dead (*cf.* I Clem. 42:3, where it is said of the apostles: "being fully assured by the resurrection of our Lord Jesus Christ"). That God raised him from the dead is a statement that, obviously quite early, was a constituent of more or less crystallized creedal statements, for without doubt Paul is alluding to a creedal formula in Rom. 10:9.

"If you confess with your mouth that Jesus is Lord and believe in your heart that God raised him from the dead, you will be saved."

II Tim. 2:8 similarly exhorts: "Remember Jesus Christ risen from the dead, descended from David, as preached in my gospel." Likewise in Pol. Phil. 12:2 the object of faith is "our Lord Jesus Christ and his Father, who raised him from the dead." Christian faith is "faith in the working of God who raised him (Christ) from the dead" (Col. 2:12, Eph. 1:20), and "who raised him from the dead" becomes a formula-like attribute of God (Col. 2:12, Eph. 1:20, Gal. 1:1, I Pet. 1:21; *cf.* Rom. 8:11, I Cor. 6:14, II Cor. 4:14; also Ign. Tr. 9:2, Sm. 7:1, Pol. Phil. 1:2, 2:2f.).

An inner causal *connection between Jesus' resurrection and the general resurrection of the dead* becomes a subject for reflection only in a different thought context which is of fundamental importance in Paul and Ignatius (see § 15, 4c). In many cases, for instance in the speeches of Acts, there is no mention of such a connection, and Christ's resurrection is regarded only as his legitimation (17:31, see above). Nevertheless, we probably should everywhere assume the implied thought that our hope is founded on the resurrection of Christ, as formulated, for instance, in I Pet. 1:3, 21—that the risen Christ has the keys of Death and Hades (thus Rev. 1:18)—that he has destroyed death by his own death or by his resurrection (Heb. 2:14f., Barn. 5:6f.). According to I Clem. 24:1, God made "the beginning" of the resurrection of the dead by raising Christ; but the idea of I Cor. 15:20ff. is not present here. On occasion, even Paul can confine himself to a simple "as . . . so" without stopping to demonstrate the inner connection: *as* God raised Christ, *so* He will also raise us (see I Cor. 6:14, II Cor. 4:14).

According to the oldest view, Christ's resurrection coincides with his *exaltation* to heavenly glory (§ 7, 3); this remains the dominant view in Paul and others of his time. But whether the exaltation was thought to be identical with the resurrection or whether it was thought to be a little later than the latter (as, for example, in Lk. 24:36ff., Barn. 15:9, Ign. Sm. 3)—in either case the two belonged most intimately together. And just as belief in his resurrection crystallized in formula-like statements, so did the conviction of his exaltation. God "exalted" Jesus Christ (Phil. 2:9f, Acts. 2:33, 5:30f.; *cf.* Jn. 3:14, 12:32, 34) and so he "sits at the right hand of God" (Rom. 8:34, Col. 3:1, Eph. 1:20, I Pet. 3:22, Acts 2:33, 7:55f., Heb. 1:3, 13; 8:1, 10:12, 12:2; *cf.* I Clem. 36:5, Barn. 12:10, Pol. Phil. 2:1), and the Symbolum Romanum summarizing this conviction calls him "he who sitteth at the right hand of the Father" (καθήμενον ἐν δεξιᾷ τοῦ πατρός).

Two proofs of the resurrection of Jesus were current: testimony of eye-witnesses (I Cor. 15:5ff., Acts 1:22, 2:32, 3:15, 10:40ff.) and discovered agreements with the Old Testament—"according to the scriptures" (I Cor. 15:4, Lk. 24:27 and 44f.; Acts 2:30ff., 13:34ff.).

It is self-evident that the preaching which proclaimed the risen Lord had also to speak in some way *of the earthly Jesus and his death.* Rom. 1:3f. and II Tim. 2:8—both formula-like traditional statements (§ 7, 5)—indicate that the risen and exalted Lord was called *Son of David* in reminiscence of his preliminary humanity. To the Gentile world this term could be neither significant nor impressive; it is indeed still current in Ignatius (Ign. Eph. 18:2, 20:2, Tr. 9:1; Rom. 7:3; Smyr. 1:1), but otherwise it has dropped out of use. Barn. 12:10 even protests against Jesus' sonship to David (§ 7, 5). But to them it was all the more significant and impressive *that the risen Lord was he who had previously died on the cross.* Here, too, formula-like expressions promptly form, as the tradition of I Cor. 15:3f. again indicates, and also the description at Rom. 4:25:

> "who was put to death for our trespasses
> and raised for our justification."

—a statement that had evidently existed before Paul and had been handed down to him (§ 7, 3).

Especially in *Ignatius,* the inter-relation between Christ's passion (πάθος) and resurrection is often emphasized. Both together belong to the οἰκονομία, the divine dispensation of salvation, according to Ign. Eph. 20:1. Faith regards both of them together—Phld. intr., 8:2, Sm. 7:2, 12:2 (see also Pol. Phil. 9:2). These two data are supplemented, according to Mg. 11:1, by Christ's preceding birth or, according to Phld. 9:2, by his "parousia" (here = into earthly life).

The same thing is shown by the predictions put into Jesus' mouth in Mk. (and also in Mt. and Lk.) carrying back the Hellenistic kerygma into the preaching of Jesus. These "predictions" speak in schematic form of Jesus' death (or of his being "delivered up"—παραδοθῆναι—as in I Cor. 11:23) and of his resurrection "after three days" (Mk. 8:31, 9:31, 10:33f.). In them we have, so to speak, a pattern of the christological kerygma, and we can see in the somewhat fuller third form how the pattern could be worked out in preaching. From the likewise highly schematic sermons of Acts we can then form a somewhat more graphic notion of concrete preaching (Acts 2:14–36, 3:12–26, 5:30–32, 10:34–43, 13:16–41). In them the focal point is the kerygma of Christ's death and resurrection (and exaltation), which, supported by scripture proofs, furnishes the basis for the call to repentance. Reference is made to the eschatological role of Jesus—in 3:20f. as a promise, in 10:42 in the description of him as "the one ordained by God to be judge of the living and the dead."

In the sermons of Acts we also see how the pattern in particular instances could be expanded by taking up this or that detail from the tradition of Jesus' life for illustrative purposes. Acts 10:37f., 13:23–25 say that Jesus' ministry attached itself to that of John the Baptist. Reference is made to Jesus' miracles in 2:22, 10:38f. The expression "that the Lord Jesus on the night when he was betrayed . . ." (I Cor. 11:23) permits us to recognize that the telling of the passion story was clothed with some details, for does that expression not imply that the reader was oriented about the events of that night? The same thing is indicated by the mention of Pilate, Acts 3:13, 13:28, and is corroborated by the description of Christ Jesus in I Tim. 6:13: "who in his testimony before Pontius Pilate made the good confession . . ." Ignatius also mentions Pilate in connection with the passion (and resurrection) of Jesus (Tr. 9:1, Sm. 1:2,

Mg. 11:1) and this tradition flows on down to "crucified under Pontius Pilate and buried" (τὸν ἐπὶ Ποντίου Πιλάτου σταυρωθέντα καὶ ταφέντα) in the Symbolum Romanum.[*]

In the case of the Hellenistic mission and its churches, as in that of the earliest Church (§ 7, 3), it is hard to say to what extent there was theological reflection on the *death of Christ;* i.e. to what extent positive significance for salvation was ascribed to it. In the beginning Christian missionary preaching was built upon motifs and concepts from the Old Testament-Jewish tradition; yet very soon views and concepts out of Hellenistic syncretism, especially the mystery religions, also show their influence. These are to be treated later (§§ 13 and 15). First, we will proceed to sketch the conceptualization of Jesus' death which was determined by the Old Testament-Jewish tradition so far as it can be grasped.

The interpretation of Jesus' death as an *expiatory sacrifice for sins,* which we found attributable to the earliest Church (§ 7, 3), was without doubt also presented in the Hellenistic-Christian mission. It finds expression in the numerous statements and formulas which describe the death of Christ as having taken place "for you" (ὑπὲρ ὑμῶν; or "for us," "for many," or "for sins," etc.). Such sentences and formulas are scattered throughout the New Testament and the immediately succeeding literature (lacking only in Acts, James, Jude, II Peter, Didache, II Clement, and Hermas), a fact which indicates that we are here dealing with a by no means specifically Pauline, but a general-Christian idea—this ὑπὲρ ("for . . ."), as everyone knows, has its solid place in the liturgy of the Lord's Supper. To this train of ideas belong those statements which expressly speak of Jesus' death as a sacrifice, or of his blood poured out for us, or where Jesus' death is described as the means of forgiveness or deliverance from sin, or of sanctification or purification, and the like. From the same tradition come the interpretations of Jesus' death as a covenant-sacrifice or passover-sacrifice. In the latter, it is still clearer than in the other cases that Jesus' death is regarded as primarily significant not for the individual, but for the Congregation, the "People" of God—a view characteristic of the Old Testament-Jewish tradition which is here determinative.

[*] On the reconstruction of the christological kerygma, see M. Dibelius, *Die Formgeschichte des Evangeliums,* 2nd ed. (1933), 14-25.

For descriptions of Christ's death as *sacrifice* (ϑυσία, προσφορά, etc.), see Eph. 5:2, Heb. 7:27, 9:26, 28; 10:10, 12, Barn. 7:3 among others; as passover-sacrifice I Cor. 5:7; as covenant-sacrifice, the texts of the Lord's Supper and Heb. 13:10. Besides the words of the Lord's Supper and texts referring to them, the following passages deal with the *blood of Christ*: Rom. 3:25, 5:9, Col. 1:20, Eph. 1:7, 2:13, I Pet. 1:2, 19, Acts 20:28, Heb. 9:11ff., 10:19ff., 29; 13:12, 20, Rev. 1:5, 5:9, 7:14, 12:11, 19:13, I Jn. 1:7, 5:6–8, I Clem. 7:4, 12:7, 21:6, 49:6; specialized mention of "sprinkling" (ῥαντισμός) with Christ's blood: I Pet. 1:2, Heb. 9:13, 10:22, 12:24, Barn. 5:1, *cf.* 8:1–3. (The Ignatian passages are of a different character.) The idea of *expiation* is expressed in the terms ἱλαστήριον (Rom. 3:25), ἱλασμός (I Jn. 2:2, 4:10) and ἱλάσκεσθαι (Heb. 2:17). That Christ's death provides *forgiveness* of sin is said in these passages among others: Rom. 3:25f., Eph. 1:7, the Matthean saying accompanying the sacramental cup (Mt. 26:28) and Heb. 9:11ff., Barn. 5:1, 8:3. The idea of *release* or *deliverance* (ἀπολύτρωσις, λύτρωσις or phrases employing verbs) is found: Rom. 3:24, I Cor. 1:30, Col. 1:14, Eph. 1:7, Heb. 9:12, 15, I Clem. 12:7, Mk. 10:45, I Tim. 2:6, Rev. 1:5, Tit. 2:14, I Pet. 1:18f., Barn. 14:5f. Similar is the idea of ransom: I Cor. 6:20, 7:23, Gal. 3:13, 4:5, Rev. 5:9, 14:3f., II Pet. 2:1. From among the many statements about *justification*, Rom. 3:24f. and I Cor. 6:11 (*cf.* 1:30!) and Herm. vis. III 9, 1 belong in this context. More characteristic for the sacrificial outlook which dominates this cluster of ideas are the statements about *sanctification*, I Cor. 6:11 (*cf.* 1:30), Eph. 5:25f., Heb. 2:11, 9:13f., 10:10, 29; 13:12, I Clem. 59:3, Barn. 5:1, 8:1, Herm. vis. III 9, 1. Likewise those on purification: Heb. 1:3, 9:13f., 22; Tit. 2:14, Eph. 5:25f., I Jn. 1:7, 9, Herm. sim. V 6, 2. The idea of *reconciliation* seems to be peculiar to Paul (Rom. 5:10f., II Cor. 5:18ff.); Col. 1:20f. and Eph. 2:16 vary the expression, each in its own way. That it is the Congregation that is founded by Christ's sacrifice comes to the fore—aside from its interpretation as a covenant-sacrifice—explicitly in Tit. 2:14, I Pet. 2:9, I Clem. 64, where "God's own (= peculiar) people" is mentioned and in Heb. 2:17, 7:27, 13:12, Barn. 7:5, 14:6, where simply "the People" is used in breviloquence for the same idea; Eph. 5:25ff., Acts 20:28 use Congregation, Church in the same sense. With still other expressions the same idea occurs: Rev. 1:5f., 5:9f., (*cf.* I Pet. 2:9).

As more and more exact and stable formulas grow out of the kerygma and gradually crystallize into creeds, so there develops out of the kerygma *the literary form: Gospel.* Its oldest exemplification is for us the Gospel of Mark. The following probable stages in the development of "the gospel" can be named: 1. The germ-cell is the kerygma of the death and resurrection of Jesus, so that the gospels have been rightly called "passion-narratives with an extensive introduction." * 2. The brief kerygma of the passion and Easter required fuller visualization, as I Cor. 11:23–26 and 15:3–7 show, and also assignment of a place in the divine plan of salvation; to fill this need, both the account of the Baptist and the proofs of fulfilled prediction were taken in. 3. The Christian "sacraments" (on which see § 13) had to be accounted for in the life of Jesus, the cultically worshiped Lord. 4. A visualization of what Jesus had done was also indispensable, since his life, considered divine, served as proof of his authority, as Acts 2:22, 10:38f. show. Hence the collecting of miracle-stories and their incorporation into "the gospel" are readily understandable. 5. Probably the apophthegms (i.e. short stories whose point is a saying of Jesus and which in part also report miracles, like Mk. 3:1–6, 22–30, etc.) also stood in the service of this visualization. These draw others after them, and the apophthegms occasion the inclusion of still other sayings of the Lord. 6. The reason that sayings of the Lord, which at first were handed down separately from the christological kerygma, came more and more to be taken up into "the gospel" (in Mark still sparingly, whereas Matthew and Luke combine the kerygma and the tradition of Jesus' sayings into a unity) is that, while missionary preaching continued, preaching to Christian congregations took on ever-increasing importance and for these already believing congregations, Jesus in the role of "teacher" had become more important again. 7. Finally both the moral exhortation and the regulations of the Congregation had to be accounted for in the life and words of Jesus (*cf.,* for example, I Cor. 7:10, 9:14). Hence, current exhortations and congregational regulations currently in force were also taken into "the gospel." Example: Mt. 18:15ff.

* M. Kähler, *Der sogenannte historische Jesus und der geschichtliche biblische Christus,* 2nd ed. (1896), 80, 1. *Cf.* Ad. Schlatter, *Der Glaube im NT,* 4th ed. (1927), 477: "For each evangelist the gospel was the account of Jesus' way to the Cross": see also Jul. Schniewind, *Th. R., NF.,* 2nd ed. (1930), 179–188, and *cf. Gesch. d. synopt. Trad.,* 2nd ed., 395–400.

5. The substantive "evangel" (τὸ εὐαγγέλιον) soon appears in Hellenistic Christianity as the technical term for the Christian proclamation, and for the act of proclaiming the verb εὐαγγελίζεσθαι was used, usually in the middle voice, sometimes also in the passive and with either a personal or a non-personal object. However, the substantive can also be used for the act of proclaiming. The meaning of noun and verb is simply "message," "news" and "proclaim," "preach." The etymological meaning "*good* news" or "to proclaim *good* news" had already worn off in the LXX (and in Philo), even though it does occasionally reappear. If the intention is to emphasize that *good* news is meant, a complementary object such as ἀγαθά (good things) is added to the verb (e.g. III Kingdoms 1:42, Is. 52:7, and, quoting the latter, Rom. 10:15). Hence, this verb can be used even where it does not mean "good" news at all (Lk. 3:18, Acts 14:15, Rev. 10:7, 14:6). Certain objects of content that are added to the verb (or objective genitives to the noun) also indicate that only the meaning "proclaim" is implied (e.g. to proclaim "the word" or "the word of the Lord," Acts 8:4, 15:35); and note especially that "preach the gospel" εὐαγγελίζεσθαι τὸ εὐαγγέλιον is, in use, completely synonymous with "to herald . . ." κηρύσσειν, "to announce . . ." καταγγέλλειν, "to speak . . ." or "to testify to" the gospel and, correspondingly, "gospel" is synonymous with "the message," "kerygma" (κήρυγμα), and "the word," ὁ λόγος.

"Evangel" (or its verb) is strictly a technical term only when it is absolute—that is, used without any object of content to designate the Christian message, but simply implying its clearly defined content. This usage of Paul, which in his footsteps became widely current, has no analogy either in the Old Testament and Judaism or in Gentile Hellenism, and the wide-spread view that "evangel" is a sacral term of the emperor-cult cannot be maintained. This absolute use of the word seems to have developed in Hellenistic Christianity gradually, but relatively quickly. In many cases "evangel" is limited by an objective genitive (e.g. "of the Kingdom," Mt. 4:23, 9:35 or "of Christ," Rom. 15:19, I Cor. 9:12, etc.) or the verb is supplemented by an object of content (e.g. the "Reign of God," Lk. 4:43, "Jesus" or an equivalent expression, Acts 5:42, 8:35, Gal. 1:15, etc.; or "faith," Gal. 1:23, etc.).

Whether the absolute use is earlier than Paul cannot be said with certainty. Evidently it does not go back as far as the earliest Church; for the substantive εὐαγγέλιον, lacking entirely in Q, is found in Mark only in secondary formations (in Matthew partly following Mark, partly in phrases peculiar to Matthew). It is absent from Luke but occurs twice in Acts. Among these occurrences it is used technically, i.e. absolutely, in these cases: Mk. 1:15, 8:35, 10:29, 13:10, 14:9, Mt. 26:13, Acts 15:7. The verb, in the passive voice, is used once in Q (Mt. 11:5 = Lk. 7:22) quoting Is. 61:1, is lacking in Mark and Matthew, but frequent in Luke and Acts, though technical only in the following cases: Lk. 9:6 (20:1), Acts 8:25, 40; 14:7, 21; 16:10. In the New Testament, outside of the synoptics, Acts, and Paul, the noun occurs in the technical use only in the deutero-Pauline writings (II Thess., Col., Eph., Past.); the verb occurs technically I Pet. 1:12, 4:6, Heb. 4:2, 6. Not infrequently (especially in Paul) "of God" as a subjective genitive or genitive of the author is added. Not only from Luke but also from the following the noun is completely absent: Jn., I–III Jn., Heb., Jas., Jd., II Pet., Rev. (here the word occurs only in a different sense, 14:6). The verb is absent from Mark and Matthew and the following: Jn., I–III Jn., Past., Jas., Jd., II Pet., Rev. In the literature of the succeeding period neither noun nor verb is found in Hermas; the noun occurs absolutely in Did. 8:2, 11:3, 15:3f., I Clem. 47:2, II Clem. 8:5, Barn. 5:9, Ign. Phld. 5:1f., 8:2 (uncertain text), 9:2, Sm. 5:1, 7:2; the verb with complementary infinitive I Clem. ·42:3, with object Barn. 8:3; absolute: I Clem. 42:1 (passive) middle voice: Barn. 14:9 (quotation of Is. 61:1), Pol. Phil. 6:3.

The technical use of κήρυγμα, "the message," and κηρύσσειν, "to herald," developed quite analogously. The verb, which can also take objects: "the Reign" (Lk. 9:2, Acts 20:25, 28:31) or "Christ" or equivalents (Acts 8:5, 9:20, I Cor. 1:23, II Cor. 4:5, etc.) is used absolutely in the technical sense: Mk. 3:14, Acts 10:42, Rom. 10:14f., I Cor. 9:27, I Clem. 42:4, Barn. 8:3, Herm. sim. IX 16, 5; 25, 2. In the spurious close of Romans (16:25) the noun has the objective genitive "of Jesus Christ"; similarly, with "of the Son of God" Herm. sim. IX 15, 4; it is used absolutely I Cor. 1:21, 2:4, 15:4, II Tim. 4:17, Tit. 1:3, Herm. sim. VIII 3, 2, IX 16, 5. "The word" (ὁ λόγος) goes through the same development. It is often qualified by an objective genitive, such as: "of the Reign" (Mt. 13:19), "of salvation" (Acts 13:26), "of grace" (Acts 20:32), "of the cross" (I Cor. 1:18), "of reconciliation" (II Cor. 5:19), "of truth" (Col. 1:5, Eph. 1:13, II Tim. 2:15); cf. Pol. Phil. 3:2; "truth" and "life," without the article, are probably qualitative genitives (Jas. 1:18 and Phil. 2:16). But "the word," absolute, also denotes the Christian message: I Thess. 1:6, Gal. 6:6, Phil. 1:14 (variant), Col. 4:3, I Pet. 2:8, 3:1, Acts 6:4, 8:4, 10:36, 11:19, 14:25, 16:6, 32; 17:11, Barn. 9:3, 14:5, 19:10, Pol. Phil. 7:2, Heϱm. vis. III 7, 3; usually, it is true, "of God" is added as a subjective genitive or genitive of the author.

Acceptance of the Message is called πίστις (*"faith"* and *"belief"*) or πιστεύειν (*"believing"* or *"having faith"*). "Faith" as the acceptance of the kerygma is described at length in Rom. 10:14–17. The object of faith is "the kerygma" (I Cor. 1:21, Herm. sim. VIII 3, 2, etc.), "the gospel" (Mk. 1:15, Acts 15:7, I Cor. 15:2, etc.), "the testimony" (II Thess. 1:10, I Jn. 5:10), "the word" (Acts 4:4, Eph. 1:13, Barn. 9:3, *cf.* 16:9), the ἀκοή (lit. "the hearing"—i.e. "what is heard," "the preaching," Rom. 10:16, Jn. 12:38). The importance of this act of believing acceptance of the message, the act which makes the believing one a member of the Congregation, had the result that the concept "faith" took on a meaning which it had not had either in the Old Testament or in other ancient religions. In Christianity, for the first time, "faith" became the prevailing term for man's relation to the divine; in Christianity, but not before it, "faith" came to be understood as the attitude which through and through governs the life of the religious man. The way for this semantic development was prepared by the missionary activity of Judaism and of Gentile religions that were spreading their propaganda in the Hellenistic world. For it is only in missionary activity that "faith" comes to be conceived as conversion to a new religion that is being preached, whereas in the Old Testament, as in all folk-religions of antiquity, the worship of a people's own divinity (or divinities) is taken for granted.

In accord with the specific content of the primitive-Christian message, "faith" or "believing" means in Hellenistic Christianity: 1. belief in the one God (I Thess. 1:8f., Heb. 6:1, 11:6, Herm. mand. I 1; see above, 2, p. 67f.); 2. belief in God's saving deed in Christ (I Cor. 15:11, Rom. 4:24). The content of such belief may be given in a subordinate clause (ὅτι-clause, Rom. 10:9, I Thess. 4:14, Jn. 20:31, etc.), or it may be intimated by abbreviated expressions like "believing in Christ Jesus" (Gal. 2:16), or "in the Lord" (Acts 14:23, Herm. mand. IV 3, 3), "in the name of the son of God" (I Jn.

5:13), or others. The development of just this abbreviated expression to "believe (or belief) in" (or "believe" alone, and "belief" plus an objective genitive), foreign both to Greek diction and to the Old Testament (LXX), is significant. It is likewise significant that soon "believe" and "belief" (= "faith") are used technically, without any qualifying phrase. "Pistis," with or without a qualifying phrase, besides meaning faith-belief, can mean the act of becoming a believer (Gläubigwerden: I Thess. 1:8, Acts 20:21, etc.), or the state of being a believer (Gläubigsein: I Cor. 2:5, Did. 16:2, Barn. 4:9, etc.), or the attitude of having faith (Gläubigkeit: Rom. 14:1, I Thess. 1:3, etc.). "To believe" likewise sometimes means to become a believer (Rom. 10:14, Acts 18:8, etc.) and sometimes, especially in the participle, to be a believer, so that "the believing" (οἱ πιστεύοντες or οἱ πιστεύσαντες) can be substituted for "Christians" (II Thess. 1:10, Herm. sim. IX 19, 1f., etc.). Finally, pistis, whose first meaning, of course, is "faith" (fides qua creditur), comes to mean also "belief" (fides quae creditur—that which is believed: Rom. 10:8, Acts 6:7); then πίστις means simply "Christianity" (I Tim. 4:1, 6)—and "after the common faith" (Tit. 1:4 KJ) means "Christian." Except for this last stage all these possibilities of usage had developed before Paul's time and continued to be worked out by his contemporaries. Only against this background of missionary terminology does Paul's distinctive understanding of faith stand out.

Nevertheless, even aside from Paul the concept of faith underwent an expansion and enrichment in earliest Christianity. That is readily explained in the first place by the fact that πιστεύειν (have faith) can mean "to trust" and that this meaning easily combines with that of the missionary terminology. As "faith" and "confidence" are combined in Eph. 3:12, I Clem. 26:1, 35:2, so "trust" πεποίθησις takes the place of "believe" (I Clem. 58:1, 60:1, Herm. sim. IX 18, 5), and I Cor. 2:9, Phil. 3:4ff. also show the affinity of the two verbs. In the second place, this kinship of meaning made it inevitable that an Old Testament-Jewish conception of man's relation to God should influence the Christian relation to God called pistis. The conception referred to is expressed by the verbs הֶאֱמִין (feel safe, trust, believe), בָּטַח (trust), חָסָה (find refuge in), קִוָּה (wait for, hope in)—i.e. an understanding of man's relation to God as one characterized both by trust and hope and by fidelity and obedience. The influence of this conception on the meaning of Christian "faith" was all the more inevitable because the regular LXX rendering of הֶאֱמִין is precisely πιστεύειν (have faith, trust); the other verbs, especially בָּטַח, are frequently rendered πεποιθέναι ("to trust").

Heb. 11 shows with special clarity the richness of nuance that the concept "faith" has under these influences. While in verse 3, and especially verse 6, the technical sense of missionary terminology emerges, in general the meaning "trust" and "hope" prevails (especially vss. 9f., 11, 13, 17), yet in such a way that in addition the meaning "obedience" and "fidelity" again and again asserts itself (vss. 5, 7, 8, 24ff., 30f., 33). Elsewhere, also, the meaning "trust" breaks through: (e.g. Rom. 4:17-20; I Clem. 26:1, 35:2, II Clem. 11:1), or that of "hope" (esp. in I Pet.; cf. 1:5-9, 21; elsewhere: I Clem. 12:7, Barn. 4:8), or that of "fidelity" (II Tim. 4:7, I Pet. 5:9, Rev. 2:13, 13:10) or that of "obedience," which is especially marked in Paul but also appears elsewhere—for instance, in the use of πείθεσθαι ("obey," "be persuaded" as synonymous with πιστεύειν (believe, trust) in Acts 17:4, 28:24, and in the designation of unbelief as ἀπειθεῖν ("disobeying" in Acts 14:2, 19:9, I Pet. 2:8, 3:1, Joh. 3:36, etc.).

Does "faith" (or "to believe") also indicate a personal relation to the person of Christ, or does it mean only a relation to God on the basis of God's deed in Christ? The expression "believe in him" (εἰς αὐτόν), at any rate, does not in itself assert a personal relation to Christ, since this expression is only an abbreviation for the fuller one "believe that . . ." followed by a clause (e.g. "that God raised him from the dead," Rom. 10:9). The LXX never describes man's relation to God as "believing in" (εἰς), and the expressions the LXX does use for this purpose occur almost nowhere in the New Testament to designate a relation to Christ. The LXX-phrases are: πιστεύειν with the dative and no preposition, and πιστεύειν ἐπί ("believe upon") with the dative. (The verb with dative alone is used of Jesus in the New Testament really only in John, with the meaning: believe him (his words); with ἐπί and the dative, I Tim. 1:16.) Rarely πιστεύειν ἐπί with the accusative, which elsewhere is also used of God, is used of Christ (Acts 9:42, 11:17, 16:31, 22:19); the use of πρὸς τὸν κύριον Ἰησοῦν, Phm. 5 ("faith toward the Lord Jesus"), is unique. So the answer that must be given to the initial question is that faith as a personal relation to the person of Christ is an idea that was at first foreign to the earliest Christian message; for such an idea to arise there must have been other factors at work.

From this survey of the message of the one God and His judgment and of Jesus Christ as Judge and Savior the *questions* that arise are: Will faith in the one God take on the character of an "enlightened" *Weltanschauung* or will God be understood as the Power who determines human existence and demands the whole will of man? Though the question seems to have been decided in the second of these two ways by the eschatological message, the question remains: To what extent will eschatological faith outgrow mythological imagination? Will it confine itself to simply waiting for a coming event, or will it understand the present in the light of an already happened eschatological occurrence? In what manner will eschatology be retained when the expectation of the imminent End pales and dies out? Further: Will the significance of Christ remain confined to the role of the future Judge and Savior? How will theological reflection understand his death and resurrection? Will theological propositions take on the character of theoretical speculation, and will "faith in him" thereby become mere belief in dogmas? How will the idea of "faith" develop and how will theological thinking be guided by it?

§ 10. Church Consciousness and the Christian's Relation to the World

1. The eschatological missionary preaching of Christians was a startling thing to at least a large part of Gentile hearers in the Greek-speaking world—especially the message of the resurrection of the dead. The account in Acts indicates this in 17:18, 32 when it lets the Athenian audience pay special attention and take offense when the theme of "resurrection" is touched (see above p. 77). Likewise I Thess. 4:13ff. and I Cor. 15 show the novelty and the offensiveness of such preaching. And yet, on the other hand, the proclaiming of an imminent eschatological drama, a cosmic revolution, was for many hearers nothing basically new or unheard of. Eschatological ideas of this sort had long since penetrated the Hellenistic world from the orient. It must be recognized, of course, that they had been largely divested of their originally mythological character either by

taking on the character of a theory of natural science, as in the Stoic teaching of the world-periods with a "conflagration" (ἐϰπύϱωσις) at the end of each, or by becoming a poetic figure for a turning-point in political history, as in the *Carmen saeculare* of Horace or in Vergil's *Eclogue* IV, which sings the birth of a coming savior of the world.

As the announcement of a cosmic turning-point the eschatological preaching of earliest Christianity could therefore count upon being rather generally understood. But so far as it was the earliest Christian view *that the imminent eschatological event was to be the closing act of a history of salvation,* the history of the Chosen People, "true Israel"—so far as it meant fulfilment of the promise for the benefit of the Chosen People—the presuppositions for understanding it were not present. How could the consciousness of the earliest Church of being the eschatological "Congregation" of the end of days, for whom the promises were now being fulfilled—how could the consciousness of being "true Israel" find a footing in Hellenistic congregations?

This is a decisive question, the question of the *Church concept.* Does the salvation proclaimed by the Christian message mean only the salvation of the individual, the release of the individual soul from the contamination of sin and from suffering and death? Or does it mean salvation for the fellowship of God's people into which the individual is incorporated? The fact that the earliest Church in its mission simply took the latter for granted essentially differentiates it from the propaganda of other oriental religions of redemption; and, viewed historically, therein lies a basic reason for Christianity's triumph over them. In Christianity, the individual believer stands within the Congregation, and the individual congregations are joined together into one Congregation—the Church. Nor is the primary motive of this joining together the practical need of organization. Rather, churchly organization arose primarily out of the consciousness that the total Church exists before local churches do. An indication of this is the terminology: "ecclesia" denotes at first not the individual church at all, but the "people of God," the fellowship of the chosen at the end of days. This was the usage not only in the earliest Church (§ 6) but also in Hellenistic Christianity. And though *in the latter* the individual Church before long is called "ecclesia," and "church" can then be used in the plural, the idea is, nevertheless, that the individual church is the manifestation of the one Church.

Paul is evidently following the common Hellenistic terminology when he uses "ecclesia" sometimes of the total Church, sometimes of the local congregation. Following Old Testament and earliest Christian usage he calls the total Church "Church of God": I Cor. 10:32, 11:22, 15:9, Gal. 1:13. "Church" by itself can also mean the total Church: I Cor. 12:28, Phil. 3:6. In Acts, the singular occurs only once where it certainly means the total Church: 9:31; perhaps also 20:28 ("the Lord's Church"); this use is frequent in Col. and Eph. and occurs also I Tim. 3:5, 16, in the Didache (in prayer to God: "thy Church," 9:4, 10:5; also 11:11), in Hermas ("thy = God's holy Church" vis. I 1, 6; 3, 4—also, sim. VIII 6, 4, IX 13, 1; 18 2f. ("of God"), and hypostatized to a mythical figure in vis. II 4, 1; III 3, 3 IV 1, 3; 2, 2; sim. IX 1, 1f.). It occurs, further, in Barn. 7:11, II Clem. 2:1, 14:1–4, and in Ignatius, who calls the Church sometimes "holy" (Tr.), sometimes "God's" (Tr. 2:3) or "Jesus Christ's" (Eph. 5:1) or "God's and Christ's" (Phld. pr., Sm. pr.) but also speaks of "the Church" without qualification, meaning the total Church (Eph. 17:1, Phld. 9:1); in his writings also occurs for the first time "the universal (catholic) Church" (ἡ καθολικὴ ἐκκλησία, Sm. 8:2).

That the local church is a manifestation of the total Church is probably meant in the expression occurring a number of times in the prefatory greetings: "To the Church (of God) so far as it is present at . . . (τῇ ἐκκλησίᾳ [τοῦ θεοῦ] τῇ οὔσῃ ἐν . . .), (I Cor. 1:2, II Cor. 1:1, Ign. Eph., Mg., Tr., Phld.), in place of which may also be said: "to the Church of God sojourning in . . . (τῇ παροικούσῃ, I Clem. pr., Pol. Phl. pr.).

The idea of the priority of the total Church over the local church is also indicated in the equating of the Church with the "body of Christ" which comprises all believers. Paul practically makes this equation in I Cor. 12; it is then explicitly made in Col. 1:18, 24, Eph. 1:22f., 5:23ff., II Clem. 2:1; but especially is this so in the speculations which early arose over the pre-existence of the Church—i.e. an existence which preceded its historical realization—Eph. 5:32, II Clem. 14, Herm. vis. II 4, 1 (cf. II, 1, 6; 3, 4).

This *Church-consciousness* likewise stands behind the effort of the Jerusalem Church to exercise a sort of oversight over the Gentile-Christian congregations of which we hear both from Paul and in Acts. It also stands behind Paul's own efforts to establish and strengthen the connection of Gentile-Christian congregations with Jerusalem. Seen from this point of view, the decree of the "apostolic council" (Gal. 2:10) that Gentile congregations should contribute funds for the poor of the Jerusalem Church is historically almost the most important decree of the council, for there was a greater danger that the unity of the congregations might be lost than that the Gentile congregations might accept an obligation to observe the Torah. That is the reason for Paul's eagerness about the collections of the Gentile Christians for Jerusalem (I Cor. 16:1–4, II Cor. 8–9, Rom. 15:26f., 31).

2. It is due not only to the efforts of Paul that a church consciousness did promptly form and develop in Hellenistic Christianity, but also to the fact that the Hellenistic congregations in part grew out of Hellenistic synagogues, and to the fact that—whether in each instance the latter was the case or not—that the *Old Testament had been transmitted to them as a holy book*. Though the influence of the Old Testament was not equally great in all congregations, yet by and large it was probably everywhere operative. The epistolary literature of the New Testament, with the exception of the Johannine epistles, shows that all the way through a certain familiarity with the Old Testament is assumed in the readers—a familiarity that, of course, may be of very uneven extent. The same thing is shown by the writings of the apostolic fathers, among which only the letters of Ignatius rarely refer to the Old Testament. Perhaps there soon existed anthologies, i.e. collections of Old Testament quotations on specific points of teaching, as the agreement among composites of quotations in various writings seems to prove. Individual writings, such as Hebrews and Barnabas, are almost entirely devoted to exegesis of the Old Testament.

While it makes a difference, of course, whether the Old Testament is read as a book of oracles serving to demonstrate the fulfilment of prophecy, or as a code of ethics and moral examples, or as the document of the history of salvation—still these various motives all work together toward creating in the Christian Congregation a consciousness *of solidarity with Israel and its history*. Abraham is the "father" of believers from the Gentile world, too (Rom. 4:1, 12, 9:7f., Gal. 3:7, 29, Jas. 2:21, I Clem. 31:2, Barn. 13:7; *cf.* Heb. 2:16,

6:13), and the Christian congregations dispersed in the world are the people "of the twelve tribes in the dispersion" (Jas. 1:1; *cf.* I Pet. 1:1, Did. 9:4, 10:5, I Clem. 59:2). They are the "Israel of God" (Gal. 6:16), the "chosen generation" and the "peculiar people" (I Pet. 2:9), "the portion of His choice" (I Clem. 29:1); they are "the true circumcision" (Phil. 3:3). So it is perfectly natural that the Old Testament witnesses of faith are their models (Heb. 11); they are to "fix their gaze" (ἀτενίσωμεν εἰς) upon the Old Testament men of faith (I Clem. 9:2); it is to them that Christians are to "cleave" (κολληθῶμεν, I Clem. 31:1, 46:4). Job is the model of patience and piety (Jas. 5:11, I Clem. 17:3), Lot and Rahab, the harlot, are examples of hospitality (I Clem. 11f.), Abraham and David are models of humility (I Clem. 17f.), etc. When in I Clem., 55 models of conduct from heathen history are ingenuously placed by the side of those from the Old Testament, it is evident to what an extent the Church has already made the history in the Old Testament its own history. No less the Old Testament furnishes them warning examples not to be followed: the disobedience and faithlessness of Israel in the desert (I Cor. 10:6ff., Heb. 3:7ff.), the jealousy of Cain, Esau, and others (I Clem. 4; *cf.* Heb. 12:16). This principle holds: "Whatever was written (in the Old Testament) in former days was written for our instruction, that by steadfastness and by the encouragement of the scriptures we might have hope" (Rom. 15:4; *cf.* I Cor. 10:11, Rom. 4:23f., I Cor. 9:9f., II Tim. 3:16).

Teaching and exhortation of this sort are an after-effect of the Synagogue's homiletic tradition, and two *conventional forms of preaching* soon appear in the earliest Church which were already present in Judaism: 1. Summaries of the history of God's People which point out the divine teleology of that history. Examples of this in the New Testament are the speech of Stephen, Acts 7:2–47, and that of Paul in Pisidian Antioch, Acts 13:17–25 (41). 2. Series of examples collected from history according to a particular catch-word. Of this nature is Heb. 11; shorter, Jd. 5–7; I Clem. contains many examples of this sort (4–6, 7–8, 9–10, 11–12, 51:3–5).

It must be recognized, however, that the *relation of the Church to Israel's history* is a peculiarly paradoxical one because the course of events from Jacob-Israel down to the present is not a continuous history but one broken by the eschatological occurrence in Christ. That is, the eschatological Congregation·is not simply the historical successor and heir of the empirical Israel of history but the heir of the ideal Israel, so to say, the people of God which the historical Israel was indeed called to be, but which, in point of fact, it never actually was. For it was indeed the elect People of God; but its election always hovered above and ahead of it, so to say, as goal and promise. Israel's election determined its history in consequence of divine guidance in bane and blessing. Still the election never came to realization—or, when it did, only in exceptions like Abraham, the strong in faith (Rom. 4, Heb. 11:8ff., etc.), David in whom God was pleased (Acts 13:22) and in whom the Holy Spirit spoke (Acts 1:16, Rom. 4:6, etc.), the prophets and men of faith who now serve as models to the Church. But as a whole, on account of its disobedience and faithlessness and especially for its rejection of Jesus, Israel itself has been rejected. The Christian Church is the true People of God.

But this contrast with the historical Israel, this eschatological break in history, does not mean discontinuity in the history of salvation but precisely the opposite—continuity. The election of the People of God, which, so to say, had been awaiting its fulfilment, is now being realized in the Christian Congregation, which in contrast to "Israel after the flesh" ('Ισραὴλ κατὰ σάρκα, I Cor. 10:18 KJ) is the "Israel of God" (Gal. 6:16), whose members are the true sons of Abraham (see above, and Rom. 9:7ff., Gal. 4:22ff.) with whom God has concluded the new covenant (II Cor. 3:6ff., Heb. 8:6ff., and see below). The rejection of the historical Israel had been foreseen from the beginning in the Old Testament, as scripture proof teaches, and the new covenant had been predicted. The worship of ancient Israel had been a foreshadowing anticipation of the occurrence of salvation in Christ (Heb. 7–10).

As this paradoxical relation of the Christian Congregation to the historical Israel is expressed in the concept of the new covenant, so also in its use of the *concept "the People"* (λαός). This word, seldom used in post-Homeric Greek literature, had become in the LXX the distinctive designation for Israel in contrast to "the nations" (τὰ ἔθνη)—so also Lk. 2:32, Acts 15:14, 26:17, 23. "The people" had meant Israel in the still undifferentiated double sense of the Hebrew people of history and the Chosen People of God. The Christian Congregation appropriates this designation to itself, retaining only the second meaning.

The peculiarities of the LXX usage recur in Christian usage: "the People" by itself in the technical sense (Heb. 2:17, 13:12, Herm. sim. V 6, 2f.); "the People of God" (or, depending upon the context, "my," "thy," "His" = God's: Heb. 4:9, 10:30, Rev. 18:14, I Clem. 59:4, Herm. sim. V 5, 3; or "his" = "of the Son of God," Herm. sim. IX 18, 4); "the holy People" (patterned after Deut. 7:6, etc.: Barn. 14:6; *cf.* ἔθνος ἅγιον, "holy nation," I Pet. 2:9); "a chosen People" λαος περιουσιος (patterned after Ex. 19:5, etc.: Tit. 2:14, I Clem. 6:4; *cf.* "a peculiar People" [KJ] or "a special People" RSV marg. [I Pet. 2:9]); "people of the inheritance," Barn. 14:4. Expressions like these recur: "they shall be to me for a people" (after Jer. 38:33, LXX = 31:32 Heb.) Heb. 8:10; *cf.* Rev. 21:3, Acts 18:10, "to take a people . . . for his name" (Acts 15:14), "to prepare himself a people" (Barn. 3:6, 5:7, 14:6). The prophecy of "not-my-people" which shall become "my people" (Hos. 1:10, 2:23 = 2:1, 25 Heb.) is applied to the Gentile Christians in Rom. 9:25, I Pet. 2:10; so is the promise of Ex. 19:5f. (I Pet. 2:9).

The idea of the *"new covenant,"* of which the death of Christ is held to be the instituting sacrifice, was evidently alive before Paul, as the liturgy of the Lord's Supper which had come down to him indicates (I Cor. 11:25). This idea, which testifies that the idea of eschatological occurrence is oriented around the Congregation as the People of God (§ 9, 4) is equally important to Paul (II Cor. 3:6ff., Gal. 4:24) and to the author of Hebrews (8:8, 9:15, 12:24) who in 8:10ff. quotes at length from Jer. 38:31ff. LXX (31:30ff. Heb. text) the promise of the new covenant made to the People of God.

The covenant idea plays a special role in *Barnabas,* with a peculiar modification, however, inasmuch as the author claims that Israel, in reality, never had a covenant with God, since by its folly of idolatry it had from the beginning trifled away the Covenant intended for it on Sinai (4:6–8, 14:1ff.). Therefore, he does not speak of a "new" covenant but of the one covenant (13–14), which, however, did not pertain to the "former people" (13:1) but to the "new People" (5:7, 7:5), the Christian Congregation.

3. Church-consciousness includes *a consciousness of separateness and delimitation from the world*. This is attested, first, by the fact that the attributes of the eschatological Congregation (§ 6, 2) are appropriated by Hellenistic Christianity, too. Believers are called "the chosen" (ἐκλεκτοί, Rom. 8:33, II Tim. 2:10, I Pet. 1:1, 2:4, etc.) or "the called" (κλητοί, Rom. 1:6, I Cor. 1:24, Jd. 1, Barn. 4:13, or κεκλημένοι, Heb. 9:15, I Clem. 65:2, Herm. sim. VIII 1, 1; IX 14, 5) or "the saints" (ἅγιοι, Rom. 8:27, I Cor. 6:2, Heb. 6:10, I Clem. 56:1, Barn. 19:10, etc.) or "the sanctified" (ἡγιασμένοι, I Cor. 1:2, Acts 20:32, 26:18, etc.) or combinations of these terms, such as "called saints" (Rom. 1:7, I Cor. 1:2) and others (Rev. 17:14, I Clem. pr., Jd. 1).

This separateness is first of all, of course, a self-exclusion from *non-Christian cults of every sort*. This is seldom mentioned in the texts because it was taken for granted. The clear-cut alternative is formulated in II Cor. 6:14–7:1. The polemic of I Cor. 10:1–22 [*] is directed against idolatry equated with participation in a heathen cult. Otherwise, idolatry (or the idolater) is only mentioned almost parenthetically among other vices as a practice that is out of the question for a Christian (I Cor. 5:10f., 6:9, Gal. 5:20, I Pet. 4:3, Rev. 21:8, 22:15, Did. 3:4, 5:1, Barn. 20:1); it simply belongs to "the time that is past" (I Pet. 4:3; *cf.* Barn. 16:7, II Clem. 17:1) and it is significant that in Christianity, as in Judaism before it, the concept is widened and transferred to other vices (Col. 3:5, Eph. 5:5). Of course, there were scrupulous souls who declared even the eating of food that had been offered to idols prohibited (Rev. 2:14, 20, Did. 6:3), and this prohibition is also the first provision of the so-called "apostolic decree" (Acts 15:20, 29; 21:25). But this provision did not go into general effect, and Paul, dealing with this matter in I Cor. 10:23–11:1, declares the eating of food offered to idols permitted so far as any principle is concerned.

[*] The contradiction between this passage and I Cor. 8:7ff. (where participation in heathen cult-meals is forbidden only out of consideration for "the weak") is probably to be explained by regarding I Cor. 10:1–22 as an excerpt from Paul's precanonical letter to Corinth (mentioned at I Cor. 5:9). Paul evidently had heard that members of the Congregation were taking part in heathen cult-meals and assumed that this participation was meant as worship of the heathen divinities. Those concerned replied that this assumption was false, and that they, having "knowledge," regarded idols as non-existent and hence could perfectly well take part in those meals. Thereupon Paul answers with 8:1–13, 10:23–11:1.

But every kind of sorcery (φαρμακεία, Gal. 5:20, Rev. 21:8, 22:15, Did. 2:2, 5:1, Barn. 20:1) or magic (μαγεία, Did. and Barn., *loc. cit.*) is forbidden as it had been in Judaism. Included under the ban of sorcery is the invoking of demons, which, according to Jewish and early Christian conceptions, the beings worshiped in idolatry really are (I Cor. 10:20f., Barn. 16:7, etc.).

4. But the separateness of the Church is above all its *delimitation from the world as the sphere of moral uncleanness and sin.* The Congregation is the holy temple of God, set apart from all that is worldly and sinful (I Cor. 3:16f., II Cor. 6:16, Eph. 2:21f., Ign. Eph. 9:1, Mg. 7:2); it is the "spiritual house" of God (I Pet. 2:5; *cf.* I Tim. 3:15, Heb. 3:6, 10:21, Herm. sim. IX 13, 9; 14, 1). The eschatological Congregation really no longer belongs to the perishing world. Its members have no home here; their πολίτευμα (citizenship) is in heaven (Phil. 3:20), their City is the one that is to come (Heb. 13:14). Here, in this world, they are away from home on a pilgrimage.

Christians in this world are "away from home," ἐπὶ ξένης, as Herm. sim. I:1 sets forth at length. They are "strangers, temporary sojourners" (παρεπίδημοι, I Pet. 1:1, 2:11), "resident aliens," not full citizens (πάροικοι, I Pet. 1:17, 2:11, II Clem. 5:1; later, Diogn. 5:5, 6:8, who, in chapter 5, deals with this theme at length). Hence a local congregation can be described as "sojourning" (παροικοῦσα) in its particular place (I Clem. pr., Pol. Phil. pr.). The basic motif of the Epistle to the Hebrews can be called "the pilgrim-people of God" [thus E. Käsemann in his book with that title: *Das wandernde Gottesvolk* (1939)]; it is thematically handled in Heb. 3:7–4:13 by parallelizing the Christian Church with Israel on its wandering toward the promised land. This foreignness of the Church is parallelized with Israel's situation in another respect when the Church is described as being in the dispersion (Jas. 1:1, I Pet. 1:1).

The thing to do, then, is "to gird up one's loins" for the pilgrimage (I Pet. 1:13, Pol. Phil. 2:1). In such expressions *the paradox of the Christian situation* comes to expression which Paul characterizes as the situation between "no longer" and "not yet" (Phil. 3:12–14). But Paul has only reduced to a brief formula what everywhere is described in a great variety of terms as the Christian situation.

For, on the one hand, the eschatological church-consciousness feels itself separated from the world—i.e. from "this age," from its own past, and from its heathen environment. For Christians are sanctified and purified (§ 9, 4, p. 85) inasmuch as Christ accomplished "purification for sins" (Heb. 1:3). Through baptism, the purification has been carried out on one and all (Eph. 5:26); it is "the bath of regeneration and renewal" brought about "by the Holy Spirit" (Tit. 3:5). As the occurrence of salvation is for Paul a new act of creation by God (II Cor. 4:6) and the Christian is "a new creation" (II Cor. 5:17), so for Barnabas it means the fulfilment of the promise, "Lo, I make the last things as the first" (6:13), namely: a new creation. It means that God renewed us by the forgiveness of sins (6:11) and created us anew: "See, then, we have been molded (ἀναπεπλάσμεθα) anew" (6:14; cf. 16:8: "We became new, being created again from the beginning"). Or, as I Pet. 1:23 says, "You have been born anew."

However, when God is called he "who has begotten us again to a living hope" (I Pet. 1:3),. that brings to the fore the paradox of which we have spoken: We are what we are in hope. For that is the other side of the Christian situation: though Christian existence can, on the one hand, be described by the indicatives—we are sanctified, we are purified—nevertheless, so long as it moves within this world, it stands under the imperative. Though, on the one hand, it is separated from its past and its environment, yet this separation must be newly made again and again. The *pure* and *sanctified* are exhorted: "Let us cleanse ourselves from every defilement of body and spirit and make holiness perfect in the fear of God" (II Cor. 7:1). Life must no longer be "conformed" (συσχηματίζειν) to the passions of one's earlier heathen period (I Pet. 1:14), one must "no longer live as the Gentiles do" (Eph. 4:17), but "be holy" and "conduct one's self in the fear of God throughout the time of one's pilgrimage" (I Pet. 1:15-17). What God wills is sanctification; thereto He called us (I Thess. 4:3-7). One must "keep one's self unstained from the world" (Jas. 1:27, II Pet. 3:14). Baptism must be kept "pure and undefiled" (II Clem. 6:9; cf. 7:6, 8:6). What has happened in principle must be brought to reality in practice: "Put to death therefore what is earthly in you . . . seeing that you have put off the old nature with its practices and have put on the new nature which is being renewed . . ." (Col. 3:5, 9f.), or "put off your old nature which belongs to your former manner of life . . . and be renewed in the spirit of your minds, and put on the new nature created after the likeness of God . . ." (Eph. 4:22–24). They who are new creations must be told: "create (reading ἀνακτίσασθε, not ἀνακτήσασθε) yourselves anew in faith" (Ign. Tr. 8:1). They who have been called out of darkness into light (I Pet. 2:9) must "cast off the works of darkness and put on the armor of light" (Rom. 13:12f., I Thess. 5:4ff.). "In the midst of a crooked and perverse generation" Christians must "shine," "blameless and innocent," "like the stars" (Phil. 2:15) and distinguish themselves from the Gentiles by their good conduct (I Pet. 2:12). They must go outside the "camp"—i.e. the world—to Christ (Heb. 13:13). We must "forsake our sojourning in this world, and do the will of him who called us, and not fear to go forth from this world" (II Clem. 5:1), and that means: "lead a holy and righteous life, and regard the things of this world as not our own (ἀλλότρια), and not desire them" (II Clem. 5:6; on the concept ἀλλότρια, "not our own, foreign" *cf.* Ign. Rom. pr., Herm. sim. I 3 and 11). The present world and the world to come are enemies, hence: "We must bid farewell to this world to consort with the one to come" (II Clem. 6:3–5).

It is not surprising that in the Hellenistic sphere, *asceticism* early became a means of delimitation from the world, for Hellenism knows many an ascetic movement. It does not mean asceticism proper, of course, when the eating of meat offered to idols is forbidden (Acts 15:20, 29; 21:25, I Cor. 8–10, Rev. 2:14, 20), or when fasting is recommended to strengthen prayer (Acts 13:3, 14:23, I Cor. 7:5 secondary koine-text, Did. 1:3), or to prepare for the reception of revelation (Acts 13:2, Herm. vis. II 2, 1; III 1, 2, etc.), or when regular fasting is prescribed on two days of the week (Did. 8:1). Did. 6:3, however, does combine the prohibition of food offered to idols with ascetic abstinence. *Food-asceticism* on principle (abstinence from meat and wine) is the standpoint of the "weak" (Rom. 14), whom Paul treats with consideration. It is not clear to what extent the demands for abstinence made by the false teachers condemned in Col. 2:16ff. were truly ascetic or whether they were simply harmless ritual commandments; the former seems to be the case with the false teachers combatted in I Tim. 4:3 (*cf.* Tit. 1:15), who also urged sexual asceticism. *Sexual asceticism* is even for Paul an ideal (I Cor. 7:7). It is evidently recommended in the merely suggestive words of Did. 6:2, and is probably meant in the enigmatic sentence Did. 11:11, *cf.* Eph. 5:32. At any rate, the ideal of chastity stands in high regard according to Rev. 14:1-5, I Clem. 38:2, 48:5, Ign. Pol. 5:2, and II Clem. 12 and 14:3 plead for it. A special form of sexual asceticism is already presupposed in I Cor. 7:25, 36f.—i.e. a "spiritual" marriage in which ascetic and virgin live together.° A vivid picture of this practice is furnished by Herm. sim. IX 11. The ascetic requirement of *renunciation of property* is not at first made, though distrust of wealth is great (I Tim. 6:6-10, Heb. 13:5, Jas. 5:1-6, and especially Herm.—e.g. vis. III 6, 5-7; 9:2-6; sim. II).

Such exhortations are naturally heightened again and again by *reference to the imminent end of this world* (e.g. Rom. 13:11f., I Thess. 5:1ff., I Pet. 1:5ff., 4:7, Heb. 10:25ff., Did. 16, Barn. 21:3, Ign. Eph. 11:1, Ign. Pol. 3:2, Herm. vis. II 3, 4). Paul expects to experience the parousia of Christ with the majority of his contemporaries (I Thess. 4:17; "we who are alive, who are left"; *cf.* I Cor. 15:51) and, of course, he was not alone in holding that view. In time, of course, the delay of the parousia becomes noticeable and references to it have to be strengthened by exhortations to be patient (Mk. 13:10, Jas. 5:7ff., Heb. 10:36ff.; indeed, even doubt of its coming must be combatted (II Pet. 3, I Clem. 23, II Clem. 11f.). The warning becomes necessary not to regard one's self as "already made righteous" (Barn. 4:10), "never to rest, as being called, and slumber in our sins" (Barn. 4:13). Nor do the exhortations "to watch" and "be sober" (§ 9, 3, p. 76) die out.

Since "forgetfulness of having been cleansed from former sins" (II Pet. 1:9) comes over many, the *exhortation to make Christian living a reality* takes on a sharper tone: "Cleanse your hands, you sinners, and purify your hearts, you men of double mind!" (Jas. 4:8). And while Heb. 6:4ff. warns: "it is impossible to restore again to repentance those who have once been enlightened" (I Jn. 1:7, 9), pointing to the blood of Christ which cleanses us, exhorts the believer to constant confession of sin. While I and II Clem. take for

° The woman in this relation was later technically known as παρθένος συνείσακτος and *virgo subintroducta* or, rarely, *synisacta*. An abstract noun seems not to have developed as a name for the practice, but German scholars have created and use the barbarism: *Syneisaktentum*. If the need for a technical term with this meaning should ever be felt in English, "subintroduction" would be more apposite.

granted that repentance is the constant accompaniment of the Christian life, according to Hermas God is just once more offering a last renewed opportunity for repentance and hence offers the possibility of a second "renewal" (ἀνακαίνωσις or ἀνανέωσις, vis. III 8, 9; 13, 2; cf. vis. III 12, 3; sim. VIII 6, 3; 14, 3). Hence, now is heard anew the exhortation: "Therefore purify your heart from all the vanities of the world" (mand. IX 4, sim. V 3, 6; cf. vis. III 8, 11, mand. IX 7, XII 3, 4; 6, 5; sim. VII 2, VIII 11, 3).

Stereotyped forms of exhortation develop. As the gods of the Gentiles are "vain" (μάταιοι, Acts 14:15, imitating the LXX) and the Gentile way of life is "vain" (I Pet. 1:18) or "a walking in futility" (ἐν ματαιότητι, Eph. 4:17; cf. Rom. 1:21), as their understanding is "darkened by vain desires" (II Clem. 19:2), so "vain" with its derivatives becomes the specification for the worldly in general. I Clem. urges the giving up of "empty and vain cares" (7:2) or of "vain toil" (ματαιοπονία, 9:1); Pol. Phil. urges the renunciation of "the futility of the many" (7:2) or "empty vanity" (κενὴ ματαιολογία, 2:1). Barnabas cries: "Let us flee from all vanity" (4:10). Hermas speaks of "the vain desire(s) of this world" (mand. XI 8; XII 6, 5) and demands purification "from all the vanities of this world" (mand. IX 4, sim. V 3, 6).

As Gentile conduct is a walking *"in lusts"* (Rom. 1:24, Tit. 3:3, I Pet. 1:14), so ἐπιθυμίαι (lusts, passions, desires) become the earmark of the world. They are called "worldly" passions (Tit. 2:12, II Clem. 17:3) or "fleshly" (I Pet. 2:11; cf. Gal. 5:16, 24, Eph. 2:3) or "carnal and bodily" (Did. 1:4). I Jn. 2:16f. combines the two descriptions: "all that is in the world, the lust of the flesh . . . is of the world. And the world passes away and the lust of it." I Clem. 28 mentions "foul desires" (ε. μιαραί). Related to "passion" is "care" or "anxiety." As Paul warns against being "anxious about worldly affairs" (I Cor. 7:32–34), so I Clem. 7:2 warns against "empty and vain cares."

Cares entangle one in the "preoccupations of daily living" (Herm. vis. III 11, 3, vis. I 3, 1, mand. V 2, 2), or the "occupations of this world" (Herm. mand. X 1, 4; cf. vis. III 6, 5, sim. VIII 8, 1f.; IX 20, 1f.)—and these are what Hermas' exhortations are directed against; his book as a whole is a penitential sermon against the secularization of Christianity.

The Christian attitude toward the world is also described in *stereotyped phrases*. A much-used term for it is "abstaining" (ἀπέχεσθαι): "abstaining from immorality" (I Thess. 4:3), "from every form of evil" (I Thess. 5:22), "from the passions of the flesh" (I Pet. 2:11; cf. Did. 1:4), "from all unrighteousness" (Pol. Phil. 2:2), or, after a catalogue of vices, "from all these things" (Pol. Phil. 5:3), "from every evil desire" (Herm. vis. I 2, 4: cf. III 8, 4, mand. XI 8, XII 1, 3; 2, 2) "from the works of the devil" (mand. VII 3), and, referring to specific vices (mand. II 4, III 5, IV 1, 3 and 9, V 1, 7; 2, 8, IX 12).

As Paul urges the believer to "cast off (ἀποθέσθαι) the works of darkness" (Rom. 13:12), so Col. 3:8 says: "now cast off also all these" (a catalogue of vices follows); Eph. 4:22 (see above) is similar. Cf. also: Eph. 4:25, I Pet. 2:1, Jas. 1:21, Heb. 12:1, I Clem. 13:1, 57:2, II Clem. 1:6. A related idea (ἀποτάσσεσθαι, "bid farewell") is expressed in II Clem. 6:4f. and 16:2.

The positive correlative to "casting off" in Rom. 13:12 is "putting on" (the armor of light), a figurative expression which also occurs in I Thess. 5:8, Eph. 6:11, 14, and, as a pure metaphor, in Col. 3:12. Col. 3:8ff. speaks of "putting on" the new man in contrast to "putting off" (ἀπεκδύεσθαι), combining this expression with the metaphorical use of "put away" (ἀποθέσθαι), while Eph. 4:22–24 mixes the two expressions. This metaphorical "putting on" (already current in the Old Testament and Judaism) is an expression especially favored in Hermas—e.g. mand. I:2, "you shall cast away from yourself all wickedness, and shall put on every virtue of righteousness"; see further: vis. IV 1, 8, mand. II 3f., V 2, 8, IX 7 and 10; X 3, 1 and 4; XI 4, XII 1, 1; 2, 4; sim. VI 1, 2 and 4; 5, 3; VIII 9, 1, IX 29, 3; also Ign. Pol. 1:2.

Christians can be and are described as "fleeing from the corruption that is in the world because of passion" (II Pet. 1:4) or "fleeing from the defilements of the world" (II Pet. 2:20), and the exhortation to "flee" (φεύγειν) occurs again and again. That from which one is to flee may be "idolatry" (I Cor. 10:14) or "fornication" (I Cor. 6:18) or the vices of greed (I Tim. 6:11, cf. 6–10) or "youthful passions" (II Tim. 2:22), or a whole list of vices (I Clem. 30:1) or "ungodliness" (II Clem. 10:1). Equivalent to this expression are "put aside (ἀπολείπειν, I Clem. 7:2, 9:1, 28:1, Pol. Phil. 2:1, 7:1) and "forsake" (καταλείπειν, II Clem. 5:1, 10:1).

Two further *types of Christian preaching* (see above, p. 96) develop in which the novelty of Christian living is described in contrast to the worldly past according to the scheme:

"formerly . . . now": 1. Once salvation (God's plan of salvation) was hidden; now it has been revealed. This motif first appears in I Cor. 2:7ff., then Col. 1:26f., Eph. 3:4f., 9f.; its overtones are heard in II Tim. 1:9f., Tit. 1:2f.; I Pet. 1:20 uses it for exhortation, and it is woven into a doxology at Rom. 16:25f. (non-Pauline!). 2. Once we were heathen, sunk in darkness and vice —now we are illumined and cleansed by God. Paul sets the pattern for this motif, too: Rom. 6:17f., 7:5f., 11:30, Gal. 4:3ff., especially I Cor. 6:9ff. in connection with a catalogue of vices. Otherwise it occurs: Col. 3:5ff., Tit. 3:3ff.; *cf.* I Pet. 4:3f.; without the vice-catalogue: Eph. 2:1ff., 11ff., I Pet. 2:25. II Clem. 1:6ff. indicates that this scheme was expanded in actual preaching.

5. Church-consciousness and the consciousness of eschatological delimitation from the world can be termed a *dualistic view*—it is the eschatological dualism of Jewish tradition. Though this contains a cosmological motif in the expectation of the great final catastrophe of the world, still it is not speculatively interested in cosmology. Nevertheless, the question arises whether the purity of the eschatological motif will be maintained or whether cosmological speculations will take root. Since a negative attitude toward the world goes hand in hand with eschatological consciousness—the attitude of "abstention" or "flight," etc.—the further question arises whether eschatological delimitation from the world will be understood as an inner de-secularization arising out of what one already positively has, or whether it will be a purely negative attitude to the world taking rise from the expectation that he who now flees the world will have his renunciation richly compensated by future heavenly goods. The historical situation of the earliest Church being such as it was, the further possibility existed that the eschatological consciousness of delimitation from the world might mingle with or even be replaced by other motifs which were also grounds for a negative attitude toward the world. *Stoic ideas* could influence Christian thought. An easy point of contact could be the Stoics' battle against "desire" and their exhortation to "renounce" (ἀπέχεσθαι) and to "regard as foreign" (ἀλλότρια ἡγεῖσθαι) to one's self all that is not truly in one's power: i.e. everything external. Indeed the occurrence of this expression (Heb. 11:9, Herm. sim. I 1, II Clem. 5:6) in itself indicates Stoic influence, at least in terminol-

ogy. Furthermore ° *the motifs of Gnostic dualism* could operate on Christian thinking even in conjunction with Stoic ideas, since for both Stoicism and Gnosticism the sphere of flesh and sensuality is degraded, although "the Spirit," which is the opposite of sensuality, is differently conceived by the two. Motifs of both kinds could become the foundation for a basically different asceticism from that of eschatological de-secularization (see above, 4).† Already in Paul the ascetic motif enters into a peculiar combination with the eschatological (espec. I Cor. 7); so also later in Hermas when, for example, he exhorts: "Guard this flesh of yours pure and undefiled" (Sim. V 7, 1). II Clem. 8:4, 6 also urges: "Keep the flesh pure and the seal (of baptism) undefiled," and presents queer, somewhat hazy ideas about the "self-control" (15:1) that is to be practiced in regard to the flesh (14:3–5). Especially Ignatius shows this influence; but with that we shall deal later (§ 15).

One is probably justified in saying that the *consciousness of the Gnostics* of constituting a community bound together in a mysterious unity and foreign to the world furnishes a certain analogy to Church-consciousness, a part of which is the consciousness of being delimited from the world. And actually the Fourth Gospel's consciousness of Church unity is influenced by Gnosticism, as we shall later show. The Epistle to the Hebrews also demonstrates how a churchly-eschatological and a Gnostic understanding of Christian existence can combine (§ 15). Nevertheless Gnosticism lacks the specific characteristics of Church-consciousness: a knowledge of its solidarity with the history of the People of God and a binding tie to the document of salvation, the Old Testament. In this detail, of course, the synagogue-congregations furnish an analogy; but otherwise the eschatological-churchly consciousness is something completely unprecedented in the Hellenistic world. That will change, of course, to the extent that the consciousness of being "the Israel of God," "the people of God" gives way to the notion of being a "third kind," τρίτον γένος, in contrast to Greeks (Gentiles) and Jews. The phrase occurs for the first time in Kerygma Petri 2: "For what the Greeks and the Jews have is antiquated, but it is we Christians

---

° *Cf.* M. Dibelius in the supplement to Lietzmann's *Handbuch* on Herm. sim. I 1. Sim. I, as a whole, is written in the style of the Cynic-Stoic diatribe.

† See above, see below = these references always refer to something which precedes or follows *within the same section* (§).

who worship Him (*sc.* God) in a new way, a third kind, τρίτῳ γένει, (of worship)." But here it means the Christian manner of worship and is not a designation for Christianity itself,° as it later became. But the next question is: how will the problem of the Church's relation to Judaism be solved—a problem arising from its consciousness of being the true Israel—and how will the authority of the Old Testament be understood?

§ 11. The Church's Relation to Judaism and the Problem of the Old Testament

1. On the one hand *the relation to Judaism* means for Hellenistic Christianity the relation to the form of *Jewish Christianity* represented by the *earliest Church* in Palestine. For it, as we have seen (§ 8, 1), had not severed itself from Judaism and had not cut the bands between the eschatological Congregation and the Jewish People. It took for granted at first that the non-Jew who wanted to belong to the Congregation of salvation had to be circumcised and place himself under the Law—i.e. had to become a Jew (§ 8, 2). In contrast to this attitude there developed out of the mission of Hellenistic Jewish-Christians a Hellenistic Christianity of which circumcision was not required and which did not obligate itself to keep the Law. This Torah-free Gentile Christianity represented by Barnabas and Paul achieved recognition by the earliest Church at the apostolic council (§ 8, 2). The fact that in spite of the agreement Jewish-Christian Torah-enthusiasts, the so-called Judaizers, propagandized for the Law in Gentile-Christian congregations and even penetrated the Pauline mission field—as Galatians testifies and Philippians hints—need not be pursued further here, since, for the history of early Christianity and the formation of its theology, it remained an episode whose only importance is that it forced Paul into the theological discussion to which we owe the letter to the Galatians.

The problem of the Church's relation to Judaism obviously took a somewhat different turn in other Hellenistic churches in which the Christian congregation had grown out of the synagogue—in that at Rome, for instance, but presumably also in many another. Here *debate with Judaism itself* was necessary, as Paul's letter to the

° On which see Ad. v. Harnack, *Mission u. Ausbreitung*, 3rd ed., I 238-267.

Romans testifies. For it does not polemize against "Judaizers," nor is it occasioned like Galatians by the intervention of rival missionaries who want to compel Roman Christians to adopt circumcision. Rather, it develops in purely theoretical fashion the principle of Christian faith in antithesis to the principle of the Jewish Torah-religion. Such debate with Judaism did not need by any means to arise out of a practical situation of conflict, but was just as likely to arise as the necessary consequence of *reflection on the part of the Christian believer* upon the essence and the foundations of his faith. To such theological reflection especially Hebrews and the Epistle of Barnabas bear witness.

The problem arose from the simple fact that Hellenistic Christianity had taken over the Old Testament and acknowledged its authority but at the same time denied the validity of the Old Testament Law for Christians. How was this denial to be backed up? How was the Law, which after all was a basic portion of the authoritative book of revelation, to be interpreted?

2. The Torah-free attitude of Hellenistic Christianity is by no means simply a result of *Paul's* struggle against the "Judaizers," and much less was his defense of freedom from the Law either then or later the *only* one in force. Side by side with his solution of the problem, other *possibilities* not only existed but were realized in practice. A survey of these possibilities comes down far beyond the time of Paul and must do so. For it is clear that all these possibilities were present from the beginning in the historical situation; the scantiness of the sources makes it impossible to say where and how soon they were realized. And it is not only possible but probable that later attested ideas were being presented before and during Paul's time. The meaning and importance of Paul's teaching on the Law can be recognized and appreciated only after a survey of all the possibilities has been made. The most important types of possibility are the following:

a. *Radical Gnosticism.* Gnosticism is not a phenomenon that first appeared within the Christian Church. It cannot be described as a speculative Christian theology under the influence of Greek philosophical tradition. It is not properly regarded as the "acute Hellenization" of Christianity, as Harnack in his time supposed. It has its roots in a dualistic redemption-religion which invaded Hellenism from the orient. Seen as a whole, it is a phenomenon parallel or competitive to the Christian religion. Each of these movements, the Gnostic and the Christian, influenced the other in many ways, but of that we shall have to speak later on. At any rate, there was very soon a Christian Gnosticism which, in its radical form, completely rejected the Old Testament, thus constituting the most extreme of the possibilities to be surveyed; that is why it is here named first.

Here the God of the Old Testament, creator of the world and giver of the Law, is distinguished from the God of Christian faith, the God of redemption whose revealer is Christ. In this, too, many differentiations are possible, depending upon whether in a particular case the Old Testament God is considered a being subordinate to the highest God, following His intentions, though with limited power, wisdom, and mercy, or whether He is thought of as a being inimical to the highest God, self-impelled and disobedient, the very Satan himself. The Old Testament with its Law is, accordingly, either an antiquated proclamation by a subordinate god or it is a Satanic law. In either case, it is no longer valid for the Christian. The practical consequence that is then drawn from such a view can be a libertinistic ethic, but not inevitably; for such a view also contains the possibility of an ascetic ethic.

b. *The Epistle of Barnabas.* This not definitely dateable document, certainly written after 70 A.D. and before 140 and very likely after 100, deals thematically with the problem of the Old Testament and claims to teach the right understanding of it which has at last been made available to Christian faith or to Christian *"gnosis"* (knowledge). For the Jews—this is its author's thesis—completely misunderstood it: "an evil angel misinstructed (ἐσόφιζεν) them" (9:4; *cf.* 10:9). Israel never had a covenant with God; for when Moses came down from Sinai with the tables of the Law and saw the people fallen into the sin of idolatry he smashed the tables "and so their covenant was broken in order that the covenant of Jesus the Beloved should be sealed in our hearts in the hope of our faith in him" (4:6–8; *cf.* 13–14). How then is the Old Testament to be understood? Allegorically. By this method two things are to be found in the Old Testament. The first is ethical instruction; that is how the cultic and ritual commandments are to be interpreted. The law of circumcision means circumcision of the heart (ch. 9); the unclean beasts that are not to be eaten mean evil men with whom one is not to associate (ch. 10), and so on. And, second, the Old

Testament contains predictions of Christ and Christian salvation (ch. 5–8). Both in cultic laws and in narratives (e.g. the 318 servants of Abraham, 9:8) the author finds the cross of Christ foretold; he reads out of the ancient texts the proclamation of the gospel (8:3), the return of Christ (7:9), the future glory of the faithful (6:16ff.), and so forth.

The real problem of the Law as the way of salvation—i.e. the problem of legalism, the problem of good works as the condition for participation in salvation—escaped the author. "The ordinances of the Lord" (δικαιώματα κυρίου, 2:1, 10:11, 21:1) have taken the place of the laws of the Old Testament. These constitute "the new law of our Lord Jesus Christ" (2:6), described, however, as "being without the yoke of necessity"—but this description is applied only in one direction: This law requires no "man-made sacrifice."

c. *The Epistle to the Hebrews.* For it the Old Testament as a whole is prediction of Christ and his work. Christ himself speaks in the Old Testament (2:12f., *cf.* Ps. 22:23, Is. 8:17f.; 10:5–7, *cf.* Ps. 40:7–9). Christ was pre-depicted in Moses as the one "faithful in all God's house" (3:1–6), and in Melchizedek as the high priest (7:1–10). But the author's chief interest is in the interpretation of the Old Testament cult. He has in common with Barnabas the method of allegorical interpretation; but in contrast to him the author to the Hebrews is certain that the Old Testament laws once were in force in their literal sense, which only Christ has abolished. "A former commandment is set aside because of its weakness and uselessness" (7:18). But why was the always weak and useless Law of the Old Testament ever given at all, then? Because it contained "the shadow of the good things to come, not the essence of these things themselves" (10:1 tr.); it typifies and presages what will perfectly appear in Christ. For "the Law appoints men in their weakness as high priests, but the word of the (divine) oath, which came later than the Law, appoints a Son who has been made perfect forever" (7:28). Christ's sacrificial blood accomplishes what the blood of the Old Testament sacrifice could not (9:15–28).

Just why all this prefiguration of Christ's deed of salvation, which no one in the time before Christ could understand, should have been instituted at all, it would probably be fruitless to ask the author in his satisfaction over his interpretation.

Nor did he any more than Barnabas reflect over the real problem of legalism. He does not mention the ethical commandments of the Old Testament; but he repeatedly emphasizes that Christians much more than Jews, or Israel, must beware of all "transgression" and "disobedience," since an incomparably sterner judgment will befall erring Christians than erring Jews (2:2f., 10:28f., 12:25). It is significant of the author's own legalistic manner of thinking that he rejects the possibility of a second repentance (6:4ff.).

d. *I Clement.* This letter was written in 95 or 96 A.D. from the Roman Church to the Corinthian. The problem we are discussing does not seem to exist for its author; rather he quite naively claims the Old Testament as a Christian book. He assumes as a matter of course that the cultic and ritual laws of the Old Testament are no longer valid. On one occasion he offers a Hellenistic idea as the reason for this: "The Sovereign (= God) . . . is in need of nothing: he asks nothing of anyone, save that confession of sin be made to him" (52:1). Yet he also assumes that the cultic laws were once a valid ordinance of God. They serve him as an analogy to the regulations of the Christian Congregation (40, 41). He has no need of allegory. Only once does he use this art—when he interprets the red thread which Rahab the harlot hung on the house as a sign to the Israelites to mean the blood of Christ (12:7f.). Rather, the knowledge" (γνῶσις, 40:1, 41:4) that he possesses is the art of making the Old Testament useful for practice and edification. For Christians it is the book of ethical models. It furnishes the "patterns" and "models," to be imitated by Christians, of the "commandments and ordinances of the Lord" (or "which are given us by God," 2:8, 58:2, etc.).

And the author knew Romans and I Corinthians! But he does not sense the Pauline problem of legalism. Like Paul (Rom. 4:7), he quotes Ps. 32:1f., "blessed are those whose iniquities are forgiven," etc. (50:6f.), but Paul's query, "Is this blessing pronounced only upon the circumcised or also upon the uncircumcised," is far from occurring to him. He perceives no difference between the Old Testament and the gospel, and still less any contrast. To him "faith" is a virtue among others; for instance, hospitality: "because of faith and hospitality" Abraham was given a son in old age (10:7) and Rahab the harlot was saved (12:1).

e. *Ptolemy to Flora.* This is a letter written by Ptolemy (140–160 in Rome), a pupil of Valentinus, to a lady to instruct her in the right understanding of the Old Testament Law. According to him, it falls into three parts: 1. the legislation of God; 2, the legislation of Moses (to it is reckoned, for instance, the law of divorce, which really is not allowed according to God's commandment, but which Moses—as the author knows from Mt. 19:6ff.—permitted on account of man's hard-heartedness); 3. the decrees of the elders, who—as the author says, echoing Mt. 15:3ff.—by their "traditions" set aside the Law of God. Therefore, "that whole Law contained in the pentateuch of Moses was not legislated by One." But even "that one part, the Law of God Himself, is divided into three," viz.: 1. the pure and perfect moral law which Jesus did not abolish but fulfilled, the decalogue; 2. the law mixed with evil, such as that of retaliation, which Jesus did abolish; 3. the ceremonial law whose spiritual meaning Jesus revealed; it is to be understood allegorically and it requires not ritualistic but ethical conduct. Nevertheless, the god who gave this three-fold Law is not the highest God, but a being standing between Him and the devil; this middle-god is not to be called "perfect," though he is to be called "righteous."

In this moderate Gnosticism of Ptolemy there is a curious combination of historical criticism and critical analysis of the content. But the latter is not oriented to the gospel but to the ideal of a spiritual ethic, and the problem of the way to salvation, or the problem of legalism, is not raised here either.

f. *Justin Martyr.* In his Dialogue with Trypho the Jew, the apologete Justin (ca. 100–165 A.D.) deals with the problem of the Old Testament in a way that later became the typical view of the Church. He, too, divides the Old Testament Law into three parts, but distinguishes them only as to content, not according to both content and history as Ptolemy did: 1. The eternal moral law: "what is by nature good and godly and righteous" or "what is universally, naturally, and eternally good" (both, 45:3f.) or "that which is always and universally just" and is acknowledged as such "by every race of mankind" (93:1f.; *cf.* also 67:10). This moral law was not abolished by Christ, the "new law-giver" (14:3, 18:3; Christ himself is called "the new law and the new covenant" at 11:4), but he summed up its content in the double commandment of love to God and to one's neighbor (93). 2. The prediction of Christ ("but some injunctions . . . were mentioned in reference to the mystery of Christ," 44:2), which is to be derived by allegory. Thus, the Passover lamb, of course, means Christ, whose two "comings" are fore-told in the two goats of the Day of Atonement (40:1ff.); the twelve bells, which according to Justin were part of the high-priest's regalia, mean the twelve apostles (42:1); physical circumcision symbolizes the "true circumcision," "by which we are 'circumcised' (cut off) from error and wickedness," and which Christians have received in baptism (41:4, 43:2, 92:4). 3. The cultic and ceremonial law in its original and (for "Israel," or "the Jews") still valid sense. It was given the Jews by God, in part "for a sign," viz. to set apart this people from all others and protect it from idolatry (16:2, 19:6, 23:5), but in part—because the people were rebellious and disobe-dient—to discipline and exhort it day by day (18:2, "on account of your transgression and the hardness of your hearts"; *cf.* 22:11, 43:1; 20:1, "in order that in your eating and drinking you might have God before your eyes"; *cf.* 92:4). For Christians, of course, the law in this sense is abolished (see, e.g. 43:1).

It is apparent that Justin did not attack the problem of legalism, either. He, too, quotes (141:2) Ps. 32:2: "Blessed is he to whom the Lord shall not reckon sin," and goes on: "that is, having repented of the sins that he may receive remission (of his transgressions) from God"—an exegesis which does not rise above the Old Testa-ment-Jewish view.

3. If one keeps in mind this range of possibilities and adds to them what is incidentally said on this theme in early Christan liter-ature, this is the resulting picture:

a. *The Old Testament Law is regarded as abolished so far as it contains cultic-ritual demands.* It is not the sacrificial cult that pro-cures God's grace, nor is it the law of cleanliness that makes clean. The usual means of coming to terms with the cultic and ritual law is allegory, which in part interprets this law as a disguise of the moral law (Barnabas, Ptolemy, and, sometimes, Justin), in part as prediction of Christ (Barnabas, Justin). A special variety of this interpretation is also that of Hebrews, which understands the Old Testament cult as "the shadow of the good things to come." Yet even when the divine origin of the Law is not contested—as it was in Gnosticism—the opinion as to what meaning the Law had for the past, varies. Though according to Barnabas the Jews had never understood it, for Hebrews, as for I Clem. and Justin, it had once been in force in all seriousness.

But the question now is whether this abolition is understood as only the nullification of an old cult and ritual or as *the complete abolition of cult and ritual as the way to salvation*. This question was nowhere clearly put, it is true, but it is clear that everywhere—and especially in Hebrews—the idea is given up that God's grace must or can be won by humanly offered sacrifices; and that led by implication to the insight that the Church does not need persons of special quality (i.e. priests) to mediate between it and God. Christ's sacrifice made God's grace operative once and for all, and he is the high priest of the Congregation (Heb. 2:17, 3:1, 4:14, 5:1ff., 7:1ff., I Clem. 36:1, 61:3, 64, Ign. Phild. 9:1, Pol. Phil. 12:2). The Congregation itself is a "holy," a "royal priesthood" (I Pet. 2:5, 9, Rev. 1:6, 5:10); it offers God "spiritual sacrifices" (I Pet. 2:5), and one and all are urged to "present your bodies as a living sacrifice, holy and acceptable to God, which is your spiritual presentation of sacrifice" (Rom. 12:1 tr.). "To visit orphans and widows in their affliction and to keep oneself unstained from the world," according to Jas. 1:27, is "religion that is pure and undefiled before God and the Father." True sacrifice is the praise of God offered by the Congregation of those who bear His name, and, along with that, doing good and sharing what one has (Heb. 13:15f.; *cf.* Justin dial. 117:2). Hence the Congregation needs no cultic building, for it is itself the temple of God (§ 10, 4). The individual likewise can be described as the temple of God in which the Holy Ghost or God Himself dwells, and which he—by his ethical conduct—must keep clean (I Cor. 6:19, Barn. 4:11: "Let us become spiritual, let us become a perfect temple for God"; Ign. Eph. 15:3). For this conception it makes no substantial difference whether "the body" (I Cor. 6:19) or "the heart" (Barn. 6:15, 16:7-10) or even "the flesh" (II Clem. 9:3, Ign. Phld. 7:2) is specified as the "temple"; the meaning remains the same since all the figure intends to do is to emphasize the demand of spiritual worship of God and ethical purity.

These ideas are specifically Christian insofar as they are the positive counterpart of the rejection of sacrificial worship. Taken by themselves they are not specifically Christian. For the Old Testament already knows the concept of spiritual sacrifice and so does Judaism, which, especially after the temple cult had ceased with the destruction of Jerusalem, had further developed out of earlier origins the "theory of equivalence," according to which the former place of sacrifice is taken by other acts, especially prayer and charity. Spiritualization of cultic concepts is still more prevalent in Hellenism, both Gentile and Jewish. That man—especially his soul—is a temple of God, is said by the Stoics and in their footsteps by Philo; and the Hermetic writer (Corp. Herm. I: 31; XIII 18f., 21) also knows that to worship the deity with prayers of praise is to worship with "spiritual sacrifices" (λογικαὶ θυσίαι; *cf.* Rom. 12:1).

Still, will this position of non-cultic worship be consistently maintained? Will not the worship of Jesus Christ as "Lord" take on cultic character? Are not baptism and eucharist in the nature of the case congregational acts with cultic character? And will this character not expand and draw far-reaching consequences after it (§§ 12, 13)? Another possible point from which a cult could develop lies in the working out of an "order" of worship for the Christian Congregation. For the exhortation, "We ought to do all things in order," I Clem. 40–42, appeals to the Old Testament with its ordering of the cult which commands that "sacrifices and services be celebrated not in just any fashion or in a disorderly way but at fixed times and hours." Therefore, "let each one of us . . . be well pleasing to God in his own rank, with a good conscience, not transgressing the fixed norm of his cultic service (τῆς λειτουργίας αὐτοῦ), with all dignity (ἐν σεμνότητι)." Here the way for a specifically cultic order to develop is more definitely prepared than in the exhortation of Paul that in the meetings of the Congregation "all things should be done decently and in order" (I Cor. 14:40), for the concern of I Clem. is for the authority of the "bishops" (and "deacons"), the official leaders of Christian worship. Thus the question arises: Will the office of priest develop anew in the Christian Congregation?

b. *The Old Testament in its entire extent is generally regarded as a book of predictions,* which in Christ are partly already fulfilled, and partly proceeding toward fulfilment. The method of interpreting the Old Testament in this way—the use of allegory, that is—is everywhere the same. It is not specifically Christian, but was taken over from Judaism, especially from its Hellenistic branch, which in turn had taken it over from Greek Hellenism, where, especially among the Stoics, it had been developed as a method of interpreting the old mythology and the old poets, such as Homer. In the present context it does not matter whether the allegorical sense of a text was regarded as its only meaning or as a deeper meaning existing side by side with the literal one. In this context the distinction can also be ignored between allegory (the art of finding prediction or deeper truths of any sort in the wording of Scripture) and typology (the interpretation of persons, events, or institutions of the past as foreshadowing prototypes). But the decisive question is whether the meaning of the Old Testament to the Christian Congregation is exhausted in being a book of oracles. Insofar as it is understood in that way, it furnished the Church a means—an effective one in that day—of polemic and defense in the battle against and the competition for Jews and Gentiles, and hence is at the same time a means of strengthening its own security. But does that not shift the real basis for the power of the gospel message and for the Christian's own security by putting a faith in the letter in place of the genuine faith which seizes the word of God's grace addressed to one's conscience and self-understanding—seizes it on the basis of having been inwardly conquered by it and not on the basis of rational proofs?

Or will the proof of prophecy play an historically inevitable and dangerous but still subordinate role? And will the real significance of the Old Testament for the Christian Congregation, then, be that it keeps alive in the Church the consciousness of being the eschatological Congregation, the goal of a history guided by God? It is *the question of the Church-concept* (§ 10, 1) over again: Will the Church understand itself to be an organization constituted by the joining together of individuals on the basis of their common understanding of general truths and of common practical goals? Or will it understand itself as the "People of God" which is "called" by God's deed in Christ? For Gentile Christianity, the danger of regarding itself as a Jewish sect will not be great. But all the greater for it will be the danger of conceiving itself simply as a "new religion" in contradistinction to the heathen and to the Jews, a new religion resting upon progress in knowledge of God. This danger can be avoided by the continuing possession of the Old Testament, since it teaches an understanding of God according to which God deals with men in *history* and man becomes aware of God and of his own nature not by free-soaring thought but by historical encounter. For to the Old Testament God is not cosmic law, available to thought and investigation, but *the God who reveals himself in the course of history*. The possession of the Old Testament will, therefore, be a counterbalance against the ideas of "natural theology" (§ 9, 2) which soon came pushing in. The idea that God reveals Himself in what He *does* will be kept, thanks to the Old Testament, and in that idea the possibility of understanding the person of Jesus and his cross will be present. For it is also out of this idea that an understanding can and must be reached of what eschatological occurrence is, if this is to be anything more than merely mythological in character. Insofar as the idea of prediction and fulfilment—even though in primitive form— includes within itself the knowledge of a meaning and goal of history that transcends historical occurrence, it is one of the factors that preserves to the Church the consciousness of being a called-in-history, history-transcending, eschatological Congregation. But that means at the same time in the fact of possessing the Old Testament, the Church is also confronted with the theological problem of reason and revelation.

c. *So far as the Old Testament contains ethical commandments* or permits such to be read out of it by the help of allegory, *its authority remains uncontested and valid*—except in radical Gnosticism. Its validity in this direction can only be strengthened the more by the authoritative words of Jesus handed down within the Church, and these at the same time lend a unified direction and a clear meaning to the manifold ethical precepts of the Old Testament by causing them to be understood from the standpoint of the master-commandment of love (Rom. 13:8–10, Gal. 5:14, down to Justin dial. 93; see above in 2f.). Indeed, it was possible for the ethical commandments of the Old Testament and the sayings of Jesus to enter into combination with the demands of Greek (especially Stoic) ethics and the bourgeois morality of Hellenism. For there are heathens who "do by nature what the Law requires," because, as their conscience testifies, they bear "what the Law requires written on their hearts" (Rom. 2:14f.). Hence the Greek notion of "virtue" (ἀρετή) very early creeps into Christian parenesis (Phil. 4:8, II Pet. 1:5, II Clem. 10:1, Herm. mand. I:2; VI 2, 3; XII 3, 1; sim. VI 1, 4; VIII 10, 3; *cf.* also 9, 2). Just as Paul had already taken over Hellenistic catalogues of virtues and vices—in which, of course, he was not the pioneer, as Hellenistic Judaism shows—so the deutero-Pauline literature takes over the Hellenistic-Stoic scheme of the "Haustafeln" (tables of household duties), and in the pastorals the ideal of Christian living is often described in accord with the bourgeois ideal of uprightness current in the Greek world and is couched in the terms used in sepulchral and honorary inscriptions.

Nevertheless, the virtue-concept does not become the dominant idea in Christian parenesis; and that also means that it is not the concept of "the ideal" that determines Christian ethics. Rather, what remains determinative is the idea *that the demand of God is the good*—that man is responsible to God and must give an accounting for his deeds before the judgment seat of God. To substantiate this insight the Church does not, it is true, first appeal to the Old Testament, still it is constantly kept awake by the Old Testament so that the possession of the Old Testament is a counterbalance against natural morality, as it is against natural theology; ethics remains theonomous. The conversion of a heathen to Christianity does mean emancipation from "idolatry" and the fear in his life, but not from the claim of God upon him, which on the contrary is intensified to the uttermost.

But then the question arises: *How is the relation between God's demanding will and the grace of God* proclaimed by the gospel understood? The very fact that the Old Testament was taken over could not help becoming dangerous by promoting the conception that obedience to God's demand for good deeds is the condition for participation in salvation—i.e. that the good deed is to be understood as a meritorious work. Describing the divine demand as a "law of liberty" (Jas. 1:25, 2:12) as a "new law of the Lord" (Barn. 2:6) or as "the commandments and ordinances of the Lord" (I Clem. 2:8, 58:2, Barn. 2:1, 10:11, 21:1) has not basically changed anything in regard to Jewish legalism, if this "new law" or these "commandments and ordinances" have the character of a way to salvation. It is as a second Moses that Christ appears when he is called the "new law-giver" (Justin dial. 14:3, 18:3) or when he is himself called "the law and word" (Kerygma Petri 1), "law of God" (Herm. sim. VIII 3, 2) or "the new law and the new covenant" (Justin dial. 11:4). Indeed, the question is raised: Has not the situation of Christians become much more responsible and dangerous than that of the devout men of the Old Testament and Judaism? Does not a much more severe judgment await them because they have received the grace of God (Heb. 2:2f., 10:28f., 12:25)?

But what does grace mean then? In what does the salvation conferred in Christ consist? Only in the remission of sins committed

[119]

before baptism, with the result that after baptism the believer must depend upon his own works (Heb. 6:4–6)? The problem of sins committed after baptism becomes a burning one, and it is not fundamentally solved when Hermas considers himself authorized on the basis of a divine revelation to proclaim the possibility of a second repentance, which however is irrevocably the last. But Hebrews and Hermas remain isolated voices in this matter. For Paul and the earliest period in general, the problem does not arise because of the expectation of the near End; but when the problem has become visible the generally prevailing conception comes to be that the grace of God which became effective in Christ remains in effect, and hence that Christians in their transgressions can and must be *constantly called to repentance* (Rev., I–II Clem., Ign., Justin; *cf.* II Tim. 2:25, II Pet. 3:9, Did. 10:6, 15:3). Though in view of Christ Christian confidence in the forgiving grace of God is incomparably more certain than the Old Testament-Jewish trust in the effectiveness of repentance, still that does not yet mean a fundamental difference from the Old Testament and Judaism until the relation between God's demand—or the obedient doing of the good and the grace of God is defined anew. Does the forgiving grace of God only supplement the human deed? Or is there no such thing as human doing of the good until God's prevenient grace makes it possible? The problem can also be formulated as that of the *relation between a man's deed* which wins God's approval *and a man's faith* which seizes the proffered grace of God. Is the faith which accepts the gospel and leads to joining the Congregation understood as only the first act of Christian conduct, or as the attitude which permeates and rules the whole life of the Christian? Does it remain present only as knowledge of the object of faith, especially as knowledge that the one God exists, so that knowledge can be distinct from love (I Cor. 8:1ff., 13:2) or so that it can be said, "Even the demons believe . . . and shudder" (Jas. 2:14)? Or so that it can be asked, "What good does it do . . . if a man says he has belief but has not works? Can belief save him?" (Jas. 2:14 tr.)? Or so that it can be said of Abraham that he was not justified by belief alone, but only because "his belief was completed by his works" (Jas. 2:21f. tr.)? Or will a new obedience be founded upon the very gift of grace, so that grace and faith become the forces that determine all of life? The answer to this question is given in one direction by the Pauline doctrine of justification by faith alone, and in another by the rise of the ecclesiastical institution of penance. The basis of the problem Augustinianism versus Pelagianism is already present in the early days of Christianity.

§ 12. Lord and Son of God

1. That the Christian congregations into which the baptized had united themselves in the Hellenistic world met for services of worship needs no explanation—neither where they were congregations grown out of synagogue-congregations, nor where they were congregations mainly or entirely of Gentile origin. But to what extent are these meetings and the services held in them to be termed cultic in the strict sense? That depends upon the definition of cult. We venture a definition in three parts: 1. *Cult* means human action—especially sacrifice, but also other acts—which influences the deity, disposes Him graciously toward the congregation, and makes His power effective for it. 2. This action takes place at fixed, holy times, in a holy place, and according to holy rules or rites. 3. This action is performed by persons of special quality, priests, who mediate between the deity and the congregation; or, in case the congregation participates more than just passively, the action is led by such persons. If that is what cult means, then the *meetings and services of the Christian Congregation* obviously *cannot be termed originally cultic.* For in Christian worship of this period there is neither sacrifice nor priest, nor is it bound to holy places or times (§ 11, 3a). As in the synagogue services the "word" must at first have dominated the service of the mission congregations, both the preached word, which could be spoken by anyone who had the gift and felt himself called thereto, and the word of prayer and song whether uttered by individuals or by the whole congregation. In many congregations preaching probably consisted in the exegesis of words of scripture, and, at least in the congregations that had grown out of the synagogue, the reading of a passage from the Old Testament must have been a regular constituent of congregational worship, though it cannot be assumed to have been so in all congregations. For at first it was simply impossible for many congregations to get possession of an Old Testament—a whole one, especially. But probably early and everywhere apostolic writings and gospels along with

Jewish apocalypses that had undergone Christian revision either took the place of the Old Testament or supplemented it.

Public reading (in these cases probably from Old Testament scripture) is explicitly attested in I Tim. 4:13, II Clem. 19:1 and indirectly at Mk. 13:14 (= Mt. 24:15). Public reading of apostolic writings is mentioned in I Thess. 5:27, Col. 4:16, Rev. 1:3. According to Justin Apol. I 67, 3, "the memoirs of the apostles" (i.e. gospels) "or the writings of the prophets" are publicly read.

Although in the Hellenistic world Christian and Jewish worship services are a peculiar phenomenon in being services of the "word," still it can *not* be said that *the cultic has been completely eliminated* from them; it is only *strongly reduced*. Sacrifice, it is true, is entirely missing, and in the apostolic and post-apostolic period the Lord's Supper is not yet by any means understood as a sacrifice; for the description of the eucharist as "sacrifice" (Did. 14) or of those administering it as "offering gifts" (I Clem. 44:4) is figuratively meant. Neither is there any priest in the Christian congregational meetings; nor, according to both Did. 7 and Justin Apol. 61, is baptism administered by specially qualified persons. But if the intent of cultic action is to bring about *the presence of the deity* for the celebrating congregation, then this intent is fulfilled in Christian services of worship, too, and the congregation's action or attitude in which God becomes present, must then also be termed cultic—though there may well be this distinction: that the act and attitude of worship in the Christian Congregation do not first summon the deity before He is there, but rest upon God's being already present. He is present in the *Spirit* by which the Congregation is conscious of being sustained and with which its speakers feel themselves filled (*cf.* I Cor. 14:25, and see § 14). But He is also present in the *word of scripture* in case such is read.

The exhortation (Did. 4:1) "to remember day and night him who speaks the word of God to thee and honor him as the Lord" is backed up by this characteristic reason: "for in the place out of which (his) Lord-ship is spoken, there the Lord is" (tr.). If this sentence belongs, as can hardly be doubted, to the Jewish "catechism" which was worked into Did. 2–6, it indicates that the synagogue service also had thoroughly cultic character. This is also attested by the fact that the removal of the Torah-roll from its shrine (the ark of the Torah) for the reading and its

[122]

replacement after the reading were solemn liturgical acts. The *Numen praesens* (divine presence) is embodied in the Torah-roll.

Furthermore, the concept of cultic action must not be too narrowly restricted. It is not limited to sacrifice and ritual acts, but also includes the recitation of holy texts, *prayers* first of all, and the singing of *hymns*—in a word, what we are accustomed to call liturgy. Now, it is true, we are not able to say how soon in Gentile Christian Congregations prayers and songs—or rather, an arrangement of such into an order of worship—achieved fixed liturgical form; but it will be shown that it was at any rate quite early. Besides, the free prayer or song of the individual also achieves a special character within the framework of the congregational celebration—precisely a cultic character. And though the young Christian Church knows neither a holy place nor holy times, purely practical reasons demand the choice of definite places and regular times; and that these gradually acquire the quality of cultic "holiness" is illustrated by the history of Sunday.

Whether Paul already knows Sunday as the day for congregational worship is not made certain by I Cor. 16:2 (*cf.* Acts 20:7). At any rate, it soon became that; and when, as such, it is called Lord's (Day), κυριακὴ (ἡμέρα), (Rev. 1:10, Did. 14:1, Ign. Mg. 9:1) and when the seer, Rev. 1:10, receives his revelation on that day, that in itself shows that as a day it possesses a special quality, even if its choice as the "eighth day" (Barn. 15:9) should have been due originally only to contrast with Jewish custom (like the choice of the Christian fast-days, Did. 8:1). Its distinction among the days is given a justification as cultic acts are, out of the history of salvation: it is the day on which Jesus "rose from the dead and having appeared ascended into heaven" (Barn. 15:9, Ig. Mg. 9:1). In the course of time, then, the sabbath laws of the Old Testament are transferred to the Lord's Day, and it has completely become a "holy" day.

2. It is taken for granted that the deity whose presence is believed and experienced in the congregational gatherings of Christians, whose word is heard, and to whom prayers are offered, is the one true God to whom the heathen have been converted from their "idols." The same thing is attested by the prayers and doxologies at Rev. 4:8, 11; 7:12; 11:17f.; 15:3f.; 19:1f.; 7f., and by the long congre-

gational prayer in I Clem. 59-61. But as in Rev. 5:13, 7:10, the praise of God and the "Lamb" sounds forth, and as in Rev. 11:15, 12:10, "God and his Christ" are praised, so the closing formula of I Clem. 61:3 reads, "we praise thee through the high priest and guardian of our souls, Jesus Christ, through whom be glory. to thee . . ." That means that Christ, too, has become a cultically worshiped figure present in the cult, and for the eschatological Congregation that is the really distinctive thing. For according to Phil. 2:10f., the saving occurrence accomplished in Christ has for its goal, "that at the name of Jesus every knee should bow, in heaven and on earth and under the earth and every tongue confess that Jesus Christ is Lord, to the glory of God the Father."

This is the distinctive feature of the eschatological Congregation in Hellenistic Christianity, for in it for the first time Jesus Christ figures not only as the eschatological savior but also as the cultically worshiped "Lord" (§ 7, 5). In place of the titles "Son of Man" and "Christ" (= messianic king), which are dying out, there appears in the Hellenistic congregations the *title* "Kyrios," Lord.

It is highly improbable that the title "Kyrios" as applied to Jesus is derived from the LXX, in which it is the usual transla- tion for Yahweh. Rather, vice versa, the already accepted des- ignation of Jesus as Kyrios made it possible for utterances of the LXX involving Kyrios to be transferred to him. But it is true that by this process the figure of Jesus as Kyrios increased in content and weight (*cf.*, for instance, the application of Is. 45:23 to Christ in Phil. 2:11; of Is. 40:13 in I Cor. 2:16; of Jer. 9:22f. in II Cor. 10:17; of Ex. 34:34 in II Cor. 3:16). Neither is the transfer of the Kyrios-title to Jesus to be understood as a counterpart to its use in the ruler-cults, or at least not pri- marily, although the adjective κυριακός (dominical) may have been taken over from it. Rather, the term Kyrios used of Christ is derived from the religious terminology of Hellenism, more specifically from that of oriental Hellenism, in which Kyrios was the Greek translation of typical terms in various languages which denoted the deity as "Lord." This usage was wide-spread in Egypt, Asia Minor, and especially in Syria, which in all prob- ability is the land of origin of the term "the Lord" used abso- lutely. This origin of the Kyrios-title comes clearly into view in the antithesis of "one Lord Jesus Christ" to the "many lords" in I Cor. 8:5f.

Kyrios in this usage (as everywhere else except in the LXX) is an appellative and hence requires completion by a proper name (unless it is evident from the context) to indicate what deity is meant. In Christianity, therefore, "Jesus Christ" is added. Kyrios indicates the respective deity not primarily in his divine majesty and power, but in his "master" relation to the speaker (the corresponding term for the worshiper is "slave," δοῦλος). With this implication it characteristically appears in the frequent phrase "our Lord Jesus Christ" or "Christ Jesus my Lord," Phil. 3:8 (*cf.* Rom. 14:4, Eph. 6:9). The fact that Kyrios occurs so often in the New Testament without the added personal name is probably due not simply to the obviousness of the implied addition but also to the influence of the LXX at just that point. It comes from LXX-usage also that Christ is not only the lord of his worshipers (or of the Church) but is "Lord of all" (Rom. 10:12), Lord, indeed, of all the cosmic powers (Phil. 2:10f.), "the Lord of all the cosmos" (Barn. 5:5); likewise from the LXX comes such an expression as "the Lord of glory" (I Cor. 2:8).

That *Paul was not the first* to give Christ the title "Kyrios" but that it was *already current in the Hellenistic Church before him* is to be concluded both from the way in which he takes the use of the title for granted and from certain other observations. The Christ-hymn in Phil. 2:6–11 was not composed by Paul for this context, but is a quotation taken over by him, as E. Lohmeyer has shown. It is not to be doubted that in Rom. 10:9 Paul is referring to a common Christian confession when he writes: "If you confess with your lips that Jesus is Lord . . ." Just this, then, is the distinctively Christian confession: "Jesus (Christ) is Lord." As such, it is also cited at I Cor. 12:3 as the criterion for distinguishing between spirits. And when Paul (II Cor. 4:5) declares: "What we preach is not ourselves, but Christ Jesus as Lord," intending thereby to legitimate himself as a genuine apostle, it is clear that just this is held to be the Christian message: to proclaim Christ as the Kyrios. Also the formula derived from Joel 2:32 LXX, "those who call upon the name of the Lord (Jesus Christ)," a formula which clearly reveals the cultic character of the Kyrios-title, became a designation for Christians, but one which Paul had evidently found already in use (I Cor. 1:2, II Tim. 2:22, Acts 9:14, 21; 22:16). When Jas. 2:7 (again using an Old Testament-Jewish formula) speaks of the "good name" as "having been called over you," this "name" is probably none other than that of "the Lord (Jesus Christ)," as we read in Herm. sim. VIII 6, 4: "the name of the Lord which was called over you," or as Christians are called (sim. VIII 1, 1) "those who are called by the name of the Lord," or (sim. IX 14, 3) "those who call upon his name." These formulas indicate the cultic meaning of the Kyrios-title. The name of the Lord is evidently "called upon" the believer at baptism and at the same time his first "calling upon" the name also takes place (Acts 22:16), but the latter is constantly repeated in the celebrations of the congregation. And the wish expressed in the greetings of Paul's letters is evidently also a liturgical formula that had come down to Paul: "Grace to you and peace from God our Father and the Lord Jesus Christ." * Hence, it is conceivable how the Christian worship-service could have been called (Acts 13:2) "worshiping the Lord (Jesus Christ, understood)."

Nevertheless, *"calling upon the Lord"* probably did not consist in liturgical prayers addressed directly to Christ. So far as we see, such prayers were preponderantly addressed to God alone; for it is hardly permissible to regard Jn. 14:14 as testimony to liturgical prayer by a congregation addressed to Jesus. For the period of the ancient Church only the apocryphal acts of the apostles attest liturgical prayers addressed to Christ. Rather, "calling upon the Lord" probably consisted in confessing him and in doxologies like II Tim. 4:18, I Clem. 20:12, 50:7, or like the ones offered to the "Lamb" in Rev. 5:9f. and 12, and also in single, formula-like invocations like the "Maranatha" interpreted as referring to Christ (§ 7, 5), which appears at Rev. 22:20 as "come, Lord Jesus." † Or at the close of the epistles, where "the grace of the Lord Jesus Christ" is wished for the readers (Gal. 6:18, Phil. 4:23, I Cor. 16:23, Rev. 22:21, I Clem. 65:2, etc.). Also in specific cases the Kyrios was probably invoked to intervene with his miraculous power.

A characteristic example for the last case is I Cor. 5:3-5, where Paul instructs the congregation to deliver to Satan the miscreant who is to be excluded. This is to happen, Paul says, "in the name of the Lord Jesus when you are assembled and my

---

* This was demonstrated by E. Lohmeyer *ZNW* 26 (1927), 162ff. by proving the divergence of this formula from the diction of Paul.

† In the table-prayer (Did. 10:6) the Coptic tradition attests the reading "let the Lord (in place of 'grace') come," which is perhaps the original text.

spirit is present with the power of our Lord Jesus Christ"; and it makes no difference whether "in the name of the Lord Jesus Christ" be connected with "when you are assembled" or with the following "deliver this man to Satan." In either case the invocation of the "name of the Lord" is to make his "power" effective in the congregation. The same point of view emerges in the legendary story of Acts 1:24. The Kyrios is implored to indicate by lot the right man to take the place among the twelve left vacant by Judas.

Related in content to the invocation of the *"name of Christ"* (I Cor. 5:3-5) is the use of the "name" for *exorcism* and miraculous deeds in general. Perhaps the earliest Church had already used the name of Jesus as a means of exorcism (§ 7, 4); at any rate this was done in Hellenistic Christianity, as the account of the Jewish exorcists who wanted to profit by the power of the "name of the Lord" (Acts 19:13-17) testify and also the editorial verse Lk. 10:17, according to which the seventy on returning to Jesus report to him, "the demons are subject to us in your name." In the same direction Mt. 7:22 also transforms the older tradition (Lk. 13:26f.): "Did we not in your name . . . cast out demons and do many mighty works in your name?" With this the outlook of the author of Acts is consistent (3:16, 4:7, 10; 16:18). But exorcistic formulas are ordinarily derived from liturgical material, and that this was true of the exorcistic use of the "name" of Christ is proved by Justin's account: "For every demon, when exorcized in the name of this very Son of God—who is the First-born of all creation, who was born of a virgin and became a man subject to suffering, who was crucified under Pontius Pilate . . . who died, who rose from the dead and ascended into heaven—is conquered and subjected" (Dial. 85:2; *cf.* 30:3, 49:8, 76:6, 121:3, 131:5). Here we see the statements of the liturgical confession of faith put into the service of exorcism. And when Justin declares (Dial. 30:3): "Thus it is apparent to all men that his Father has given him such power that even the demons are subjected by his name and by the dispensation of the suffering that he suffered," he, of course, does not mean that that had not been true before his, Justin's, time.

But *"calling upon the Lord"* has its place in liturgy, especially in the phrase "in his name" which accompanies prayers and doxologies addressed to God (Eph. 5:20; *cf.* also 3:21; Jn. 14:13, 15:16, 16:24,

26). Or prayers are offered to God "through him," for, as Paul says, clearly referring to liturgical usage, "that is why we utter the Amen through him, to the glory of God" (II Cor. 1:20). So it is *through him* that thanks is given to God (Rom. 1:8, 7:25, Col. 3:17) or praise (Did. 9:4, I Clem. 58:2, 61:3, 64, 65:2). And the formula which occurs in the letters of Ignatius, "I greet you in the name of Jesus Christ," probably also comes from liturgical usage (Ign. Rm. pr., 9:3, Sm. 12:2) and presumably likewise the "appeal through the name of our Lord Jesus Christ" (I Cor. 1:10, Rom. 15:30; *cf.* II Cor. 10:1). When the Kyrios-name is spoken every being must bow in homage to the glory of God (Phil. 2:10f.).

Outside of formal, liturgical worship, prayers evidently were said directly to Christ in the personal lives of individuals. Paul besought "the Lord" for his own person (II Cor. 12:8) and he prays to him for the weal of the Congregation (I Thess. 3:12; so also in the non-Pauline II Thess. 3:3, 5, 16, where the parallel passages in I Thess. 3:11, 5:23f. have 'God').

3. What is true of the name "Kyrios" is also true of the other name conferred on Christ: *He is the "Son of God."* Whereas according to Phil. 2:11 it is the Kyrios-name that crowns his work of salvation, according to Heb. 1:4 the "more excellent name" which God has conferred upon the exalted Christ and which lifts him above all angels is undoubtedly the name of "Son." Hence, Herm. sim. IX 14, 5 says, "the name of the Son of God is great and incomprehensible and supports the whole world." Both names occur in the exorcistic formulas (see above). They belong together inasmuch as Son of God denotes the divine nature of the Kyrios which is his as a cultically worshiped figure, and inasmuch as "Kyrios" correspondingly specifies the rank and function of him who by nature is Son of God.

The title "Kyrios" was first conferred upon Christ in the Hellenistic Church. But Hellenistic-Jewish Christians had brought along the *title "Son of God"* embedded in their missionary message; for the earliest Church had already called Jesus so (§ 7, 5). But one must recognize that the title, which originally denoted the messianic king, now takes on a new meaning which was self-evident to Gentile hearers. Now it comes to mean *the divinity of Christ, his divine nature,* by virtue of which he is differentiated from the human sphere; it makes the claim that Christ is of divine origin and is filled with divine "power."

That this meaning of the title was the one taken for granted in Hellenism is evident from a double fact. One part of it is that to the mind of Hellenistic Christians the salvation-event consists precisely in the paradoxical fact that a figure, divine by nature, appears as a man and suffers the fate of man (*cf.* the Christ-hymn quoted by Paul in Phil. 2:6–11), with the result that what had been a stumbling-block to the earliest Church—i.e. that Christ should be subject to, and subjected to, suffering (χριστὸς παθητός)—is no longer a stumbling-block to the Hellenistic Church, though it is a mystery (μυστήριον). The other part of the double fact is that the problem of how the humanity of the Son of God can be conceived becomes troublesome, and that the reality of Christ's humanity has to be defended (precisely for the sake of that paradox which the salvation-event is) against Gnostic heresy. While the term "Son of God" secondarily serves to differentiate Christ from the one true God and to indicate Christ's subordinate relation to God, it also serves—and this is the primary thing—to assert his divinity. So it is not surprising that II Clem. begins, "We must think of Jesus Christ as God"; for Heb. 1:1–14 had already taught Christ's elevation above the angels and described him as "the effulgence of the glory (of God) and the very stamp of His substance" (1:3 tr.).

In *describing* Christ as "*God*" the New Testament still exercises great restraint. Except for Jn. 1:1, where the pre-existent Logos is called God, and Jn. 20:28, where Thomas reverences the risen Christ with the exclamation, "My Lord and my God!" this assertion is made—at least by any probable exegesis—only in II Thess. 1:12, Tit. 2:13, II Pet. 1:1. Ignatius ° on the contrary speaks of Christ as God as if it were a thing to be taken quite for granted (Tr. 7:1, Sm. 1:1, 10:1); usually he says "(Jesus Christ) our God" (Eph. pr., 15:3, 18:2, Rom. pr. twice, 3:3, Pol. 8:3). And that what concerns him is precisely that paradox is shown by such expressions as: "incarnate God" (ἐν σαρκὶ γενόμενος θεός, text of GL, Eph. 7:2, "God manifested himself as man" (Eph. 19:3), the mention of "God's blood" Eph. 1:1), of the "passion of my God" (Rom. 6:3) or of "the bread of God, that is, the flesh of Jesus Christ" (Rom. 7:3).

° The doxology in Rom. 9:5 is scarcely to be referred to Christ; in Jn. 1:18 and I Tim. 3:16 "God" is a secondary variant.

That the proclamation of "Christ, the Son of God," was so understood, is not to be wondered at; *the figure of a Son of God was familiar to Hellenistic ways of thinking,* familiar in several variations. One among them was an inheritance from the Greek tradition, which applied the mythological idea of being begotten by a god to men who seemed by their heroic deeds, mental accomplishments, or benefactions to humanity to transcend ordinary human proportions. The Hellenistic period knows a whole series of such "divine men" (θεῖοι ἄνδρες), who claimed to be sons of (a) god or were regarded as such, and some of whom were also cultically worshiped. In their case, there is no emphasis, or almost none, on the paradoxicality of the divine appearing in human form; moreover, this was no problem at all to Greek thinking in general, for which every man's soul is a divine entity. Hence, here the interest lies not in the (paradoxical) fact of the divine son's humanity but in the content of his life (βίος) marked by miracles and other divinely conferred phenomena. Another variation was the conception of divine sonship which was common in oriental Hellenism as an inheritance from old oriental mythology: the idea of son-divinities, upon whom cultic worship was bestowed and who were regarded as saviors. About such divinities, worshiped in "mysteries," their myths related that they had suffered the human fate of death but had risen again from death. But according to the belief of their worshipers, the fate of these divinities establishes a salvation which is imparted to those who experience with the deity his death and resurrection in the rites of the mysteries. Akin to these divine figures, whose origin lies in ancient vegetation-gods, is the figure of the "Redeemer" in the Gnostic myth—whatever historical connections may underly this kinship—to the extent that in that figure the paradox that a divine being (a son-deity) should become man and suffer a human fate is most emphatically expressed.

The Gentile-Christian conception of Christ as Son of God varies according to which tradition influences it more. The synoptic gospels essentially represent the first type, inasmuch as they picture Jesus as the Son of God who reveals his divine power and authority through his miracles. This is a way of thinking which was also capable of being appropriated even by such Christian thought as was determined by Jewish tradition; this was done when it attributed the "power" in the life of the "divine man" to the divine Spirit,

by analogy with David and the prophets. This is the vein in which
the Gospel of Mark tells its story. According to it, Jesus becomes
the Son of God by the Spirit conferred upon him at the baptism.
The same view clearly emerges in the "western" text (D it, etc.)
of Lk. 3:22, according to which the heavenly voice says, "Thou art
my son; to-day have I begotten thee." In keeping with this line of
thinking Acts 2:22 calls Jesus "a man attested . . . by God with
mighty works and wonders and signs which God did through him."
But also the mythological conception of a divine son begotten by
some deity—an idea which not merely Greek tradition knows, but
which is also current in the Babylonian and especially the Egyptian
king-legend—was evidently taken over by Jewish Hellenism in
Egypt and transferred to the devout men of the Old Testament.
Hence, it is no wonder that early in Hellenistic Christianity the
legend springs up that Jesus was begotten by the Holy Spirit (Mt.
1:20) or by the "power of the Most High" (Lk. 1:35) and was born
of a virgin. The fact that it was unknown to Paul, of course, does
not prove that it may not have been current in circles other than
Paul's even before his time. In the New Testament the virgin-birth
concept does not occur outside of Mt. 1 and Lk. 1, and the understanding of Son of God which underlies it was surpassed by the
second type of understanding, according to which Jesus Christ is
the pre-existent Son of God become man. Paul (like John) takes
this understanding for granted, and the pre-Pauline Christ-hymn
(Phil. 2:6–11) proves that he was not the first to introduce it into
Christian thinking. This view is also consonant with the recognition of the paradoxicality of the salvation-event; all emphasis lies
upon the fact of the humanity and the human fate of the Son of
God who became man. To this fact, the idea that Jesus proved himself to be God's Son in his earthly life by miracles is really contradictory, as Phil. 2:6–11 clearly shows. It is correspondingly foreign to
Paul himself to conceive of Jesus' life as filled with the miraculous.

But in Hellenistic Christianity these two christologies joined
together in a somewhat strained union. With the synoptic gospels
is preserved their picture of the Son of God as the wonder-worker.
In Ignatius "the virginity of Mary and her accouchement along with
the death of the Lord" constitute the "three mysteries of a cry" (Ign.
Eph. 19:1; *cf.* Sm. 1:1); although otherwise it is precisely Ignatius

who emphasized the paradoxicality of the pre-existence christology (see above).

But still a *third type* of the son-of-God figure must be recognized. The son-divinity of Gnosticism often possesses not only soteriological but also cosmological significance; indeed, this was probably its primary meaning, and it was independently developed in mythologies and in religious-philosophical speculations like those of Philo, whose cosmic Logos is the "son" of God, and a similar development is found in the Hermetic writings. A parallel phenomenon is the cosmic figure of Wisdom which had already crept into the Wisdom-literature of the Old Testament and had become an object of speculation in Judaism, especially in Hellenistic Judaism. Very early this Logos and Wisdom speculation penetrated into Hellenistic Christianity. Already in I Cor. 8:6 Christ appears as he "through whom all things (are) and through whom we (exist)," a formula in which the cosmological and the soteriological roles of Christ are combined. Whether Paul was the first *to ascribe to Christ this cosmic role as mediator of creation,* cannot be said; the way he speaks of it as if it were a matter of course rather inclines one to conclude that he was not alone in doing so. The matter-of-fact way in which he terms Christ "the likeness of God" (II Cor. 4:4) makes the same impression; for this concept belongs in the context of the cosmological Son-of-God speculation and appears in that connection in Philo and in the Hermetic and Gnostic literature. After Paul, this cosmological significance of Christ is presented especially in Col. 1:15ff., where Christ is characterized as "the image of the invisible God, the first-born of all creation; for in him all things were created . . . and in him all things hold together (exist)." Ephesians, also, knows this speculation, but its author has turned it from cosmology to ecclesiology (1:20ff.), a change which Colossians had already begun to make. Besides Jn. 1:1ff., Hebrews attests that Christ as Son of God was regarded as a cosmic figure by others than Paul and his school; Heb. 1:3 describes Christ as "upholding the universe by his word of power" after having called him "the effulgence of the glory (of God) and the very stamp of his nature," which is only a paraphrase of the concept "image" (εἰκών). Similarly Hermas says (sim. IX 12, 2): "The Son of God is older than all his creation, so that he was the Father's counsellor of creation," behind which, of course, Prov. 8:27ff. hovers. But especially in sim. IX 14, 5, the cosmological role

of the Son of God finds expression: "the name of the Son of God is
great and incomprehensible and supports the whole world. If then
the whole creation is supported by the Son of God . . ." The answer
to the question here begun by Hermas draws an ecclesiological conclusion from this cosmological premise.

§ 13. The Sacraments

1. In the worship (the Kultus) of the congregation, the Lord
Jesus Christ is present. An individual gets into the congregation
through *baptism*; and that means that in this way he enters into
relation with the Lord. In all probability it was as a rite of initiation into the eschatological Congregation that baptism had been
practiced in the earliest Church (§ 6, 3), a sacramental bath which
washes away the guilt of sin, and it was so that the missionaries had
brought it to the Hellenistic Congregations. That baptism is the
indispensable condition for admission to the Congregation and for
participation in salvation is self-evident, and is at least indirectly
expressed in Acts 4:12: "And there is salvation in no one else, for
there is no other name under heaven given among men by which we
must be saved" (supply: "than the name of Jesus Christ")—even if
the author should not here be thinking of the "Name" spoken at
baptism. According to Did. 9:5 and Justin Apol. 66:1, no unbaptized
person may participate in the eucharist, and according to Herm.
sim. IX 12, 4f. "no one shall enter the Reign of God unless he shall
have received the name of the Son of God"—i.e. been baptized. In
fact, according to sim. IX 16, even the righteous of the Old Testament can participate in salvation only after they have been baptized; for this purpose, apostles and teachers after death preached
and baptized in the underworld.

As to the *rite of baptism*, it was normally consummated as a
bath in which the one receiving baptism completely submerged,
and if possible in flowing water as the allusions of Acts 8:36,
Heb. 10:22, Barn. 11:11 permit us to gather, and as Did. 7:1-3
specifically says. According to the last passage, it suffices in
case of need if water is three times poured on the head. The
one baptizing names over the one being baptized the name of
"the Lord Jesus Christ," later expanded to the name of the
Father, the Son, and the Holy Spirit (first attested in Did. 7:1,

3, Justin Apol. 61: 3, 11, 13; also found in Mt. 28:19, but this is perhaps a case of later interpolation). That the "Name" was spoken over the person being baptized is implied by the formula "baptized in (into, εἰς) the name" (indirectly attested I Cor. 1:13, 15; directly in Acts 8:16, 19:5, Did. 9:5, Herm. sim. III 7, 3; "in," ἐν, in place of "into," εἰς: Acts 10:48; "to," ἐπί, Lk. 24:47—if "repentance" here implies baptism) and Acts 2:38 (cf., besides these passages which speak only of "the name of the Lord," the passages cited above containing the trinitarian formula); it is corroborated by the formula "the name which has been spoken over you" (Jas. 2:7) or "over them" (Herm. sim. VIII 6, 4), and it is explicitly stated by Justin (Ap. 61:11). In keeping with this are also the expressions "receive the Name" (Herm. sim. IX, 12, 4 and 8; 13, 2 and 7) or "bear the Name" (Herm. sim. IX 14, 5; 15, 2). The one being baptized, on his part, speaks—either just before or just after the bath of baptism—the confession: "Jesus Christ is Lord," and belongs thereby to "those who call upon the name of the Lord" (§ 12, 2). If the "confession" of I Tim. 6:12 made "in the presence of many witnesses" is the baptismal confession, then it is surely to be thought of as preceding baptism. It would accord well with this if the act of baptism was preceded by the question and answer which O. Cullmann, *Urchristentum und Gottesdienst*, pp. 79–88, deduces out of Acts 8:36, 10:47, 11:17, Mt. 3:14, Gospel of the Ebionites in Epiphanius 30, 31—i.e. the question: "What is to prevent?" and the answer: "It is permitted" (or "nothing prevents"). In the scarcity of sources, it is impossible to say how early such ritual formulas developed. At any rate, according to Justin Apol. 61, 2, baptism is preceded by the commitment of the candidate that he "is able to live thus" (i.e. in accordance with the teachings he has received). Though in the earliest period baptism certainly often followed immediately upon the conversion which had taken place under the impression of missionary preaching (illustrated, for instance, by Acts 2:41, 8:12, 16:33, 18:8), later some instruction preceded baptism, as Heb. 6:2, Did. 7:1, Justin. Ap. 61:2, 65:1 presuppose. Since when a fast of one or two days mentioned by Did. 7:4, Justin Apol. 61:2 (here prayer is also mentioned) preceded baptism, we do not know. Neither do we know anything definite about the ritual act of laying on of hands, which, according to Heb. 6:2, Acts 19:5f. (cf. 8:17), belongs to baptism; but probably this was a regular component of it from the beginning, perhaps accompanying the speaking of the Name. It should be taken for granted that only adults were baptized (Joach. Jeremias, *Hat die älteste Christenheit die Kindertaufe geübt?* (1938), to the contrary notwithstanding). He who performed the baptism had no distinguishing quality, i.e. no priestly quality, see § 12, 1; only, according to Ign. Sm. 8:2, baptism is not to be permitted "without the bishop."

The meaning of baptism is determined by various factors which in part work together, in part independently. But in every case it is regarded as a *sacrament*—i.e. an act which by natural means puts supranatural powers into effect, usually by the use of spoken words which accompany the act and release those powers by the mere utterance of their prescribed wording. Indeed, the sacramental act may confine itself completely to the speaking of a word or a formula. The concept "sacrament" rests upon the assumption that under certain conditions supranatural powers can be bound to natural objects of the world and to spoken words as their vehicles and mediators. If the conditions are fulfilled (if, for instance, the prescribed formula is correctly spoken and the material is thereby "consecrated"—i.e. laden with supranatural power), and if the act is consummated according to the prescribed rite, then the supranatural powers go into effect, and the act, which apart from these conditions would be only a purely worldly, natural one like a bath or a meal, is itself a supranatural ceremony which works a miracle. Though in the primitive stage of the history of religions sacramental action can hardly be distinguished from magic, still in the course of history the difference becomes ever greater, depending upon what conditions must be fulfilled by those for whom the sacrament is to be effective and upon what supranatural powers are to be put into effect. The presupposed condition may be a specified state of the body, or it may be a state of spiritual preparedness. The powers may be such as only serve the enhancement of physical life, or such as promote the life of the spirit. In the latter case, it is true, the paradoxicality of the sacrament is increased: How can spiritual powers be bound to material elements as their vehicles? Finally, a sacrament can be etherealized into a symbol; then a psychological effect results instead of a miraculous one.

It is clear that in earliest Christianity the sacrament was by no means a symbol, but a miracle-working rite—most strikingly shown for the sacrament of the Eucharist in I Cor. 11:29ff. (see below), and for baptism in I Cor. 15:29. When people have themselves baptized for the dead, as they did in Corinth—i.e. when their intention is to have the supranatural powers that the sacrament bestows made effective for the dead—then no distinction is made between the sacrament and a magical act. It is of course self-evident that neither Paul nor other Jewish-Christian missionaries introduced this practice, and it is no less understandable that it was eliminated by the Church, though Gnostic sects still practiced it for a while. But it is significant that Paul mentions the custom without any criticism whatever; for the mode of thought behind it is precisely his own, too, as it was for earliest Christian thought in general (with the exception of John).

What is expected as the effect of baptism (corresponding to its origin; see above) is first: *Purification from one's sins,* and it is several times expressly said, from one's sins committed in the past (II Pet. 1:9, Herm. mand. IV 3, 1, Justin Ap. 61:10). Paul undoubtedly means purification by baptism when after describing the sinful heathen past of the readers he continues: "But you were washed, but you were made holy, but you were made righteous in the name of the Lord Jesus Christ and in the Spirit of our God" (I Cor. 6:11). All three verbs describe the sacramental bath of purification; and in this series "made righteous" is not meant in the specific sense of Paul's doctrine of justification, but, corresponding to "made holy," is meant in the general-Christian sense: cancellation of sin (§ 9, 4, p. 85). The related passages also show that Paul is here presenting the general-Christian view of baptism. In the deutero-Pauline literature such passages include: Eph. 5:26, where the purpose of Christ's work of salvation is "that he might make her (the Church) holy, having cleansed her by the washing of water with the word"; or I Pet. 3:21, where baptism is interpreted as "not a removal of dirt from the body," i.e. the bath of baptism is no external purification, but creates the possibility (by cleansing the believer of his sins) of "calling upon God with the consciousness of purity" (*cf.* Heb. 9:14, 10:2, 22). Similar passages occur in literature nearly or entirely independent of Paul. Since baptism takes place "for the forgiveness of sins" (Acts 2:38), Saul-Paul is commanded to "rise and be baptized and wash away your sins, calling upon his name" (Acts 22:16). According to Heb. 10:22 we, as Christians, have "our hearts sprinkled clean from an evil conscience and our bodies washed with

pure water" in which "body" is separated from "heart" only for the
sake of the rhetorical parallelism of members; for the washing is, of
course, not limited to the "body," but applies just as much to the
"heart." The "cleansing from one's old sins," II Pet. 1:9, is, of course,
the cleansing received in baptism. According to Barn. 11:11 "we go
down into the water full of sins and foulness, and we come up bearing the fruit of fear in our hearts and having hope on Jesus in the
Spirit"; and according to 16:8f. we become a temple of God by "the
remission of sins" (received in baptism). "When we went down
into the water," Hermas says (mand. IV 3, 1), "we received remission of our former sins" (*cf.* Justin Ap. 61:10).

With the cleansing bath of baptism *the naming of "the name of
the Lord"* is combined. Here a second factor joins the first, but it is
hard to say when the combination took place (§ 6, 3). The calling
of the Name is not what it became in the later Church, an *epiclesis,*
a special prayer which summons the power of Christ into the water
to give it the ability to purify and sanctify, but is a naming of the
Name over the candidate, which imparts its power to him. Hence,
at bottom, the naming of the Name is an independent sacrament
competing with the bath of baptism. Still, since their effects more
or less coincide, their combination is understandable enough. The
meaning of this naming of the Name is first of all this: that by it the
candidate is stamped as property of the Kyrios and placed under his
protection. This is proved by the use of the term *"seal"* (σφραγίς),
which Paul clearly presupposes, for baptism.

The statement made of God in II Cor. 1:22: "he has sealed
(σφραγισάμενος) us and given us his Spirit in our hearts as a
guarantee," undoubtedly alludes to baptism. Even if Paul does
not necessarily imply the actual use of the noun, "seal"
(σφραγίς) for baptism, at any rate, behind the cognate verb
used by him lies the idea that did lead to this terminology in
later sources. The same is true of Eph. 1:13: "having believed
in it (*sc.* the gospel), you were sealed (ἐσφραγίσθητε) with the
promised Holy Spirit." But later on, in II Clem. 7:6, 8:6, Herm.
sim. VIII 6, 3, IX 16, 3–7; 17, 4; 31, 1, the designation of baptism by the noun, "seal," is perfectly familiar; furthermore, in
Hermas it is quite clear that baptism is called "seal" because it
places the one baptized under the authority and protection of
the Name; his phrase "receive the seal" (sim. VIII 6, 3, IX 16,

3; 17, 4) is equivalent to "receive the Name" (see above, p. 134). Perhaps Judaism already referred to circumcision as a "seal" before Paul did so (*cf.* Rom. 4:11, in which, however, "seal" could be a mere metaphor for "ratification"; likewise in Barn. 9:6); but that can be proved only for a later period. In the mystery-religions, too, "seal" was a technical term for the rite of initiation. But even though here Christian language may possibly have been influenced from that direction, the root meaning of the term has not died out. W. Heitmüller (*Neutest. Studien für G. Heinrici* [1914], 40–59) has demonstrated that just as in secular use so also in sacral use the word "seal" means the brand or trade-mark which indicates ownership and owner's rights, and that it is in this sense that the Name serves in baptism as a "seal."

The bath of baptism as a purification has a negative meaning (cancellation of past sins), but the naming of the Name has a double effect, both negative and positive. Negatively, it drives out evil spirits (widely regarded as the cause of sins) by its exorcistic power (see above, 2, p. 127). Positively, it puts the baptized under the protection of the Kyrios for the future, too, and secures him against demonic influences—and that means against sins, too, though also against other evils. In Col. 1:13f.—for this passage is probably alluding to baptism—this view is clearly expressed: "He has delivered us from the dominion of darkness and transferred us to the kingdom of his beloved Son, in whom we have redemption, the forgiveness of sins." Likewise in Barn. 16:7f.: once our heart was a "house of demons," but by virtue of the Name it has become a temple in which God dwells. The fast which soon came to be associated with baptism (see above) probably is connected with this view, for fasting is a means of driving out demons (e.g., Mk. 9:29 variant).

A positive effect of baptism important for the future is that *it bestows the Holy Spirit.* This also is a general-Christian view presupposed by Paul when he appeals to it as a thing to be taken for granted (I Cor. 12:13, II Cor. 1:22); also present in Eph. 1:13, 4:30 (see above). According to Tit. 3:5 baptism is a "bath of . . . renewal (brought about) by the Holy Spirit." In baptism the Holy Spirit is received (Acts 2:38; *cf.* 9:17f.), and it is in this that the Church sees the specific difference of its baptism from that of John (Acts 19:1–6; *cf.* Mk. 1:8). Water and Spirit, according to the traditional text of Jn. 3:5, bring about re-birth. Barn. 11:9–11 presupposes the same view, and Herm. sim. IX 13 expounds in broad allegory that a condition for salvation is to be clad by the twelve virgins with their garments; these virgins are building the tower of the Church, and Hermas interprets them as "holy spirits" and "powers of the Son of God."

The passages, Acts 8:14–17, 10:44–48, in which the receipt of the Spirit and baptism are not contemporaneous, are only an apparent exception. In reality, the intent of both passages is to teach precisely the inseparability of baptism and the receipt of the Spirit. A baptism which does not bestow the Spirit is no proper baptism and hence must be supplemented by the receiving of the Spirit (8:14–17). The bestowal of the Spirit by God means that baptism must be given to the one so favored (10:44–48).

The bestowal of the Spirit is a third factor in the meaning of baptism. This is also recognizable in the fact that it was attached to the special ritual act of laying on of hands—at least it is in Acts 8:17, 19:6, and presumably was from the beginning as soon as bestowal of the Spirit was associated with baptism at all. Since when that was the case we admittedly do not know. At any rate it was scarcely true in the earliest Church (§ 6, 3), because there, where Jewish tradition was dominant, the baptismal water-bath can scarcely have been conceived otherwise than negatively—i.e. as a purification. For Heb. 6:2, at any rate, the doctrine of baptism and of the laying on of hands belongs to the matter handed down by tradition. In its meaning the bestowal of the Spirit (by the laying on of hands) is more closely related to the naming of the Name than to purification by the water-bath; and perhaps it was from the beginning associated with the former rather than with the latter. It would be in line with this that, in Eph. 1:13, 4:30, the "sealing" is described as the work of the Spirit—i.e. in the mind of the author the naming of the Name (= the "sealing") and the impartation of the Spirit are identical. In fact, the driving out of demons and endowment with the Holy Spirit are correlates; exorcistic effect is likewise attributed to the laying on of hands, as it is to the Name. Of course, the cooperating factors are not differentiated in the general consciousness; hence, forgiveness of sin can also be connected with the naming of the Name and "forgiveness of sins" can be said to be received "through his name" (Acts 10:43), in which the Name is probably used *a parte potiori* (chief part for the whole) for the baptismal act as a whole.

But to the three interpretations of the sacrament of baptism—purification, sealing by the Name, and bestowal of the Spirit—still a fourth and very important one is added: *Baptism imparts participation in the death and resurrection of Christ.* This interpretation undoubtedly originated in the Hellenistic Church, which understood this traditional initiation-sacrament on analogy with the initiation-sacraments of the mystery religions. The meaning of the latter is to impart to the initiates a share in the fate of the cult-deity who has suffered death and reawakened to life—such as Attis, Adonis, or Osiris.

This interpretation, by which baptism was furnished with a hitherto missing reference to the salvation-occurrence, is clearly a secondary one, for the ceremony of baptism was in no wise adapted to serve as a reproduction or dramatization of what had happened at Jesus' death and resurrection. Jesus did not die by drowning; neither did the earliest Church consider baptism "a drowning of the old Adam," as Luther did. This interpretation could attach itself to baptism only because it was, after all, the Christian sacrament of initiation; and so it came to be explained as a Hellenistically understood initiation-sacrament. Such an interpretation is foreign to Old Testament-Jewish thinking, for it knows no cultic acts based on the fate of the Deity and intending to bring its effect into the present, but only such as have their basis in the history of the People. To understand Jesus fate as the basis for a cult, and to understand the cult as the celebration which sacramentally brings the celebrant into such fellowship with the cult-divinity that the latter's fate avails for the former as if it were his own—that is a Hellenistic mystery-idea.

Correspondingly, the effect of baptism so understood is not considered to lie in purity from sins, the protection of the Kyrios, and the bestowal of the Spirit, but in conquest over death and the acquisition of life. In Rom 6:2ff., it is true, Paul makes an effort to bring freedom from sin into relation with the latter by teaching the reader to understand the future resurrection guaranteed by baptism as an already present resurrection which realizes itself in ethical conduct. But the artificial turn of this understanding is obvious in v. 4: "We were buried therefore with him by baptism into death, so that as Christ was raised from the dead . . . we too"—not: "might be raised from the dead," as we would expect if the sentence were logical, but "might walk in newness of life." But the explanation added in v. 5 clearly indicates the understanding to which Paul is appealing: "For if we have been united with him in a death like his, we shall certainly be united with him in a resurrection like his." The same relation exists between vss. 6 and 8.

Thus Rom. 6:2ff. clearly implies that Paul was not the first to give baptism this mystery interpretation, but that it was already current before him in Hellenistic congregations, as his question (v. 3), "or do you not know . . ." might indicate by itself. It is implied by the additional fact that when he intends to explain the origin of the new ethical way of life in baptism he does not take as his point of departure the bestowal of the Spirit (one of its meanings), as one would expect from Rom. 8:11ff. or Gal. 5:25, e.g. Instead he simply makes use of the mystery-interpretation, which he feels free to presuppose in his readers. Actually, Paul's own particular interpretation of baptism is still another one, specifically, one determined by Gnostic thought, that the baptized is incorporated into the "body of Christ" (I Cor. 12:13, Gal. 3:27f.), which will be discussed later. It is also implied, finally, by I Cor. 15:29; for what else did this vicarious baptism for the dead, which Paul already found in use, intend but just this: to give even those who had died the benefit still of the life provided by Christ's resurrection?

The school of Paul follows his thought that the life mediated by baptism is already at work in the present. Col. 2:12ff. does so by saying that being "buried with him in baptism" is the basis of forgiveness of sin and emancipation from the spirit powers. From this, then, in 2:16ff. emancipation from cultic and ritual regulations is deduced: "If with Christ you died to the elemental spirits of the universe, why do you live as if you still belonged to the world?" (2:20). It is apparent how the various motifs here flow together. More closely connected with Rom. 6:2ff. is Col. 3:1ff.: "If then you have been raised with Christ, seek the things that are above . . . for you have died . . ." Similar is the use of the terminology of the baptismal mystery in Eph. 2:5f., where, however, the idea has considerably paled. For here, though being "made alive with Christ" and being "raised up with him" are spoken of, dying with Christ is no longer mentioned (rather the contrast is expressed as being "dead through our trespasses"). But the original mystery idea reappears (though without explicit mention of baptism) in II Tim. 2:11: "If we have died with him, we shall also live with him." Similar to this is the interpretation of the tower allegory in Herm. sim. IX 16, 1: "They had need . . . to come up through water that they might be made alive. For 'they could not' otherwise 'enter into the Kingdom of God' unless they put away the mortality of their (former) life." This is the more clearly a reference to a traditional interpretation of baptism as mystery thinking is otherwise foreign to Hermas. The wide circulation of the mystery idea is also implied by such brief allusions as the interpolation in Jn. 19:34b, 35: from the wound of the crucified flowed (blood and) water. For the meaning is evidently this: In Jesus' death lies the foundation of the sacrament (of the Lord's Supper and) of baptism. The same idea lies in the statement of Ignatius Eph. 18:2: ". . . who was born and baptized that by his passion he might purify the water."

It is in harmony with the mystery interpretation of baptism that its effect is also called *re-birth*, a usage which has parallels in the mysteries. Baptism, according to Tit. 3:5, is a "bath of re-birth." This is also the conception of the text of Jn. 3:3ff. as it has come down to us when it speaks of being "born (again) by water and the Spirit," i.e. by baptism. That is an echo of an apocryphal saying of Jesus which Justin quotes in Ap. 61:4: "Unless you are born again you cannot enter the Reign of God"; moreover, Justin quotes this saying to substantiate the conception of baptism as "re-birth" (61:3, 66:1). So, according to Justin Dial. 138:2, Christians are "(a race) regenerated by him (*sc.* Christ) through water, and faith, and wood." This terminology is also echoed when I Pet. 1:3 describes God as He "who has begotten us anew to a living hope through the resurrection of Jesus Christ from the dead." So Christians can be described (1:23) as "born anew, not of perishable seed . . ." in which fact here as in Paul lies their foundation for ethical living. This terminology is not found in Paul, but the same idea lies in II Cor. 5:17: "if any one is in Christ, he is a new creature"; for "being in Christ" comes about by "being baptized into Christ" (Gal. 3:27, Rom. 6:3; *cf.* I Cor. 12:13). Barn. 6:11 similarly says: "Since he has made us new by the remission of sins (i.e. by baptism) he made us another type, that we should have the soul of children (*cf.* I Pet. 2:2) as though he were molding us anew." Likewise 16:8: "When we received the remission of sins and put our hope on the Name, we became new, being created again from the beginning."

Calling baptism *"illumination"* or using "to illumine" for "to baptize" has this same meaning. The mystery term "illumination" specifically designating baptism first occurs in Justin Ap. 61:12 (the verb occurs at 61:12f.; 65:1; Dial. 39:2: "illumined through the Name of Christ"; 122:1ff.; 123:2). Justin interprets it as an "illuminating of the mind" (Ap. 61:12; *cf.* Dial. 39:2), whereas the term originally meant not the illuminating of the mind but transformation into a divine nature which is "Light" (= "Life"). As Heb. 6:4 shows, the term in this sense had already been taken over by Christianity at a much earlier time. "Those who have once been enlightened" can by the context here only mean the baptized, and that "to be enlightened" means "to be filled with divine powers" is shown by the additional description, "who have tasted . . . the powers of the age to come." The baptized are also called "the enlightened" in 10:32. Whether the figurative use of the expression in Eph. 1:18; 3:9; II Tim. 1:10 goes back to baptismal terminology may be left an open question.

Naturally, *the other interpretations of baptism were combined with the mystery interpretation.* When the effect of baptism, understood as purification from sins, is attributed to the "resurrection of Jesus Christ" in I Pet. 3:21—i.e. to the fate of the cult-divinity—two interpretations have flowed together. Or, once the relation of the baptismal bath to Jesus' death had been worked out, a mode of thought that moved within Jewish tradition and understood Christ's death as sacrifice (§ 9, 4) could easily combine the idea of a sprinkling with the blood of Christ with that of the purifying bath of baptism, as Heb. 10:22 does. Or, again, forgiveness of sin and renewal or rebirth are combined in Barn. 6:11; 16:18; Justin Ap. 66:1; and in Justin Dial. 39:2, the "illumination" is attributed to the Name and connected with the bestowal of the Spirit. Rebirth and bestowal of the Spirit are united in Tit. 3:5; Jn. 3:5; and, correspondingly, to the heavenly powers bestowed by the sacrament, according to Heb. 6:4f., belongs primarily the Spirit.

The decisive thing that had happened in the mystery interpretation of baptism is this: The Christian initiation sacrament of baptism had been given a relation to Jesus' death and resurrection—i.e. to the occurrence of salvation—which it did not originally have. What Ignatius expresses in enigmatic brevity by saying "that by his passion he might purify the water" Barnabas 11 developed more fully: "water" (= baptism) and "the cross" belong together. From Ps. 1:3-6 Barnabas draws the conclusion: "Mark how he (sc. God) described the water and the cross together. For he means this: Blessed are those who hoping on the cross descended into the water." It cannot be denied that this whole interpretation brought along with it the danger that Christian existence might be built up entirely upon Hellenistic sacramental magic instead of being understood as eschatological existence. But, on the other side, the possibility seized by Paul was also given: to interpret it as an existence determined by Christ's death and resurrection and hence to understand the sacrament as an actualization, here and now, of the occurrence of salvation.

2. Besides the initiation sacrament of baptism Hellenistic Christianity knows one other sacrament, *the Lord's Supper*; its celebration is regularly repeated by the congregation.

Paul calls this meal "the Lord's supper" (κυριακὸν δεῖπνον, I Cor. 11:20), but the term that became prevalent is "Eucharist" (εὐχαριστία, a giving of thanks). This term is found in Didache, Ignatius, and Justin, and means at first, as Didache clearly indicates, the prayers spoken at the celebration of the meal and then the whole sacramental celebration. In addition to the latter, Ignatius knows the name "Agape" (Sm. 8:2; Rom. 7:3? ἀγαπᾶν, Sm. 7:1 = "hold the Agape") which also occurs in Jd. 12. It is very doubtful whether "the breaking of bread" (Acts 2:42) or "to break bread" (Acts 2:46; 20:7, 11) was ever a technical designation of the Lord's Supper. So far as the latter was a meal, "breaking of bread" could be used of it, even though the phrase in itself did not denote the sacramental meal (thus I Cor. 10:16; Did. 14:1); in itself the phrase means simply a meal (e.g. Acts 27:35). It cannot be definitely said how frequently the Lord's Supper was celebrated or in what relation its celebration stood to worship by the word. According to Did. 14:1 the whole congregation celebrated the Eucharist "each (κατὰ) Lord's Day of the Lord"; but probably there were celebrations of the Supper in smaller groups besides. Whether the meal on "the first day of the week" in Acts 20:7 is the Lord's Supper, must remain in doubt; Barn. 15:9 speaks of the celebration of the "eighth day," as the day of Jesus' resurrection, without mentioning the Eucharist. According to Justin Ap. 65, a Eucharist follows immediately after a baptism, and according to Ap. 67, the whole congregation celebrates the Eucharist (but it is no longer a real meal; see below) just after worship by the word on "the day called Sun's day." When Pliny in his letter to Trajan (ep. X 96, 7) reports of the worship and the meal-celebrations of the Christians that they take place *stato die* (on a fixed day), he undoubtedly means Sunday.

As long as the Eucharist was a real meal (see below), it probably took place only in the evening, as the expression "Supper" (δεῖπνον) itself suggests; whether it was at that time connected with a service by the word, we do not know. So far as congregations had come out of the synagogue or followed its traditions, at least the services of worship by the word took place in the morning, while the Eucharist was celebrated in the evening (Pliny: *rursusque coeundi ad capiendum cibum*, "to convene again to take food").* Probably varying customs were in practice in different places and times; and there is as little foundation for saying that worship by the word and the celebration of the Supper always and everywhere took place separately as for saying that the celebration of the Supper was always and everywhere "the cause and purpose of all congregating" (Cullmann). With certainty, only Justin Ap. 67 testifies that in Sunday worship proclamation of the word and the Eucharist were combined; but here the Eucharist is no longer a real meal but is only a liturgical ceremony.

In addition to this, we know that only baptized persons were admitted to the Eucharist (Did. 9:5; Justin Ap. 66:1). According to Did. 14 a confession of sin precedes the celebration and none may participate who has an unreconciled quarrel with his brother. The celebration of the Supper was accompanied by prayers (Did. 9f.; Justin Ap. 65:3; 67:2; Dial. 41:1).

The liturgical words which make the Lord's Supper a sacrament have been handed down to us by Paul and Mark in essential agree-

---

* The morning celebrations, which according to Pliny take place *ante lucem* (before daybreak), are probably not services of the word but baptisms; see H. Lietzmann, *Geschichtl. Studien für Albert Hauck* (1916), 34–38.

ment with each other; Matthew and Luke are dependent upon Mark, Luke also upon Paul.

The text of I Cor. 11:23–25 in comparison with Mk. 14:22–24 has evidently been smoothed out. In Mark's saying over the cup the modifiers placed after "my blood"—"of the covenant" and "poured out"—collide with each other; but especially does "of the covenant" collide with "my" (literal Greek order: "This is the blood of me of the covenant . . ."), indicating that "of the covenant" is a secondary addition. The Pauline text has eliminated "poured out, etc." from the words said over the cup and has compensated for it by adding "for you" (τὸ ὑπὲρ ὑμῶν) to the words said over the bread; it avoids the collision of "blood of me" with "blood of the covenant" by the formulation: "This cup is the new covenant in my blood." The much-debated Lucan text (22:14–20) with its many textual variants is not to be regarded as having the value of independent tradition in any of its forms.

This liturgy contains *three motifs*: 1. the really sacramental interpretation of the act, which is expressed in the repeated phrase "this is," by which bread and wine are offered the partaker as flesh and blood of Jesus; 2. the words "of the covenant" which interpret Jesus' death as the sacrifice of the (new) covenant; 3. the words "poured out for many" (Mk. 14:24) or "for you" (I Cor. 11:24), which interpret his death as an expiatory sacrifice for sins, of which Matthew's addition "for the forgiveness of sins" (26:28) is a correct exegesis. There can scarcely be a doubt that the first interpretation is the original one, for the act is first and foremost a meal. Then, not only "of the covenant," which has already been shown on linguistic grounds to be an addition, but also "poured out for many" or "for you" is the result of secondary interpretation, and the original liturgical words are only:

"This is my body,
This is my blood."

And that is the wording in Justin Ap. 66:3, introduced by these words only: "This do in memory of me." The primary element of the text must be the words which interpret the act.

But what, then, is the *original meaning of the act*? When the

participants by partaking of bread and wine take into themselves
the body and blood of Jesus, the basic idea is that of *sacramental
communion*—communion of the partakers with the Kyrios. The
question asked in this connection whether the sacrament bestows
participation in the crucified physical body of Jesus or in the spiritual
body of the exalted Christ is wrongly put. The "glory-body" of the
exalted Christ is identical with the body put to death on the cross.
That is just what the sacramental idea is: that the killed body of the
cult-divinity is simultaneously the body filled with power and mighty
in effect. This is also apparent in the warning at I Cor. 11:27: Whoever partakes unworthily of the sacramental body and the sacramental blood of the Kyrios makes himself guilty of the Lord's death.
And when Rom. 7:4 says: "you have died to the law through the
body of Christ," this "body" is the crucified body of Christ, which,
as such (by virtue of the resurrection) is at the same time the glory-
body, mighty in effect.

That sacramental communion is the real meaning of the Lord's
Supper is also indicated by I Cor. 10:16: "The cup of blessing which
we bless, is it not a participation (or communion) in the blood of
Christ? The bread which we break, is it not a participation (or communion) in the body of Christ?" Paul's rhetorical questions indicate
that he assumes this meaning to be the one self-evident to his readers. The following v. 17 confirms this by a peculiarly Pauline turn
of thought: "Because it is *one* loaf, we who are many are *one* body,
for we all partake of *one* loaf"; i.e. by sacramental communion the
participants are united into one "body"—in which "body" is not a
figurative term for unity, but means Christ's body. The unity of the
celebrating congregation is explained by the unity of the bread only
if the bread is the body of Christ (as v. 16, in fact, had said).

The same conception is expressed in Jn. 6:51b-58, a passage
which is secondary within the Gospel of John. At the same time,
this passage expresses what the effect of the sacrament for the participants is: Whoever eats the flesh ("flesh" as in Ignatius and Justin,
instead of "body") and drinks the blood of Jesus thereby achieves
Life. Ignatius, who in Phld. 4:1 defines the purpose of the cup as
being "for union with his blood (*sc.* of Jesus Christ)," and for whom
the Eucharist is "the flesh of our Savior" (Sm. 7:1), quite in this
sense calls the eucharistic bread "the medicine of immortality, the
antidote that we should not die, but live forever in Jesus Christ"

(Eph. 20:2). And in the same sense Justin Ap. 66:2 says that the elements of the Eucharist by the power of the prayer spoken become the flesh and blood of Christ and that by this nourishment "our flesh and blood are transformingly (κατὰ μεταβολήν) fed"—i.e. are transformed into a supranatural nature.

In Hellenistic Christianity the Lord's Supper, like baptism, is understood *as a sacrament in the sense of the mystery religions.* The idea of communion brought about by the sacramental meal is in itself not a specific idea of the mysteries, but is wide-spread in primitive and classic cults. But in the mysteries it plays a special role; in them it is communion with a once dead and risen deity, in whose fate the partaker receives a share through the sacramental meal, as we know from the mysteries of Attis and Mithra. Paul himself shows that the sacrament of the Lord's Supper stands in this context in the history of religions. He does so not only by calling the Lord's Supper "the table of the Lord," thereby using a Hellenistic term for cultic banquets (I Cor. 10:21; on which see Lietzmann in the *Handbuch zum NT*), but especially by the way he contrasts the cup and table of the Lord with heathen sacrificial meals: as these make the partakers "partners (or communicants) with demons," the Lord's Supper brings about "communion" (or partnership) with the Lord. And Justin declares the sacramental meal of the Mithra-initiates, in which bread and a cup of water are set before them with words of blessing, to be a demonic aping of the Eucharist (Ap. 66:4).

Like baptism, the Lord's Supper also is attributed, in keeping with the mode of thinking characteristic of the mystery religions, to the fate of the Kyrios as its founding cause—especially to Jesus' last meal with his disciples. That is the meaning of the prefatory words in I Cor. 11:23: "the Lord Jesus on the night when he was betrayed . . ." And it is in this direction that Mark cast his account of the last supper in the form of an etiological cult-narrative by working the eucharistic liturgy into an older traditional account which reported the last supper as a Passover meal. At bottom, it is the death of the Kyrios that is specified as the real foundation of the cultic meal when it is attributed to Jesus' last supper, for the body and blood of Jesus distributed by him at this meal are, of course (as precisely the secondary words of interpretation corroborate), in mysterious anticipation the body and blood of the crucified, sacrificed Christ. Paul clearly indicates that in the sentence added by him

(I Cor. 11:26): "For as often as you eat this bread and drink the cup, you proclaim the Lord's death."

That is, he conceives the eucharistic meal as a representational rite (δρώμενον) like the "acted rites" (δρώμενα) of the mysteries; the ceremony acts out the death of the Lord. And it is significant that Ignatius does not even mention the last supper of Jesus; for him the real institution of the Eucharist is the passion of Christ.

Quite understandably, the sacramental meal also received *other interpretations*. It was accompanied by various prayers, and in them "the proclamation of the Lord's death" which took place in the sacred act could be verbally expanded. It is not to be wondered at that such interpretations were then also adopted into the liturgy. The interpretations of Jesus' death as covenant sacrifice and as expiatory sacrifice were current, as we have seen (§ 9, 4, p. 84); and how easily such thoughts arose is indicated, e.g. by Jn. 6:51b ("for the life of the world") or Ign. Sm. 7:1 (Jesus' eucharistic "flesh" conceived as "having suffered for our sins") or by Justin Dial. 41:1. Though the additions "of the covenant" and "(poured out) for" are derived from the Jewish-Christian tradition, the sentences I Cor. 11:24f., which are without parallel in Mark, had their origin in the Gentile-Christian sphere—namely, the repeated instruction: "Do this in memory of me." They are apparently to be attributed to the fact that the Lord's Supper was conceived in analogy to Hellenistic memorial-ceremonies, for in the deeds of bequest for such ceremonies similar formulas occur (see Lietzmann on I Cor. 11:41f. in the *Handbuch zum NT*). According to Justin Dial. 41:4, also, the Eucharist is celebrated "in memory of the passion." "Out of these ideas grew the so-called Anamnesis,* in the most ancient liturgies."

In the course of development the *Eucharist came to be conceived of as a sacrifice*. It is called "sacrifice" in Did. 14:1, but there, it must be admitted, it is still meant figuratively—or rather the Eucharist is thereby designated as a cultic act which in the Christian congregation has taken the place of actual sacrifice. Ignatius, too, uses sacrificial terminology when, in urging unity upon the congregation gathered together under the bishop, he speaks of the "altar" or the "altar space" (θυσιαστήριον) within which the "bread of God" is dis-

---

* The "commemoration"-section of the eucharistic liturgy; (for examples see Lietzmann's commentary on I Cor. 11:26 and Lietzmann: *Messe und Herrenmahl*, pp. 50ff.).

tributed (Eph. 4:2), or when he speaks of the "one altar" which must be the only one in the congregation (Philad. 4). I Clem. prepares for this development of meaning in a different way when he places the Christian cultic officials in analogy with the priests of the Old Testament (I Clem. 40). Justin specifically calls the Eucharist a sacrifice (Dial. 41:3; 117:1), though he leaves us in doubt what he conceives the thing sacrificed to be. Only at a later stage of the development will that be made definite.

But another development, a presupposition for the last named one, takes place still earlier: *the divorce of the sacramental meal from an actual meal.* That the Lord's Supper was originally framed by a real meal for the satisfaction of the participants' hunger, or was itself the frame for such a meal, is attested by I Cor. 11; in a different way Didache also attests this combination (see below). But I Cor. also indicates that this arrangement led to irregularities; hence, Paul directs that hunger be satisfied by a meal at home before the sacramental celebration (11:21, 34). We do not know how soon in the various areas the real meal for hunger was eliminated from the cultic celebration; in Justin it has already been accomplished and the Eucharist has been combined with the service of the word (see above). But social meals continued to be held in the churches, and the title "Agape" stuck to them; they were occasions of sociability and charity.

The earliest witness to the sacrament of the Lord's Supper is Paul; but he created it no more than he did baptism; rather *he found it already present in Hellenistic Christianity.*

When, in I Cor. 11:23, he introduces the liturgical words with the sentence: "For I received from the Lord . . ." he is not appealing to a personal revelation from the Lord, though this is frequently assumed, but to a tradition that has been handed down to him, being ultimately derived from the Lord. Our comparison of I Cor. 11:23-25 with Mk. 14:22-24 has shown that Paul's text represents an older one which has undergone editorial smoothing; and the analysis of the liturgical sentences showed that they imply a development in the course of which the various motifs combined. Another indication that Paul found the liturgical words already in existence is the fact that they speak of a "communion" with the (body and the) blood of the Lord. Can Paul, for whom "flesh and blood" are excluded from the Reign of God (I Cor. 15:50), have created this text? He also speaks in I Cor. 10:16 of sacramental communion as something self-evident for Christians; the "we" of these sentences is evidently the same as that of Rom. 6:2ff.

But did *Hellenistic Christianity* itself create the sacramental meal of communion—or is it, analogous to the mystery interpretation of baptism—the interpretation of a traditional custom, i.e. the fellowship meals derived from the earliest Church (§ 6, 4 and § 8, 3)? This question cannot be answered with certainty. It would be comprehensible if such meals, which were not really cultic ceremonies but were a bond and expression of fellowship in keeping with the tradition of Judaism and of the historical Jesus himself, should have been transformed into sacramental celebrations in Hellenistic Christianity. That may be regarded as the probable process. But in any case it must be borne in mind that the development in one place may have been different from that in another. The Didache apparently implies that at various places in Hellenistic Christianity, too, those fellowship meals continued to be held without developing into the sacramental Lord's Supper.

From Did. 9 and 10 we get a picture of a meal-celebration quite in keeping with Jewish tradition (§ 6, 4), in which there is no reference whatever to the death of Jesus and no mention of sacramental communion. It does appear to be true that the words of 10:6 are to be understood as a transition to the sacramental Eucharist, the liturgy of which does not need to be set down because it is familiar to all. But then it is clear that two celebrations of entirely different kind have been secondarily combined. Therefore, the celebration implied in Did. 9 and 10 existed at first by itself, and it must have been from it that the Lord's Supper took over the title "Eucharist" ("Thanksgiving"), which is a very strange term for the sacrament of the Lord's Supper.

3. Out of the facts set forth in §§ 12, 13 arise a number of questions for the future. First of all is the question already raised in § 11, 3a *whether a sacrificial cult and a priesthood will develop in the Christian Church.* At the same time the question arises *whether the cult will come to be considered one-sidedly as the means to salvation,* corresponding to Ignatius' conception of the Eucharist

as the "medicine of immortality" (see above p. 147)—that is to say, also corresponding to the conception of the Hellenistic mystery religions—or whether its meaning will remain that of being the self-representation of the eschatological Congregation, for which salvation is already present as anticipated future.

So far as salvation is held to be present in the cult, there is also the question how this presence is to be understood. Is the transcendent world present in the cult as a thing to be experienced and enjoyed, a reality of which one becomes aware by ecstasy and all sorts of "pneumatic" phenomena (§ 14)? That also means *how will the relationship between cult and eschatology be settled?* When Christ is worshiped as the present Lord, will the expectation of the coming Christ remain alive? Or will it fade out and thereby push the eschatological expectation clear into the background? Will the end of the world be postponed into an indefinite future, resulting in the reduction of Christian hope for the future to the hope for individual "immortality"? Or will the conception that the cult is the appropriate form for representing the eschatological transcendence of the Church win out? If so, will it do so through the idea that the congregation at worship is also a demonstration of God's judgment over the world, as Paul holds (I Cor. 14:21-25)? Will it win out by regarding the cult as that which calls the worshipers into question as earthly men and points them to that which they are not yet and yet, regarded from the view-point of the eschatological occurrence, already are, and which they must make manifest in their lives in order—as Paul puts it—to "shine as lights in the world" (Phil. 2:15)?

That also contains the question *in what relation will the cult and every-day life be placed to each other?* Is the cult—and with it "religion"—an interrupting and occasional thing within secular living? Is it to be understood as a guarantee of life after death and as having no relation to the present? Or is the whole person in his present every-day living determined by the cult? And if so, is his conduct negatively determined by regulations, either ritualistic or ascetic (§ 10, 4)? Or is one's conduct of life positively determined by the cult in this sense: that both the congregation and the individual are regarded as the temple of God and of His Spirit, a fact which each must confirm by ethical conduct so that one's whole life becomes service of God, or "cult," or "sacrifice" (§ 10, 4, p. 101f.; § 11, 3a, p. 115)? Similar questions will soon arise again.

§ 14. The Spirit

1. In baptism, the Spirit has been conferred upon all Christians (§ 13, 1, p. 138); it shows itself to be alive in them in the worship services of the congregation (§ 12, 1, p. 122). What is meant by "the Spirit"? How is Christian existence determined by it? Neither the conceptions of the Spirit (πνεῦμα) nor those of the individual's possession of the Spirit are entirely homogeneous.

The variation in *terminology*, however, does not imply variation in content of meaning. The same thing is meant whether "Holy Spirit" (ἅγιον πνεῦμα, on the basis of the Old Testament-Jewish רוּחַ הַקֹּדֶשׁ, "Spirit of Holiness") is used, or simply "Spirit," or "Spirit of God." Since the gift of the Spirit was brought about by the salvation-occurrence accomplished in Christ, the Spirit can be regarded as God's and also as Christ's gift, hence one may also speak of the "Spirit of Christ" or "of the Lord."

So far as the *Spirit-concept* is concerned, the basic notion underlying it, is, to be sure, homogeneous. Right comprehension of it has often been hindered by the choice of "Spirit" to translate *pneuma*, inasmuch as "spirit" in modern languages, especially in German (*Geist*), can also mean "mind." *Pneuma* does not mean "spirit" in the Greek-Platonic and the idealistic sense; i.e. it does not mean mind in contrast to body (regarded as the vehicle of sensuous life), or in contrast to nature. "Mind" in this sense, the active subject in "mental" or "spiritual" life, is called in Greek νοῦς, or ψυχή ("soul"), or λόγος ("reason"). Rather, *pneuma* is the miraculous divine power that stands in absolute contrast to all that is human. This comes out in Paul when he denies that the Corinthians are "spiritual men" (πνευματικοί) and asks them in view of their conduct, "are you not (ordinary) men?" (I Cor. 3:1-4). Or again Ignatius expresses it (Eph. 5:1) when he describes his "fellowship" with the bishop of Ephesus as "not human, but spiritual." Generally, the sphere of the human is termed "flesh" (σάρξ) to indicate its contrast to *pneuma*— a usage which, though not peculiar to Paul, was especially developed by him and need not here be treated (see § 23). The manifestations of the Spirit are that in a man's conduct which is extraordinary, mysteriously or terrifyingly mighty, and seems inexplicable as coming from merely human capabilities and powers. This, then, constitutes the concept of *pneuma*: *it is the miraculous—insofar as that takes place in the sphere of human life—either in what men do or in what is done to them.* To the *pneuma* are attributed miracles and extraordinary psychic phenomena but also brilliant insights and deeds of heroism or of moral power—but such are regarded as "pneumatic" (spiritual) not because they are phenomena of the inner or ethical life but because they are miraculous.

Such phenomena are called "spiritual [gifts]" (πνευματικά, I Cor. 12:1, 14:1) or "gifts" (χαρίσματα, Rom. 12:6, I Cor. 12:4, 9, 28, 30f.; I Tim. 4:14; II Tim. 1:6; I Pet. 4:10; I Clem. 38:1; Ign. Sm. pr., 2:2). Specified as such gifts are: the "word of wisdom" and the "word of knowledge" (I Cor. 12:8); the two are probably joined together in the "gift of teaching" (Rom. 12:7; I Cor. 12:28f.; 14:26; *cf.* Acts 6:10). The "faith" in I Cor. 12:9 is certainly the faith that is capable of working miracles (*cf.* I Cor. 13:2). Not clearly distinguishable from this are the "gifts of healing" (I Cor. 12:9, 28, 30) and the "working of miracles" (I Cor. 12:10; *cf.* 12:28f.; Gal. 3:5; *cf.* Rom. 15:18f.; Heb. 2:4; Acts 6:8); in fact, as a rule the distinction between related gifts must not be too precisely made. The "gift of prophecy" is often mentioned (Rom. 12:6; I Cor. 12:10, 28f.; 13:2, 8f.; 14:5f.; I Thess. 5:20; Acts 19:6; *cf.* Rev. as a whole, espec. 22:9, for instance; also Ign. Philad. 7). How "revelation" (I Cor. 14:6, 26, 30) is related to this gift or to the "word of knowledge" can scarcely be said. Especially sought after by the Corinthian church is the gift, also highly regarded by Paul, of "tongues," ecstatic "speaking in tongues" (I Cor. 12:10, 28, 30; 14:18, 26; Acts 19:6; is it also meant by the Spirit that is not to be "quenched"? I Thess. 5:19), a gift which finds its complement in the "interpretation of tongues" (I Cor. 12:10, 30). Finally, Paul mentions the gift of "distinguishing between spirits" (I Cor. 12:10). This list of gifts, to the enumeration of which Paul restricts himself in I Cor. 12:7–10, evidently includes those generally recognized as such. Other gifts include prayers uttered "in the Spirit" (I Cor. 14:14f.; Eph. 6:18? Jd. 20; Mart. Pol. 7:2f.) and songs sung "in the Spirit" (psalms, hymns, spiritual songs; I Cor. 14:15, 26; Col. 3:16; Eph. 5:18f.), while it is a peculiarity of Paul that he reckons "services of help" and "powers of administration" (I Cor. 12:28), "service" (Rom. 12:7f.) and similar activities to the "gifts" of the Spirit. On the other hand, it is evidently a common Christian opinion that man is guided by the Spirit in important decisions (Acts 13:2, 4; 16:6f.; *cf.* Gal. 2:2); and when Paul regards the unmarried state as a special "gift" (I Cor. 7:7) that probably also corresponds to general Christian opinion.

There is also agreement that *the bestowal of the Spirit is an eschatological gift* and that its coming into effect in the Church is an eschatological event. The earliest Church had so understood the Spirit (§ 6, 5), and the Hellenistic Church likewise did. When Paul calls the Spirit "the first fruits" (Rom. 8:23) or the "guarantee" (II Cor. 1:22; 5:5) of future glory (in which Eph. 1:13f. follows his lead), he is only expressing the common Christian conviction. According to Heb. 6:4f., the baptized, who have become partakers of the Holy Spirit, have already "tasted . . . the powers of the age to come." That is perhaps also what is meant in Barn. 1:7, where it is said that God "has given us a foretaste of the things to come." At any rate, it is clear that for Barnabas, too, it is being filled with the Spirit (1:2f.) which makes the Congregation into the eschatological temple of God (16:5ff.). The outpouring of the Spirit at Pentecost is the fulfilment of Joel's prophecy for the end of days (Acts 2:16ff.). And for I Pet., it is self-evident (1:3ff.) that "sanctification by the Spirit" (1:2) makes the sanctified heirs-apparent of the eschatological salvation soon to appear.

Over against these agreements *the differences in conception relating to the Spirit* are relatively unimportant; nevertheless, one important matter is expressed in them, as will appear.

In *animistic thinking pneuma* is conceived as an independent agent, a personal power which like a demon can fall upon a man and take possession of him, enabling him or compelling him to perform manifestations of power. In *dynamistic thinking*, on the contrary, *pneuma* appears as an impersonal force which fills a man like a fluid, so to say. One or the other of these ways of thinking may be distinctly present in a given passage; but in general little emphasis is placed upon the distinction, and the two conceptions can intertwine in the same author.

The *animistic* conception is present, e.g. in Rom. 8:16; I Cor. 2:10–16; 14:14; likewise Acts 5:32; 10:19; 16:6f.; 20:23; Ign. Philad. 7:1f.; and also in John—though here it has faded to a figure of speech—14:26; 15:26; 16:8, 13–15. It is also apparent in the use of the plural for spirits that work in individual persons (I Cor. 14:12, 32; esp. in the Mandata of Hermas); or also from the fact that a spirit is mentioned which evokes a specific effect (as in the Old Testament also—thus, the "spirit of stupor" (Rom. 11:8 quoting Is. 29:10; also the "spirit of gentleness" I Cor. 4:21; *cf.* further: II Cor. 4:13; Gal. 6:1; Eph. 1:17; II Tim. 1:7; Rev. 19:10). Often, it is true, the original concrete idea no longer remains but has been sublimated to a mere form of speech (as in I Cor. 4:21; Gal. 6:1). The *dynamistic* conception is the usual one; and it is evidently present wherever the "giving" (διδόναι or δοθῆναι), the "gift," the "pouring out," or the "supplying" of the Spirit is mentioned (Rom. 5:5; II Cor. 1:22; 5:5; I Thess. 4:8; Acts 2:38; 10:45; Heb. 6:4—Tit. 3:6; Acts 2:17f.; 10:45; I Clem. 2:2; 46:6; Barn. 1:3—Gal. 3:5; Phil. 1:19). This conception is also clear cut in Rom. 8:11, or also where "Holy Spirit" is coordinated with definite terms like "wisdom," "faith," "joy" (Acts 6:3, 5; 11:24; 13:52), and especially where "Spirit" and "power" are united in a hendiadys (I Cor. 2:4; I Thess. 1:5; Lk. 1:17); but also where the "power of the (Holy) Spirit" is mentioned (Rom. 15:13, 19; Ign. Sm. 13:1; *cf.* also Herm. sim. IX 1, 2 "empowered by the Spirit"). It can almost be said that "Spirit" and "power" are synonymous; that is the case in Herm. sim. IX 13, 2 where the "holy spirits" are soon after called "the powers of the Son of God." It is also very significant that in Heb. 7:16 the contrast to "after the law of a carnal commandment" (KJ) is not formed by means of the concept "spiritual," as one would expect according to the usual antithesis of "flesh" and "spirit," but is formulated: "after the power of an endless life" (KJ). Since "power" and "glory" can be synonymous (*cf.* Rom. 6:4 with I Cor. 6:14), so "spirit" is also related to "glory," the life-giving power from heaven; the "spiritual body" (I Cor. 15:44) is the "body of glory" or "glorious body" of Phil. 3:21); the resurrection of "the spiritual body" is a raising up "in glory" and "in power" (I Cor. 15:43). The textual variants of I Pet. 4:14 ("spirit of glory" or "spirit of glory and of power") beautifully illustrate the kinship of the concepts "spirit," "glory," and "power." The synonymity of πνευματικόν ("spiritual gift") and χάρισμα ("gift"; lit. "token of grace") indicates that "grace" can also be synonymous with "spirit"—or that "grace" can be conceived as a spiritual "power." See I Cor. 15:10; II Cor. 12:9; this is very clear in Acts 6:8 where "full of grace and power" corresponds to "full . . . of the Holy Spirit" in 6:5. *Cf.* also Ign. Mg. 8:2 ("inspired, ἐμπνεόμενοι, by his grace"); Rm. pr., Pol. 1:2 (*cf.* Mart. Pol. 7:3).

Neither conception is foreign to the Old Testament. Nevertheless the animistic one must be regarded as characteristic for Old Testament thought. The same is true of another distinction which to a certain extent coincides with the animistic-dynamistic one. The Spirit can be conceived *as the power which seizes a man, or is given to him, for a specific situation or moment,* causing in him a temporary condition or eliciting specific deeds for that sole time. Or it can be conceived *as a power permanently allotted to him, resting in him, so to say,* which, of course, goes into effect on special occasions, but which also gives his whole mode of life a special character, imparting a supranatural quality to his nature. The former conception is that of the Old Testament and Judaism. The latter is apparently present there, too, in embryo, but it is characteristic of the Hellenistic world. Hellenism, in turn, also knows the former conception, especially the phenomenon of ecstasy, in which, for moments, divine power lifts a man out of the sphere of the earthly. Nevertheless, the typical "pneumatic" in Hellenism is the "divine man" (θεῖος ἀνήρ), who is of higher nature than ordinary mortals, filled with mysterious, divine power, which makes him capable of miraculous insights and deeds. The term for the power in him is not, it is true, as a rule *pneuma,* but *dynamis,* power ("grace" also occurs); but in substance it means the same thing as the *pneuma* of early Christianity (dynamistically understood).

2. The variety in regard to these points accounts for certain inconsistencies or contradictions in Hellenistic Christian conceptions of the Spirit. On the one hand, the general conviction is *that all Christians have received the Spirit in baptism* and have thereby been transformed into a new nature (§ 13, 1, p. 138). The Spirit thus possessed is ordinarily latent, so to say, but can manifest itself in miraculous deeds (Gal. 3:5); according to Paul, it is above all the power for ethical living. But this is an idea peculiar to him. Generally accepted, however, appears to be the view which is also self-evident to Paul—that possessing the Spirit, which is God's life-giving power, lends the assurance of triumph over death, *the certainty of the resurrection and of eternal life* (Rom. 8:10f.; *cf.* Gal. 6:8). The Spirit "gives life" (II Cor. 3:6); it is a "life-giving Spirit" (I Cor. 15:45; Jn. 6:63) or a "Spirit of life" (Rom. 8:2). The resurrection body is a "spiritual body" (I Cor. 15:44). Contrasted to the "service of death" stands the "service of the Spirit" (II Cor. 3:7f.).

"Sealing" by the Spirit guarantees future salvation (Eph. 1:13f.; 4:30), whose "first-fruits" or "pledge" is precisely the Spirit (see above; *cf.* also Heb. 6:4f.). Did. 10:3 gives thanks that God has bestowed upon the Church in the Eucharist "spiritual food and drink and eternal life." Whoever has received the Spirit in baptism is, according to Barn. 11:11, sure of eternal life; and II Clem. 14:5 even formulates the idea in such a way that the very flesh participates in "life" and "incorruption" when the Spirit has united with it. The angel of repentance in Hermas bases his promise of heavenly glory in fellowship with the Son of God upon these words: "for of his Spirit you have received" (Sim. IX 24, 4).

But elsewhere the fact of common possession of the Spirit is ignored—ignored in various respects. First, it is rather often mentioned *that there are people who are to be regarded as bearers of the Spirit* (πνευματικοί) *in a special sense,* or who so regard themselves. Paul (I Cor. 2:13–3:3) distinguishes between people in the Church who are Spirit-endowed (πνευματικοί) and those who are "unspiritual" (ψυχικοί; KJ: "natural") or "men of flesh" (σαρκικοί; KJ: "carnal")—contrary to the proposition that all the baptized have received the Spirit. He similarly distinguishes between the Spirit-endowed in the Church and those whom some trespass has overtaken and who therefore cannot be regarded as Spirit-endowed (Gal. 6:1). It means the same thing when he makes a distinction between "the mature" (τέλειοι, Phil. 3:15) and others; for according to I Cor. 2:6 (compared with 2:13ff.) "the mature" are identical with the "Spirit-endowed." Now this view that there are people specially marked as endowed with the Spirit, is evidently not peculiar to Paul —regardless of whether he ascribed this dignity to the same persons as others did, or not. It may be regarded as especially the view of gnosticizing Christians (§ 15); at any rate, it was wide-spread. For, since Paul can say, "If any one thinks that he is a prophet, or one Spirit-endowed" (I Cor. 14:37 tr.), he presupposes a usage of speech according to which the ecstatic speaker in tongues (in the context it can mean only him) is the "Spirit-endowed" *par excellence,* as if ignoring the fact that prophecy is also a gift of the Spirit.

One must ask whether in an inconsistency of this sort there does not appear a difference in the conception of what the Spirit is. When some in the Church as "Spirit-endowed" are distinguished from others, the Spirit is obviously not understood as the power that governs the Christian as Christian. How that can be understood must be shown further on. The conception *that one may possess the Spirit in varying quantity or intensity* is more easily reconciled with the idea that all Christians have the Spirit. When individuals are described as being "full of the Spirit and of wisdom" or "full of faith and the Holy Spirit" (Acts 6:3, 5; 11:24), that intends to affirm nothing more than that they are especially richly and powerfully endowed with the Spirit. Barn. 1:2f., for instance, shows how this conception is compatible with that of baptismal grace; the author rejoices that the readers have received (by baptism) "the implanted grace of the Spirit-gift" in such high degree (οὕτως) "that I truly see in you the Spirit of the Lord, whose fountain is rich, poured out upon you" (tr.).

Related to this conception is the view that there are not only *various gifts of the Spirit* ("apportionings of the Holy Spirit" Heb. 2:4; "distributions" KJ mg.), but that these also *vary in value*—a view which Paul assumes to be current in Corinth (I Cor. 12, 14), and which he also shares, himself, when he outlines a value-gradation among spiritual gifts, as it were (I Cor. 12:28), or exhorts: "earnestly desire the higher gifts" (12:31). That really contradicts the view that the Spirit has been bestowed upon all Christians at baptism. For it is the Spirit that accomplishes the decisive thing: It makes Christians new creatures. But in the conception under discussion the Spirit is spoken of as the miraculous power which grants the capacity for certain particularly excellent deeds or attitudes, and its operation is perceived in specific "gifts" so that Paul under certain circumstances has occasion to emphasize the unity of origin of the various gifts (I Cor. 12:4ff.).

But the Spirit not only shows differences in its particular gifts, *it also manifests its activity at particular moments*. It is at special times that a person is "filled with the Spirit" (Acts 4:8, 31; 13:9) or is "full of the Spirit" (Acts 7:55) or is "transported by the Spirit" (γίνεσθαι ἐν πνεύματι, Rev. 1:10; 4:2; *cf.* 17:3). In this, too, the possession of the Spirit by all Christians is ignored—and devout Jews can be spoken of in the same way (Lk. 1:41; of the Baptist, Lk. 1:15; of Jesus himself, Lk. 4:1). The same is true of the formula "speak (or "pray," or the like) in the Spirit" or "by the Spirit" (I Cor. 12:3; 14:2, 14ff.; Did. 11:7), which, of course, does not at all mean just speaking that is Christian, but rather a speaking in momentary seizure by the Spirit.

Finally, it is curious—and again not in harmony with the general view of baptism—that by the side of the ordinary view that the Spirit is the origin of all distinctly Christian phenomena, another view can find room: *that an effort or an appropriate attitude on man's part is needed to bring about the gift of the Spirit or of a particular spiritual gift*—or at least to increase or strengthen it. This is already implied in "earnestly desiring spiritual gifts" (I Cor. 12:31; 14:1) and in the exhortation: "strive to excel" (I Cor. 14:12) or "earnestly desire to prophesy" (I Cor. 14:39). So Barn. 4:11 directly urges: "Let us be spiritual" (somewhat different from the paradoxical exhortation at Gal. 5:25!), whereas II Tim. 1:6 more modestly urges the "rekindling" of "the gift of God" (in this case it is the specific gift of the teaching office that is meant). The means of achieving a particular gift of the Spirit is prayer, according to I Cor. 14:13. Fasting, according to Acts 13:2, is the preparation for revelation by the Spirit. This agrees with the traditional Jewish view. According to II Clem. 14:4, asceticism is the presupposition for the receipt of the Spirit. But according to I Clem. 2:2, it was on account of its model conduct that the Corinthian church had experienced a "full out-pouring of the Holy Spirit."

3. In the inconsistency—in fact, the contradictoriness—of these conceptions a significant fact in regard to the Spirit is reflected. Once it has been seen, this inconsistency can to a large extent be called appropriate to the nature of Spirit.

The view that all Christians receive the Spirit in baptism does not rest upon the idea that the individuals baptized have special "spiritual" or emotional experiences during the act of baptism, however much that may occasionally have been the case. Rather, it rests basically upon the fact *that the Spirit is given to the Church*, into which the individual is received by baptism. Hence, the Spirit bestowed upon the Church is often dwelt upon, or the gifts that are at work in the Church (I Cor. 1:4ff.; I Clem. 2:2; Barn. 1:2f.; Herm. mand. XI 14). Whoever imposes upon the Church deceives the Holy Spirit (Acts 5:3), and what the Church (through its leaders) decides and proclaims is thereby the Spirit's proclamation (Acts 13:2; 15:28). For the earliest Church there was no problem here at all, but for the Hellenistic Church there now arises the question how participation in the Spirit becomes a reality in all individuals. Do they possess the Spirit only in faith?—i.e. only in the conviction that in a manner at present hidden from view they are no longer of earthly nature but by the power of the Spirit dwelling within them will not perish with this world but in a changed form, a "spiritual body," will participate in the glory of the world that is soon to appear? Or, in case they die before the *parousia* of the Lord, that they will be awakened from the dead? Or do they already feel indications of possessing the Spirit? Is its life-giving power already at work in them?

The common Christian conviction is that the last of these is the case, and quite naturally *the workings of the Spirit are experienced above all in the service of worship*, in which the eschatological Congregation takes present form. It understands everything that is given it here as the gift of the Spirit, especially what transcends the limits of the ordinary—the 'word of instruction, which dispenses wisdom and knowledge, as well as prophecy, which uncovers the mystery of future events but which also reveals what lurks in the heart—prayers and songs and especially ecstatic speaking in tongues. However, it is clear that the criterion by which these utterances are judged to be gifts of the Spirit is not how Christian they may be, but how extraordinary their symptoms—the phenomena that accompany or precede them—may be. Doubtless the content of such enthusiastic utterances, except where they are completely unintelligible, is always assumed to be appropriate, but that is not what makes them "spiritual gifts." And we must think of the range between what was intelligible and significant in content and what was unintelligibly ecstatic or irrelevant in content as a wide one. Prayer may be anything from clear conscious speech to stammering in ecstatic tongues (I Cor. 14:14f.); it may be a wordless sigh (Rom. 8:26) or an ecstatic cry of "Abba" (Rom. 8:15; Gal. 4:6).

But the workings of the Spirit extend beyond these phenomena, which belong, primarily at least, to the cultic gathering. Its power manifests itself in all extraordinary achievements and modes of conduct. First of all, in *missionary activity* for which the Spirit gives instructions (Acts 13:2, 4; 16:6f.) and whose bearer, the *apostle* (I Cor. 12:28), is legitimated as a bearer of the Spirit by miracles (II Cor. 12:12; *cf.* Rom. 15:18f.; I Cor. 2:4; I Thess. 1:5; I Pet. 1:12; Heb. 2:4; I Clem. 42:3). *Prophecy and teaching* appear not only within the worship service as momentary gifts to one individual or another; they can also be the permanent possession of certain persons (for both prophets and teachers, see I Cor. 12:28; Eph. 4:11; Acts 13:1; Did. 11–13; for prophets, also Rev.—e.g. 22:9; Herm. mand. XI; for teachers, Jas. 3:1; Barn. 1:8; 4:9; Herm. vis. III 5, 1; mand. IV 3, 1; sim. IX 15, 4; 16, 5; 25, 2). But just as the gifts of prophecy and teaching can be given to any member of the congregation, so can the capacity for special acts, such as *healing and other miracles* (I Cor. 12:8ff., 28ff.). To these, Paul also reckons *gifts of "help" and "administration"* and various kinds of assistance, but that is peculiar to him. It is somewhat different when the officials of the congregation (by virtue of the laying on of hands) are later regarded as bearers of the Spirit. Also peculiar to Paul is the attribution of *ethical* conduct to the Spirit (Gal. 5:22–25; Rom. 8:4); outside of Paul and writings influenced by him ethical conduct is everywhere placed one-sidedly under the imperative. Very strange are the remarks of Herm. sim. IX 13 about the "virgins" who are building the tower of the Church (IX 2ff.); according to IX 15, 2f., they are "virtues," but in IX 13 they are interpreted as "holy spirits" or "as powers of the Son of God." Still, no serious attempt to found ethical conduct upon the Spirit is present here. Still less is that the case in the mandata (esp. mand. V) of Hermas; in them the idea of good powers dwelling in man as "spirits" is only precariously combined with the Christian conception of the Holy Spirit.

To sum up, *a double understanding of pneuma is discernible.* On the one hand, it is the power conferred in baptism which makes the Christian a Christian—a power which already in the present takes him out of this perishing world and "seals" him for the one to come. On the other hand, it is the power given now and again for the occasion to the Christian, enabling him to accomplish extraordinary things. If, now, it is taken seriously that the Spirit given in baptism truly determines Christian existence and is not just "believed in" in the sense that its possession guarantees resurrection or an eternal life, then—until a thinker like Paul takes hold of the problem—*inconsistent and contradictory statements will inevitably arise, because they are inherent in the matter itself.* For the statements which conceive the Spirit as a power given for the occasion and accomplishing extraordinary things are attempts to understand it as the power that determines Christian existence. In this contradiction it comes to

light that the baptized Christian who, as such, belongs to the world
to come, is, in his temporary present existence, not yet what he is to
be and in the sight of God already is, but that his belonging to the
world to come nevertheless determines his present existence. And
in the contradiction that on the one hand the Spirit is the origin of
a new attitude and capacity in the Christian, and on the other hand
that his attitude qualifies him for ever-new endowment with the
Spirit and that he must strive after spiritual gifts, an expression is
provided for the insight that the might of the Spirit is not a magically (mechanically) working power, but is one that equally demands and presupposes a transformation of the will—although this
paradoxical situation is clearly recognized only by Paul (Gal. 5:25).

Now the question arises, however, *how an understanding of existence founded and upheld by the eschatological divine power of
the Spirit will develop.* It is the problem of delimitation from the
world and of eschatological dualism (§ 10, 4 and 5). Insofar as the
Christian's delimitation from and opposition to the world are believed to be founded and guaranteed by the gift of the Spirit and are
so experienced, dangers arise for the Church. If the activity of the
Spirit is seen in special deeds of power which are regarded as unambiguous signs of Spirit endowment, the existence of a Christian is in
danger of being conceived as that of a Hellenistic "divine man"
(θεῖος ἀνήρ), and the eschatological history of salvation comes to be
regarded in the light of edifying legend—a danger which is already
apparent in the New Testament, but which shows its full consequences in the apocryphal acts of the apostles. Simultaneously, the
Spirit-endowed become arrogant, as the exhortations of I Cor. 12 already indicate. But if, instead, the real essence of Christian existence
is held to lie in subjective emotional experiences and the activity of
the Spirit accordingly to be the producing of emotional experiences,
then an individualistic sort of Spirit-endowment will arise which
may, of course, also express itself in deeds of power, but culminates
in ecstasy. Then the Spirit will no longer be understood as the gift
conferred upon the Church, nor will it any longer be the "first-
fruits" or the "guarantee." Rather, eschatological de-secularization
will be interpreted in terms of mysticism. I Cor. 12–14 and II Cor.
especially indicate that these dangers existed. A sense of such a
danger is shown also by the yet unsettled question which the Corinthian church evidently had asked Paul: By what criterion can divine

and demonic ecstasy be distinguished from each other (I Cor. 12:2f.)? In other words, ecstasy is no unambiguous phenomenon in itself.

§ 15. Gnostic Motifs

PRELIMINARY REMARKS

In the Hellenistic world it was a historical necessity that the gospel should be translated into a terminology with which that world was familiar—this gospel of the one true God and of Jesus the Messiah-Son-of-Man with its eschatological message of imminent judgment and salvation, all of which had at first been embodied in the concepts of the Old Testament-Jewish tradition. How the Messiah-Son-of-Man, whose parousia was expected, became the cultically worshiped Kyrios has been shown in § 12. To express convincingly to Hellenistic ears his eschatological meaning and also the whole eschatological message and the eschatological dualism involved in it (§ 10, 5), Gnosticism and its myth offered a stock of terms that were intelligible to great numbers of people. Several times before now we have caught sight of Gnosticism (§ 10, 5; §11, 2a and e; § 12, 3; § 14, 2) and have had to call attention sometimes to its kinship with the Christian message, sometimes to its contrast with it. Here our task is to set forth connectedly the extent to which the understanding of the Christian message in Hellenistic Christianity was unfolded by means of Gnostic terminology.

Such a process does not, in the nature of the case, take place without some effect on the content of the ideas involved. As the development of the Kyrios-cult drew Hellenistic Christianity into *the syncretistic process,* the development, under Gnostic influence, of the doctrine of redemption did so still more. The extent to which that was the case varied greatly in different social levels and different localities; and side by side with positive influence from Gnosticism we also find rejection of it. But sometimes Christianity and Gnosticism combined. On the whole, one could be tempted to term Hellenistic Christianity a syncretistic structure. The only reason one may not do so is that it is not just a conglomerate of heterogeneous materials; in spite of all its syncretism in detail it retains from its origin an inherent drive toward an independent understanding, all its own, of God, world, and man. But the question is: Will this drive triumph and achieve clear form in a genuinely Christian theology? For the time being, all that is necessary here is to set forth the problematical situation and the issues arising therefrom.

1. For Christian missions, *the Gnostic movement* was a competitor of the most serious and dangerous sort because of the far-reaching relatedness between them. For the essence of Gnosticism does not lie in its syncretistic mythology but rather in a new understanding—new in the ancient world—of man and the world; its mythology is only the expression of this understanding. Whereas to ancient man the world had been home—in the Old Testament as God's creation, to classic Greece as the cosmos pervaded by the deity—the *utter difference of human existence from all worldly existence* was recognized for the first time in Gnosticism and Christianity, and thus the world became foreign soil to the human self (§ 10, 4); in fact, in Gnosticism, his prison. Gnostic thought is so radical that to it the impulses of one's own senses, instincts, and desires, by which man is bound to the world, appear alien and hostile—hostile to man's real self, which cannot achieve its own nature in this world at all, and to which this world is a prison in which his real self, related to and derived from the divine world of light, is shackled by the demonic powers of darkness.

To know of the heavenly origin of one's self (not of the "soul"—that would be misleading, for Greek-speaking Gnosticism distinguishes between the real self, the spark of light derived from the divine world and consisting of *pneuma* and the *psyche*, "soul," which, like the "body," is a garment imposed upon the real self by the demonic powers and holding it captive; this "soul" is the worldly vital urge, the urge that is found in the senses, instincts, and the will) to know of one's world-foreignness, the heavenly origin of one's self, and the way of redemption out of this world—*that is the definitive "knowledge," the Gnosis* ("knowledge") which gives the Gnostic movement its name. Salvation is bestowed upon the Gnostic ("knower") who has come to knowledge of himself, of his heavenly home, and of the way back to it, when the self separates at death from body and soul and soars, released, into the heavenly world of light.

This knowledge gives the Gnostic *his consciousness of superiority to the world.* The Gnostic—in whom the spark of heavenly light is alive—is the "spiritual man," the "pneumatic," who disdainfully looks down upon others who do not bear within them the spark of light but are mere "men of soul" (in the derogatory sense, as above), "men of flesh" or "men of matter." ° Conscious of being already emancipated by his *Gnosis*, he demonstrates this freedom either by asceticism or libertinism, or even by a peculiar combination of both. By a meditative contemplation which culminates in ecstasy, he is able even now to enjoy the world of light which he is to enter after death, and he can demonstrate the power of the Spirit that dwells within him by miraculous deeds.

The history of the individual self stands in intimate relation *with that of the entire cosmos*. The individual self is only a spark or fragment of the light-treasure which is held prisoner by the demonic world-rulers in this world of darkness; and its redemption is only a detail of the redemption of all the sparks of light fettered here in prison but united with each other and with their origin by a "kinship of nature" (συγγένεια). Individualistic eschatology—i.e. the doctrine of the emancipation of the individual self at death and of its journey to heaven—stands within the context of a cosmic eschatology—i.e. the doctrine of the emancipation of all the sparks of light and their elevation into the light-world, after which this present world of mingled light and darkness will sink back into the primeval chaos of darkness, and the demonic rulers of the world will be judged.

The Gnostic myth depicts the cosmic drama by which the imprisonment of the sparks of light came about, a drama whose end is already beginning now and will be complete when they are released. The drama's beginning, the tragic event of primeval time, is variously told in the several variants of the myth. But the basic idea is constant: The demonic powers get into their clutches a person who originates in the light-world either because he is led astray by his own foolishness or because he is overcome in battle. The individual selves of the "pneumatics" are none other than the parts or splinters of that light-person. Hence, in their totality they constitute that person—who is frequently called Primal Man—and for whose total redemption they must be released and "gathered together." Inasmuch as the world structure made by the demonic powers will necessarily crash when the sparks of light are withdrawn from it, the

---

° The three-fold division of mankind found in churchly Gnosticism: *pneumatic, psychic, hylic* (or *sarkic*)—men of spirit, soul, matter (or flesh)—is secondary.

demons jealously guard their booty and attempt to stupefy the heavenly selves by the bustle and noise of this world, make them drunk and put them to sleep so as to make them forget their heavenly home.

Redemption comes from the heavenly world. Once more a light-person sent by the highest god, indeed the son and "image" of the most high, comes down from the light-world bringing *Gnosis*. He "wakes" the sparks of light who have sunk into sleep or drunkenness and "reminds" them of their heavenly home. He teaches them concerning their superiority to the world and concerning the attitude they are to adopt toward the world. He dispenses the sacraments by which they are to purify themselves and fan back to life their quenched light-power or at least strengthen its weakened state—by which, in other words, they are "reborn." He teaches them about the heavenly journey they will start at death and communicates to them the secret pass-words by virtue of which they can safely pass through the stations of this journey—past the demonic watchmen of the starry spheres. And going ahead he prepares the way for them, the way which he, the redeemer himself, must also take to be redeemed. For here on earth he does not appear in divine form, but appears disguised in the garment of earthly beings so as not to be recognized by the demons. In so appearing, he takes upon himself the toil and misery of earthly existence and has to endure contempt and persecution until he takes his leave and is elevated to the world of light.

What form the Gnostic religion took in its various groups and congregations, or how, in one place and another, doctrines developed and rites evolved, are secondary questions not to be dealt with here. We have little information—especially for the older period—about *Gnostic congregations*. At any rate the Gnostic movement did take a concrete form in various baptizing sects in the region of the Jordan; these also drew certain Jewish groups into their orbit. The movement evidently attached itself to local cults in the Near East, and in a syncretistic process melted together with them in the form of mystery-congregations; this happened, e.g. when the Gnostic Redeemer was identified with the Phrygian mystery-god, Attis. In this manner the movement also crept into Christian congregations, or the converse also happened—that Gnostic congregations adopted elements of Christianity. But the effect of Gnosticism extends beyond the circle of specifically religious groups: Its ideas were also at work in the speculations of Hellenistic religious philosophy down into neo-Platonism—likewise in the Jewish philosopher of religion, Philo of Alexandria.

2. Insofar as Christian preaching remained true to the tradition cf the Old Testament and Judaism and of the earliest Church, *definitive contrasts between it and Gnosticism* are straightway apparent. In harmony with that tradition the Christian message did by and large hold to the idea that *the world is the creation of the one true God,* and hence that the creator-God and the redeemer-God are *one.* That immediately results in a contrast in *anthropology.* For in the genuinely Christian view, man is, body and soul, the creature of God, and no pre-existent spark of heavenly light—as if that were his real being—is to be distinguished from his psychosomatic existence. Hence, that division between those who bear the spark of light within, the "spiritual ones" (who, Gnostically speaking, are φύσει σωζόμενοι: "by nature saved") and the mere "men of soul" or "men of flesh" who lack the heavenly self, was not considered *a priori* to run through all mankind, though this Gnostic differentiation was taken over in another way (see below). Correspondingly, a contrast in *eschatology* persists almost consistently, insofar as the Christian proclamation does not know the idea of the heavenly journey of the self made possible by Gnosis and sacraments, but does teach the resurrection of the dead and the last judgment. However, the Gospel of John is peculiar in this respect, and in general it must be said that the Christian conception of the reception of the righteous into heaven and the idea of heavenly bliss were strongly influenced by Gnosticism. These differences entail a contrast in *christology,* since Gnosticism cannot acknowledge the real humanity of Jesus. Apparent humanity to a pre-existent heavenly being is only a disguise; and where Gnosticism adapts the Christian tradition to its own use, if it does not insist upon declaring Jesus' flesh and blood to be only seemingly a body, it has to make a distinction between the Redeemer and the historical person Jesus and assert some such thing as that the former was only transiently united with the latter (in the baptism) and left him before the passion.

The struggle against Gnosticism consists in part in mere warnings against "stupid, senseless controversies" (II Tim. 2:23; Tit. 3:9), "disputes about words" (I Tim. 6:4), "myths and genealogies" (I Tim. 1:4; 4:7; II Tim. 4:4; Tit. 1:14; 3:9), "the contradictions of falsely named *Gnosis*" (I Tim. 6:20). In very pale fashion Gnostic teachers are combatted in Herm. sim. VIII 6, 5; IX 19, 2f.; 22, 1ff. But elsewhere there is spirited polemic and controversy against or confutation of specifically Gnostic propositions. Christian congregations evidently first felt the contrast in *eschatology* and *christology*. I Cor. 15, early as that is, is already a great polemic against the gnosticizing party in Corinth which declares, "There is no resurrection of the dead." Paul, one must admit, misunderstands his opponents in attributing to them the view that with death everything is over (I Cor. 15:19, 32). That, of course, was not their view, as the custom of vicarious baptism (15:29) by itself suffices to show; they were only contending against the realistic teaching of the resurrection as contained in the Jewish and primitive-Christian tradition.* This view could also take the form of saying: "the resurrection has already occurred"; i.e. the resurrection doctrine could be spiritualized (II Tim. 2:18; but *cf.* also Jn. 5:24f. and Eph. 5:14).

The detailed proof of the resurrection in I Clem. 23–26 is evidently not occasioned by Gnostic opposition, nor is the refutation of doubt in the parousia, II Pet. 3:1–10, but by doubts of a general nature. On the other hand, those who, according to Pol. Phil. 7:1, deny the resurrection and the judgment are Gnostic teachers; and II Clem. 9:1 also has such in view in the warning: "And let none of you say that this flesh is not judged and does not rise again." The warning emphasis upon the certainty of the parousia in II Clem. 10–12 is probably also motivated by Gnosticism. Later Justin Ap. I 26, 4; Dial. 80, 4; Iren. I 23, 5; II 31, 2 bear witness to the same motivation.

The true humanity of Christ is defended against the Gnostics in I Jn. 2:22; 4:2, 15; 5:1, 5–8; II Jn. 7. I Jn. 5:6 seems to be specifically directed against the Gnostic proposition that the Redeemer, though united with Jesus at his baptism, separated from him before his passion. Similarly Ignatius does battle against the Gnostic christology, which he encounters in the form of the claim that Christ had only a seeming body (Eph. 7:2; 18–20; Mg. 11, Tr. 9f.; Sm. 1–3, 7); Polycarp does the same (Pol. Phil. 7:1).

---

* It appears that in II Cor. 5:1–5, Paul, having been better informed in the meantime, combats the Gnostic view that man's self at death will be released from the body (and from the "soul") and will soar in the state of "nakedness" into the heavenly world.

The contrast in the *doctrine of God and creation*, which constituted a main point for the later opponents of heresy, seems not to have come to the fore at first. The reason for this probably is that Gnosticism first crept into Christian congregations by the mediation of a syncretistic Judaism, a form of Gnosticism, that is, in which this contrast was not prominent. An additional reason may well have been that the Gnostic opinion of the world as it factually is did not greatly differ from the Christian; for both it is true that the world is ruled by Satan and "lieth" utterly "in wickedness" (I Jn. 5:19 KJ). I Jn. 1:5 probably contains polemic against Gnostic teachings which regarded the lower world of darkness as having originated by gradual emanations from the world of light, when it asserts, "God is light and in him is no darkness at all." Jd. 8–11 is unclear because of its merely allusive formulation; it appears to contain polemic against the Gnostic conception of the angel-world as a realm of enemy powers, which, however, are conquered by the Gnostic. It is probably gnosticizing Christians that are castigated in Rev. 2:2, 6, 14–16, 20–24 as "Nicolaitans" and as the (evidently identical) partisans of the prophetess "Jezebel." When these people claim for themselves knowledge of "the deep things of Satan" (Rev. 2:24), probably theogonic and cosmogonic speculations are meant. At any rate I Tim. 4:3–5; Tit. 1:14f. are aimed against Gnosticism's dualistic understanding of the world and the ascetic rules deduced therefrom.

3. Now it must be carefully noted that in all this Gnosticism is combatted not as if it were a foreign, heathen religion into which Christians are in danger of apostatizing. Rather, it is only dealt with so far as it is a *phenomenon within Christianity.* And it is also clear that the Gnostics here opposed by no means regard the Christian congregations as a mission field which they want to convert from Christianity to Gnosticism. Rather, they consider themselves Christians teaching a Christian wisdom—and that is the way they appear to the churches, too. Of course, the Gnostic apostles are regarded as interlopers by the representatives of the old tradition, and the author of Acts makes Paul predict (20:29): "I know that after my departure fierce wolves will come in among you . . ." But v. 30 lets Paul continue: "and from among your own selves will arise men speaking perverse things, to draw away the disciples after them." To Paul the apostles who have kindled a pneumatic-Gnostic movement in Corinth are interlopers, it is true—not, however, interlopers into the

Christian Churches as a whole, but into *his* Church, over which, since
it is of his own founding, he alone has authority. It is perfectly clear
that to the Church they have the standing of *Christian* apostles,
though to Paul they are ministers of Satan "disguising themselves as
apostles of Christ" (II Cor. 11:13). They proclaim Christ, though
according to Paul "another Jesus than the one we preached" (11:4).
In the churches of Ephesus, Pergamum, and Thyatira the false
teachers opposed in Rev. 2 evidently dwell, or dwelt, as recognized
teachers—recognized by a part of the churches, at least—as apostles
and prophets.

Naturally Gnosticism, just like Christianity, is also spread by
wandering teachers. It is against such false teachers coming into a
church from without that II Jn. 10 and Did. 11:2 warn. But in I Jn.
2:19 it is said of the Gnostics: "They went out from us, but they were
not of us; for if they had been of us, they would have continued with
us." The case is no different with the false teachers at Colossae, and
the polemic of the pastorals clearly shows that Gnosticism is an
infra-ecclesiastical phenomenon. The Gnostics are such as have
"fallen" from the faith (I Tim. 4:1; *cf.* 1:6; 6:21; II Tim. 2:18; 3:8);
they are not heathens but "faction-makers" (αἱρετικοί, Tit. 3:10; *cf.*
II Pet. 2:1). The letters of Ignatius and that of Polycarp reveal the
same picture: False teaching is being imported into the churches by
wandering teachers, and the churches are warned against receiving
such teachers (Sm. 4:1; *cf.* Mg. 11). But they are Christian teachers
and their doctrine has its advocates in many a church.

It is clear: Hellenistic Christianity is in the maelstrom of the
syncretistic process; the genuinely Christian element is wrestling
with other elements; "orthodoxy" does not exist at this early period
but is still to develop.

At first, Gnosticism probably penetrated into the Christian congregations mostly through the medium of a Hellenistic Judaism that
was itself in the grip of syncretism. The Gnostic Spirit-enthusiasts
whom Paul opposes at Corinth are of Jewish origin (II Cor. 11:22).
Whether the false teachings advanced in Colossae are also derived
from a syncretistic Judaism, is not quite certain (*cf.* Col. 2:11, 14
and espec. 2:16). But in the case of the pastorals it is probably a
Jewish-Christian Gnosticism that is involved (I Tim. 1:7; Tit. 1:10,
14). Ignatius polemizes against Ἰουδαϊσμός (Mg. 8–11; Phld. 6–9)
"Judaism," but since its representatives are evidently identical with

the opponents elsewhere inveighed against in his letters, it must be a Jewish-Christian Gnosticism that is meant by the term. Hence, it is doubly conceivable that Gnosticism could be regarded not as a heathen faith, but as a form of Christianity.

4. Now we must ask: In what manner did Gnosticism's thought, myth, and terminology influence Christian thinking and contribute to the development of Christian theological language?

a. It did so first of all by *further developing the concept of eschatological dualism* by carrying the latter beyond the dimensions of history-of-salvation thinking into those of cosmological thinking— or, better expressed, by further developing *cosmological thinking* in a more consistent manner. For even in Jewish eschatology, hopes for the future had already reached cosmic scope under the influence of Persian and Babylonian mythology, which were the sources of mythological thinking for Gnosticism also. It was from this influence that the differentiation between this age or world (עוֹלָם הַזֶּה, αἰών οὗτος) and the age or world to come (עוֹלָם הַבָּא, αἰών μέλλων) was derived—terms that were still unknown to the Old Testament. In this view, the forces that threaten Israel in the present are only superficially foreign nations or world empires; back of these are demonic powers or Satan himself. Accordingly, not revolutions on the plane of history (as is still the case in Deutero-Isaiah in spite of all its miraculous details) but a cosmic catastrophe will usher in the time of salvation, and the resurrection of the dead and the judgment of the world will bring the great change about. Here the judgment of the world is conceived as a "forensic" act—the act of a Judge in court—while the Old Testament (with the exception of Daniel and the late passage·Is. 24-27, in which for the first time the ideas of cosmological eschatology occur) thinks of the judgment as taking place in the course of historical events. The figure of the Davidic king who was to appear in the time of salvation was more or less replaced by the figure of the Son of Man who was to come from heaven as the judge and salvation-bringer (§ 7, 5). The colors of the national political ideal had more or less faded in the popular conception of the time of salvation. The opinion that this world is the sinister stamping-ground of Satan—who in this role is still unknown to the Old Testament—and of his demonic hordes had spread abroad. And though the belief that the world had been created by

God was retained in accord with Old Testament tradition, that could be done only with a certain inconsistency. And if the difficulty was in a measure cleared up in apocalypticism by attributing to Adam's fall the consequence (still unknown to the Old Testament) of having brought upon Adamitic man and "this Aeon" the curse of sin, distress, and death, probably Gnostic ideas had already influenced this solution.

Under Gnostic influence such views could not help being further developed in Hellenistic Christianity. That is already quite apparent even in Paul; only it cannot be determined how much of this he may have brought along out of his Jewish past and how much Gnosticism may have influenced him at a later period.

It is Gnostic language when Satan is called "the god of this world" (αἰῶνος) (II Cor. 4:4), the "ruler of this world" (Jn. 12:31; 14:30; 16:11), "the prince of the power of the air" (Eph. 2:2), or "the ruler of this Aeon" (Ign. Eph. 19:1). Both in name and meaning "the rulers of this age" who brought "the Lord of glory" to the cross (I Cor. 2:6, 8) are figures of Gnostic mythology—viz. those demonic world-rulers who are also meant by the terms "angels," "principalities," "authorities," "powers" (Rom. 8:38f.; I Cor. 15:24, 26; Col. 1:16; 2:10, 15; Eph. 1:21; 3:10; 6:12; I Pet. 3:22) and are at least included in the "many gods and many lords" of I Cor. 8:4. As in Gnosticism, they are conceived to be in essence star-spirits; as such they are called "elemental spirits of the universe" (Gal. 4:3, 9; cf. Col. 2:8, 20) who govern the elapse and division of time (Gal. 4:10). Also Gnostic are the "world rulers of this present darkness" and the "spiritual hosts of wickedness in the heavenly places" (i.e. in the region of air, the lower sphere of the firmament, Eph. 6:12).

Aside from the terms for mythological figures, the *terminology* in which dualism is expressed shows extensive Gnostic influence. This is most apparent in John, whose language is governed by the antithesis "light—darkness." But the rest of the New Testament also knows this contrast (Rom. 13:12; I Thess. 5:4f.; II Cor. [6:14]; Col. 1:12f.; Eph. 5:8ff.; 6:12; I Pet. 2:9; cf. I Clem. 36:2; II Clem. 1:4; Barn. 14:5f.; 18:1; Ign. Rom. 6:2; Phld. 2:1). In this category also belongs the use of "truth" (and its opposite, "falsehood") to denote true (divine) reality in contrast to the seeming reality of the earthly. Here again this usage gives John its peculiar stamp—especially the related use of the adjective "true" (ἀληθινός), which occurs in this sense not only in John but also in Hebrews (8:2; 9:24). Hebrews expresses this same contrast in the antithesis "heavenly" (8:5; 9:23) as opposed to the earthly "shadow" (8:5; 10:1; *cf.* Col. 2:17) or to the "earthly" (9:1).

b. Gnostic mythology lies behind the allusion to the *fall of creation* in Rom. 8:20ff., which, because of its allusiveness, is difficult to explain in detail. According to it, creation "was subjected to futility" and has fallen into "bondage to decay," under which it groans in expectation of release. Rom. 5:12ff. interprets Adam's fall quite in keeping with Gnosticism, as bringing (sin and) death upon mankind; I Cor. 15:21, 44-49 goes even further when it derives Adamitic man's plight from his inborn quality of Adam, who, without any reference to his fall, is ψυχικός and χοϊκός—a man of mere "soul," not spirit (see § 14, 2) and "a man of dust." The contrast "psychic–pneumatic" ("man of soul"–"man of Spirit") to designate two basically different classes of men—a contrast which can be explained neither from Greek usage nor from the Old Testament but only from Gnostic anthropology—is an especially clear indication that Paul's anthropological concepts had already been formed under the influence of Gnosticism (I Cor. 2:14f.; 15:44-46; see further: Jas. 3:15; Jd. 19). It is likewise a piece of Gnostic thinking when Jn. 8:44 attributes enmity to Jesus to the descent of the unbelieving from the arch-liar, the devil. In fully Gnostic fashion those who are "of the devil" (Jn. 8:44; I Jn. 3:8)—or are "of the evil one" (I Jn. 3:12), "from below" (Jn. 8:23), "of this world" (Jn. 8:23 and elsewhere), or "of the earth" (Jn. 3:31)—are contrasted with those who are "from God" (Jn. 7:17; 8:47), "of the truth" (Jn. 18:37), "from above" (Jn. 8:23), or are "begotten of God" (I Jn. 2:29; 3:9; 4:7; 5:1).

Thus, Gnostic mythology serves to characterize *man's situation in the world* as a life which by its origin is destined for destruction, a life that is prone to be ruled by demonic powers. Paul even ventures in his polemic against Jewish legalism to contradict his basic view that the Torah comes from God (Rom. 7:12, 14) by appropriating the Gnostic proposition that on the contrary it was given by subordinate angel-powers (Gal. 3:19).

Correspondingly, the *terminology of parenesis* is to a large extent Gnostic when—in connection with the concepts "light" and "darkness"—it says that men have "fallen asleep" or are "drunk" and must be "awakened" or be "sober" (Rom. 13:11-13; I Thess. 5:4-6; I Cor.

15:34; 16:13; Col. 4:2; Eph. 5:14; II Tim. 2:26; 4:5; I Pet. 1:13; 5:8;
Ign. Sm. 9:1; Pol. 1:3; 2:3; II Clem. 13:1—though, of course,
γρηγορεῖν, "be awake" or "watch," is also already found in the
Jewish-Christian tradition: Mk. 13:35; Rev. 3:2f.; Did. 16:1, etc.).
The hymn (a fragment) in Eph. 5:14 is cast quite in Gnostic
terms:

> "Awake, O sleeper,
> And rise from the dead,
> And Christ shall give you light."

c. But most of all the Gnostic stock of concepts served to clarify
the history of salvation. According to these concepts the Redeemer
appears as a cosmic figure, the pre-existent divine being, Son of the
Father (§ 12, 3), who came down from heaven and assumed human
form and who, after his activity on earth, was exalted to heavenly
glory and wrested sovereignty over the spirit-powers to himself. It is
in this conception of him that he is praised in the pre-Pauline Christ-
hymn which is quoted in Phil. 2:6–11. This "mythos" is also briefly
alluded to in II Cor. 8:9. The Gnostic idea that Christ's earthly garment of flesh was the disguise in consequence of which the world-
rulers failed to recognize him—for if they had recognized him, they
would not have brought about their own defeat by causing his crucifixion—lurks behind I Cor. 2:8. Further on, it will be indicated
how the Gnostic Redeemer-myth of the incarnation of the pre-
existent Son, and of his exaltation, by which he prepares the way for
his own into the world of light, provides the terminology for the
christology of John.

The descent and re-ascent of the Redeemer is the subject of Eph.
4:8–10. The expression, "descended into the lower parts of the
earth," does not mean the descent into Hell, but corresponds to "he
ascended" and means the pre-existent Son's journey to earth. And
the idea that he conquered the inimical spirit-powers by his journey
to heaven the author finds expressed in the words of the Psalter
(68:19): "When he ascended on high he led a host of captives"
(Eph. 4:8). That the exalted Lord won dominion over the realm of
the cosmic powers, is also said in Col. 2:15: "He (God) disarmed
the principalities and powers and made a public example of them,
triumphing over them in him (Christ)." So, according to I Pet. 3:22,

also, Christ's ascent to heaven is simultaneously the act of subjugating the demonic world-rulers; and 2:19f., whose original meaning * no more deals with the descent into Hell than does Eph. 4:9, follow the Gnostic myth, according to which the prison of the dead is not in the interior of the earth but in the region of the air, where the spirits of the stars, or of the firmament, keep them confined. This cosmic event is very briefly alluded to in Jn. 12:31: "Now is the judgment of this world, now shall the ruler of this world be cast out" (cf. 16:10f.). These words are spoken by Jesus as he prepares to go to his passion, which for John, however, means nothing less than his "exaltation" (12:32) or "glorification" (12:28).

Hence the whole cosmos—heavenly, earthly, and subterranean beings—must pay homage to the exalted "Lord" (Phil. 2:10f.). Thereby, God has appointed an end for the cosmic disorder which originated in the primeval fall and through him has "reconciled all things" (i.e. the universe) to Himself, as the hymn underlying Col. 1:20 says—a hymn which the author has rather strongly accommodated to the Christian tradition by his editing of it. The cosmic "peace" bestowed by the work of salvation is still more radically Christianized in Eph. 2:14ff., which interprets the "dividing wall of hostility," which according to the Gnostic myth divides the earthly from the heavenly world, as applying both to the enmity between Jew and Gentile (v. 14) and to the enmity between God and man (v. 16). Hebrews also follows the Gnostic Redeemer-myth: The pre-existent Son, who is here termed "the effulgence of the glory of God" and "the very stamp of his (God's) character" (1:3) in keeping with the Gnostic "image"-idea, abased himself (2:9) in becoming man and then was exalted above the angels; 1:5 applies to the enthronement of the exalted Redeemer. But here the figure is modified in the direction of Jewish-Christian eschatology by postponing the subjection of the total cosmos to him until the future parousia (1:6; 2:8). The myth is also contained in the lines of the hymn found at I Tim. 3:16:

---

* A Christ-hymn underlies I Pet. 3:18–22 (as in the case of Col. 1:15–20). As I Pet. 4:6 shows, the author of this epistle understood 3:19 as referring to the descent into Hell, a subject that is later treated in Ign. Mg. 9:3 and Herm. sim. IX 16, 5–7. On I Pet. 3:18–22 see R. Bultmann, *Coniectanea Neotestamentica* XI (1949), 1–14; on Col. 1:15–20 see E. Käsemann, *Bultmann-Festschrift* (1949), 133–148.

"Who was manifested in the flesh,
Vindicated in the Spirit
Seen by angels . . .
Taken up in glory."

What is here hinted at is more extensively expressed in Ign. Eph.
19. Here we encounter again the motif that "the Prince of this
world" is deceived. From him the "three mysteries of a cry" were
kept hidden: the virginity of Mary, her giving birth, and the death
of "the Lord." His death is followed by his glorious manifestation
to the "Aeons" (by this Gnostic term the cosmic powers are here
called; Lake translates misleadingly) as he triumphantly ascends on
high—a drama whose goal and end is the destruction of "the old
kingdom" (viz. that of the "Aeons" and of their Prince). Christ's
passion and cross are conceived as a cosmic event by Ignatius, partly
in Gnostic terms, partly in polemic against them.

d. For believers the cosmic triumph of Christ means *emancipation from the demonic world-rulers,* from sin, and especially from
death; hence the declaration that "the resurrection has already
occurred" (II Tim. 2:18; see p. 169 above) is comprehensible. In
this connection the Gnostic idea is frequently utilized that the Redeemer by his ascent has prepared the way through the spheres of
the spirit powers into the heavenly world. The exalted Redeemer
will draw after himself his own (Jn. 12:32); he is, himself, the "way"
(Jn. 14:6). The idea is expressed in Hebrews by the term "pioneer"
(ἀρχηγός, 2:10; 12:2, *cf.* Acts 3:15; 5:31; II Clem. 20:5—same word
in all five cases). Christ is the pioneer-guide to heaven; being, himself, "made perfect" by attaining heaven (τελειωθείς, 2:10, 5:9), he
is also the "perfecter" (τελειωτής, 12:2) of his own. However, Hebrews re-interprets the Gnostic idea of the self's ascent to its heavenly "resting-place" (κατάπαυσις) into the idea that the People of
God on earth is on pilgrimage to its heavenly home (3:7–4:11).

The Gnostic teaching of the "kinship" between the Redeemer
and the redeemed by virtue of their mutual heavenly origin is so
applied by Hebrews that the redeemed appear as brothers of the
Redeemer (2:11f., 17), though they can also be called his children,
since he has the priority. In the same sense, Paul calls the exalted
Lord "the first-born among many brethren" (Rom. 8:29). Paul expresses Christ's meaning as Redeemer especially by paralleling him,

as "the last Adam," with the (fallen) Primal Man Adam. As Adamitic man in his earthly-unspiritual (ψυχικός) nature, in his servitude to Death, is determined by Adam, so those who believe in Christ are determined by Christ, and that means by Spirit and Life. However, in so speaking, Paul does not draw the consistent Gnostic conclusion that "the resurrection has already occurred," but champions, instead, the old realistic resurrection-hope against the gnosticizing Corinthians; but in so doing, he gets into the difficulty of having to work out a paradoxical concept of Life—a life that is already present reality and yet is still future (Rom. 5; see §§ 18, 29). John, however, gives up the old realistic eschatology of the future parousia, resurrection, and last judgment.*

The Gnostic notion of the pre-existence of souls (or rather, thinking gnostically, the pre-existence of human selves) was, by and large, given up in the Christian congregations, and likewise the related idea of those who are "by nature saved," i.e. the idea that redemption has its foundation in a kinship between Redeemer and redeemed which antedates the decision of faith. But it recurs in John with a new interpretation when believers are held to be the ἴδιοι of the incarnate Logos ("his own," Jn. 1:11; supply: people, or relatives) whom he calls to himself and who hear and know his voice (Jn. 10) because they are "of the truth" (18:37b).

e. Hebrews takes *the Gnostic idea* that all "men of Spirit" who are delimited from the world *constitute a unity* (§ 10, 5) and combines it with the Old Testament-Jewish tradition of the People of God (besides 3:7–4:11, see 13:12–14). But Paul explains the inner unity of believers with each other and with the Redeemer by using the Gnostic term "body" (i.e. in the phrase "body of Christ," Rom. 12:4f.; I Cor. 12:12–27; also I Cor. 6:15–17) and in so doing very materially determines *the development of the Church-concept*.

Stimulated by Paul but also influenced, themselves, by Gnostic tradition, the authors of Colossians and Ephesians further developed this idea. Especially in Colossians the originally mythological or cosmological nature of the "body" concept of the Church is apparent. In Col. 1:15–20, the author builds upon a hymn which originally was in praise of the cosmic rank of Christ and understood the "body" whose "head" is Christ to be the cosmos, while the author interprets

---

* In the text that has come down to us churchly editing has "corrected" John by re-introducing the realistic eschatology; on this point, see Vol. II.

the "body" as the "Church" (by means of the addition in v. 18 and again in v. 24), thereby giving "the Church"—quite in keeping with Gnosticism—the character of a cosmic entity.

The same thing can be perceived in Ephesians. Here, however, in order to express Christ's relation to the Church, not only the "head" concept is used but also the Gnostic idea of the "divine marriage" (συζυγία): the Church is the bride, or the wife, of Christ (Eph. 5:25ff.; espec. 29–32).°

Though the idea this suggests—that the Church is pre-existent— is not expressed in this Ephesians passage—in fact, there may even be polemic against it in the emphatic words of v. 32: "but *I* mean . . ."—the author of II Clem. does draw this conclusion, speaking of "the first, the spiritual Church which was created before sun and moon" and "was made manifest at the end of days." The "body of Christ" (II Clem. 14:1f.) for him is the pre-existent Church.

In Hermas likewise (vis. II 4, 1) the Church, appearing in the guise of an old woman, is pre-existent: "she was created first of all things . . . and for her sake [or: through her] was the cosmos established." But the divine-marriage idea is not present here, and the "body" concept is only faintly echoed when the unity of the Church is described with the expression "one spirit and one body" (sim. IX 13, 5 and 7; cf. 17, 5; 18, 4). It is a Gnostic motif that is used when the virgins who are building the tower of the Church are called "holy spirits" and "powers of the Son of God" (sim. IX 13, 2); both the number of the virgins (seven in vis. III 8; nine in sim. IX 12ff.) and the description of the tower also betray the originally cosmological meaning of this presentation.† No very strong Gnostic influences affected the vague ecclesiological and christological arguments of Hermas.

The Gnostic myth also influenced the view of the Church found in Ignatius. The Church is the "body of Christ" (Sm. 1:2); he is its "head" (Tr. 11:2); Christians are "Christ's members" (Eph. 4:2; Tr. 11:2). Just as in the Gnostic myth the occurrence of salvation culminates in the gathering together of the sparks of light and their

° This conception is scarcely behind so early a passage as II Cor. 11:2, where the Corinthian church is regarded under the figure of the bride of Christ. It is more plausible at Rev. 19:7; 21:2, but there, too, it is doubtful.

† See Käsemann, *Leib und Leib Christi,* 85f.; Dibelius, *excursus on Hermas* vis. II 4, 1; III 2, 4; sim. V 6, 7 in the supplement to Lietzmann's *Handbuch,* IV, 451f., 459f., 572–575.

union into that figure of light, Primal Man, so for Ignatius the "unification" (ἕνωσις, or ἑνότης, "unity") of the Church is the goal that God had promised (Tr. 11:2; *cf.* Eph. 5:1; Pol. 8:3), and this "unification" is the constant refrain of his exhortation (Eph. 4:2; Mg. 7:2; Pol. 1:2); it is at the same time "unification" with Christ (Mg. 1:2; 13:2; Phld. 4:1). The concept of the divine marriage does not occur, for the statement that Christ "loved" the Church (Pol. 5:1) is probably a reminiscence of canonical Eph. 5:25, 29.

f. To come from polytheism to faith in the one true God was called "to come to knowledge of the truth" (§ 9, 2)—emancipating knowledge was a thing the Christian and the Gnostic had in common, and the Christian preacher could say in Gnostic terminology: "You will know the truth, and the truth will make you free" (Jn. 8:32). Paul in place of "faith" could speak of the "knowledge" which surpasses all that he once held to be gain ("the surpassing worth of *knowing* Christ Jesus," Phil. 3:8) and could set as his goal: to "be found in him" and to "*know* him and the power of his resurrection . . ." (Phil. 3:9f.). It is no wonder, then, that Christian and Gnostic zeal for "knowledge" united, and that in Corinth an eagerness after "knowledge" was unleashed (I Cor. 1:18). Nor is it any wonder that pride flourished over the fact that "we (all) have knowledge" (I Cor. 8:1ff.). Neither is it surprising that the Christian consciousness of delimitation from the world and of superiority over unbelievers should have taken on the Gnostic form of claiming to be "men of Spirit," because possessed of a higher nature, and hence of looking down upon mere "men of soul" (ψυχικοί) or "the weak" (ἀσθενεῖς). All this is the less to be wondered at because of the Christian awareness of possessing the Spirit through baptism (§ 13, 1).

This consciousness flaunted itself not only in the phenomena of enthusiasm and ecstasy (§ 14, 3) within the meeting of the congregation but also and especially in the genuinely Gnostic claim to have "*liberty*" and "*authority*," on the strength of which the "man of Spirit" disdained to be bound to the concrete ecclesiastical fellowship (I Cor. 8:1ff.) and also made light of being bound morally—"all things are lawful to me" (I Cor. 6:12ff.; *cf.* 10:23). In the struggle against false teachers, the accusation of immorality (Pastorals; Jd.; II Pet.; Herm. sim. V 7, 1ff.) and lovelessness (I Jn.) became so stereotyped that one cannot always be certain that it is a libertinism with a genuinely Gnostic basis that is meant. Yet precisely out of the conventionality of such accusations it follows that such libertinism had its representatives in Christian circles. How this consciousness of being a "knower" (i.e. a Gnostic) results in getting "puffed up" (I Cor. 4:6, 18f.; 5:2; 8:1) is shown by II Cor. 10–13: It causes men to "boast," to judge others arrogantly and to regard their own manifestations of "pneumatic" power as proof of their superiority to the Apostle, who only pursues his task "in weakness."

But Paul himself, obviously, also regards the Gnostic terminology as the appropriate form of expression for the Christian understanding of existence. He indicates this not merely by referring to the "knowledge" that is his foundation. Rather, being himself a *pneumatikos* (man of Spirit), he considers himself also to have at his disposal a "wisdom" which penetrates into the mysteries of the divine wisdom, "the deep things of God" (I Cor. 2:6ff. KJ). He feels himself exempted from others' judgment while he, as one who has the "mind (= Spirit) of Christ," has the right to judge others (I Cor. 2:15f.). He accepts not only the proposition that "we (all) have knowledge" (I Cor. 8:1) but also that "all things are lawful (to me)" (I Cor. 6:12; 10:23)—though with a specifically Christian correction, it is true (see below). He is just as proud of his "liberty" and "authority" as the Gnostics are—recognizing, however, the paradoxical character of this liberty (I Cor. 9:1–23). He declares himself to be "not in the least inferior to these superlative apostles" (II Cor. 11:5; *cf.* 10:3–5, 8; 13:3, 10)—pointing out, nevertheless, the paradoxicality of Christian "boasting" (II Cor. 11:16ff.; 12:1ff.). He belongs to the "mature" or "perfect" (τέλειοι, Phil. 3:15; *cf.* I Cor. 2:6)—but immediately assures the reader "Not that I have already obtained or am already perfect" (Phil. 3:12).

g. Undoubtedly, the Gnostic myth and its terminology offered the possibility of elucidating the eschatological occurrence as one inaugurated by the history of Jesus Christ and now at work in the present in process of consummation, and the possibility of comprehending the Church and the individual as placed in the grand context of a process of disaster and salvation. But the question now is whether this cosmic occurrence is to be understood as only a sublime process of nature which takes place by-passing, so to say, my conduct, my responsibility, my decisions—a process which has me at its mercy for better or for worse. *Will human history be conceived as natural process, or as genuine historical happening?* Is *Gnosis* only a speculative knowledge that exists alongside of all other knowledge and points of view, a knowledge the possession of which reassures me concerning my future after death? Or is it a genuine understanding of myself which dominates and determines my life in its every manifestation, especially in my conduct? Undoubtedly Gnosticism's intent is such an understanding of one's self; that is what comes to expression in the Gnostic consciousness of "liberty" and "authority." But the question is whether this liberty is to be conceived *as the liberty of responsibly existing man—man living, that is, in responsibility to and for his actual existence*—or whether it is to be conceived as man's withdrawal from his real existence. If it is to be conceived in the latter way, then, since such withdrawal is fundamentally impossible, man's "liberty" becomes a mere assertion or a meaningless theorem. In other words, the question is whether or not the paradoxical character of "liberty" is recognized. Or, asked in still another way, this is the question whether the state of being *pneumatikos* (a man of Spirit) is to be understood as if that were a quality of nature, or whether that state is kept in existence by an ever-repeated responsible decision because of the fact that the possibility of being *sarkikos* (a man determined by flesh), in accord with genuine existence in true history, continues to exist. Only in the latter case is liberty genuinely understood as liberty. Wherever this is not the case, the consequence will either be asceticism, which strives either to demonstrate or anxiously to preserve the "pneumatic" quality of liberty, or it will be libertinism, which either strives to demonstrate "liberty" or uses it as a pretext. Failure to recognize the reality of human existence in actual history involves a non-paradoxical misunderstanding of one's possession of the Spirit and of the liberty it brings, and this misunderstanding carries with it the surrender of the *idea of creation*. But retaining both the idea of the world as creation and the idea of de-secularization (Ent*welt*lichung—inward divorce from the world) through participation in the eschatological occurrence must establish such a dialectic (paradoxical) relation to the world as will be expressed in Paul's "as if . . . not" (I Cor. 7:29ff.). This Gnostic failure to recognize true human existence as fulfilling itself in one's actual history leads also to a non-historical interpretation of the "kinship" idea—

i.e. to a misconception of what *fellowship in the Church* is. Under this misconception, "knowledge" (γνῶσις) seeks its culmination in "de-historizing" ecstasy (i.e. an ecstasy which divorces its subject from his concrete existence) instead of finding it in the *Agape* which is its perfect realization—its genuine demonstration in the knower's actual history.

PART TWO

THE THEOLOGY OF PAUL

§ 16. The Historical Position of Paul

The historical position of Paul may be stated as follows: Standing within the frame of Hellenistic Christianity he raised the theological motifs that were at work in the proclamation of the Hellenistic Church to the clarity of theological thinking; he called to attention the problems latent in the Hellenistic proclamation and brought them to a decision; and thus—so far as our sources permit an opinion on the matter—became the founder of Christian theology.

Paul originated in Hellenistic Judaism; his home was Tarsus in Cilicia (Acts 9:11; 21:39; 22:3). There, without doubt, he received his first training in the rabbinic scriptural learning to which his letters bear witness. According to Acts 22:3 he is said also to have been a pupil of Gamaliel (the Elder) in Jerusalem; but the correctness of this information is debated and (in the light of Gal. 1:22) is at least doubtful. At any rate, in his home city he came into contact with Hellenistic culture and became acquainted with popular philosophy and the phenomena of religious syncretism. It remains uncertain, however, to what extent he had already appropriated in his pre-Christian period theological ideas of this syncretism (those of the mystery-religions and of Gnosticism) which come out in his Christian theology.

Not having been a personal disciple of Jesus, *he was won to the Christian faith by the kerygma of the Hellenistic Church.* The question thrust upon him by this kerygma was whether he was willing to regard the crucified Jesus of Nazareth, whom the kerygma asserted to have risen from the dead, as the expected Messiah. But for Paul, the fervent champion (ζηλωτής) of the traditions of the fathers (Gal. 1:14), straightway recognizing how basically the Torah was called into question by the Hellenistic mission, that meant whether he was willing to acknowledge in the cross of Christ God's judgment upon his self-understanding up to that time—i.e. God's condemnation of his Jewish striving after righteousness by fulfilling the works of the Law. After he had first indignantly rejected this question and become a persecutor of the Church, at his conversion he submitted to this judgment of God.

[187]

For just this is what his conversion meant: In it he surrendered his previous understanding of himself; i.e. he surrendered what had till then been the norm and meaning of his life, he sacrificed what had hitherto been his pride and joy (Phil. 3:4–7). His conversion was not the result of an inner moral collapse (which it is frequently assumed to have been on the basis of a misinterpretation of Rom. 7:7ff. as autobiographical confession). It was not rescue from the despair into which the cleavage between willing and doing had allegedly driven him. His was not a conversion of repentance; neither, of course, was it one of emancipating enlightenment. Rather, it was obedient submission to the judgment of God, made known in the cross of Christ, upon all human accomplishment and boasting. It is as such that his conversion is reflected in his theology.

His conversion brought him into the Hellenistic Church; it was in Hellenistic territory that he was soon working as a missionary in company with another Hellenistic missionary, Barnabas, who had sought him out and taken him to Antioch to collaborate with him (Acts 11:25f.). In company with him, Paul was the advocate of Hellenistic Christianity against the Palestinian Church at the "apostolic council" (§ 8, 2), and in company with him he undertook the so-called "first missionary journey" (Acts 13–14).

After his conversion he made no effort toward contact with Jesus' disciples or the Jerusalem Church for instruction concerning Jesus and his ministry. On the contrary, he vehemently protests his independence from them in Gal. 1–2. And, in fact, his letters barely show traces of the influence of Palestinian tradition concerning the history and preaching of Jesus. All that is important for him in the story of Jesus is the fact that Jesus was born a Jew and lived under the Law (Gal. 4:4) and that he had been crucified (Gal. 3:1; I Cor. 2:2; Phil. 2:5ff., etc.). When he refers to Christ as an example, he is thinking not of the historical but of the pre-existent Jesus (Phil. 2:5ff.; II Cor. 8:9; Rom. 15:3). He quotes "words of the Lord" only at I Cor. 7:10f. and 9:14, and in both cases they are regulations for church life. It is possible that echoes of words of the Lord are present in Paul's parenesis; e.g. Rom. 12:14 (Mt. 5:44); 13:9f. (Mk. 12:31); 16:19 (Mt. 10:16); I Cor. 13:2 (Mk. 11:23). The tradition of the Jerusalem Church is at least in substance behind the "word of the Lord" on the parousia and resurrection in I Thess. 4:15–17, though it is not certain whether Paul is here quoting a traditionally transmitted saying, or whether he is appealing to a revelation accorded to him by the exalted Lord. But of decisive importance in this connection is the fact that Paul's theology proper, with its theological, anthropological, and soteriological ideas, is not at all a recapitulation of Jesus' own preaching nor a further development of it, and it is especially significant that he never adduces any of the sayings of Jesus on the Torah in favor of his own teaching about the Torah. The concept, Reign of God, which was basic for the message preached by Jesus has lost its dominant position in Paul and occurs only at Rom. 14:17; I Cor. 4:20; 6:9f.; 15:50; Gal. 5:21 (*cf*. I Thess. 2:12); neither does Paul's description of the essence of salvation as "the righteousness of God" have a parallel in Jesus' preaching.

In relation to the preaching of Jesus, the theology of Paul is a new structure, and that indicates nothing else than that Paul has his place within Hellenistic Christianity. The so often and so passionately debated question, "Jesus and Paul," is at bottom the question: Jesus and Hellenistic Christianity.

But merely to recognize this historical fact does not in itself, of course, decide anything about the relation in content between Paul's theology and Jesus' message. This question, however, cannot be set forth and answered in advance, but must be developed and answered in the presentation of Paul's theology itself.

CHAPTER IV

Man Prior to the Revelation of Faith

PRELIMINARY REMARKS

1. As sources for Paul's theology only the undoubtedly genuine letters of Paul may serve: Rom., I–II Cor., Gal., Phil., I Thess., Phlm.

2. Paul did not theoretically and connectedly develop his thoughts concerning God and Christ, the world and man in an independent scientific treatise as a Greek philosopher or a modern theologian. He only developed them fragmentarily (except in Romans), always broaching them in his letters for a specific and actual occasion. Even in Romans, where he expresses them connectedly and with a degree of completeness, he does so in a letter and under the compulsion of a concrete situation. These facts must not be allowed to lead one to the false conclusion that Paul was not a real theologian, nor to the notion that to understand his individuality he must be regarded, instead, as a hero of piety. On the contrary! The way in which he reduces specific acute questions to a basic theological question, the way in which he reaches concrete decisions on the basis of fundamental theological considerations, shows that what he thinks and says grows out of his basic theological position—the position which is more or less completely set forth in Romans.

Nevertheless, this basic position is not a structure of theoretical thought. It does not take the phenomena which encounter man and man himself whom they encounter and build them into a system, a distantly perceived *kosmos* (system), as Greek science does. Rather, Paul's theological thinking only lifts the knowledge inherent in faith itself into the clarity of conscious knowing. A relation to God that is only feeling, only "piety," and not also a knowledge of God and man together is for Paul unthinkable. The act of faith is simultaneously an act of knowing, and, correspondingly, theological knowing cannot be separated from faith.

Therefore, Pauline theology is not a speculative system. It deals

[190]

with God not as He is in Himself but only with God as He is significant for man, for man's responsibility and man's salvation. Correspondingly, it does not deal with the world and man as they are in themselves, but constantly sees the world and man in their relation to God. Every assertion about God is simultaneously an assertion about man and vice versa. For this reason and in this sense Paul's theology is, at the same time, anthropology. But since God's relation to the world and man is not regarded by Paul as a cosmic process oscillating in eternally even rhythm, but is regarded as constituted by God's acting in history and by man's reaction to God's doing, therefore every assertion about God speaks of what He does with man and what He demands of him. And, the other way around, every assertion about man speaks of God's deed and demand—or about man as he is qualified by the divine deed and demand and by his attitude toward them. The christology of Paul likewise is governed by this point of view. In it, Paul does not speculatively discuss the metaphysical essence of Christ, or his relation to God, or his "natures," but speaks of him as the one through whom God is working for the salvation of the world and man. Thus, every assertion about Christ is also an assertion about man and vice versa; and Paul's christology is simultaneously soteriology.

Therefore, Paul's theology can best be treated as his doctrine of man: first, of man prior to the revelation of faith, and second, of man under faith, for in this way the anthropological and soteriological orientation of Paul's theology is brought out. Such a presentation presupposes, since theological understanding has its origin in faith, that man prior to the revelation of faith is so depicted by Paul as he is retrospectively seen from the standpoint of faith.

A. THE ANTHROPOLOGICAL CONCEPTS

PRELIMINARY REMARK

Paul, of course, did not draw up a scientific anthropology as if to describe man as a phenomenon in the realm of the objectively perceptible world. He sees man always in his relation to God. Still, it is in relation to God that he sees all that is or happens, and in this respect man has nothing to distinguish him from other beings. What, then, is the specifically human—that which gives man's relation to God its peculiar character? Precisely for the sake of understanding this relation, it is necessary that we clarify for ourselves the peculiarity of human existence, i.e. the formal structures of this existence.

§ 17. "Soma" (Body)

The most comprehensive term which Paul uses to characterize man's existence is *soma*, body; it is also the most complex and the understanding of it is fraught with difficulty. That *soma* belongs inseparably, constitutively, to human existence is most clearly evident from the fact that Paul cannot conceive even of a future human existence after death "when that which is perfect is come" as an existence without *soma*—in contrast to the view of those in Corinth who deny the resurrection (I Cor. 15, especially vv. 35ff.). However, the resurrection body will no longer be a body of flesh (I Cor. 15:50), not a "physical" (ψυχικόν) body or one of "dust" (I Cor. 15:44–49), but a "spiritual" (πνευματικόν) body, a "body of glory" (Phil. 3:21; *cf*. II Cor. 3:18). Hence, it was natural for interpreters to conceive *soma* to mean the body-form which could be stamped upon various materials—of fleshly or spiritual kind; and I Cor. 15:35ff. was a downright temptation so to conceive it. But it is a methodological error to choose this passage as the point of departure for the interpretation of *soma*; for in it Paul lets himself be misled into adopting his opponents' method of argumentation, and in so doing he uses the *soma*-concept in a way not characteristic of him elsewhere. In these verses only the underlying idea is genuinely Pauline: The only human existence that there is—even in the sphere of Spirit—is somatic existence; but the use of *soma* as "form," "shape" is un-Pauline. This is at once apparent when certain important statements are considered. When Paul warns, "Let not sin therefore reign in your mortal *soma*" (Rom. 6:12), or when he exhorts the Romans "to present your *somata* as a living sacrifice, holy and acceptable to God" (Rom. 12:1), it is clear that *soma* does not mean "body form" nor just "body," either, but that by "body" he means the whole person—undoubtedly in some specific respect which we have yet to define more exactly.

How little it is true that for Paul *soma* means "form," "shape," can be seen from the fact that he uses the words having the primary meaning of form and shape to designate the essence of a thing: the words *morphē* and *schema*. *Morphē* is the shape, the form, in which a person or thing appears, and in the LXX it is used synonymously with εἶδος (shape, form), ὁμοίωμα (likeness), ὅρασις (appearance), and ὄψις (appearance), not, however, in contrast to its essence, but precisely as the expression thereof. Hence, it is understandable that in Hellenistic usage *morphē* can be used to designate the divine nature (see Reitzenstein, *Hellenistische Mysterienreligionen*, 3rd ed., 357f.). It is used in the same way by Paul. Being "changed from glory to glory into the same image (with him)" which, according to II Cor. 3:18, takes place as a result of beholding the Lord, is an alteration not of one's form, but of one's nature. If the elect of God are to be "conformed to the image of his Son" (Rom. 8:29), that means that their nature will be, like his, a glory-nature. And Phil. 3:21 means the same thing: (Christ) "who will change our lowly body into conformity with his glory-body." The "form of God" in which the pre-existent Christ existed is not mere form but the divine mode of being just as much as the "form of a servant" is the mode of being of a servant (Phil. 2:6f.). The same is true of *schema*. He who "was found in human form" (Phil. 2:8) did not merely look like a man but really was a man "obedient unto death." The "change" (μετασχηματίζειν) of Phil. 3:21 (see above) denotes change of nature, and in Rom. 12:2 "conformed" (συσχηματίζεσθαι) and "transformed" (μεταμορφοῦσθαι) correspond in the same way. It is apparent that the perishing "form of this world" (I Cor. 7:31) means the world itself, not just its form. Only in II Cor. 11:13–15 is μετασχηματίζεσθαι (transform) used in its original sense of changing form; perhaps it is also so used in the obscure passage, I Cor. 4:6—i.e. instead of "applied" (RSV) perhaps "transformed this to apply . . ."

In defining the concept *soma,* the place to begin is the naive popular usage in which *soma* means *body*—as a rule, man's—which in a naive anthropological view can be placed in contrast with the "soul" or the "spirit" (I Thess. 5:23; I Cor. 5:3; 7:34). The body has its members, which comprise a unity within it (Rom. 12:4f.; I Cor. 12:12–26). Personal, physical presence is the "presence of the body" (II Cor. 10:10). Paul bears about on his body the "marks of Jesus" (Gal. 6:17)—evidently scars (resulting from mistreatment or accidents) which mark him physically—and he can describe his constant enduring of danger and sufferings as "carrying in the body the death of Jesus" (II Cor. 4:10). There are people who "deliver their bodies to be burned" (I Cor. 13:3); Paul "pommels and subdues his body" (I Cor. 9:27). In the *soma*, sexual life has its seat. Abraham beheld his body "dead"—i.e. no longer capable of procreation (Rom. 4:19). A wife does not rule over her body, nor a husband over his (I Cor. 7:4). Unnatural lust (homosexuality) is a "dishonoring of the body" (Rom. 1:24); unchastity in general is a sin which concerns the body (I Cor. 6:13-20, espec. v. 18).

But in a number of the above passages it is clear that the *soma* is not a something that outwardly clings to a man's real *self* (to his soul, for instance), but belongs to its very essence, so that we can say man does not *have* a *soma*; he *is soma*, for in not a few cases *soma* can be translated simply "I" (or whatever personal pronoun fits the context); thus, I Cor. 13:3; 9:27; 7:4 (see above), or Phil. 1:20 KJ ". . . Christ shall be magnified in my body (= me) whether by life, or by death." The same is thoroughly clear in the already mentioned exhortation, Rom. 12:1: "Present your bodies (= yourselves, or: your selves) as a living sacrifice, etc." Rom. 6:12f. is also instructive:

"Let not sin therefore reign in your mortal *soma* . . .
Do not yield *your members* to sin as tools of wickedness,
But yield *yourselves* to God . . .
And *your members* to God as tools of righteousness." (tr.)

Here "your members," which is a synonymous variation of "your body," stands parallel to "yourselves"; and in the following verses, both within v. 13 and in vv. 16 and 19, "yield yourselves" and "yield your members" are used synonymously. Likewise I Cor. 6:15, "Do you not know that your bodies are members of Christ?" and I Cor. 12:27, "Now you are the body of Christ and individually members of it," correspond to each other. In the former case, the subject of "being the members of Christ" is "your bodies"; in the latter case it is "you" without difference in meaning. In this usage, the word "members" denotes the individual faculties of human existence which are comprised in the *soma* as the whole, just as, correspondingly, the individual man, provided he is baptized, belongs to Christ's *soma* as a member.

The nuances of meaning in the word *soma* melt into one another in a strange fashion in I Cor. 6:13-20. "The body is not meant for immorality" (v. 13), evidently means that the body, insofar as it is the seat of sex-life, is not to be defiled by immorality. But when it goes on to say, ". . . but for the Lord, and the Lord for the body," this sexual implication of "body" can scarcely still be present. Moreover, when v. 14 says, "And God raised the Lord and will also raise us up," the word "us" has taken the place of the expected phrase "our bodies"; i.e. the equation "*soma* = self, person" hovers in the background. And when v. 15 begins, "Do you not know that your bodies are members of Christ," "your bodies" means "you" (*cf.* 12:27, see above). But when it continues, "Shall I therefore take the members of Christ and make them members of a prostitute?" the other meaning of *soma* as the physical body sounds through again. And when according to v. 16 he who joins himself to a prostitute becomes "one *soma*" with her, "*soma*" once more means physical body, even though the meaning tends toward the figurative in that it also means "unity," "one-ness." In v. 18 the meaning of *soma* is hard to determine; nevertheless, this much is clear: *Soma* here means that which is most intimately connected with man and amounts to the same thing as "self." In this formulation Paul is probably dependent upon the rabbinic idiom "to sin with the body," a term that can be used to denote unchastity. In v. 19, again, the meaning of *soma* fluctuates strangely, for when the *soma* is called the temple of the Spirit that dwells within the Christian, one is at first inclined to think of his physical body as the temple (*cf.* Rom. 8:11) in keeping with the basic tenor of the exhortation—that the Christian keep his body clean from immorality. But then it says, "*You* are not your own" instead of saying "your *bodies* are not your own property." Hence, the *soma* that is the Spirit's temple must be the Christian's whole person, not just his body. On the other hand, *soma* in the exhortation, "So glorify God in your *soma*" (v. 20), probably means "body"—i.e. within the whole context it means: do not yield your body to unchastity.

2. The result of all the foregoing is this: *Man, his person as a whole*, can be denoted by *soma*. It may also be significant that Paul never calls a corpse *soma*, though such a usage is found both in profane Greek and in the LXX. But what is the specific respect in which man is regarded when he is called *soma*? *Man is called soma in respect to his being able to make himself the object of his own action or to experience himself as the subject to whom something happens.* He can be called *soma*, that is, *as having a relationship to*

himself—as being able in a certain sense to distinguish himself from himself. Or, more exactly, he is so called as that self from whom he, as subject, distinguishes himself, the self with whom he can deal as the object of his own conduct, and also the self whom he can perceive as subjected to an occurrence that springs from a will other than his own. It is as such a self that man is called *soma*. Since it belongs to man's nature to have such a relationship to himself, a double possibility exists: to be at one with himself or at odds (estranged from himself). The possibility of having one's self in hand or of losing this control and being at the mercy of a power not one's own is inherent to human existence itself. But in the latter situation the outside power can be experienced as an enemy power which estranges man from himself or as the opposite, a friendly power that brings the man estranged from himself back to himself.

The fact that *soma* can denote both the body and the whole man, the person, rests upon a point of view that is current both in the Old Testament (where the same holds true for בָּשָׂר, "flesh," "body," "self") and in Judaism. The reason for it is that for a person his body is not a thing like the objects of the external world, but is precisely *his* body, which is given to him, and he to it. He gets his primary experience of himself by experiencing his body, and he first encounters his thraldom to outside powers in his bodily dependence upon them. So the inward aspect of the self and the outward (its sensory given-ness) remain at first undiscriminated as phenomena.

That man is called *soma* in respect to his being able to control himself and be the object of his own action, is shown by the passages quoted above: he pommels or subdues *himself* (I Cor. 9:27); he can give *himself* to be burned (I Cor. 13:3); he can yield *himself* to the service of sin or of God (Rom. 6:12ff.; 12:1); he can expend *himself* for Christ (Phil. 1:20). Also, the statement that marriage-partners do not rule over themselves (I Cor. 7:4) ultimately belongs here, for the meaning is that though they can withhold themselves from each other, yet they are to place themselves mutually at the other's disposal; hence, it is up to them whether or not they make real the statement "he (she) does not rule . . ." The *soma* can be described as the actual tool of action; thus II Cor. 5:10 says, "that each may receive according to what he has done through the (= his) *soma*" (tr.). This has no other meaning than "according to his own deeds" —i.e. according to what he has done not with his body, but with himself, what he has made of himself.

Soma appears only once in Paul as the implied subject of an action: Rom. 8:13, where "deeds of the *soma*" are mentioned.* But these "deeds of the *soma*" recede strangely into the distance in reference to the acting human subject; these deeds are the object of his conduct ("if . . . you put to death the deeds of the *soma*"). So the expression is to be understood as arising from the fact that the *soma*-self (a self distinguished from the subject-self) has become so independent in Paul's thought that he can speak of *its* deeds. But that means nothing else than that the *soma*, so far as it brings forth deeds of its own, is under the sway of an outside power, which has seized from the self the power of control over itself; it simply means that in the "deeds or the *soma*" man no longer has himself in hand. The context shows that the outside power is "the flesh"; for the "deeds of the *soma*" correspond to "living according to the flesh." The same thing is indicated by the fact that Paul can speak of the "passions" of the *"soma"* (Rom. 6:12), for here, too, it is clear that what is meant by *soma* is that self which has fallen under the sway of "flesh"; precisely that self from which the real self distinguishes itself, or rather is urged to distinguish itself. The "passions of the *soma*" are nothing else than the "passions of the flesh" (Gal. 5:16f., 24; *cf.* Rom. 7:7ff.; 13:14). In the same sense, Paul can also speak of the *"soma* of sin" (Rom. 6:6)—i.e. the sinful self (the self that is under the sway of sin), while in Rom. 8:3 he speaks of the *"flesh* of sin" (= sinful flesh). In addition, *soma* receives adjectives and other qualifiers which express its captivation by an outside power, whether of destructive sort or of emancipating and beneficial sort. As subject to transitoriness and death, the *soma* is called *psychikon* (animate, but bound to lose its life, I Cor. 15:44), or "mortal" (Rom. 6:12; 8:11) or a *"soma* of humiliation" (Phil. 3:21); as the resurrection-body, it is a "spiritual body" (I Cor. 15:44), or a "glory-body" (Phil. 3:21).

The characterization of man as *soma* implies, then, that man is a being who has a relationship to himself, and that this relationship can be either an appropriate or a perverted one; that he can be at

---

* This *lectio difficilior* is to be preferred to the reading of DG *et al.*: πράξεις τῆς σαρκός (deeds of the flesh).

one with himself or at odds; that he can be under his own control or lose his grip on himself. In the latter case, a double possibility exists: that the power which comes to master him can make the estrangement within him determinative, and that would mean that it would destroy the man by entirely wresting him out of his own hands, or that this power gives him back to himself, that is, brings him to life. That man is *soma* means that he stands within such possibilities. The fact that he is *soma* is in itself neither good nor bad. But only because he is *soma* does the possibility exist for him to be good or evil—to have a relationship for or against God.

It can now be understood why Paul so zealously defends the resurrection of the *soma* against his Corinthian opponents—it must be understood from the basic meaning that the concept *soma* has as a characteristic of human existence. If man were no longer *soma*—if he no longer had a relationship to himself—he would no longer be man. Since Paul's capacity for abstract thinking is not a developed one, and he therefore does not distinguish terminologically between *soma* in the basic sense of that which characterizes human existence and *soma* as the phenomenon of the material body, he connects the idea of somatic existence in the eschatological consummation with a mythological teaching on the resurrection (I Cor. 15). In it *soma* must appear somehow or other as a thing of material substance, or as the "form" of such a thing. And since the substance of the resurrection-body cannot be "flesh and blood" (I Cor. 15:50), the unfortunate consequence is that *pneuma* must be conceived as a substance of which that *soma* consists. In distinction from this mythology the real intention of Paul must be made clear. It is that he asserts specific human existence, both before and beyond death, to be a somatic existence in the basic sense defined above.

It could be objected, to be sure, that in the resurrection-life the possibility seems to have dropped out that man could become estranged from himself, could get to be at odds with himself and fall victim to an inimical power that would tear him out of his own hands and destroy him. In fact, this has dropped out as a factual (ontic) possibility, for sin and death are destroyed at the consummation (I Cor. 15:26, 55f.). But that does not mean that the ontological structure of human existence will be destroyed, for if it were, no continuity at all would exist between a man before his death or resurrection and the resurrected individual. Actually, the statement that faith, hope, and love abide in the consummation (I Cor. 13:13) also testifies that Paul regards human nature as such (in its ontological structure) as unchanging, for in faith, hope, love man always also has a relationship to himself, since in them he makes up his mind about something, adopts a definite attitude. And the sa ne conclusion results from the concept *soma pneumatikon* ("spiritual body"), rightly interpreted: "It does not in the end mean a body formed of an ethereal substance, but it does mean that the self is determined by the power of God which reconciles the cleft between self and self within a man and hence does presuppose a relationship of man to himself. But this cannot be cleared up until the concept *pneuma* (Spirit) is discussed.

3. Insofar as man is *soma* and thereby has a relationship to himself, he can distinguish himself from himself, and he will do this all the more as he experiences outside powers trying to wrest him out out of his own control or even having done so. Then the temptation exists to let the perceived separation between himself and himself become a divorce—to misunderstand his relationship to himself as that between his self and a totally foreign being, a "not-I." In such misunderstanding the original naive meaning, *soma* = body, can come to the surface again so that the "double" to which the self is bound is regarded to be the material body. That is the understanding of the self that is found in (Gnostic) dualism, according to which man's self is imprisoned in the body, a prison foreign to its own nature, from which it yearns to be set free. To this view such a somatic existence as Paul expects to find at the consummation is, of course, unthinkable. And this dualism's attitude in practical life is mysticism and asceticism, that is, a turning aside from bodily (somatic) existence—a flight from the uncomfortable tension of a human existence in which a person unavoidably has a relationship to himself.

From the very fact that Paul conceives the resurrection-life as somatic, it is apparent that his understanding of the self was not shaped by this dualism. But, on the other hand, he sees so deep a cleft within man, so great a tension between self and self, and so keenly feels the plight of the man who loses his grip upon himself and falls victim to outside powers, that he comes close to Gnostic dualism. That is indicated by the fact that he occasionally uses *soma* synonymously with *sarx* ("flesh").

This does not refer to the use of *soma* or *sarx* to denote the physical body as in the following examples. II Cor. 4:10f. ". . . so that the life of Jesus may also be manifested in our bodies"; but in v. 11 the same statement ends ". . . in our mortal *flesh*"—synonymous parallelism of members. In Gal. 6:17, Paul bears on his "body" the marks of Jesus, but "body" can hardly mean anything else than "flesh" does in the phrase "ailment of the flesh" (Gal. 4:13 tr.), or the "thorn . . . in the flesh" (II Cor. 12:7). I Cor. 6:16 uses the two words synonymously, but only because Gen. 2:24 LXX "the two shall become one *flesh*" (tr.), is cited to prove that he who joins with a prostitute "becomes one *body* with her." In all such cases Paul is following the example of the LXX, in which בָּשָׂר is rendered sometimes *soma*, sometimes *sarx*, with no difference in meaning.

The passages named above (p. 197) which deal with the "passions" or the "deeds" of the *soma* (Rom. 6:12; 8:13) use *soma* in the sense of *sarx*—a sinful power at enmity with God. Here *soma* is to be understood as the self under the rule of *sarx*—and the "passions" and "deeds" that are meant are precisely those of *sarx* ("flesh"). The correspondence of the two clauses in Rom. 8:13— "if you live according to the flesh . . . if you put to death the deeds of the body"—shows that when the *soma* is under the sway of *sarx*, Paul can speak of the *soma* in just the same way as he does of *sarx* itself. The case of Rom. 7:14ff. is similar. Here the sin leading man to death is first attributed to the *sarx* (vv. 14, 18), but later the "law of sin" is spoken of as ruling in the "members"—i.e. in the *soma* (v. 23). Then when the question is asked, "Who will save me from this *soma* of death?" *soma* means the sin-ruled self, the self under the sway of sin—and that cry applies not to release from the *soma* absolutely, but release from this *soma* as it is ruled through and through by "flesh," and that really means release from "flesh" itself. According to Rom. 8:9, "flesh" is deposed, and when the next verse says "if Christ is in you, although your *soma* is dead because of sin," that means that the *flesh-ruled soma* (again equivalent to *flesh* itself) is eliminated (and it is eliminated "because of sin"—i.e. because sin has been condemned; *cf.* v. 3). Hence the estrangement between the self which is the bearer of man's real will (the "inmost self" of Rom. 7:22) and the self which slips away from this will and falls under the sway of flesh—exactly the cleft which Rom. 7:14ff. depicts—is regarded as so far-reaching that this second self seems almost a foreign one, not belonging to the same person. It is so completely ruled by flesh that the difference between *soma* and *sarx* is at the point of disappearing. And yet, the *soma* remains that self which is indissolubly bound to the willing self, as Rom. 7:14ff. also shows, and the basic difference between *soma* and *sarx* remains valid. For the Christian, the flesh is dead and deposed (Rom. 8:2ff.); it is excluded from participation in the Reign of God (I Cor. 15:50), while the *soma*—transformed, i.e. released from the dominion of flesh—is the vehicle of the resurrection-life. The *soma* is man himself, while *sarx* is a power that lays claim to him and determines him. That is why Paul can speak of a life κατὰ σάρκα (according to the flesh) but never of a life κατὰ σῶμα (according to the body).

Thus, Paul did not dualistically distinguish between man's self (his "soul") and his bodily *soma* as if the latter were an inappropriate shell, a prison, to the former; nor does his hope expect a release of the self from its bodily prison but expects instead the "bodily" resurrection—or rather the transformation of the *soma* from under the power of flesh into a spiritual *soma*, i.e. a Spirit-ruled *soma*. As the rescue from the "*soma* of death," for which Rom. 7:24 yearns, means release from the flesh (see above), so does the hope for the "redemption τοῦ σώματος" in Rom. 8:23 mean redemption from the *soma* as ruled by *sarx*, if it really means redemption *from* the *soma* (genitive of separation) and not just the *soma's* redemption (objective genitive).

The case of II Cor. 5:1ff. is different. Here Paul comes very close to Hellenistic-Gnostic dualism not merely in form of expression, by speaking of the *soma* under the figure of the "tent-dwelling" and "garment," but also in the thought itself. Here the *soma* appears as a shell for the self (the "inner nature," ἔσω ἄνθρωπος, of 4:16), moreover as an inappropriate shell, inasmuch as it is the earthly tent-dwelling in which the self at present still sighs with longing for a heavenly garment that would be appropriate to the self. Here, quite dualistically, to be "at home in the body" and its correlate to be "away from the Lord, our home" (tr.), confront their opposites: to be "away from (move out of?) our body-home and be at (move into our) home with the Lord" (vv. 6, 8, tr.). Furthermore, it is not the *soma* ruled by flesh (and sin)—ultimately sin itself, in other words—from which the self here desires to be freed, but the physical body distressed by care and suffering, the body mentioned at 4:10f. whose sufferings are described in 4:8f., the body that is an "earthen vessel" (4:7). So the Christian desires to be and will be redeemed from the *soma* in this sense. But that does not mean that this expectation contradicts the special sense of *soma* worked out above. It does not imply release from somatic existence altogether. Rather, the arguments of 5:1ff. contain indirect polemic against a Gnosticism which teaches that the naked self soars aloft free of any body. The Christian does not desire, like such Gnostics, to be "unclothed," but desires to be "further clothed" (ἐπενδύσασθαι, v. 4); he yearns for the heavenly garment, "for we will not be found naked when we have divested ourselves (of our present physical body)" (Blt., reading ἐκδυσάμενοι with D* etc. in v. 3).

In the same sense, as the physical body, *soma* is probably also to be understood in II Cor. 12:2–4, where Paul is speaking of a pneumatic experience of his, doubtless an ecstasy as mysticism uses the word. When he twice professes not to know whether this experience happened to him "in the body or out of the body," he is clearly reckoning with the possibility that the self can separate from the *soma* even in this present life, and this *soma* can only be the physical body. It would be meaningless here to think of the "*soma* of sin."

Though Paul shows himself to be influenced in II Cor. 5:1ff. and 12:2–4 by the Hellenistic-dualistic depreciation of the body conceived as physical corporeality, this influences goes still deeper in his treatment of the marriage question (I Cor. 7:1–7). For here, in keeping with ascetic tendencies of dualism, he evaluates marriage as a thing of less value than "not touching a woman" (v. 1); indeed, he regards it as an unavoidable evil ("on account of fornication," v. 2, tr.). It is to be noted, however, that he does not derive these ideas from the *soma*-concept, so that the latter remains quite in the background.

Nevertheless, it would be an error in method to proceed from such passages as these to interpret the *soma*-concept that is characteristic of Paul and determines his fundamental discussions. This characteristic concept, first meaning the physical body, comes to serve, as we have shown, to denote man's person in the respect that having a relationship to one's self belongs essentially to being man. More accurately, man is *soma* when he is objectivized in relation to

himself by becoming the object of his own thought, attitude, or conduct; he is *soma* in that he can separate from himself and come
under the domination of outside powers.

§ 18. *Psyche, Pneuma, and Zoe*

1. What does Paul call man, and how does he regard him, when
he is the *subject* of his own willing and doing, when he is his real
self who can distinguish himself from his *soma*-self? In Rom. 7:22
and II Cor. 4:16 as a formal designation for that self he uses the
term "the inner man" (ὁ ἔσω ἄνθρωπος), an expression that appears
to be derived from the anthropology of Hellenistic dualism. But it
has a purely formal meaning in Paul, as may be seen from the fact
that it means two things of different content in the two passages
cited. In Rom. 7:22, "the inner" is man's real self in contrast to the
self that has come under the sway of sin: "the *soma* of death" (7:24)
or "the *soma* of sin" (§ 17, 2, p. 200). In II Cor. 4:16 "the inner man
is still the real self, it is true, but in contrast to the physical body
(§ 17, 3, p. 201f.). Rom. 7:22 deals with unredeemed man under the
Law, II Cor. 4:16 with the Christian, in whom God's power is at
work (4:7), and in whom the Spirit dwells (5:5). The "inner man"
of Rom. 7:22 is identical in content with the *nous* ("mind"), which
belongs to man's essence (note how "inner man" is picked up, v. 23,
by the term "mind"), but "the inner man" of II Cor. 4:16 is the self
transformed by the Spirit (3:18). Thus the term "inner man" as
formal designation for the subject-self confirms our conception,
derived from the interpretation of *soma* (§ 17), of Paul's view of
human existence as the having of a relationship to one's self. But
the investigation of other anthropological terms of Paul must teach
us how he more specifically understands that real self.

2. The term *psyche* (soul), so often used with *soma* to designate
man in his entirety, occurs relatively seldom in Paul—in connection
with *soma* in I Thess. 5:23, where *pneuma* is used in addition, so
that a trichotomous anthropology appears to be present. The investigation of Paul's use of *soma* has already shown that he does not
dualistically set body and soul in opposition to each other. Just as
Paul does not know the Greek-Hellenistic conception of the immortality of the soul (released from the body), neither does he use
psyche to designate the seat or the power of the mental life which

animates man's matter, as it had become the custom to do among the Greeks. Rather, *psyche* in Paul means primarily the Old Testament נֶפֶשׁ (rendered *psyche* in the LXX)—"vitality," or "life" itself.

This corresponds, furthermore, with the older Greek usage. This is his use in Rom. 11:3 (quoting III Kingdoms 19:10), 16:4 ("risked their necks for my life"); II Cor. 1:23; Phil. 2:30; I Thess. 2:8. That is why lifeless instruments of music, which have no voice until the breath gives it to them, can be called "lifeless (ἄψυχα, 'soul'-less) things giving sound" (I Cor. 14:7). The use of "every soul" in the sense of "everyone" corresponds to Old Testament idiom (Rom. 2:9; 13:1). In this use it is already apparent that *psyche*, too, can take on the meaning "person," "self" (like נֶפֶשׁ). The *psyche* already mentioned in II Cor. 1:23, I Thess. 2:8 could be understood in this way and in any case must be so understood in II Cor. 12:15 ("I will most gladly spend and be spent for your souls" = for you).

It is very peculiar that Paul is influenced in addition by Gnostic usage, with the result that he uses *psyche* in a depreciatory sense. In I Cor. 15:45 he quotes Gen. 2:7: "The (first) man (Adam) became a living *psyche* (לְנֶפֶשׁ חַיָּה)" —quite in keeping with the Old Testament meaning, inasmuch as ψυχὴ ζῶσα (living "soul") denotes a living being, an animate person. But at the same, a foreign idea is smuggled into these words when "living soul" is qualified by the contrasting phrase "life-giving spirit." *Psyche* is now (as in Gnosticism) the merely natural, earthly vitality in contrast to the divinely given capacity for eternal life. And so the derived adjective *psychikos* can take on the meaning "second-rate," "limited," "transitory" (I Cor. 2:14; 15:44, 46; see § 15, 4b).

Nevertheless, where the contrast with *pneuma* is not involved, Paul uses *psyche* altogether in the sense current in the Old Testament-Jewish tradition; viz. to designate human life, or rather to denote man as a living being. But how his conception of this "life" is to be more adequately grasped is indicated by a number of passages. First, Phil. 1:27 ". . . that you stand firm in one spirit, with one mind (*psyche*) striving side by side for the faith of the gospel." The phrase "with one *psyche*" (like "in one spirit") means "in agreement"—i.e. having the same attitude or the same orientation of will; and there is no difference between *psyche* here and other expressions that mean the tendency of one's will, one's intention (*cf.* I Cor. 1:10, "united in the same mind—*nous*—and the same judgment"). Words compounded with the root *psych-* indicate the same thing: *Sympsychos* means "being in agreement" ("of one mind," Phil. 2:2 RSV); the *isopsychos* (Phil. 2:20) is the "like-minded." *Eupsychein,* "be of good cheer, hopeful, confident" (Phil. 2:19), offers a somewhat different nuance. It does not mean the willing of something, it is true, but it does also express the intention element of that vitality which is denoted by *psyche.* Hence, it is incorrect to understand *psyche* in Paul as meaning only the "principle of animal life" and as standing in close relation to "flesh" understood as the matter enlivened by that *psyche.* Rather *psyche* is that specifically human state of being alive which inheres in man as a striving, willing, purposing self. And even where *psyche* is depreciated in contrast to *pneuma,* it does not mean mere animal life but full human life—the natural life of earthly man, of course, in contrast to supranatural life. The man who is *psychikos* (I Cor. 2:14 "natural man" KJ; "unspiritual man" is RSV's interpretive rendering) is not a person who has only biological needs, but the person whose life is directed toward, and limited to, the earthly.

3. Just as in the Old Testament, נֶפֶשׁ (soul, life, self) and רוּחַ (spirit) are to a large extent synonymous, Paul, too, can use *pneuma* in a sense similar to that of *psyche.* This use, of course, must be carefully distinguished from his predominant use of *pneuma* for the Holy Spirit or the Spirit of God. In Rom. 8:16 the divine *pneuma* which Christians have received (v. 15) is expressly distinguished from "our *pneuma.*" Likewise, in I Cor. 2:10f., which is a case of conclusion by analogy—as only a man's "spirit" knows what is within him, so also the depths of God are available only to the divine "Spirit" (which has been bestowed upon Christians). When the unmarried woman or the maiden (I Cor. 7:34) is said to be anxious "how to be consecrated in body and spirit," "body and spirit" are evidently intended as a summary designation of the totality of a human being;* likewise, the wish (I Thess. 5:23) that "your spirit and soul and body may be kept sound and blameless" evidently means only that the readers may be kept sound, each in his entirety. So far as form is concerned, this is a trichotomous scheme of anthropology; but the formulation is to be explained as coming from litur-

---

* The totality of a person is designated in quite the same fashion by "flesh and spirit" in II Cor. 7:1; this verse, however, is non-Pauline like the whole of the inserted passage II Cor. 6:14–7:1.

gical-rhetorical (perhaps traditional) diction, so that nothing more is to be gathered from this passage than that Paul can also speak of a *pneuma* that is human.

In this use, *pneuma* can mean the person and take the place of a personal pronoun just as *soma* and *psyche* can. When I Cor. 16:18 says of the messengers from the Corinthian congregation, "they refreshed my *spirit* as well as yours," that means simply "me and you." That Titus' *pneuma* was set at rest (II Cor. 7:13) means only that he himself was set at rest. When Paul says in II Cor. 2:13, "I had no rest in my spirit" (KJ), he means that he found no inward rest (for there can be no thought of a distinction between his self and his "spirit"); but in the end the meaning is quite the same as that of II Cor. 7:5, "our flesh had no rest" (KJ). Both sentences mean, "I could not come to rest," and from them it is apparent how casual from case to case the choice can be of the anthropological term to designate the person. It is due to rhetorical pathos that in the closing wishes of some of the letters instead of the usual formula, "God . . . (or grace . . .) be with you all (or, with you)," we read the conclusion, "with your *spirit*," Gal. 6:18; Phil. 4:23; Phlm. 25. Probably Rom. 1:9 ("God . . . whom I serve with my *spirit*") should be included in this category; "with my spirit," in keeping with the pathos of the whole sentence, only emphasizes that Paul puts his whole person into the service of the gospel. Rom. 12:11 "fervent in *spirit*" (KJ), on the contrary, probably means "aglow with the Spirit" (RSV), since *pneuma* here seems to be the Holy Spirit conferred upon the Christian.

When Paul speaks of the *pneuma* of man he does not mean some higher principle within him or some special intellectual or spiritual faculty of his, but simply his self, and the only question is whether the self is regarded in some particular respect when it is called *pneuma*. In the first place, it apparently is regarded in the same way as when it is called *psyche*—viz. as the self that lives in a man's attitude, in the orientation of his will. Standing "in one *spirit*" (Phil. 1:27) is synonymous both with striving "with one mind" (*psyche* in the same verse; see above, 2) and with "in the same mind" and "the same judgment" of I Cor. 1:10. Phil. 2:1, also, scarcely means "participation in the Spirit" (RSV) or "unity bestowed by the Spirit," but simply unity of mind—i.e. unanimity of will. At any rate, this meaning of *pneuma* does occur in II Cor. 12:18 when Paul asks,

"Walked we not in the same spirit?" (KJ)—i.e. "Did we not (Titus and I) conduct ourselves in the same attitude (with the same intention)?" In distinction from *psyche*, *pneuma* seems also to mean the self regarded as conscious or aware. Thus Rom. 8:16: the divine Spirit "bears witness" to our spirit that we are God's children—i.e. makes us conscious of it, confers the knowledge of it upon us. And in the statement of I Cor. 2:11 that "man's *spirit* knows what is within him," *pneuma* approaches the modern idea of consciousness. It is apparent, therefore, that the meaning of *pneuma* departs from that of *psyche* and approaches that of *nous* ("mind"). Observe in this connection that in I Cor. 14:14 instead of the contrast between the divine *pneuma* and the human *pneuma* we find the contrast between the (divine) *pneuma* and the human *nous*, "mind," (for "my *pneuma*" here is not the human mind but the divine Spirit bestowed upon man)—exactly in a passage where it is essential to designate the conscious self.

Since the human self as a willing and knowing self can be called by the same term ("*pneuma*") as the marvelous power of divine action (§ 14, 1), then the formal meaning of *pneuma* must possess this double possibility. As a matter of fact, a glance at what *pneuma* means as divine Spirit confirms what we have worked out for its meaning as human spirit. Paul does not conceive the divine Spirit as an explosively working power, so to say, but conceives it as guided by a definite tendency, a will, so that he can speak of its "endeavor" (φρόνημα, Rom. 8:6, 27) or even of its "desires" (ἐπιθυμεῖ, Gal. 5:17). It acts like a conscious subject certain of its goal (Rom. 8:26; I Cor. 2:10; II Cor. 3:6). Hence, to be "led by the (divine) Spirit" means to have one's will oriented in a particular direction (Rom. 8:14; Gal. 5:18). The same conclusion results from the fact that in I Cor. 2:16 Paul can let the expression νοῦς (κυρίου), which means "the planning (of the Lord)" (see below, § 19), take the place of *pneuma* (of God) because he wants to confirm his statement about the Spirit of God with the quotation from Is. 40:13.

It is from this point of view that certain passages are to be understood in which Paul, using an animistic terminology such as is frequently met in the Old Testament, speaks of a special *pneuma* which determines conduct in a specific case. It is clear that *pneuma* here means a special orientation of the will, although it cannot be said with certainty, whether *pneuma* in these passages is conceived as a specialization—a particle, so to say—of the divine Spirit, or whether it is simply a very pale locution approaching our own expression: "in the spirit of . . ."—i.e. "with the tendency of . . ." Thus Paul speaks of a "spirit of gentleness" (I Cor. 4:21; Gal. 6:1) or "of faith" (II Cor. 4:13). To this category, also, belongs the expression "the spirit of the world" in I Cor. 2:12. It must be left unanswered whether in this expression Paul is really imagining a concrete "power" inspired by the cosmos (a notion which, strictly speaking, is required by the contrast to "the Spirit which is from God"), or whether the formulation of the contrast is merely rhetorical, so that "spirit of the world" means *only* the worldly way of thinking and willing—a meaning which it would *include*, of course, in the other case, *too*.

I Cor. 5:3–5 presents difficulties. The contrast "absent in body—present in spirit" seems at first sight simply to contrast physical, personal absence (§ 17, 1) with presence in wish or will.* But v. 4 ("when you and my *pneuma* are gathered together") shows that for Paul it is not a matter of "mental" presence in his thoughts, but that his *pneuma* will be present as an active "power." Evidently a fluid transition takes place from one meaning of *pneuma* to another. Neither can the meaning of *pneuma* in v. 5 be determined with certainty: "for the destruction of the flesh, that his *pneuma* may be saved . . ." Is this *pneuma* the person, his real self, in contrast here to "the flesh" regarded as physical life (as in II Cor. 5:1ff., it is contrasted with the *soma*, § 17, 3)? Or is it the divine *pneuma* bestowed upon man in contrast to sinful flesh? Probably the former.

Rom. 8:10 and I Cor. 6:17 offer merely seeming difficulties which are due to their pointed, rhetorical formulation. Rom. 8:10: "(if Christ is in you), although your *bodies* are dead because of sin, your *spirits* are alive because of righteousness." This antithesis means that the flesh-ruled self is dead because sin is condemned (§ 17, 3); the new self ruled by the divine *pneuma* is alive because uprightness (of conduct; see "walk," v. 4) has now become reality. Still *pneuma* here does not mean simply the self, the person, but the divine *pneuma*, which has become the subject-self, so to say, of the Christian; the contrast

* In this sense Col. 2:5 says, "For though I am absent in the flesh, yet am I with you in the spirit" (KJ).

of *pneuma* to *soma* ("the *soma* of sin") requires this under-standing. Hence, we have here a rhetorical paraphrase of the simple thought: "If Christ dwells in you, then the life-giving Spirit also dwells in you" (*cf.* v. 11). In I Cor. 6:16f. Paul sup-ports his statement, "he becomes one body with her" with Gen. 2:24: "they shall become one flesh." In so doing, he gives "flesh" the meaning of *soma* (§ 17, 3), but, of course, this *soma* is one of "flesh." Then follows the contrasting statement, "But he who is united to the Lord becomes one Spirit with him"; in com-pressed form this expresses the thought, "But he who joins him-self to the Lord constitutes one body with him—a pneumatic body."

4. In summary, this may be said: The various possibilities of regarding man, or the self, come to light in the use of the anthropo-logical terms *soma, psyche,* and *pneuma.* Man does not consist of two parts, much less of three; nor are *psyche* and *pneuma* special faculties or principles (within the *soma*) of a mental life higher than his animal life. Rather, man is a living unity. He is a person who can become an object to himself. He is a person having a relation-ship to himself (*soma*). He is a person who lives in his intention-ality, his pursuit of some purpose, his willing and knowing (*psyche, pneuma*). This state of living toward some goal, having some atti-tude, willing something and knowing something, belongs to man's very nature and in itself is neither good nor bad. The goal toward which one's life is oriented is left still undetermined in the mere ontological structure of having some orientation or other; but this structure (which for Paul is, of course, the gift of the life-giving Creator) offers the possibility of choosing one's goal, of deciding for good or evil, for or against God.

This analysis is also substantiated in the concept *zoe* (life), wherever it is used as an anthropological term denoting the life that is man's in the nature of the case when he has *psyche.* That man is given natural *zoe* by God, that it is temporally limited and finds its end in death, does not hit the meaning of the formal (ontological) concept *zoe.* The supranatural life that is conferred upon the man who is accounted righteous, or which stands in prospect for him, is also *zoe* and has the same formal meaning as the concept *zoe* when used to designate natural life. That is, what was said of the concept *soma* (§ 17, 2) also applies here.

The way in which the verb "to live" (ζῆν) is used shows clearly that Paul does not understand life as a phenomenon of nature; but neither does he understand it in the Greek sense of "genuine" or "true" life—i.e. "mental" life. Rather, he understands it as the life a man leads in his concrete existence, the intentionality of human existence. His concept of life as lived by men is paradoxical in that *zoe* on the one hand means the life that a man lives as the subject of his own actions, his living self (i.e. his striving, willing self) and on the other hand, that this self-hood is not, like God, self-creative but is a thing entrusted to him—hence, that he factually lives only by constantly moving on, as it were, from himself, by projecting himself into a possibility that lies before him. He sees himself confronted with the future, facing the possibilities in which he can gain his self or lose it. This finds expression in the fact that he does not simply "live," but is always "leading his life" in some particular way. Living is always a "walking" (περιπατεῖν) and like the latter word is usually qualified by an adverb (to live "heathenishly" or "Jewishly," Gal. 2:14 tr.; *cf.* "to walk worthily . . ." I Thess. 2:12; "becomingly," Rom. 13:13; I Thess. 4:12) or by an adverbial phrase ("to live according to κατά—the flesh," Rom. 8:12; *cf.* "to walk . . . according to the flesh," Rom. 8:4; II Cor. 10:2; *cf.* "according to love," Rom. 14:15, tr.; "according to man," I Cor. 3:3 KJ mg.). Life is lived in some sphere and that sphere gives it its direction ("live in *it*"—by the context; in sin—Rom. 6:2; "in faith," Gal. 2:20; *cf.* "walking in craftiness," II Cor. 4:2; "by a spirit," II Cor. 12:18; Gal. 5:16). At the same time, man always lives "for" or "to" something (Rom. 14:7f.; II Cor. 5:15; Gal. 2:19), and just such statements show that a man's life can go astray in the illusion that he can live "for or to himself" instead of in dedication or self-surrender, renouncing the possibility of holding onto himself. In contradistinction to this aberration of "living for one's self," Paul admittedly does not set up a variety of possible ways of devoting one's self to a cause, but only the one basic possibility of living for God (Gal. 2:19) or for "the Lord" (Rom. 14:17f.) who for us died and rose again (II Cor. 5:15). But in these statements, which describe specifically Christian life, all that concerns us in this context is the bare ontological meaning they presuppose for "life" as a form of existence.

§ 19. Mind and Conscience

1. That being man means being a specific self that is the subject of its own willing and doing, is perhaps most clearly expressed by the term *nous* (usually translated "mind" or "understanding"). By it is meant not the mind or the intellect as a special faculty, but the knowing, understanding, and judging which belong to man as man and determine what attitude he adopts—except in the case that the human self is replaced by the divine Spirit in the state of ecstasy.

As the opposite of speaking in a "tongue," Paul speaks of speech "with the understanding" (τῷ νοΐ, I Cor. 14:14f., 19)—intelligent and intelligible speech. God's "peace" exceeds "all understanding," i.e. all that human "comprehension" (*nous*) understands—whether it be what man can think out or what he can receptively grasp (Phil. 4:7). The "unseen things" (KJ) of God, "his invisible nature" (RSV), have since the creation of the world been νοούμενα—i.e. perceived with the eye of νοῦς, "understanding thought" (Rom. 1:20).

Though in these passages the contemplative aspect inherent in the structure of *nous* is prominent, other passages show that *nous* is by no means just a contemplative attitude, but that it includes— like the Old Testament לֵב or לֵבָב ("heart," "mind") which it often represents in the LXX—the taking of a stand, a conscious or uncon- scious volition; it is an understanding intention, a "planning." In this sense, it is said of God's *nous*: "Who has recognized God's won- drous plan of salvation?" (Rom. 11:34 Blt., quoted from Is. 40:13, whose Hebrew text here has רוּחַ, Spirit). The same question occurs at I Cor. 2:16, where *nous* (16a and 16b) takes the place of the *pneuma* in the whole preceding discussion (vv. 10–15; *cf.* § 18, 3). Correspondingly, the ἀδόκιμος νοῦς to which God has given the heathen up (Rom. 1:28) is their "depraved inclination," their "mis- erable bent." Likewise, the exhortation to the Corinthian Church to be firm "in the same *mind* and the same judgment" (I Cor. 1:10; *cf.* § 18, 2 and 3) shows that *nous* is "what one has a mind to," the aim of one's will, the intent—i.e. *nous* is thinking that "has some- thing in mind" or is making a plan for action. And when Rom. 12:2 exhorts: "Be transformed by the renewal of your *mind*," it is once more clear that what is meant is not a theoretical re-learning, but the renewal of the will. (Here as in Rom. 1:28 *nous* could almost be translated: "character.") Rom. 14:5, "Let every one be fully convinced in his own *nous*," means "in his own judgment"—his judgment, that is, as to what is to be done and what not. Just as there is no willing and planning without knowing and understanding, so for Paul, knowing-and-understanding is everywhere of the sort that plans something, that contains an aim toward action.

The full meaning of *nous* is shown by Rom. 7:23: "But I see in my members another law at war with the law of my *nous*." The term *nous* takes up the term "inner man" (KJ) or "inmost self" (RSV) of v. 22 (§ 18, 1); the *nous*, therefore, is man's real self in distinction from his *soma*, the self which has become objectivized in relation to himself (§ 17, 2). And this self (the *nous*) is an understanding self that hears God's will speaking through the Law, agrees with it, and adopts it as its own. The *nous* is that self which is the subject of the "willing" in v. 15f. and 19–21, its aim is "the good" or "what is right," but its "doing" is frustrated by sin, which dwells "in the members." *

Admittedly there are grounds to wonder whether *nous* in Rom. 7:23 may not have lost its formal-ontological meaning, according to which it is an understanding volition that can turn toward either the good or the bad, while here it is presupposed that *nous*, as *nous*, turns toward the good. However, in Rom. 7:14ff. the ontological point of view (*nous* as a formal, neutral possibility capable of taking either direction) and the ontic point of view (*nous* already pointed in one specific direction) are peculiarly intertwined. It belongs to the nature of man (i.e. to his ontological structure) to desire "what is good," inasmuch as this good is nothing other than "life" itself. Since man can fail to achieve this thing that to him is "good," it also lies ahead of him as the requirement which he must fulfill if he is to achieve what he really desires. Factually, then, (ontically) the man who is under the Law—for that is *his* "ontic" situation—must actualize his human will for "good" by willing what the Law requires; for v. 10 says what the Law was given for: It was given "for life" (on which see § 27). Thus, behind the ontic meaning of v. 23 lies the ontological meaning. In the *nous* which affirms God's demand in the Law lurks the human *nous* whose innate inclination is toward

---

* In v. 25b, *nous* has the same meaning; but this sentence is very likely a gloss, which, in addition, has landed in the text at the wrong place; it belongs to v. 23.

"what is good," but as "depraved inclination" (Rom. 1:28), may factually be striving toward the bad, having in itself, as *nous,* the possibility of heeding or rejecting God's demand.

The very expression "being understood" (νοούμενα), they "are clearly seen" (Rom. 1:20 KJ), shows the same thing. For Paul so takes for granted that the understanding perception of God's nature includes knowledge of God's demand that he can describe the knowledge of God which is given (as possibility) to the heathen as "knowing God's demand (δικαίωμα)" (Rom. 1:32 Blt.); indeed, this is already implied by the fact that he can describe the sin of the heathen thus: "although they knew God, they did not honor him as God or give thanks to him" (v. 21). Knowledge of God is a lie if it is not acknowledgment of Him. Thus, it is clear that the *nous,* as such, is understanding will with the alternative of being for God or against Him. Man's volition is not an instinctive striving but is an understanding act of will which is always an "evaluating" act and therefore necessarily moves in the sphere of decisions between good and evil. It can go wrong in its judgment as to what is good or evil; it can become blind and be a "depraved intent." Hence, *nous* is not a higher principle in man any more than *psyche* or the human *pneuma* is, but is inherent to man as man and thereby has all the possibilities that human existence has.

2. The other derivatives of the root νο- indicate the same thing. The verb νοεῖν (understand) occurs in Paul only in the passage Rom. 1:20 already discussed; νόημα occurs more frequently. The *noemata* of Satan, II Cor. 2:11, are very clearly his "plots," his "designs" (RSV). When the *noemata* of the Jews are said to be hardened (II Cor. 3:14), the element of understanding thought is more prominent; but the very next verse "the veil is upon their *heart*" (KJ) indicates that the element of attitude or purpose is included, for that is just what is more clearly expressed by "heart" (§ 20, 1). Thus, both terms are combined into a hendiadys in Phil. 4:7: "The peace of God . . . will keep your *hearts* and your *minds.*" In II Cor. 4:4, the element of will is again more prominent when unbelief—which for Paul simultaneously means disobedience—is attributed to the fact that "the god of this world has blinded the *minds* of the unbelievers." This meaning is also clear in the description of the apostle's work, II Cor. 10:5: "taking captive every will (νόημα) to obey Christ" (tr.). Nor is it any different in 11:3: "I fear

. . . lest your *wills* (νοήματα) be led astray from single-hearted devotion to Christ" (tr.).

The terms διάνοια and διανοεῖσθαι (to consider, to purpose) do not occur in Paul; *metanoia* (repentance) occurs at Rom. 2:4 and II Cor. 7:9f., and *metanoein* (repent) at II Cor. 12:21. Its meaning here ("rue," "repent") clearly indicates that it is an act of the will that is meant.

A survey of the words on the root *phren*- can be added in confirmation of the above results. Φρένες in the sense of "understanding" appears only in I Cor. 14:20, where the context shows that what is meant is not just theoretical thinking but an intelligent (as opposed to childish) stand, or intelligent judgment. Φρονεῖν frequently occurs, and characteristic locutions indicate that it means one's "attitude" in which thinking and willing are one: τὸ αὐτό (or: τὸ ἕν) φρονεῖν, "have the same (or, one common) attitude" (RSV usually paraphrases: "live harmoniously" or "agree") Rom. 12:16; 15:5; II Cor. 13:11; Phil. 2:2; 4:2; "take a lofty attitude" (tr.), Rom. 11:20; 12:16; "adopting an earthly attitude," Phil. 3:19; "give way to the will of the flesh" (Blt.), Rom. 8:5. In the expression "be helpfully concerned for . . ." (Phil. 4:10 Blt.) the element of attitude is especially prominent. That φρόνημα means "intent" is clearly indicated by Rom. 8:6f., 27, where the *phronema* of the flesh and of the Spirit are mentioned. Φρόνιμος (wise, sensible) designates the one who has that intelligence or insight which has judgment as to right conduct (I Cor. 10:15; II Cor. 11:19); the "wise in their own conceits" (Rom. 11:25; 12:16) are the conceited ones who pride themselves on their own merits. The ἄφρων ("un-wise," "fool") is not just a dunce in thinking (I Cor. 15:35), but is a fool especially in attitude and conduct (II Cor. 11:16–19; 12:6, 11; "foolishness" in the same sense, 11:1, 17, 21); specifically the heathen are regarded categorically as "fools," Rom. 2:20. That σωφρονεῖν (have a sober or sane mind, Rom. 12:3; II Cor. 5:13) means an attitude of character, is self-evident.

3. According to Rom. 12:2, *nous* has for one of its functions δοκιμάζειν ("prove," "make a judgment"); when the judgment in question is a value-judgment, this word means "to consider worth" or "consider worthy." The element of will included in this meaning emerges clearly in Rom. 1:28: "since they did not *see fit* to acknowl-

edge God"—i.e. the heathen despised, rejected the acknowledgment of God. Elsewhere, with persons as object, this verb means "find worthy in the test" (I Cor. 16:3; II Cor. 8:22; said of God I Thess. 2:4; *cf.* also II Cor. 8:8: "to prove the genuineness of your love"). As the *nous* has the possibility of recognizing the demand for the good, so the faculty of δοκιμάζειν ("proving," "approving") has the ability to recognize τὰ διαφέροντα—i.e. "that which is essential" (Rom. 2:18; Phil. 1:10 Blt.)—or "what is the good and acceptable and perfect will of God" (Rom. 12:2, RSV mg.). In Rom. 14:22, this verb obviously means deciding for what is required. Though the verb also has the more specific meaning "test," this meaning, too, is subordinate to the question concerning what is "good" (I Thess. 5:21: "test everything, hold fast what is good"); this is true in a special way when the object to be tested is he who is to do the testing, himself ("himself" I Cor. 11:28; II Cor. 13:5; "his own work" Gal. 6:4), in which it once more is apparent that the *nous* is the self that makes itself the object of its own judging.

A special form of judging is κρίνειν, which in certain cases can be almost synonymous with δοκιμάζειν (*cf.*, for instance, I Cor. 10:15: "judge for yourselves what I say" or 11:13 with I Thess. 5:21). It often means censorious judgment of others (Rom. 2:1f.; 14:3f., 10, 13; I Cor. 5:12; from the context also I Cor. 4:5, where it is used absolutely; *cf.* also I Cor. 10:29. It is also used in this meaning, of course, of the decision of a judge I Cor. 6:2f. and often of God's judging). Also, the self-condemnation that results from self-examination belongs here (Rom. 14:22). In II Cor. 5:14 judgment concerning a subject under discussion is meant: "making this judgment: that one died for all" (tr.; *cf.* I Cor. 10:15); discriminating judgment is meant in Rom. 14:5 ("judges one day to be better than another," etc., tr.). It means judgment concerning a course to be chosen in Rom. 14:13 ("judge this rather, that no man put a stumbling-block . . . in his brother's way" KJ) and in I Cor. 2:2 ("I reached the judgment not to know anything among you but Jesus Christ," tr.)—also I Cor. 5:3f.; 11:13. Hence, κρίνειν can mean almost "decide" (II Cor. 2:1, "I *made up my mind* not to make you another painful visit," RSV; also, I Cor. 7:37) (RSV directly renders it "decide" at Rom. 14:13; I Cor. 2:2, at least).

In part closely related to κρίνειν (and δοκιμάζειν) is λογίζεσθαι. It likewise can denote judgment of a matter of fact ["we *hold* that

a man is justified by faith," Rom. 3:28 RSV; "*consider* yourselves
dead to sin" (Rom. 6:11); "I *consider* that the sufferings . . . are
not worth comparing" (Rom. 8:18); "who *considers* it unclean"
(Rom. 14:14 tr.); "I do not *consider* . . ." (Phil. 3:13 RSV)]. Judgment about a person can also be meant: I Cor. 4:1 ("regard"),
II Cor. 10:2b; (a little differently, with a figurative use of a mercan-
tile expression): II Cor. 12:6 (λ. εἰς ἐμέ = "give me credit"). In
other passages ·one can waver in opinion whether this verb means
judgment concerning a matter of fact or only means "think," "weigh,"
"ponder"; such cases are Rom. 2:3; II Cor. 10:2, 7 (RSV: "let him
remind himself that as he is Christ's, so are we;"); 10:11 ("let such
people understand," etc.); 11:5 ("I *think* that I am not in the least
inferior . . ."). At any rate, in II Cor. 3:5 it means "consider" (not
"think something up"); but in Phil. 4:8, on the contrary, it means
merely "ponder," "think about," and in I Cor. 13:11 ("as a child")
simply "think."

4. Other terms for "understanding" or "knowing" such as
γινώσκειν and εἰδέναι have no specifically anthropological significance; i.e. they do designate acts that belong to man, but mean
specific acts or states, from case to case, and neither characterize
human existence as such nor contain the possibility of good or evil.
Only the concept συνείδησις (conscience) belongs to the fundamental anthropological concepts. This word, which originally meant
joint knowledge (συν-ειδησις) with another, had in Paul's time long
since come to have the meaning of knowledge shared with one's self.
Hellenistic Judaism had already appropriated the word in this sense,
but any such term was still foreign to the Hebrew Old Testament
(though not the phenomenon denoted by it; note, moreover, LXX
Job 27:6: οὐ γὰρ σύνοιδα ἐμαυτῷ ἄτοπα πράξας, "for I am not conscious of having done wrong" = almost "my conscience does not
accuse me of having done wrong"; LXX Eccles. 10:20 uses the
noun, but in its original sense). It is in this sense that it is used by
Paul, through whom, perhaps, it was first introduced into Christian
language.

This term, too, denotes a relationship of a man to himself, though
in a different way than *soma* does. While *soma* serves to distinguish
the objectivized self from the real self and to characterize the *soma*-
self as the object of one's own action or that of outside powers,
συνείδησις ("conscience") is a man's knowledge ("consciousness")

of his conduct as his own. Unlike *nous*, it is not a state of mind that includes an intent but one that, reflecting and judging, scrutinizes precisely this intent of one's own mind. Conscience judges; i.e. it is a knowledge about one's own conduct in respect to a requirement which exists in relation to that conduct. Hence, "conscience" is at one and the same time a knowledge of good and evil and of the corresponding conduct. This knowledge may point toward still unaccomplished conduct, a duty to be fulfilled, as well as critically judge already happened conduct. Both are involved in I Cor. 8:7–12; 10:25–30. For the idea is, on the one hand, that "conscience" forbids "the weak" to eat food that has been offered to idols, but on the other hand, Paul's thought evidently is that if "the weak" nevertheless eat it and thereby get their conscience "defiled" (8:7), they will have "a bad conscience." Rom. 2:15, also, probably refers first of all to the demanding, binding conscience, since "conscience" is to be regarded as a proof that the requirements of the Law are written in the hearts of the heathen. If, then, the added words apply not to social discussion (in which case one would translate: "while their discussions among themselves accuse or perhaps excuse," tr.) but to the conflict within a man, interpreting the term "conscience," as they probably do ("their conflicting thoughts accuse or perhaps excuse them," RSV), the consequence is that Paul is also thinking of the judging conscience which accuses the doer with an accusation which he (at times) resists.* If, according to Rom. 13:5, the citizen is to yield obedience to the government "for the sake of conscience," then it is the conscience that prescribes what is to be done. And when Paul as an apostle commends himself "to every man's conscience" (II Cor. 4:2), he means that the conscience of those who come to know him as an apostle forces them to an approving verdict as to his sincerity. Likewise, when he hopes not to be misunderstood by the Corinthians ("I hope to be revealed [for what I *am*] in your *consciences*," II Cor. 5:11, tr.), if they let themselves be guided by their "conscience." That is, conscience demands in each case a specific attitude. Elsewhere, the word means the judging conscience that can either condemn or acquit. Thus, I Cor. 4:4: "for my conscience (συνοῖδα) has nothing against me" (tr.)—here the verdict is acquittal. Likewise, Rom. 9:1: Paul's "conscience"

* In any case v. 15 must not be combined with v. 16 into one sentence; v. 16 is a secondary gloss.

testifies that he is telling the truth. Also, II Cor. 1:12: his "conscience" testifies to him the sincerity of his way of life.

As Rom. 2:15 indicates, Paul considered conscience a universal human phenomenon—consistent with his view of human existence as we have thus far unfolded it. For if it is inherently human to have knowledge of one's self, and if the life a man has to lead lies ahead of him and can be won or lost (§ 18, 4), and if, therefore, the good that he seeks takes on the nature of requirement (see 1, above), then it is inherently human to have conscience. Paul takes it for granted that the heathen have a conscience. That he understands conscience as knowledge of the demand that is incumbent upon man, is to be concluded from the circumstance that this very fact of their having conscience testifies to him that the heathen know the demands of the Law, even though they do not have the Law; they are "written in their hearts," i.e. it is just by virtue of their "conscience" that they know them.

Insofar as the conscience's knowledge applies to *that which is demanded* of man, the decisive thing is that conscience knows that there *is* such a thing *at all*; for it is possible for it to err in regard to the *content* of that demand. That is true of the conscience of those in Corinth who suppose themselves to be obligated not to eat food offered to idols (I Cor. 8:7-12; 10:25-30); their conscience is called "weak," and they themselves, lacking correct "knowledge," are "weak." Nevertheless, the verdict of conscience which falls upon a man's conduct in view of what is demanded cannot err, but is valid. Those Corinthians, according to Paul, are really bound to the verdict of their conscience and may not be forced into conduct which their conscience condemns. Likewise, the certainty with which Paul appeals to the testimony of his conscience in defense of his conduct shows that its verdict is not subject to doubt (Rom. 9:1; II Cor. 1:12). But that rests upon the fact that the demand perceived by conscience has its foundation in a sphere transcendent to man; to acknowledge *that sphere* is in the end the decisive thing, though man may err in what he believes he hears as its demand. That is why Paul can motivate the duty of obedience to the government in a peculiarly double way (Rom. 13:5): The citizen owes the government obedience not only "for the sake of wrath," i.e. for fear of its power to punish (*cf.* v. 4; "*God's*" in v. 5 RSV is an interpretative addition!), but also "for the sake of conscience," i.e. for fear of the transcendent source of authority that stands behind conscience— for Paul, of course, God. And just as here "conscience," which was originally man's knowledge, is conceived as independent of him and used by metonomy for that authority of which the knowledge in "conscience" knows, so in Rom. 9:1; II Cor. 1:12 the conscience is accorded separate existence ("personified") as an authority beyond man—which indicates that the essential thing about "conscience" is just this obligation to its transcendent source of authority. Conscience, so to say, steps in as an independent witness with the man whose binding obligation she is.

Here again we see that Paul understands a man's self as the specific self which becomes his by his assuming responsibility, irrespective of the judgments of men, for the particular life turned over to him from outside himself. Precisely in "conscience," which a man has by virtue of a power which transcends it, his self constitutes itself as his specific self. The verdict of conscience is absolutely valid, inasmuch as in it obedience to the transcendent power takes place, hence, precisely in "conscience" man has his "freedom" (I Cor. 10:29). No other person has the right to force his judgment upon me: "for why is my freedom decided by any other conscience [than my own]?" (tr.)

This sentence is not to be taken as the objection of an opponent (Lietzmann). V. 27 (and 25, too,) had said, one need not ask for conscience' sake whether meat served at a meal has been offered to idols (i.e. there is no obligation to refuse such meat under any and all circumstances). If, however, the heathen host points out (with good or evil intent) that the meal served is sacrificial meat (v. 28), it is to be declined—declined not only for the informer's sake, but also for conscience' sake. V. 29 then comments on the motive for declining—not because one's own conscience demands it, but for the sake of the other's (i.e. the "weak" one's) conscience, lest he be caused to act contrary to his conscience. If "I" (Paul) supposed that I had to decline for the sake of *my* conscience, I would have submitted to another's judgment and surrendered my freedom; in principle, I am free to eat anything that I can eat with thanksgiving (i.e. with a "good conscience"; v. 30); but I do not surrender my freedom either, if I decline out of consideration for another's conscience.

The situation is the same when what is involved is not judgment concerning a duty still to be fulfilled but judgment of conduct already carried out. He whose conscience acquits him is no longer subject to any human authority—or rather such judgment is indifferent to him (I Cor. 4:3f.).

Since Paul takes for granted that the transcendent authority, whose demand and verdict conscience knows, is known by Christians as God, he can substitute "faith" for "conscience," insofar as faith (on whose complete structure see § 32) is obedience to God's demand. It is through this insight that the fact is to be understood that Paul argues on the basis of "faith" in the analogous question of Rom. 14 quite as he does on the basis of "conscience" in I Cor. 8 and 10. "One man has the faith (πιστεύει) that he may eat anything" (Rom. 14:2, tr.) means exactly that the verdict of one man's conscience permits him to eat anything. And the concluding statement, "and whatever does not proceed from faith is sin" (v. 23b, tr.), corresponds to the assertion that it would be a "stumbling-block" (i.e. seduction to sin) to cause "the weak" to act against his conscience (I Cor. 8:9) and that "the weak" would thereby fall into "ruin" (I Cor. 8:11; *cf.* Rom. 14:15). Thus, the verdict of "conscience" coincides for the Christian (as a man of "faith") with the verdict of "faith"; and the verdict of faith, like that of conscience, has validity even if it is mistaken as to what is required of it. He who is "weak in faith" (Rom. 14:1f.) corresponds to the weak in conscience (I Cor. 8:7, 9, 12). And when the term *nous* (mind, judgment) takes the place of the term "faith" ("Let every one be fully convinced in his own *judgment*," Rom. 14:5, tr.; see 1, above), that is only possible because the term "faith" includes just that element of conscious judgment which is present in the term "conscience." Vice versa, the analogy between "conscience" and "faith" confirms our conclusion that conscience means the self's knowledge of itself (the conduct that is demanded of it, or its conduct subject to the Judge's verdict) in responsibility to the transcendent power (of God).

§ 20. Heart

1. Just as in the LXX לֵב (heart) is rendered either by καρδία (heart) or by νοῦς (mind), Paul uses "heart" to a large extent synonymously with *nous*; viz. to designate the self as a willing, plan-

ning, intending self. In II Cor. 3:14f., "minds" and "heart" are parallel in content (RSV renders both: "minds"), and in Phil. 4:7, the two terms constitute a hendiadys (§ 19, 2). Just as the *nous* (or the νοήματα, "minds," "wills") can be detestable, hardened, blinded, or corrupted (Rom. 1:28; II Cor. 3:14; 4:4; 11:3), so can "the heart" (Rom. 1:21; 2:5; 16:18); and as the *nous* must be renewed (Rom. 12:2), so must "the heart" be illumined (II Cor. 4:6). Since the "heart" is called "impenitent" (Rom. 2:5), it is apparent that penitence (μετάνοια, change of mind) is a matter of the "heart."

Like *nous*, "heart" is a man's self, and in most cases where it is used it performs the service of a personal pronoun. For the "heart" is the subject that desires (Rom. 10:1), lusts (Rom. 1:24), purposes (I Cor. 4:5), decides (I Cor. 7:37; II Cor. 9:7), grieves (Rom. 9:2), suffers (II Cor. 2:4), and loves (II Cor. 7:3; 8:16; Phil. 1:7). Clearly the "heart" is not a higher principle in man, any more than *nous* is, but just the intending, purposing self—which decides within itself or is moved from without—which can turn to either the good or the bad. As it can be "darkened," and "hardened" (Rom. 1:21; 2:5), it can also be the victim of deception (Rom. 16:18) or have evil desires (Rom. 1:24). God "who searches hearts" (Rom. 8:27) or "tests" them (I Thess. 2:4, after Jer. 11:20), will bring to light the purposes of men's hearts and judge them (I Cor. 4:5).

Moreover, the heart doubts as well as believes (Rom. 10:6–10). As refusal of faith is hardening of the *heart* (II Cor. 3:14f.), so faith arises when God causes light to dawn in the *heart* (II Cor. 4:6). It is God who can "establish" hearts (make them firm, I Thess. 3:13); he confers the gift of the Spirit upon our hearts (II Cor. 1:22; Gal. 4:6); his love has been poured into the hearts of believers by the Spirit (Rom. 5:5). Everywhere "heart" stands for the self (*cf.*, for example, II Cor. 1:22 with 5:5). The statement that "the demands of the Law are written in the heart of the heathen" (Rom. 2:15) simply means that in their "conscience" they know these demands (§ 19, 3).*

Paul can use (τὰ) σπλάγχνα ("bowels," KJ) almost synonymously with "heart," except that "bowels" is confined to a much narrower territory, viz. to denote the self as moved by love,

---

* The expression "from the heart"—i.e. with dedication of one's whole person—occurs in a secondary gloss: Rom. 6:17; *cf.* Mk. 12:30, 33 parr.; I Tim. 1:5; II Tim. 2:22; I Pet. 1:22.

II Cor. 6:12 (RSV: "affections"; here the word is parallel with "heart"); 7:15 and Phlm. 12 (RSV here renders it "heart"!). By metonymy, σπλάγχνα stands for "love" itself in Phil. 1:8; 2:1. In Phlm. 7 and 20 ("refresh the heart") it substitutes for a personal pronoun in the very phrase in which *pneuma* does the same (at I Cor. 16:18; II Cor. 7:13).

The difference between *nous* (mind) and *kardia* (heart) lies in the fact that the element of knowing which is contained in "mind" and can be prominently present is not emphasized in "heart," in which the dominant element is striving and will and also the state of being moved by feelings (pain and love). Another nuance of difference exists in this: the term "heart" can express the idea that the self's intent and will may be a hidden thing; "heart" is the "interior" in contrast to the "exterior," the real self in contrast to what a man appears to be. As in I Thess. 2:17, the external separation of the apostle from the congregation is contrasted as being a separation "on the surface" (ἐν προσώπῳ) with a separation "in the heart," so in II Cor. 5:12 a "boasting about the exterior" (ἐν προσώπῳ, i.e. on the basis of externally visible, impressive merits) is contrasted with a "boasting about the interior" (ἐν καρδίᾳ, i.e. on the basis of invisible qualities). Similarly, in Rom. 2:28f. "external, physical circumcision" and "inward (καρδίας) circumcision" confront each other in contrast. The "purposes of hearts" (I Cor. 4:5) are hidden until God brings them to light; the "secrets of the heart" are disclosed by the prophet-inspiring Spirit (I Cor. 14:25).

II Cor. 3:2 is complicated and not entirely clear (that is why the text-tradition is also uncertain): The Corinthian Church is Paul's letter of recommendation—a letter that can be universally seen and read, since anyone can perceive that Church ("known . . . by all men"); and yet Paul also calls this a letter "written in your hearts" (read "your" following ℵ pc., not "our") because he wants to contrast it with a literal document of recommendation; to that extent, therefore, it is an invisible letter, a letter not written with ink, as v. 3 proceeds to say, but with the divine Spirit. But now another thought is woven in: The recommendation with which God has equipped Paul is not written on "tablets of stone" but on "hearts of flesh" (read: ἐν καρδίαις σαρκίναις!); now it is contrasted with the Law of Moses, and with a formulation determined by reminiscences of the Old

Testament. That is, the description of "hearts" as "fleshly" which means "living hearts" (in contrast to the "tablets of stone") is derived from Ezek. 11:19; 36:26. At any rate, "heart" is clearly regarded to be that inward sphere which is the seat of life.

The exterior and the interior, separately named, can also be combined to designate the totality of man. Thus, "mouth" and "heart" stand in parallelism of members in Rom. 10:9f.; II Cor. 6:11 (for which "we" is introduced in v. 12), quite as "eye," "ear," and "heart," combined in the apocryphal quotation, I Cor. 2:9, describe man's possibilities of perception.

2. The strivings of the "heart" can actualize themselves in conscious volition. The words that designate this possibility are primarily θέλειν (to will) and θέλημα (will).

Θέλειν means "to will" in various nuances, and its meaning is frequently incapable of being very precisely defined. A willing, which is definite decision, is meant in these places (disregarding the passages where it is said of God): Rom. 9:16; I Cor. 4:21 ("what do you wish?" = decide!); 10:27; Gal. 4:9; Phlm. 14; it is expressly distinguished from execution (ποιῆσαι, "do" or ἐνεργεῖν, "work"): II Cor. 8:10f.; Phil. 2:13. Elsewhere, it means "desire," "long for": II Cor. 5:4; 11:12; 12:20; Gal. 4:17 or a wishing which may be ardent: Rom. 16:19; I Cor. 7:32; 10:20; Gal. 4:20; I Thess. 2:18, or may be less ardent, "like": "I should like . . .": I Cor. 7:7; 14:5; Gal. 3:2 or "I prefer," I Cor. 14:19; finally, it can be used quite unemphatically as in phrases like "I *would* not have you ignorant," KJ: Rom. 1:13; I Cor. 10:1, etc.

Θέλημα is used mostly of God's will, his deliberative decree (in such phrases as "by the will of God," Rom. 15:32; Gal. 1:4, etc.) or his demanding will (Rom. 2:18, etc.). It is also used of the decision or the intention of man (I Cor. 7:37; 16:12).

It is important to note that human "will" can aim at the "good" (Rom. 7:15–21) as well as at the bad or perverse (Gal. 1:7; 4:9, 21; 6:12), but especially that "will" need not penetrate into the field of consciousness at all, but may designate the hidden tendency of the self. The rhetorical question (Rom. 13:3): "*Would* you have no fear of him who is in authority?" presupposes that everyone "wills" to live without fear of the public authorities without necessarily being conscious of this will. When Paul characterizes his opponents in

Gal. 6:12 as "those who want to make a good showing in the flesh," he is not naming their conscious intention but their secret motive hidden even from themselves; likewise, when he says of them (6:13): "they desire to have you circumcised that they may glory in your flesh." The willing of the "good" in Rom. 7:15–21 is the self's innermost tendency which is covered up and hidden by the conscious desires which bring forth deeds. And if the consequence of the battle between Flesh and Spirit over man, according to Gal. 5:17, is that man does not do what he "wills" to do, then this passage also does not have in mind what man in the specific case actually does will but what he wills *at heart,* an intention which can be perverted in his concrete will (through the influence of Flesh). The case of Gal. 4:21 is somewhat different. "You who *desire* to be under law" does not, it is true, pertain to the Galatians' conscious will, but neither does it mean the real desire of their "heart"; rather, it means the "unintentional" consequence of their purpose to combine obedience to the Law (or at least certain of its regulations) with faith; for they do not perceive the exclusive antinomy between "life under Law" and "life under grace." Gal. 1:7 is a related case; here Paul's opponents are called they who "want to pervert the gospel of Christ." The perverting of the gospel into its opposite is, of course, not the intention of these people, but is the hidden meaning of their willing —hidden even from themselves.

A few times Paul uses βούλεσθαι (decide, purpose) for human intention (II Cor. 1:15, 17) or wish (Phil. 1:12; Phlm. 13). The "strivings (βουλαί) of hearts" (I Cor. 4:5) are purposes that need not be actualized in conscious will. God's βούλημα (will) is mentioned in Rom. 9:19.

The expression "desires of their hearts" (Rom. 1:24) indicates that "desire" is·an activity of "the heart." Admittedly, Paul frequently uses the verb or the noun (ἐπιθυμεῖν, ἐπιθυμία) not as an anthropological term denoting desire in general, but in a qualified sense, in which "desire" (used absolutely) is in itself evil. This is the case in the formula, "Desire not!" (Rom. 7:7 tr., 13:9; also I Cor. 10:6b, though here it is easy to supply the object "evil" from 6a). "Desire," as such, is also evil in Rom. 1:24; 7:7f.; I Thess. 4:5, and in Rom. 13:14; Gal. 5:16, 24 is attributed to the flesh (as in Rom. 6:12 to the flesh-dominated "body"). Nevertheless, the very fact that Spirit as well as Flesh can have "desires" (Gal. 5:17) by itself indicates that the original meaning of "desire" is simply the direction in which one yearns. This is its meaning in Phil. 1:23: "My desire is to depart and be with Christ," and in I Thess. 2:17: "we endeavored . . . with great desire to see you face to face." In both cases "desire" has the meaning of "longing," and in itself therefore is nothing evil.

Θυμός in classic Greek frequently meaning, among other things, "desire," "appetite" and any "passion," occurs in Paul only in the qualified meaning, "wrath" (Rom. 2:8; II Cor. 12:20; Gal. 5:20); but the derivatives προθυμία ("readiness," "zeal for the good," II Cor. 8:11f., 19; 9:2) and πρόθυμος ("eager," Rom. 1:15) occur in the old, neutral sense.

Other verbs that denote striving and purpose with various nuances are the following:

Σκοπεῖν (II Cor. 4:18) means "focus upon . . ." i.e. upon an object as the goal worth striving for, just as σκοπός is the "goal" which guides the "onward pressing" of Phil. 3:14. Selfish striving is meant by τὰ ἑαυτοῦ σκοπεῖν, Phil. 2:4—looking to one's own interests. When σκοπεῖν is used in the sense of "wary attention to . . ." or of "bewaring of . . ." (Rom. 16:17; Gal. 6:1; Phil. 3:17), it still has the basic meaning of a conduct-guiding "viewing" in one's own interest. Ζητεῖν (to seek), too, means striving as such—after either good or evil. Its object may be "incorruption" (Rom. 2:7) or "wisdom" (I Cor. 1:22). Paul and Peter are "endeavoring to be justified in Christ" (Gal. 2:17). Paul exhorts: "strive to excel in building up the church" (I Cor. 14:12); he describes his relation to the Corinthians: "I seek not what is yours, but you" (II Cor. 12:14). Foolish "seeking" would "seek glory from men" (I Thess. 2:6) or seek "the favor of men" (Gal. 1:10); the Jews "seek to establish their own (righteousness)" (Rom. 10:3). "Seeking one's own" (τὰ ἑαυτοῦ ζητεῖν, I Cor. 10:24, 33; 13:5; Phil. 2:21) is selfish purpose; its opposite is "seeking (the advantage) of the many" (I Cor. 10:33 tr.). Intense purpose is called ζηλοῦν (be zealous after), whose object likewise can be good or evil. Paul is "zealous" (or "jealous"—ultimately both are the same word) for the Church with "a divine zeal" (or "jealousy"), II Cor. 11:2, while the preachers of the Law in Galatia are "zealously after" ("make much of," RSV) the Galatians in order that the latter in turn may "make much of" them. The apostle urges that "spiritual gifts" be "zealously sought after" (I Cor. 12:31; 14:1, 39). Like "desire," ζηλοῦν can also be used absolutely; when it is, it is used with a qualified (pejorative) meaning (I Cor. 13:4: "Love is not jealous"), and ζῆλος, "jealousy" (likewise, used absolutely), is, correspondingly, a vice characteristic of heathen nature (Rom. 13:13; I Cor. 3:3; II Cor. 12:20; Gal. 5:20). But the fact that ζῆλος, "zeal," can be directed toward either right or wrong ends indicates that its basic meaning is that of a non-qualified striving. Paul concedes to the Jews that they have "a zeal for God" and he himself is "zealous with a divine zeal" (II Cor. 11:2, see above), and he praises the "zeal" of the Corinthians for the collection (II Cor. 9:2). There is such a thing as "zeal" for another's welfare (II Cor. 7:7: "for me"; cf. v. 11); but there is also reprehensible "zeal" (Phil. 3:6: "as to zeal a persecutor of the church"). The same is true of ζηλωτής (one who is zealous, I Cor. 14:12; Gal. 1:14). Διώκειν (to pursue) in the figurative sense means, much like ζηλοῦν, eager striving, but it is not used absolutely in a qualified (pejorative) sense, but in itself is neutral, receiving any qualification only from its object—as it happens (accidentally), always a good qualification (Rom. 9:30f.: "righteousness" or "the Law of righteousness"; 12:13: "hospitality"; 14:19: "what makes for peace"; I Cor. 14:1: "love"; I Thess. 5:15: "the good"; figurative Phil. 3:12, 14). Μεριμνᾶν (be anxious about), finally, denotes solicitous care of a thing or a person. That it can operate in opposite directions, is indicated by I Cor. 7:32-34, where "worldly affairs" and "the affairs of the Lord" are named as its objects. It means "solicitude," "care for another's welfare" in I Cor. 12:25 ("for one another") and Phil. 2:20 ("anxious for your welfare"), and the noun is used in the same sense in II Cor. 11:28. Still, Paul can also use μεριμνᾶν, like "desire," absolutely in the qualified sense of something wrong in itself (Phil. 4:6), and hence he can write, I Cor. 7:32: "I want you to be free from all anxieties (ἀμερίμνους)."

So far as the "heart" is the self which is stirred by feelings and emotions, it may express itself in χαίρειν (rejoicing), λυπεῖσθαι (sorrowing), or κλαίειν (weeping). All these verbs describe human conduct simply as such, not as either good or bad, as particularly Rom. 12:15 and I Cor. 7:30 show in the case of joy and sorrow. I Cor. 13:6 shows that joy can relate to either good or bad. Analogously, II Cor. 7:9-11 distinguishes between "godly grief" and "worldly grief." Specifically, Christian joy is joy "in" (Rom. 14:17) or "of" (I Thess. 1:6) "the Holy Spirit."

B. FLESH, SIN, AND WORLD

§ 21. Creation and Man

1. As the investigation of the term *soma* showed (§ 17, 2), man, according to Paul, is a being who has a relationship to himself, is placed at his own disposal, and is responsible for his own existence. But this existence of his, as the investigation of the terms *psyche, pneuma, zoe, nous,* and *kardia* showed (§§ 18–20), is never to be found in the present as a fulfilled reality, but always lies ahead of him. In other words, his existence is always an intention and a quest, and in it he may find himself or lose his grip upon himself, gain his self or fail to do so. This brings in the possibility that man can be good or bad; for just because he must first find his life (that which is "good"—meaning the existence that at heart he wants), this existence comes to have for him the character of the "good"—in the sense of that which is required of him (§ 19, 1).

If, up to this point, the ontological structure of human existence, as Paul sees it, has been clarified, this, nevertheless, only affords the presuppositions for his ontic statements about man in which his real interest lies. It has already become apparent that several anthropological terms which have a primarily unqualified ontological meaning are at times used by Paul in a qualified ontic sense. *Soma,* since it is factually dominated by "flesh," can be used synonymously with "flesh"; i.e. ontically regarded, the *soma* is a "*soma* of sin" (§ 17, 2, 3). *Vice versa, nous* can mean the affirmation, though a fruitless one, of the demand for the good (§ 19, 1), while "desire," in the other direction again, can have the qualified sense of *evil* desire (§ 20, 2); so can ζηλοῦν ("be zealous," but also "be jealous") and μεριμνᾶν ("be solicitous," but also "be anxious," § 20, 2).

These phenomena indicate that Paul is of this opinion: *Man has always already missed the existence that at heart he seeks,* his intent is basically perverse, evil. Indeed, the view that all men are sinners, which he develops at length in Rom. 1:18–3:20, is a basic one for his doctrine of salvation; through Adam, sin and death came into the world as dominant powers (Rom. 5:12ff.); "the scripture consigned all men to sin" (Gal. 3:22, tr.).

[227]

In order to understand this view it is necessary to clarify what the meaning of evil is according to Paul. And since in his cogitations the presupposition is taken for granted that evil is in any case "sin"—rebellion against God, guilt toward God—his idea of God, so far as it is pertinent to this context, must first be presented.

2. Paul constantly sees man as placed before God. The ontological possibility of being good or evil is simultaneously the ontic possibility of having a relationship to God; and God, for Paul, is not the mythological designation for an ontological state of affairs but the personal God, man's Creator who demands obedience of him. The ontological possibility of being good or evil is ontically the choice of either acknowledging the Creator and obeying Him, or of refusing Him obedience. The demand for good which is made upon man is God's demand, which, as such, is a "life-giving demand" (Rom. 7:10, tr.); and disobedience is, therefore, sin.

In accordance with the Old Testament tradition Paul speaks of God as the Creator. It is God who once commanded light to shine forth out of darkness (II Cor. 4:6 from Gen. 1:3), and created man (I Cor. 11:8-12; *cf.* 15:45, 47). The earth with its contents is His, as I Cor. 10:26 in allusion to Ps. 24:1 says. God's creatorship is not, for Paul, a cosmological theory which professes to explain the origin of the world and its existence as it is. Rather, it is a proposition that concerns man's existence. It concerns him, for instance, in the fact that the earth as God's creation is at man's disposal for his needs, as the Old Testament creation-story (Gen. 1:26) had already said; hence, there is nothing on the earth that is unclean or untouchable (I Cor. 10:25f., 30; Rom. 14:14, 20).

"All things are yours" (I Cor. 3:21f.), is not relevant here, because it applies specifically to Christians and has a different meaning. Neither can it be said (see W. Gudbrod, *Die Paulinische Anthropologie*) that the goal of God's work of creation is stated in I Cor. 15:28: "that God may be all in all" (KJ); for the drama described in I Cor. 15:20-28 does not come from the tradition of the creation-story, but from Gnostic cosmology and eschatology. What I Cor. 15:28 deals with is the end of the battle against the Powers that are at enmity with God.

But knowledge of God as Creator contains primarily knowledge of man—man, that is, in his creatureliness and in his situation of being one to whom God has laid claim. Yes, Paul does use familiar ideas of Stoic "natural theology" in Rom. 1:19f., but not in order to prove the sheer existence of God and His world-dominating providence so that he may thereby enlighten man and free him from "ignorance of God" and from fear. Rather, he uses them in order to accuse, specifically to expose, the guilt of the heathen: With evil will they refused to pay heed to the possibility of knowing God that was given to them. To know God means in itself to acknowledge God, obey His demand (δικαίωμα, 1:32), bow before Him in grateful adoration (1:21; *cf.* I Cor. 10:31).

That God's existence is not an objectively perceptible, mere existing like that of a thing, is indicated by I Cor. 8:4–6. If God were being spoken of as only a cosmic Thing, the statement, "there is no God but one," would not be right at all; for in this sense of "is," other "gods" and "lords" "are." The "uniqueness" of God is His εἶναι ἡμῖν, His being "*for us.*" That is, His being (existence) is understood aright only when it is understood as significant-for-man being; hence, it is not understood aright unless at the same time man's being is also understood as springing from God ("from whom are all things") and thereby oriented toward Him ("and toward whom we exist," I Cor. 8:6).

Here, as also in Rom. 11:36, "for from him and through him and to him are all things," Paul is using a formula of Stoic pantheism. But in this Romans passage it is especially clear how far Paul is from orienting his concept of God to the cosmos in the Greek sense. For, as the closing sentence of chapters 9–11, the formula has lost its original cosmological meaning and serves the purpose of expressing Paul's theology of history: The history of nations is salvation-history, and its origin, its guidance, and its goal are all in God.

3. For Paul, the word *cosmos,* accordingly, has in the great majority of cases a meaning different from that of the Greek conception of the world (§ 26). As the created world, here and now existing, Paul calls it "creation," with reference to its Creator (Rom. 1:25). When the world is so regarded, man is excepted from it, even though as "mortal man" (Rom. 1:23) he belongs to it. But as a being endowed by God with special dignity and responsibility (*cf.* I Cor. 11:3, 7, "he is the image and glory of God"), man stands between God and the creation and must decide between the two.

The "creation" is characterized by creaturely transitoriness (φθαρτόν, Rom. 1:23; 8:20f.). In obscure words, which evidently go back to a myth, Paul hints that it was not always so, but that the creation was involuntarily subjected to "futility," "bondage to decay" —subjected, moreover, by "him who subjected it"—but that some day it, like "the children of God," will be set free from the curse of transitoriness (Rom. 8:20f.). Since it is unclear whom Paul means by the "subjector" (God? Satan? Adam?), we cannot understand this in detail; all that is clear is that the "creation" has a history which it shares with men—a fact which once again indicates how completely the cosmological point of view recedes for Paul behind that of his theology of history.

When Rom. 8:20f. speaks of the "creation" subject to transitoriness and longing for freedom, what is meant is evidently the earth and its creatures subordinate to man, not the *cosmic powers* which are enumerated in 8:38f. Although this enumeration strings together heterogeneous elements when it combines "death" and "life" (the former of which, it is true, could conceivably be a cosmic power in keeping with I Cor. 15:26) and "things present" and "things to come" with the cosmic powers, still in the case of "angels," "principalities" and "powers" at least, and probably also in the case of "height" and "depth," it does name cosmic powers which belong to the world created by God. This would be the case even if the additional remark, "nor any other created thing," did not directly say so. While this sentence testifies on the one hand that the activity of such powers is restricted by the will of God, nevertheless it presupposes, on the other hand, that there is an area of the creation in which rebellious powers, at enmity with God and man, hold sway.

Thus, the creation has a peculiarly ambiguous character: On the one hand, it is the earth placed by God at man's disposal for his use and benefit (I Cor. 10:26, see above, 2); on the other, it is the field of activity for evil, demonic powers. The historical observation, correct as far as it goes, that Old Testament tradition and Gnostic tradition have flowed together here, does not sufficiently explain the facts. Paul is able to appropriate the cosmological mythology of Gnosticism because it enables him to express the fact that the perishable "creation" becomes a destructive power whenever man decides in favor of it instead of for God (Rom. 1:25, see above); i.e. when he bases his life upon it rather than upon God. Hence, it owes to man himself such independence as it has toward God; how this is so, must be clarified later by investigation of the term "flesh" (sarx). But this much is already clear: Paul's conception of the creation, as well as of the Creator, depends upon what it means for man's existence; under this point of view the creation is ambivalent.

4. As God and the creation are regarded as being within the horizon of a theological view of history—i.e. in regard to their significance for man and his history—correspondingly *man's being* is understood in its relatedness to the Creator and the creation.

Only rarely does Paul use the word "man" (*anthropos*) to designate the species man as one of the creatures of this world in distinction from other living beings, such as beasts (I Cor. 15:39) or angels (I Cor. 4:9; 13:1).

We here leave out of account the passages where *anthropos* is used unemphatically for "some one," "any one" or "one" (Rom. 7:1; I Cor. 4:1; II Cor. 12:2f.; Gal. 6:1, 7) or where πᾶς ἄνθρωπος with no definite antithesis means "everyone" (Gal. 5:3) or where its plural means simply "all" (Rom. 12:17f.; I Cor. 7:7; 15:19; II Cor. 3:2; Phil. 4:5; I Thess. 2:15).

In most passages, *anthropos* means man in his creaturely humanity, and that means also man in his relation to God. It is in his creatureliness that man is regarded when Paul rhetorically says that the "foolishness of God" is wiser than men and the "weakness of God" stronger than men (I Cor. 1:25), or when he asks, "O man, who are you to answer back to God?" (Rom. 9:20 tr.). Before God, every human complaint must become dumb: "Let God be true though every man be false" (Rom. 3:4). God's authorization puts Paul's legitimation beyond doubt as "an apostle not from men nor through man, but through Jesus Christ and God the Father" (Gal. 1:1; *cf.* 1:11f.). It is to God and not to man that one must look to find the right norm for apostolic activity (I Thess. 2:4, 6; Gal. 1:10), and the apostle's word is God's word, not man's (I Thess. 2:13); whoever disdains it, despises not men but God (I Thess. 4:8).

Before God, all human distinctions vanish; before him Jew and Greek stand alike as "man" (Rom. 3:28f.). Human greatness and human evaluations are nil before God. It would be madness for one chosen by God as a slave of Christ to make himself a slave of men by orienting himself according to human evaluations (I Cor. 7:23). It would be madness to boast of men (I Cor. 3:21). Praise from

God alone, not from men, has any importance (Rom. 2:29). Wherever jealousy and strife still find room, there things are still going in human fashion (I Cor. 3:3). The paradoxicality of the salvation-occurrence finds expression in the Christ-hymn which had been taken over by Paul (Phil. 2:6f.): he who had been in the form of God (= of divine nature) appeared on earth as a man, in human form; in so doing he "emptied himself"—therefore, there is nothing divine about man or in him! This understanding of man is the background of the formula, "I speak in a human way" (Rom. 3:5; I Cor. 3:3; 9:8; Gal. 3:15; *cf.* Rom. 6:19), which designates the form of a statement about things divine as really inappropriate to its content; the apostle must so speak only "on account of the weakness of the flesh" (RSV paraphrases interpretively: "because of your natural limitations," Rom. 6:19).

§ 22. The Term "Flesh" (Sarx)

Evil, our investigation of Paul's anthropological terms has shown (§§17-20), is perverse intent, a perverse pursuit, specifically a pursuit which misses what is good—i.e. misses "life," what man at heart is after—and it is evil, because the good it misses is also that which is required of a man. But to miss what is required is also sin, rebellion against God, who as Creator is the origin of life and whose commandment is a "commandment unto life" (§ 21). Hence, the alternative to lay hold of one's true existence or to miss it is synonymous with the alternative to acknowledge God as the Creator or to deny Him. And denial of God means failure to acknowledge one's own creatureliness. And since all pursuit, even the perverted sort, is, in intention, pursuit of life, this means seeking life where it is not —in the created world. For to deny God as Creator is to turn away from Him to the creation (§ 21). But the creation stands at man's disposal; hence, to seek life in it means to have the presumption to seek life in the disposable, i.e. to presume to have life at one's own disposal. Hence, the ultimate sin reveals itself to be the false assumption of receiving life not as the gift of the Creator but procuring it by one's own power, of living from one's self rather than from God.

Paul developed this train of thought neither so abstractly nor so compactly as this; but it underlies his discussions of sin, as is apparent in his statements about creation and man (§ 21), and as investigation of the term "flesh" will above all make clear.

2. *Sarx* means, first of all, "flesh" as man's material corporeality. In contrast to κρέας ("meat," animal flesh intended for food, Rom. 14:21; I Cor. 8:13), it is the animate flesh of man, active in its sensual manifestations and perceptible to the senses. *Sarx,* therefore, (in spite of I Cor. 15:39; see § 17, 1) does not mean simply "matter" (ὕλη) in contrast to "form"; while, though it does primarily mean a material, it means a material only as it is formed and animated in the human body. That is the only reason that *sarx* can occasionally be used synonymously with *soma* (§ 17, 3). Bodily sickness is "infirmity of the flesh" (Gal. 4:13 KJ); physical suffering is denoted by the figure of "the thorn in the flesh" (II Cor. 12:7). Circumcision, an operation on the body, is "circumcision which is outward, in the flesh" (Rom. 2:28 KJ). The outward cares of living are "trouble in the flesh" (I Cor. 7:28 KJ). Flesh is mortal (II Cor. 4:11), and death, as the end of physical life, is "destruction of the flesh"(I Cor. 5:5).

Inasmuch as man in his earthly existence is bound to fleshly corporeality, *sarx,* using Old Testament terminology, can mean man in general in the phrase "all flesh" (πᾶσα σάρξ = כָּל בָּשָׂר = everyone, Rom. 3:20; I Cor. 1:29; Gal. 2:16; *cf.* "every soul," § 18). In fact, like *psyche* and *pneuma* (§ 18, 2 and 3), *sarx* can even be used to designate the person himself (II Cor. 7:5 KJ: "our flesh had no rest" = "I found no rest"). In this usage the humanity of the person can be emphasized by adding "blood" to "flesh" in Jewish fashion (בָּשָׂר וָדָם) as in Gal. 1:16: "I did not confer with flesh and blood." While in this passage "flesh and blood" means a person in his humanness, in I Cor. 15:50 it means humanity as such, human nature: "flesh and blood cannot inherit the kingdom of God." *Sarx* by itself can also have this meaning, as Rom. 6:19 shows: "I speak after the manner of men because of the infirmity of your flesh" (= because of your limitations of human nature), which is synonymous in content with "I speak in a human way" (Rom. 3:5; I Cor. 9:8; § 21, 4, p. 232). "To remain in the flesh" means "to remain alive"— alive in the sphere of earthly life—in contrast to the wish "to depart and be with Christ" (Phil. 1:23f.).

Further examples indicate that *sarx* can denote not only the concrete body of flesh but also "fleshliness," carnality, meaning the nature of the earthly-human in its specific humanness—i.e. in its weakness and transitoriness, which also means in opposition to God and His Spirit (*cf.* espec. Gal. 1:16; I Cor. 15:50). Not Abraham's "children of the flesh" (Rom. 9:7f. KJ), i.e. his natural, earthly offspring, are to be regarded as the "children of God," the true "seed of Abraham." The meaning of *sarx* undergoes an extension, however, in the fact that it means not only human nature as it is perceived at work in and on man himself but that the sphere of the human is expanded to include the environment with which man has to do. Thus, *sarx* can mean *the whole sphere of that which is earthly or "natural."* According to Rom. 2:28f. it may be termed the sphere of the "outward":

> "For the true Jew is not he who is outwardly a Jew
> but he who is a Jew deep within;
> nor is true circumcision the outward flesh-circumcision
> but a spiritual, not a literal, heart-circumcision" (tr.).

"Flesh" here means, first of all, simply the physiological flesh on which circumcision is performed, and flesh in this sense by the juxtaposition of "outward" is brought into the wider sphere of "the outward." But the antithesis, especially by using "spirit" as a contrasting term, makes it clear that the sphere of "the outward" is precisely the sphere of "flesh." It will later be explained (§ 23, 1) that this is also the sphere of "the letter" or "the literal." "The seen" or "the visible" is synonymous with "the outward" (which, itself, should literally be translated "the visible"). The men of faith who surrender their "outward man" (II Cor. 4:16 KJ) to destruction—and that means their "body," their "mortal flesh" (II Cor. 4:10f.)—fix their gaze not on "the things that are seen," but on the "things that are unseen" (II Cor. 4:18); and when it is said, "for the things that are seen are transient," that is a direct characterization of the sphere of the "flesh." Those who by faith are no longer "in the flesh" (Rom. 8:9) live in a hope which hopes for that which is not visible (Rom. 8:24f.). While in Rom. 2:28f. the antithetical term to "the outward" is "the heart" (as the "hidden" sphere within a man), the contrast in II Cor. 5:12 to "priding one's self on a man's heart" is "priding one's self on appearance" (ἐν προσώπῳ)—i.e. on his externally visible merits; but that means glorying "after the flesh" (II Cor. 11:18 KJ); "boasting of worldly things" (RSV). Hence all that is "outward" and "visible," all that has its nature in external "appearance" belongs to the sphere of "flesh." In this sense, "flesh" becomes synonymous with the term "world" (κόσμος), insofar as *cosmos* denotes the world of created things which is the stage and the life-condition for "natural" life, the world which is at man's disposal, giving him the possibility to live from it and to be anxious about it (for further discussion of "world," see § 26). The "wisdom of this world" at I Cor. 1:20; 3:19 is the wisdom of those who are "wise . . . after the flesh" (I Cor. 1:26 KJ). Life in worldly affairs with all its hustle and bustle, its weal and woe, is "using the world" (I Cor. 7:31 KJ; "mixing in the world," Moffatt) and the care of husband or wife for the other is being "anxious about worldly affairs" in contrast to being "anxious about the affairs of the Lord" (I Cor. 7:32–34). "Worldly grief" is contrasted with "godly grief" (II Cor. 7:9f.). To Paul, the "world" is crucified in the cross of Christ (Gal. 6:14); this is synonymous in substance with the other statement (Gal. 5:24): "And those who belong to Christ Jesus have crucified the *flesh* with its passions and desires."

This is also the way to understand the phrase "in the flesh" (except where it means "on the body," as in Rom. 2:28), a phrase which can be explained neither from the Old Testament nor from Greek usage. This formula shows that according to Paul a man's nature is not determined by what he may be as to substance (in the way the Old Testament says man is flesh) nor by what qualities he may have (as Greek thinking would put it), but that his nature is determined by the sphere within which he moves, the sphere which marks out the horizon or the possibilities of what he does and experiences. The meaning of "in the flesh" becomes clear in the fact that it corresponds antithetically to the formula "in the Spirit," in which Spirit means the miraculous, life-giving power of God (§ 14, 1); its territory is the "hidden interior" (τὸ κρυπτόν), the "unseen," the "heart."

"In the flesh"—i.e. in the sphere of the obvious, or the earthly-human, or the natural—takes place man's "living" (Gal. 2:20; Phil. 1:22), or "walking" (II Cor. 10:3)—also Christian man's in this aeon. Or, differently said, "to live" or "to walk in the flesh" means nothing else than simply "to lead one's life as a man," an idea which in itself does not involve any ethical or theological judgment but simply takes note of a fact; not a norm but a field or a sphere is indicated by "in the flesh." Only it must be borne in mind that with this phrase there hovers in the air the opposite possibility that there is also another dimension in which life can move. Thus, Paul may speak of Onesimus as a brother "both in the flesh and in the Lord" (Phlm. 16 KJ)—i.e. both as a person and as a Christian. And insofar as the believer, having his true existence by faith, is already beyond the sphere of the merely human and belongs to the sphere of the Spirit, his "existence in the flesh" can be proleptically denied, and Paul can say: "when we *were* in the flesh . . ." (Rom. 7:5 KJ) and: "ye are not in the flesh but in the Spirit" (Rom. 8:9 KJ).

Whatever pertains to natural human life and is necessary for it can be called "fleshly" in contrast to "spiritual." Accordingly, Paul motivates his exhortation to Gentile Christians to contribute to the collection for the Jerusalem Church: "for if the Gentiles have come to share in their spiritual blessings, they ought also to be of service to them in material blessings" (σαρκικοῖς, lit.: "fleshly things"—Rom. 15:27 RSV). In the same way, he defends his apostle's right to support by the Churches: "If we have sown spiritual good among you, is it too much if we reap your material (σαρκικά) benefits?" (I Cor. 9:11).

While "flesh" in itself only means the human sphere as that of the earthly-natural and of the weak and transitory, nevertheless the use made of the formula "in the flesh" in Rom. 7:5; 8:8f. indicates that life "in the flesh" is a spurious life; in fact, everywhere the formula expresses an explicit or implicit antithesis to a life "in the Spirit" (Rom. 8:9), "in Christ" (Phlm. 16), "in faith" (Gal. 2:20), or the like. The sentence Rom. 8:8, "those who are in the flesh cannot please God," especially indicates that the sphere of "the flesh" can also be regarded as the sphere of sinning. So regarded, it is not merely the earthly-transitory contrast to the transcendent-eternal God but opposes God as His enemy. In this sense, Rom. 8:7 says: "The attitude of flesh is enmity to God" (tr.). How "flesh" comes to have this meaning comes into view when we examine the use of the phrase "according to the flesh."

3. The formula κατὰ σάρκα ("after the flesh" KJ) is used in a double sense, characterizing primarily a person, or a human relation-

[236]

ship, in regard to facts present within natural life and verifiable by everyone. However, it is true of this formula, as of "in the flesh," that a contrast between it and another possible point of view hovers behind it or is expressed. Abraham is "our forefather according to the flesh" (Rom. 4:1)—i.e. the natural progenitor of the Jews. The Jews are Paul's "kinsmen according to the flesh" (Rom. 9:3; or, abbreviated: "my flesh," 11:14)—in contrast, of course, to his "brothers in Christ." The Israelitic people of the Old Testament is "Israel after the flesh" (I Cor. 10:18 KJ) in contrast to the "Israel of God" (Gal. 6:16). Ishmael, Abraham's son born without God's promise, is called "he who was born according to the flesh" (Gal. 4:29; *cf.* v. 23: "But the son of the slave was born according to the flesh, the son of the free woman through promise"); i.e. he is Abraham's son only in the sense of natural human progeny in contrast to Isaac who was miraculously begotten "through the promise." Christ, too, can be described according to what he humanly is. "According to the flesh" he is a descendant of David and is from the people of Israel (Rom. 1:3; 9:5) in contradistinction to what he is "according to the Spirit of holiness": "Son of God" (Rom. 1:4). That in all these cases nothing more is meant than the sphere of the "natural" —that which is given and present in earthly fact—becomes clear in the insight that "we who are Jews by nature" (Gal. 2:15 KJ) would mean just the same thing if it read: "we who are Jews according to the flesh," or that instead of "uncircumcision which is by nature" (Rom. 2:27 KJ) Paul could just as well have said "uncircumcision according to the flesh."

"According to the flesh" in this sense serves as a rule (Gal. 4:23, 29 are exceptions) to modify substantives (including proper names). As a modifier of verbs the phrase has an altogether different meaning: It stamps *an existence or an attitude* not as natural-human, but *as sinful.* In this meaning we read of "purposing according to the flesh" (II Cor. 1:17 KJ), "knowing" (II Cor. 5:16), "walking" (II Cor. 10:2; Rom. 8:4), "warring" (II Cor. 10:3), even "being" after the flesh (Rom. 8:5)—and the last is given what amounts to a definition: "for they who exist according to the flesh are they who have the attitude of the flesh" (tr.). The antitheses here implied or expressed are: "according to the Spirit" (Rom. 8:4f.), "according to the Lord" (II Cor. 11:17 tr.), "according to love" (Rom. 14:15 tr.), and the like.

Σαρχιχός ("fleshly," see above) can also have the meaning of κατὰ σάρκα (I Cor. 3:3; II Cor. 1:12; 10:4), and one might say that κατὰ σάρκα fills the place of an adverb σαρκικῶς (which occurs in Ignatius, but not in the New Testament). Paul uses σάρχινος also in this same sense (Rom. 7:14; I Cor. 3:1), though it properly means "consisting of flesh (as matter)" (so used in II Cor. 3:3).

Now it is of decisive importance to comprehend that in such usage the word "flesh" does not, as might be assumed, have another meaning than it has in those other cases where it designates the sphere of the humanly natural and transitory. That is to say, we do not have here, as it might seem, a mythological concept, as if "flesh" were conceived as a demonic being. Neither do we have a physiological concept, as if "flesh" here meant sensuality. Rather, the sinful has its origin in "flesh" in this respect: That that conduct or attitude that directs itself according to "flesh," taking "flesh" for its norm, is sinful—as the cited sentence, Rom. 8:5, clearly says: "existence in the flesh" realizes itself in "setting the mind on the things of the flesh" (RSV), i.e. in the pursuit of the merely human, the earthly-transitory.

A comparison of Rom. 9:5 with I Cor. 1:26 makes clear the difference between the two uses of "according to the flesh." When Christ is here qualified as "according to the flesh," that means Christ regarded as an empirical phenomenon within the world—in that respect he was of the Jewish race. But when the "wise" are called "wise after the flesh," the addition does not mean "so far as they are empirical phenomena within the world," but "(wise) so far as a wisdom according to the norms of 'flesh' is concerned"; "the wise" is equivalent to a verb in the above discussion. What corresponds in the former case to the recognition of a "Christ according to the flesh" is the manner in which such a Christ is perceived; this manner itself is also "according to the flesh"—i.e. Christ as a phenomenon in the world is perceived in the worldly manner of seeing.

The old debate over II Cor. 5:16 can be decided in a similar way: "Wherefore henceforth know we no man after the flesh: yea, though we have known Christ after the flesh, yet now henceforth know we him no more" (KJ). The question is, does "after the flesh" in these two clauses modify the objects ("no man" and "Christ") or the verbs? The latter is the more probable, it seems to me. But this decision means nothing for the sense of the total context, for a "Christ regarded in the manner of the flesh" is just what a "Christ after the flesh" is.

§ 23. Flesh and Sin

1. Man, and hence the Christian, too, lives his natural life "in flesh" (§ 22, 2). But the crucial question is whether "in flesh" only denotes the stage and the possibilities for a man's life or the determinative norm for it—whether a man's life "*in* flesh" is also life "*according* to the flesh" (§ 22, 3)—or, again, whether the sphere of the natural-earthly, which is also that of the transitory and perishable, is the world out of which a man thinks he derives his life and by means of which he thinks he maintains it. This self-delusion is not merely an error, but sin, because it is a turning away from the Creator, the giver of life, and a turning toward the creation—and to do that is to trust in one's self as being able to procure life by the use of the earthly and through one's own strength and accomplishment. It is in this sense, then, that "fixing the mind on the things of flesh" is to be at war against God (Rom. 8:7).

The sinful self-delusion that one lives out of the created world can manifest itself both in unthinking recklessness (this especially among the Gentiles) and in considered busy-ness (this especially among Jews)—both in the ignoring or transgressing of ethical demands and in excessive zeal to fulfill them. For the sphere of "flesh" is by no means just the life of instinct or sensual passions, but is just as much that of the moral and religious efforts of man.

The "passions and desires" of the flesh, which, according to Gal. 5:24, the man of faith has crucified, are the "vices" of sensuality and self-seeking which are enumerated in 5:19–21 as the "works of the flesh." When 5:13 warns against misusing Christian freedom as an "opportunity for the flesh," the antithesis in vv. 14, 15 shows that what is meant is natural human self-seeking, to which Christian freedom is not to give free rein. The same thing, in all likelihood, is meant by the "sinful passions" which were at work in us when we were "in the flesh" (Rom. 7:5), and probably also by the "deeds of the body" in which living "according to the flesh" (Rom. 8:13) consists. The accusation that the Corinthians are still "of the flesh" (σαϱϰιϰοί) is evidenced by the fact that "jealousy and strife" prevail in the congregation (I Cor. 3:3). The complaint made against Paul of "fleshly wisdom" (KJ, II Cor. 1:12) or of "walking according to the flesh" (II Cor. 10:2) consisted in accusations of unreliability and insincerity and of arrogance and the will to dominate, as his debate with his opponents shows.

Elsewhere, it is not always clear what specific attitude Paul had in mind when he spoke of fleshly attitude or conduct. It may be an "anxiety for things of the world," but this need not be immoral conduct; rather it may consist of normal human affairs whenever a man devotes himself to them without the reservation of "as if . . . not" (I Cor. 7:29ff.). To the category of conduct "according to the flesh" belongs above all zealous fulfillment of the Torah; it does so because a man supposes he can thereby achieve righteousness before God by his own strength. The Galatian Christians who want to adopt the Torah and be circumcised are indignantly asked: "Having begun with the Spirit, are you now ending with the flesh?"—ending, that is, not in sensual passions but in observance of the Torah (Gal. 3:3). In fact, not only zeal for the Law but also pride in all the pious Israelite's merits and titles of honor belongs to the attitude of flesh—or, the Torah and the merits and dignities of Israel fall within the concept "flesh" as belonging to the sphere of the visibly occurring and the historically demonstrable (Phil. 3:3-7). This passage makes it especially clear that the attitude which orients itself by "flesh," living out of "flesh," is the self-reliant attitude of the man who puts his trust in his own strength and in that which is controllable by him. For the renunciation of this attitude means, according to Phil. 3:9, renunciation of one's own righteousness; and according to Rom. 10:3, the basic sin of the Jews is that they want—even though motivated by "zeal for God"—to establish "their own righteousness." Thereby it also becomes clearer why "the letter" (i.e. the Law of Moses) constitutes the antithesis to Spirit and belongs to the sphere of "flesh" (Rom. 2:29; 7:6; II Cor. 3:6). It does so to the extent that it serves man as a means for that effort to win "righteousness" and "life" by his own strength through "works"—that is, through what he accomplishes (see §27). The Torah is "letter" as the code of formulated and defined rules which can be discharged by performing definite acts corresponding to them.

Arrogance, which in the Jewish world takes the form of zeal for fulfilling the Torah and of pride over one's accomplishments in doing so and over Israel's titles to honor, appears in the Hellenistic world *as a striving after wisdom and as pride in knowledge and pneumatic endowment.* The "wise after the flesh" (I Cor. 1:26) are the wise who trust in themselves, who are not willing to smash their wisdom before God and let it become foolishness. The opponents against whom Paul writes in II Cor. 10–13, who boast "after the flesh" (11:18) and, as the allusion 10:4 implies, conduct their campaign with "fleshly weapons," are the people who boastfully compare themselves with others and commend themselves (10:12–18), and who give themselves airs with their "visions" and "revelations" (12:1). When they demand of Paul a "certification" (δοϰιμή 13:3), they thereby betray their position that a tangible accomplishment capable of being presented for inspection is to them the proof of possessing the Spirit.

Whether, then, it is a matter of giving one's self up to worldly enticements and pleasures, either in frivolity or swept along by the storm of passion, or whether it is the zealous bustle of moral and religious activity that is involved—life in all of these cases is apostasy from God—a turning away from Him to the creation and to one's own strength, and is, therefore, enmity toward God (Rom. 8:6) and disobedience to the will of God (Rom. 8:7; 10:3; II Cor. 10:5). All human wisdom, power, and greatness must come to naught in the presence of God (I Cor. 1:26–31).

2. This judgment about flesh and sin finds characteristic expression, further, in the verbs Paul uses to describe this specifically human attitude. This purpose is served by the verb *"desire"* when used in Paul's negatively qualified sense (§ 20, 2). The divine commandment says: "You shall not desire," but it thereby only arouses sinful desire (Rom. 7:7f.). And it has its seat in "flesh," so that Paul can go so far as to make "flesh" (or the fleshly *soma,* § 17, 2) the subject which "desires" or has "desire" (Gal. 5:16f., 24; Rom. 6:12; *cf.* Rom. 13:14). The evil "desires of hearts" are the desires of such as have turned to the worship of creation (Rom. 1:24), and the vices to which they have given themselves up (1:26ff.) are none other than the "works of the flesh" of Gal. 5:19f. Clearly a life "after the flesh" is a life of "desire"—a life of self-reliant pursuit of one's own ends.

This self-reliant attitude of man likewise lurks in his μεριμνᾶν (*"care,"* § 20, 2). In it, through his will to dispose over the world, he factually falls victim to the world. Natural human "care," except as it may mean worrying dread of the future, is the pro-vision, foresight (behind which, of course, that dread always lies), which self-reliantly strives to forestall the future. The intention of such "care" is to insure one's self for the future, or also, to keep what now is for the future. This attitude is care "about worldly affairs" (I Cor. 7:32ff.), which rests upon the illusion that a man can insure his life by that which is worldly, controllable. As antithesis to this sort of "care" stands "care about the Lord's affairs"—and to have the latter, is to be "care-free" (I Cor. 7:32) or to be "care-ful for nothing" (Phil. 4:6 KJ). (In both these cases, "care" has the qualified sense of worldly care.)

The attitude of sinful self-reliance finds its extreme expression in man's "*boasting*" (καυχᾶσθαι). It is characteristic both of the Jew, who boasts of God and the Torah (Rom. 2:17, 23), and of the Greek, who boasts of his wisdom (I Cor. 1:19–31). It is also a natural tendency of man in general to compare himself with others in order to have his "boast" thereby (Gal. 6:4). How characteristic "boasting" is for the Jew, Rom. 3:27 shows. After Paul has stated his thesis of righteousness by faith alone without works, he clarifies the meaning of this thesis by the rhetorical question, "then what becomes of our boasting?—It is excluded," and then refers to Abraham, who, having believed God, had no "boast." In "boasting" is revealed a misconstruing of the human situation, a forgetting of the fact implied by the question, "What do you have that you have not been given? And if it has been given you, why do you boast as if it had not been given you?" (I Cor. 4:7 tr.). And God insists upon this: All standards of human greatness must be shattered "so that no human being may boast before God" (I Cor. 1:29 tr.). There is only one valid boast: "Let him who boasts, boast of the Lord" (I Cor. 1:31; II Cor. 10:17). Therefore, the Christian must be warned also against haughtily looking down on others (Gal. 6:4; Rom. 11:17f.). And when Paul does once boast, he does it in the "fool's" role (II Cor. 11–12) which he has adopted; and yet in so doing he turns his "boasting after the flesh" into a paradoxical "boasting," by boasting of his "weakness" (II Cor. 11:30; 12:9; *cf.* Rom. 5:2). Thus he confesses, "Far be it from me to boast except in the cross of our Lord Jesus Christ, by which the world has been crucified to me, and I to the world" (Gal. 6:14; *cf.* Rom. 5:11).

[242]

Very closely related to "boasting after the flesh"—in fact even synonymous with it—is *putting one's confidence in the flesh.*" In Phil. 3:3 it constitutes the antithesis to "boasting in Christ Jesus." [*] While the latter means the surrender of all worldly accomplishments and titles of honor as mere "loss" and even "refuse" (Phil. 3:4-8) and also means the renunciation of a righteousness of one's own (3:9), "confidence in the flesh" is the supposed security which a man achieves out of that which is worldly and apparent, that which he can control and deal with. It is the rebellious pride which in the Jew expresses itself in his "boasting in the Torah" (Rom. 2:23) and misleads him to be "confident of being a guide to the blind, etc." (Rom. 2:19). "Putting confidence in the flesh" is nothing else than man's confidence in himself, and this is just what must come to naught before God; as there should be a "boasting" only "in the Lord," so there should be a "reliance" (= confidence, πεποιθέναι) upon God alone. When God caused Paul to despair of his life he learned by experience "that we should not rely upon ourselves but upon God who raises the dead" (II Cor. 1:9 tr.).

3. The hidden side of "boasting" and "putting confidence in the flesh" is the *fear* which the man who is concerned for himself has, a fear which arises both from zeal in the works of the Law and from zeal in wisdom. This fear may remain hidden from the man himself, even though it unmistakably manifests itself in "care" (μεριμνᾶν). That the worldly man is full of fear (φόβος) is indicated by Paul's reminder to the believers, "for you did not receive the spirit of slavery to fall back into fear" (Rom. 8:15). The period before faith, that is, was under the sway of fear. This sentence also shows that it was a period of "*slavery.*" And that holds true not only insofar as both Judaism and paganism are under slavery to the "elemental spirits of the universe," which for the Jews are represented by the Torah, for the Gentiles by "beings that by nature are no gods" (Gal. 4:1-10), but it especially holds true insofar as "life after the flesh" leads into slavery to "flesh" and "sin." Both he who "desires" and he who is "anxious with care," both he who "boasts" and he who "relies upon" something, in reality makes himself dependent upon that

[*] The affinity between "boasting" and "confidence" is also attested by a comparison of II Cor. 1:12 with 3:4; the same conclusion is to be drawn from the interchange between "confidence," or "be confident," and "boast" in II Cor. 10:2, 7f.

which he supposes he can control. Hence, the warning to the Galatians who want to achieve their own righteousness by observing the Torah, or who want to get to the goal "by flesh" (Gal. 3:3; see above, 1): "For freedom Christ has set us free; stand fast, therefore, and do not submit again to a yoke of slavery" (Gal. 5:1). The wisdom-proud Corinthians must be reminded: "all things are yours" (I Cor. 3:21f.); i.e. they must be warned against delivering themselves into dependence upon human authorities—that would be dependence upon "flesh and blood." And whoever has the notion that he has to shape his life according to the norms of human evaluations must hear the warning: "You were bought with a price; do not become slaves of men" (I Cor. 7:23). And when those who, by a misunderstanding of Christian freedom, regard unrestricted sexual intercourse as permitted are warned: "You are not your own; you were bought with a price" (I Cor. 6:20), that brings to light the whole paradox that he who apparently belongs to himself and has himself at his own disposal is a slave. Man is "bought free" from his previous slavery; but even so, he nevertheless does not belong to himself; for there is for man no absolute belonging-to-one's-self, but belonging to God or "the Lord" is man's freedom—namely, freedom from "flesh" and "sin" (Rom. 6:15ff.; 7:5f.). Indeed, one might say, he who lives "after the flesh" makes "flesh" his god; for Rom. 16:18 (KJ) gives a warning against those who "serve not our Lord Christ but their own belly," and Phil. 3:19 polemizes against those "whose god is their belly" (KJ).

The fact that *"flesh,"* and through it also *"sin," can become powers* to which man falls slave finds especially clear expression in the circumstance that Paul can speak of both as personal beings as if they were demonic rulers—but in such a way that we do not have the right actually to ascribe to him a mythological concept of "flesh" and "sin." Man is in danger of becoming a "debtor" to the "flesh" (Rom. 8:12) or of opening the door to it, so to say, or of offering it his hand (Gal. 5:13, tr.: "do not [offer] your freedom to the flesh as a base of operations"). Paul can even attribute "desire" to the "flesh" itself (Gal. 5:17: "for the desires of the flesh are against the Spirit"). Or he can speak of the "intent (φρόνημα) of the flesh" (Rom. 8:6f. tr.), or of its "passions" and "desires" (Gal. 5:24) and its "works" (Gal. 5:19) or "deeds" (Rom. 8:13; § 17, 3). Moreover, he can personify the world in the same way when he speaks of its "wisdom"

[244]

and its "knowing" (I Cor. 1:20f.). "Sin" particularly appears in this way as if it were a personal being. It "came into the world" (Rom. 5:12) and "achieved dominion" (Rom. 5:21 Blt.). Man is enslaved to it (Rom. 6:6, 17ff.), sold under it (Rom. 7:14); or man places himself at its disposal (Rom. 6:13) and it pays him wages (Rom. 6:23). Sin is also thought of as if it were a personal being when it is said to have been dead but to have revived (Rom. 7:8f.), or to have used the Torah to rouse desire in man and to have deceived and killed him (Rom. 7:8, 11, 13), or to "dwell" and act in man (Rom. 7:17, 20).

Little as all this constitutes realistic mythology—it is not that, but figurative, rhetorical language—it is, nevertheless, clear that this language stamps *flesh and sin as powers to which man has fallen victim* and against which he is powerless. The personification of these powers expresses the fact that man has lost to them the capacity to be the subject of his own actions. The strongest expression of this is found in Rom. 7:14, "I am carnal (= flesh-ly), sold under sin," and Rom. 7:18, "for I know that nothing good dwells within me, that is, in my flesh." While it may be that "that is" possibly has a limiting meaning here ("so far as I am flesh") and that the true, willing self is thereby dissociating itself from this self that is fallen victim to flesh, it is, nevertheless, significant that "I" and "my flesh" can be equated. Under the viewpoint of "doing," they are identical; but if they can be opposed to each other in regard to "willing," then it is apparent that the subject-self, the true self of a man, is inwardly split. That self which in Rom. 7:17, 20 distinguishes itself from the "sin which dwells within me," is flatly labeled in v. 14 as "carnal" and "sold under sin"—just as the first person is used throughout vv. 14–24 both in regard to willing and to doing. Therefore "I" and "I," self and self, are at war with each other; i.e. to be innerly divided, or not to be at one with one's self, is the essence of human existence under sin.

This inner dividedness means that man himself destroys his true self. In his self-reliant will to be himself, a will that comes to light in "desire" at the encounter with the "commandment," he loses his self, and "sin" becomes the active subject within him (Rom. 7:9). Thereby the self—the "I"—dies; selfhood, of course, belongs to the nature of man, and it is just the "commandment," given "for life," that ought to bring his selfhood to reality. Man fails to achieve it by attempting self-reliantly to realize it in "desire." In this false will toward selfhood man's destination to be a self—his will toward "life" —is pervertedly preserved; that is just the reason why it is possible to describe human existence as the struggle between "self" and "self" within a man. In the fact that man is a self—that he is a being to whom what matters and should matter is his "life," his self—lies the possibility of sin. In the fact that God's commandment is meant to give man "life" lies the possibility of misunderstanding: Man, called to selfhood, tries to live out of his own strength and thus loses his self—his "life"—and rushes into death. This is the domination of sin: All man's doing is directed against his true intention—viz. to achieve life.

§ 24. Sin and Death

1. Since all man's pursuit ultimately aims at life, even though in each case it seeks some specific end, it follows that a false, aberrant pursuit walks the way that leads to death.

For Paul, in the train of Old Testament-Jewish tradition, it is axiomatic that sin draws death after it. The "sting" of death is sin, whose power lies in the Torah (I Cor. 15:56); i.e. the transgressing of the Torah, which is occasioned by sin, draws death after it. *Death is the punishment for the sin a man has committed;* sinners are "worthy of death" (Rom. 1:32 KJ), they have "earned" death. So Paul can also say that sin pays her slave his "wage" with death (Rom. 6:16, 23), or that the sinner by his death pays his debt, atones for his sin (Rom. 6:7). In such statements, death, we must recognize, is first thought of as the death which is natural dying, as Rom. 5:12ff. shows, according to which death as the punishment for sin was brought into the world by Adam's sin. Nevertheless, they also presuppose that this death will be confirmed—made final, so to say— by the verdict condemning them to "destruction" which God will pronounce over sinners on the judgment day (Rom. 2:6-11).

2. Still Paul's thoughts on flesh and sin lead beyond this traditional juristic conception of death as punishment. If as we have concluded sin is man's false pursuit of life, and if this consists in leading one's life "after the flesh,"—i.e. living out of the created, the earthly-natural and transitory—*then sin leads with inner necessity into death:* "If you live according to the flesh you will die" (Rom. 8:13).

[246]

He who derives life out of the transitory must, himself, perish with the perishing of the transitory. "He who sows to his own flesh will from the flesh reap corruption" (Gal. 6:8). "Anxiety for the affairs of the world" clings to "the world," whose σχῆμα ("substance," not just "form") "passes away" (I Cor. 7:31); he who so lives clutches at emptiness, so to say, and all he gets himself is death. "Worldly grief" brings death to him who has it (II Cor. 7:10). Why? Because in it he clings to that which is doomed to death.

Thus, death grows out of flesh-ly life like a fruit—organically, as it were: "While we were living in the flesh, our sinful passions, aroused by the law, were at work in our members to bear fruit for death" (Rom. 7:5). Death is the "end" of the "fruit" of sinful life (Rom. 6:21 KJ). The *soma* of flesh in which sin "dwells" is thereby a "*soma* of death" (Rom. 7:24; § 17, 3). When II Cor. 3:6 says: "for the written code kills, but the Spirit gives life," there is no reflection in this context over the question whether the individual under the reign of Law brings death upon himself by transgressing the Law or by his zeal for it. But the sentence is spoken not in regard to Jewish transgressions of the Law, but in polemic against the Jewish esteem for the Torah as an eternal Law diffused with glory. In opposition to this esteem Paul says that the ministry of Moses is a "ministry of death" and its "splendor" or "glory" a fading one. The Torah, therefore, belongs to the sphere of "flesh" (§ 23, 1, p. 240) in contrast to the "new covenant," which is a "covenant of the Spirit." Hence, serving the Torah leads with inner necessity to death.

The perversion of human striving that pursues life and yet only garners death is described at length in Rom. 7:7-25, a passage in which Paul so depicts the situation of man under the Torah as it has become clear to a backward look from the standpoint of Christian faith. V. 10 says that the commandment was given to man "for life"; and man, whose longing is to have life, completely agrees with this intention (v. 16: "I agree . . ."; v. 22: "I delight in . . ."). But the commandment nonetheless leads factually into death; it does so by arousing "desire" in man (vv. 7–11).

It may be that in these verses Paul does not reflect over the question whether "desire" tempts man to transgress the Law or whether it misleads him to a false zeal for fulfilling it. Yet the latter must at least be included; for if 7:7-25 describes the situation of being under the Law in a way that holds true for everyone who is under it, then the attitude (described in Phil. 3:4–6) of being "blameless" "as to righteousness under the Law" must be contained in it. In this case, then, the "desire" aroused by the Law is the "unenlightened zeal for God" of Rom. 10:2 (tr.).

Sin's "deceit" (Rom. 7:11) consists in deluding man to think that if he follows his "desire" he will gain life, whereas he only acquires death. Victimized by this deceit, man does not know what he is doing: "for what I am bringing about I do not know (v. 15a tr.); i.e. he does not know that by what he is doing he is only reaping death.

These words cannot mean: "I don't know how it happens that my good resolutions always get broken," in the sense of Ovid's line, *video meliora proboque, deteriora sequor* (I see the better and approve; the lower I follow, *Metamorphoses* 7, 21). For nothing is said about good resolutions that come to nothing in actual conduct. What the encounter with the commandment arouses is not good will, but "desire"! Rather, the point of the passage in its context is that what man brings about is an "evil," whereas according to his intention (which is the guiding factor in "desire"), it was to be a "good." Since κατεργάζεσθαι in v. 13 does not mean "do," but "bring about" or "reap," it is natural to take it to mean the same in v. 15 (and then also in v. 17 and v. 20 in spite of 2:9f.) and to supply there the object named in v. 13—"death" (*cf.* also II Cor. 7:10: "worldly grief brings about —κατεργάζεται—death"); then "the good thing" which is the object of the same verb in v. 18 is "life." Then the "doing" (πράσσειν, vv. 16, 19, or ποιεῖν, vv. 19, 20, 21) of evil and good must be correspondingly interpreted as meaning the bringing about of the evil thing (= death) and of the good thing (= life), which might be a conceivable locution in pointed speech. But even if the simple verbs (πράσσειν and ποιεῖν) are understood literally (linguistically the more natural assumption) as the "doing" of evil or of good (in which case κατεργάζεσθαι would also have to be so understood, at least in vv. 17, 18, and 20), the basic meaning still remains the same: In pursuing his "desire" man thinks he is doing something good (i.e. life-bringing) and actually is doing something evil (i.e. life-destroying). In either case, the gruesome contradiction which characterizes human striving is being described: It wants to gain life and only achieves death.

[248]

Fundamentally, then, death is already a present reality, for man "sold under sin" (v. 14) has lost himself, is no longer at one with himself (§ 23, 3). This is clearly expressed in the formulation of vv. 9–11: ". . . but when the commandment came, sin revived and I died . . . for sin . . . deceived me and . . . killed me" (see § 27).

3. The juristic conception of death as the punishment for sin and the conception of death as a fruit organically growing out of sin are not harmonized with each other. Nor does either conception agree with the view set forth in I Cor. 15:45–49 that Adamitic man was created "earthy," and being earthy is flesh and blood (v. 50), and therefore "perishable" (v. 53f.). The disagreement between this view and the two preceding is obscured only by the fact that Paul here avoids the term "fleshly" (σαρκικός) and uses ψυχικός ("animate"–but non-spiritual) instead–which, however, amounts to the same thing (cf. I Cor. 2:14 with 3:1, 3; § 18, 2).

§ 25. The Universality of Sin

1. *The power of sin* operates not only in the fact that it completely dominates the man who has become its victim, but also in the fact that it forces all men without exception into slavery: "for all have sinned" (Rom. 3:23; cf. 3:9, 19), "scripture has encompassed all men under the power of sin" [Gal. 3:22 tr.–πάντα, "all," is probably a generalizing neuter referring to persons; (see Blass-Debrunner, § 138, 1)].

What reason is given for this proposition? Rom. 8:3 seems to give a reason by saying that "what the law could not do" (i.e. the Law's incapacity to bring man life) has its cause in the "flesh." Though that is understandable, still the question, Does not "flesh" first achieve its power when man lives "according to the flesh"? remains. And is there a necessity that natural human "life in the flesh" must without exception become "life in the flesh" in the negatively qualified sense–i.e. must it become "life according to the flesh"?

That is evidently Paul's opinion. In man–because his substance is flesh–sin slumbers from the beginning. Must it necessarily awaken? Yes, because man encounters the Torah with its commandment: "you shall not desire" (Rom. 7:7ff.).

Although, judging from the whole train of thought in this epistle, Paul is thinking only of the Jewish Law, the same holds true for the Gentiles, too, among whom the place of the Law of Moses is taken by the demands of conscience (Rom. 2:14f.). And it is quite possible that in Rom. 7:7-11 Paul has Adam in mind, the prototype of mankind, who, of course, also lived without the Law of Moses.

If, now, the demand of the "commandment" is this "you shall not desire," its intent is to snatch man out of his self-reliant pursuit of life, his will to rule over himself. When it is further said that by this very demand, sin is awakened, that rests upon a conviction that man fundamentally strives in the wrong direction. The life that the Torah offers him (v. 10: "for life") he wants to attain himself, by his own power.

2. Can reasons be given for this conviction, or is it simply derived from experience? Unless the guilt-character of sin were to be denied, it obviously could only have its origin in experience. For its guilt-character would be sacrificed if the universality of sin were attributed to some quality necessarily inhering in man—for instance, thinking Gnostically, to a sensuality having its basis in the matter of which man consists, or, Gnostic again, to a fateful event which occurred in the hoary past, because of which the curse of sin weighs upon all men. Paul's statements on this subject are not consistent with each other.

When Paul prefaces the thesis of righteousness by faith without works with *a demonstration of the universality of sin* in Rom. 1:18–3:20, he does not have recourse to a cause lying behind the factual sinning of men nor does he speak of a curse existing since primeval times, but only sets forth the fact that all men—both Gentiles and Jews—are factually sinners. To be sure, God did give them up to sin (1:24ff.), but only as a punishment for the proto-sin of apostasy from the Creator—and this, of course, does not take away the guilt-character from sinning, but only means that apostasy, the sin of sins, necessarily draws the vices after it. If sin is here a curse, it is "the curse of the evil deed" which, "begetting, must bear evil" (Schiller, "Piccolomini" 5, 1). That sin of sins is not elicited by matter nor by a primeval fate, but is real guilt. Neither, obviously, is this proto-sin meant as the sin of mankind's first parents at the beginning of time, but as the proto-sin of apostasy which repeats

[250]

itself in every Now in the face of that possibility of knowing God which is open to every Now. Consistent with this is Rom. 2:1ff., where Paul refuses to get involved in argument with those who set themselves up as judges over notorious sinners, but simply tells them to their faces that they likewise are sinners.

But the case is quite different in Rom. 5:12–19; here *the sin of all men is attributed to Adam's sin*; i.e. the idea of "original sin" (*Erbsünde:* "inherited sin") is enunciated: "for as by one man's (Adam's) disobedience the many were made sinners . . ." (v. 19). Here, in describing the curse that lies upon Adamitic mankind, Paul is unquestionably under the influence of the Gnostic myth (§ 15, 4b).

However, he avoids slipping off into Gnostic thinking by not letting Adam's sin be caused by something lying behind it, either by the matter of which Adam consists, or by Satan, or—following a rabbinic teaching—to "the evil tendency." Instead he holds to the idea that sin came into the world by sinning; and to this extent Rom. 5:12ff. is compatible with 7:7ff.—i.e. Adam's "transgression" (v. 14) or "disobedience" (v. 19) is the violation of the divine "commandment," which woke the sin slumbering within him.

I Cor. 15:44ff., however, is not applicable here. According to it Adam was ψυχικός and χοϊκός (non-spiritual and earthy) and hence had no possibility whatever of perceiving God's will (§ 24, 3) because the "unspiritual man" has no perception of the Spirit (I Cor. 2:14) whereas God's commandment is "spiritual" (Rom. 7:14). According to the Corinthian passage, further, Adam was doomed to death by his origin in "dust"; and, consequently—if it is to hold true that death is punishment for sin (§ 24, 1)—he must have been sinful by nature. Otherwise, one would have to say—if it could be justified—that death as the natural end of physical life pertained to Adam even before he sinned, but did not get its true death-character (as "destruction") until he sinned. But Paul makes no such distinction.

Nevertheless, it cannot be denied that in Rom. 5:12ff. the sin of humanity after Adam is attributed to Adam's sin and that it therefore appears as the consequence of a curse for which mankind is not itself responsible. At the most, men sinning under the curse of Adam's sin could be regarded as guilty only in a legal sense, inasmuch as law deals only with the guilty deed; but then we would have no right to speak of guilt in the ethical sense.

Now it must be noted that the real theme of Rom. 5:12ff. is not the origin of sin but the origin of death; more accurately, even the origin of death is the theme only as the negative aspect of the positive theme, the origin of life, for the meaning of the passage in its context is this: The certainty of the Christian hope set forth in 5:1–11 has its foundation in the fact that Christ has obtained life for the mankind instituted by him, and obtained it with the same certainty with which Adam brought death upon Adamitic mankind (so also in I Cor. 15:21f.). Then, since death is held to be the punishment or the consequence of sin, *Adam's* sin had to be brought in, too. For the context, it would have been sufficient to mention only Adam's sin; there was no need to speak of the sin of the rest of men, for whether they were sinners or not, through Adam they had simply been doomed to death—an idea that was expressed not only in Judaism but also by Paul himself (v. 14). However, Paul gets into obscurity here because he also wants to have the death of men after Adam regarded as the punishment or consequence of their own sin: "and so death spread to all men—because all men sinned" (v. 12)! Verse 13 is completely unintelligible: "sin indeed was in the world before the law was given, but sin is not counted where there is no law." What sort of sin was it if it did not originate as contradiction of the Law? And how can it have brought death after it if it was not "counted"? These questions cannot be answered. Suffice it to say that because Paul regards death as the punishment or consequence of sin, he cannot content himself with speaking of the inherited death brought about by Adam but is prompted to go on to the proposition of inherited sin (v. 19).

If one takes one's bearings from what is said of Christ, the antitype of Adam, then it becomes clear that the effect of Christ's "obedience" is by no means regarded as one that takes place with inevitable necessity. Not all men since Christ, it is clear, receive life, as all since Adam became the victims of death, but only those who have faith (= "those who receive," v. 17). Through Christ, that is, there was brought about no more than the *possibility* of life, which, however, in men of faith becomes certain reality. That suggests, then, that one should assume by analogy that through Adam there was brought about for Adamitic mankind the *possibility* of sin and death—a possibility that does not become reality until individuals become guilty by their own responsible action. Whether that may be regarded as Paul's real thought must, to be sure, remain a question; at any rate the universal fallenness of Adamitic mankind to sin and death is beyond all question to Paul.

It might seem that Abraham is an exception and hence a source of difficulties. He need not be, for the special position that he occupies (also David? *Cf.* Rom. 4:6; possibly the prophets, too?) is his not as one who is sinless, but as one who has faith—and that a faith in "him who rightwises the ungodly" *
(Rom. 4:5 tr.).

In Rom. 5:13f. it is perhaps possible to discover a differentiation between sin for which man is responsible and sin for which he is not responsible and from that insight to make this inference: At the base of the idea of inherited sin lies the experience that every man is born into a humanity that is and always has been guided by a false striving. The so-derived understanding of existence applies as a matter of course to every man; and every man brings himself explicitly under it by his concrete "transgression," thereby becoming jointly responsible for it. Since human life is a life with others, mutual trust is destroyed by a *single* lie, and mistrust—and thereby sin—is established; by a *single* deed of violence defensive violence is called forth and law as organized violence is made to serve the interests of individuals, etc.—ideas at least hinted at by I Cor. 5:6: "do you not know that a little leaven ferments the whole lump of dough?" So everyone exists in a world in which each looks out for himself, each insists upon his rights, each fights for his existence, and life becomes a struggle of all against all even when the battle is involuntarily fought. So sin is always already here, and the divine command always encounters man as a "thou shalt" or "thou shalt not" which he must transform into an "I will" or "I will not" by first conquering himself. The fact that the good always demands a sacrifice testifies that in his living man has a tacit understanding of himself that is basically sinful. Paul, it is true, never expounds this train of thought, but our right to develop it for the understanding of his statements is suggested by his conception of "world."

* The translator has ventured to revive and to use here and especially in § 28 an obsolete Middle English verb "rightwise(n)"—the true English counterpart of the adjective "righteous" (Anglo-Saxon: rihtwīs) and the noun "righteousness" (Anglo-Saxon: rihtwisnes). The only alternative seems to be to use consistently the Latin cognates just, justify, and justification—but they are alive in English with other very misleading meanings.

§ 26. The Term "World" (Cosmos)

1. In Greek antiquity, the conception "universe" was expressed by the word "*kosmos.*" They conceived it as a totality bound together by rationally comprehensible relationships of law into a unified structure containing heaven and earth and all living beings, including gods and men. This conception is foreign to the Old Testament; it contains no term corresponding to the Greek "kosmos." It does occasionally speak of the "all" (הַכֹּל) and, much oftener, of "heaven and earth"—but always in such a way that God himself is not included in it, but is always distinguished from it as the Creator. In this restricted sense, Hellenistic Judaism took over and used the term "kosmos," and it is in this sense that the New Testament, inclusive of Paul, uses it.

From the phrase "since the creation of the world" (Rom. 1:20) it is apparent that for Paul "kosmos" can mean "the creation"; and, in keeping with Old Testament thought, he can place "in heaven . . . on earth" (I Cor. 8:5) in parallelism with "in the 'kosmos'" (v. 4). Probably Gal. 4:3 ("the elemental spirits of the 'kosmos'") and Phil. 2:15 ("as lights in the 'kosmos'") are to be reckoned to the few passages in which "kosmos" denotes the (total) world of creation.

Since statements about the "kosmos" as a rule have a bearing on men, it is quite understandable that "kosmos" occasionally means "world" in the restricted sense of the stage on which human life is played—that is, the "earth." That is the case when Abraham is called "the inheritor of the earth" (Rom. 4:13 tr.), and probably also in the reference to the many "sorts of languages" that there are "in the kosmos" (I Cor. 14:10 tr.).

However, "kosmos" does not always mean "earth" as the mere stage for man's life and living but often denotes the *quintessence of earthly conditions of life and earthly possibilities.* It embraces all the vicissitudes included between the pairs of polar terms "life . . . death," "things present . . . things future" (I Cor. 3:22). Accordingly, human life in its worldly aspects, in its hustle and bustle, in its weal and woe, is a "dealing with the world" (I Cor. 7:31)—and as the antithesis to the "affairs of the world," "the affairs of the Lord" hover in the background (7:32–34; see § 22).

As "kosmos" is *not a cosmological term here, but an historical one,* so it also is in the numerous passages where it is used in the

sense of *"the world of men," "mankind"*—a usage, moreover, which
Hellenistic Judaism also knows. Such a passage as Rom. 1:8 shows
the transition to it: "your faith is proclaimed in all the world,"
which is evidently synonymous in substance with 16:19: "for your
obedience is known to all." When Paul declares he has behaved
with sincerity "in the 'kosmos'," he is not thinking of "kosmos" as
the cosmic stage, but as the sphere of human relationships, as his
added remark, "especially toward you," itself indicates (II Cor.
1:12). I Cor. 4:9 in naming angels in addition to men ("we have
become a spectacle to the 'kosmos,' to angels and to men") also
shows that when "kosmos" is used it can mean not the stage, but
the persons existing upon it.

When it is said that God will judge "the world" (Rom. 3:6), or
that before God every mouth must be stopped and all "the world"
stand guilty (3:19; *cf.* v. 20 "all flesh"), "world" denotes men in
their entirety. God's chastening is said to have the purpose, in
Christians, that they may not fall under the verdict of condemnation "along with the world" (I Cor. 11:32); that means, with the
rest of mankind. When it is said that by a man sin came into the
"world" (Rom. 5:12f.), once again "world" does not mean the
stage, but mankind; likewise, in the statement that God reconciled
"the world" to Himself, for the comment follows: "not counting their
(= the world's!) trespasses against them" (II Cor. 5:19). The
"reconciliation of the world" (Rom. 11:15) is to be understood in
the same sense. "Riches for the world" and "riches for the Gentiles"
stand in parallelism (Rom. 11:12); similarly "refuse of the world"
and "offscouring of all (men)" (I Cor. 4:13). The "wisdom of the
world" (I Cor. 1:20) is human wisdom in contrast to God's; "the
foolish of the world" (μωρά the generalizing neuter for the mascu-
line!) with what follows (I Cor. 1:27) denotes the despised and
outcast among men (v. 28).

2. Most important of all, however, is the fact that the term
"kosmos" often contains a definite *theological judgment.* In many
of the already cited passages, "kosmos" constitutes the implicit or
explicit antithesis to the sphere of God or "the Lord," whether
"kosmos" denotes the totality of human possibilities and conditions
of life (I Cor. 3:22, 7:31ff.), or whether it implies persons in their
attitudes and judgments (I Cor. 1:20, 27f.) or in their sinfulness
and enmity toward God (Rom. 3:6, 19; 11:15; II Cor. 5:19). But

this is especially true where Paul says "*this world*." The human wisdom which shuts itself off from divine wisdom is "the wisdom of this world" (I Cor. 3:19). Sinners are described as "the immoral of this world" (I Cor. 5:10). The present is characterized by the sentence: "the *schema* (essence) of this world is passing away" (I Cor. 7:31b). But "kosmos" alone, which can interchange with "this 'kosmos,' " has the same meaning (I Cor. 1:20f., 27f.; 2:12; 7:31a, 33f.; also II Cor. 7:10; Gal. 6:14).* "This world" can also interchange with "this age" (αἰών). The "wisdom of this age" (I Cor. 2:6, 8; 3:18) is the "wisdom of the world" or "of this world"; the wise who exemplify the wisdom of this world are the wise men, the scholars, the investigators "of this age" (I Cor. 1:20). "The *schema* of this world" (I Cor. 7:31) is "the present evil age" of Gal. 1:4.

Now this means that "kosmos"—used in the above sense—is much more a time-concept than a space-concept; † or, more exactly, it is an *eschatological concept*. It denotes the world of men and the sphere of human activity as being, on the one hand, a temporary thing hastening toward its end (I Cor. 7:31), and on the other hand, the sphere of anti-godly power under whose sway the individual who is surrounded by it has fallen. It is the sphere of "the rulers of this age" (I Cor. 2:6, 8) and "of the god of this age" (II Cor. 4:4).

This power, however—and this is the distinctive thing about Paul's view—does not come over man, either the individual or the race, as a sheer curse of fate, but grows up out of himself. The "kosmos," as the sphere of earthly life's conditions, achieves power over the man whose caring is directed toward "the affairs of the world" (I Cor. 7:32–34), as "flesh" does over him who lives "after the flesh" (§ 22). As a matter of fact, let us recall that the terms "flesh" and "kosmos" can be synonymous (§ 22, 2). Then the eerie fact is that the "kosmos," the world of men, constituted by that which the individual does and upon which he bestows his care, itself gains the upper hand over the individual. The "kosmos"

---

* In some of these passages various textual witnesses understandably (and correctly so far as the meaning is concerned) supply the demonstrative pronoun.

† This corresponds to the fact that in later Judaism the terms "kosmos" and עוֹלָם (originally a time-concept, "age," but gradually shading over into the meaning "world"), mutually influenced each other. I Cor. 5:10 indicates how the time-concept and the space-concept can interpenetrate each other: It is not at all "the immoral of this world" (with whom you are not to associate)— "since then you would need to go out of the world."

comes to constitute an independent super-self over all individual selves. In Paul's usage this clearly emerges in the fact that what is actually practiced or felt by individuals is attributed to the "kosmos" as the active or sentient self. It is the "world" that through its wisdom did not come to know God (I Cor. 1:21); and as the "world" has its "wisdom" (I Cor. 1:21; 3:19), it also has its "grief" (II Cor. 7:10). Indeed, Paul can even express the fact that the world masters those who constitute it by speaking of the "spirit of the world" (I Cor. 2:12)—no matter whether that is only a rhetorical phrase as an antithesis to "the Spirit which is from God," or whether "the spirit of the world" is conceived as an actual mythical reality. In modern terms, "the spirit of the world" is the atmosphere to whose compelling influence every man contributes but to which he is also always subject.

This sense of "kosmos" is also apparent wherever it is said that even though Christians are still in "the world" (considered as the stage and sphere of earthly life) because they are still "in the flesh" (§ 22, 2) and cannot flee out of the world (I Cor. 5:10), they are, nevertheless, already beyond "the world"—"the world" this time regarded as the anti-divine power that controls men. With all its menacing and tempting possibilities, it lies, so to say, beneath their feet; they have mastered it (I Cor. 3:21f.: "for all things are yours . . . whether . . . the world, etc."). They have received not "the spirit of the world" but "the Spirit which is from God" (I Cor. 2:12). To them "the world" is crucified on the cross of Christ and they to it (Gal. 6:14). For them the "elemental spirits of the 'kosmos'" to which they were once enslaved, have been unmasked as "the weak and beggarly elemental spirits" (Gal. 4:9). Therefore, they will someday be judges over the world (I Cor. 6:2f.). All this is true because, in point of fact, they have become new persons (II Cor. 5:17).

3. This eschatological-historical meaning of "kosmos" and along with it the understanding of man's situation as an enslavement to powers for whose dominion he nevertheless is himself responsible, comes out, finally, in the interpretation of Paul's *mythological statements* about these powers.

The "kosmos," although on the one hand, it is God's creation, is, on the other hand, *the domain of demonic powers*: the "angels," "principalities" and "powers" (Rom. 8:38; I Cor. 15:24; see § 21, 3), "the rulers of this age" (I Cor. 2:6, 8), "the elemental spirits of the 'kosmos'" (Gal. 4:3, 9; see §15, 4a). These are "the enemies of God," the last of whom is "death" (I Cor. 15:26). The head of these anti-divine powers is Satan (Rom. 16:20; I Cor. 5:5; 7:5; II Cor. 2:11; 11:14; I Thess. 2:18), the "god of this age" (II Cor. 4:4).

Like the character of the "kosmos," *the character of the spirit powers has a peculiar ambiguity,* for it is clear, in the first place, that Paul does not think in the dualistic manner of Gnosticism, recognizing side by side with the divine world of light an equally eternal, competing, devilish world of darkness (§15). Instead, he considers the spirit powers also to belong to God's creation (Rom. 8:39); God can make use even of an angel of Satan (II Cor. 12:7). It is clear, in the second place, that the "existence" of these powers has significance only for those who let it be an existence "for us"—in which sense, in reality, only God exists (I Cor. 8:5; see §21, 3). Hence, ultimately it is from men that they derive their power, and for the Christian they are already "dethroned" (I Cor. 2:6 Moffatt). In reality, they can no longer harm him. To be sure, the Christian, too, still lives "in the world," "in the flesh," and the ultimately unmythological meaning of the "powers" is also manifested in the fact that their "dethronement" is conceived unmythologically. A Christian's existence is not magically transformed but even after he becomes a Christian his life continues to be an historical existence as long as he is "in the flesh." His existence is ever threatened by danger; and if he, too, must still suffer under the enmity of those "powers," what is expressed in such statements is nothing else than the state of constant threat that menaces his existence. The "powers" come upon the Christian in the vicissitudes of his particular lot—i.e. in his "tribulations" and "distresses," etc. (Rom. 8:35; *cf.* I Thess. 2:18: "Satan hindered us")—which, however, can no longer basically harm him (Rom. 8:31-39). They also come upon him in his temptations; Satan is the "tempter" (I Thess. 3:5) against whom one must be on guard (I Cor. 7:5; II Cor. 2:11).

Hence, the mythological notions of the spirit powers and Satan do not serve the purpose of cosmological speculation nor a need to explain terrifying or gruesome phenomena or to relieve men of responsibility and guilt. When Paul speaks of the event by which death came into the world he takes recourse not to the devil, as Wis. 2:24 does, but to Adam's sin (Rom. 5:12ff.; §25, 3). Though

Death does appear in the mythological role of the "last enemy," I Cor. 15:26, yet in 15:56 it is "sin" that is the "sting of death." It is out of man's deeds that death grows as their fruit (§ 24, 2). Paul may indeed speak in naive mythology of the battle of the spirit powers against Christ or of his battle against them (I Cor. 2:6–8; 15:24–26). In reality, he is thereby only expressing a certain understanding of existence: The spirit powers represent the reality into which man is placed as one full of conflicts and struggle, a reality which threatens and tempts. Thus, through these mythological conceptions the insight is indirectly expressed that man does not have his life in his hand as if he were his own lord but that he is constantly confronted with the decision of choosing his lord. Beyond this, they also contain the conviction that natural man has always already decided against God, his true Lord, and has let the threatening and tempting world become lord over him.

§ 27. The Law

1. The true will of man—the "inward man" (§ 18, 1)—insofar as it is νοῦς, (understanding intent, § 19, 1) strives toward life as that which to him is "good"; and since he can miss this "good," it straightway takes on for him the character of the "good," in the sense of that which is demanded (§§ 19, 1; 21, 1). *God's demand* encounters man concretely in the νόμος, *the Law of the Old Testament*, the purpose of which is no other than to lead man to life (Rom. 7:10; *cf.* Rom. 10:5; Gal. 3:12b).

By νόμος (whether with the article or without) Paul understands the Old Testament Law or the whole Old Testament conceived as law, except in a few passages where νόμος has the general meaning of norm or of compulsion, constraint, as in Rom. 7:2f., 22–8:1. Here there is a play on the term νόμος (the "law of God" is contrasted with the "law in my members"; the "law of my mind" with the "law of sin and death"; and the latter, finally, with the "law of the Spirit of life"). Other such passages are Rom. 3:27 (νόμος, "principle of faith") and Gal. 6:2 ("the law of Christ"). Elsewhere, Paul's νόμος means the Old Testament Law or the whole Old Testament. Pentateuch passages from Moses' time are regarded as νόμος as much as the actual Law of Moses is: Rom. 4:13–16 (Gen. 17:10f.; 18:18; 22:17f.); 7:7ff. (Gen. 2:17); I Cor. 14:34 (Gen. 3:16). In Rom. 3:10–19, passages from Psalms and the prophets are put together and regarded as νόμος. In I Cor. 14:21, Is. 28:11f. figures as νόμος. Nor is any distinction made between the cultic or ritual commandments (Gal. 4:10; 5:3) and the ethical requirements (Rom. 7:7ff.); both are called νόμος. In place of νόμος, Paul may also say ἐντολή, "commandment" (Rom. 7:8ff.), whereas in strict usage the Law contains a multitude of "commandments" (*cf.* Rom. 13:9; I Cor. 7:19).

The Old Testament Law is conceived in the meaning it has for the Old Testament and Judaism. That is, it is not conceived as the principle of an ideal of man, individual or social, which is unfolded in specific requirements. In other words, it is not the rational moral law inherent in man's intellect and giving rise to discussion of such problems as education and the itemized content of "the good." Rather, the Law is *the totality of the historically given legal demands,* cultic and ritual as well as ethical; and the human attitude demanded by it is not that of Goethe's "ever-striving endeavor" (Faust II, Act V)—orientation to an ideal—but is obedience, obedience again and again in the concrete case.

To be sure, except when Paul has specific occasion to speak of the ritual law as in Galatians, in his statements about the Law he is thinking essentially of its *ethical* demands, in particular of the decalogue, as Rom. 2:1–3:20 proves (*cf.* especially 2:21f.); likewise, Rom. 13:8–10; Gal. 5:14 (*cf.* 5:23). This is also indicated by his assertion that for the heathen the demands of the Law are attested in their conscience (Rom. 2:14f.); for what their conscience hears is certainly not the cultic-ritual regulations of the Old Testament. Again, the δικαίωμα τοῦ Θεοῦ, "God's decree" (Rom. 1:32), or the δικαίωμα τοῦ νόμου, Rom. 2:26 ("precepts of the law"); 8:4 ("just requirement of the law") can also only mean the ethical demand.

Nevertheless, Paul, unlike the prophets and Jesus, did not define the nature of obedience under the demand of God by contrasting the ethical demand of the cultic-ritual demands and by criticizing the latter from the standpoint of the former. In his battle against false obedience to the Law he never appeals to a saying of Jesus (§ 16, p. 189). He did not ask how it is that fulfilment of cultic-ritual commandments can be regarded as obedience offered to God at all—a question which it seems superfluous to ask in the case of the ethical demands. The reason why no difference between them is

apparent to Paul is that, thinking Jewishly, he does not evaluate the
cultic-ritual commandments in regard to their content, but considers
them only in regard to the fact that they, like the ethical commandments, are *demands*. Nevertheless, it is apparent from the matter-
of-fact way in which he names the ethical demands of the decalogue
(Rom. 13:8–10; Gal. 5:14) as the abiding content of the Law obligatory even for the Christian, that the identity of meaning in the cultic-
ritual and the ethical demands exists only for the man who has not
yet come to faith, and that in faith itself an unconsciously-working
principle of criticism is provided.

Under God's demand stand the Gentiles as do the Jews, except
that for the former this demand has not taken shape in the Law of
the Old Testament. But Paul explicitly says that when the Gentiles,
who do not have the "Law," do "by nature" (φύσει) the demands of
the Law—so Gentile fulfilment of the Law does occur, no matter
how rare or how frequent it may be—they testify that the "work of
the Law," i.e. the deed demanded by the Law, is 'written in their
hearts. Conscience also, which they have, too, testifies the same
thing (Rom. 2:14f., § 19, 4).* Of course, Paul does not mean "practical reason," (Kant) which unfolds a rational moral law out of
itself, when he speaks of conscience in the Gentiles; rather, he
means that the Gentiles can hear the command of God which confronts them in the specific case. It takes concrete form for them, for
instance, in the state, whose regime is ordered by God and serves
Him, and is therefore to be obeyed for conscience' sake (Rom.
13:1–5). It also takes concrete form in convention—in all that is
regarded as "true, honorable, just, pure, lovely, and gracious," all
that is in repute as a "virtue" or "worthy of praise" (Phil. 4:8).

2. *Naturally, the Law had been given by God in order to be fulfilled.* According to Rom. 2:20, it is "the embodiment of knowledge
and truth," and the "inward man" (man's "inmost self" RSV) approves of it (Rom. 7:14ff.). From the fact that the Law, being
unable to lead to "righteousness" and leading, rather, only to death,
is radically abolished for the man of faith (Rom. 1:18–7:6; Gal.
3:1–5:12) it is not to be inferred that it does not contain *God's
obligatory demand.* Paul himself counters such misunderstanding
(Rom. 7:7) with the question, "What then shall we say? That the

* Rom. 2:26 ("if the uncircumcision keeps the precepts of the Law") probably refers not to the heathen but to Gentile Christians.

law is sin?" (τί οὖν ἐροῦμεν; ὁ νόμος ἁμαρτία); and shortly after
(v. 12) avers: "So the law is holy and the commandment is holy and
just and good" and characterizes the Law as "spiritual" (v. 14). The
"legislation" (νομοθεσία) accorded to Israel is one of Israel's titles of
honor of which Paul is proud (Rom. 9:4). As the Law was given
"for life" (with life-giving intent), the keeping of it would bestow
life (Rom. 10:5; Gal. 3:12). The doers of the Law will be "rightwised" * (Rom. 2:13), and "eternal life" and all salvation will be
accorded him who is faithful in "well-doing" (Rom. 2:7) or "who
does good" (Rom. 2:10)—i.e. in the context, to him who fulfills the
Law.

The presupposition for understanding the proposition that not
works lead to "righteousness," but only faith, is the acknowledgment that the Law's demand is just, *that God is the Judge who
demands good deeds of man* (Rom. 1:18–3:20). The preaching of
faith does not introduce a new concept of God as if God were not
the Judge who requires good works but were only the Merciful. No,
we may speak of God's "grace" only when we also speak of His
"wrath." That is how it happens that Paul, in words that sound open
to misunderstanding, can refer the Christian, who achieves "righteousness" not by works of the Law but by faith, to the judgment in
which recompense is made according to works (I Cor. 1:8; 3:12–15;
4:4f.; I Thess. 3:13; 5:23, etc.; especially II Cor. 5:10: "For we must
all appear before the judgment seat of Christ, so that each one may
receive good or evil, according to what he has done in the body").
Though the Christian in a certain sense is no longer "under Law"
(Gal. 5:18; Rom. 6:14), that does not mean that the demands of the
Law are no longer valid for him; for the *agape* demanded of him is
nothing else than the fulfilment of the Law (Rom. 13:8–10; Gal.
5:14). Having received the possibility of proving "what is the good
and acceptable and perfect will of God" by the "renewing" of his
'mind" (Rom. 12:2), he is able to know by himself what the Jew
can know as one "instructed in the law": "know the will (of God)
and approve what is excellent" (Rom. 2:18). The will of God revealed to the Christian is identical with the demand of the Law.

The reason why man's situation under the Law is so desperate is
not that the Law as an inferior revelation mediates a limited or even
false knowledge of God. What makes his situation so desperate is

* See footnote p. 253.

the simple fact that prior to faith *there is no true fulfilment of the Law.* "For all who rely on works of the law are under a curse; for it is written, 'Cursed be every one who does not abide by all things written in the book of the law, and do them'" (Gal. 3:10). The arguments of Rom. 1:18–2:29 are summarized in 3:9: "I have already charged that all men, both Jews and Greeks, are under the power of sin." Then, after he has substantiated that by a composite of quotations, vv. 10–18, he concludes, "for no human being will be justified in his sight (God's) by works of the Law" (v. 20)—the primary meaning of which is that no man *can* procure his own "rightwising" by works of the Law. He cannot because he cannot exhibit "the works of the Law" in their entirety. That is why the "ministration of the Law" is a "ministration of death" or "of condemnation" (II Cor. 3:7, 9); that is why "the written code kills" (II Cor. 3:6); that is why the Law is "the law of sin and death" (Rom. 8:2). The reason why man under the Law does not achieve "rightwising" and life is that he is a transgressor of the Law, that he is guilty before God.

But Paul goes much further still; he says not only that man *can not* achieve salvation by works of the Law, but also that he is not even *intended* to do so. Paul thinks in this manner in consequence of his concept of God, according to which whatever factually is or happens, is or happens according to divine plan. In its context, Rom. 3:20—"no human being will be justified . . . by works of the law"—means, "no one can be justified on the basis of works of the Law," but that this impossibility was also *intended* is indicated by Gal. 2:16, where the same sentence means in this context: "no one *is to be* justified on the basis of works of the Law." A Jew would contradict Paul's assertion that a man can be justified only on the basis of absolutely perfect keeping of the Law ("who . . . abides by all things . . ." Gal. 3:10), still more would he contradict the proposition that *justification by works of the Law and justification by divine grace appropriated in man's faith exclude each other.* But that is the decisive thesis of Paul: "for Christ is the end of the law, that every one who has faith may be justified" (Rom. 10:4); i.e. "Christ means the end of the Law; he leads to righteousness everyone who has faith." Paul reminds the Galatians, who are by no means giving up their faith in Christ or rejecting the grace of God but only wish to combine with it the taking over of circumcision,

"You are severed from Christ, you who would be justified by the law; you have fallen away from grace" (Gal. 5:4). The way of works of the Law and the way of grace and faith are mutually exclusive opposites (Gal. 2:15–21; Rom. 4:4f., 14–16; 6:14; 11:5f.).

But why is this the case? Because *man's effort to achieve his salvation by keeping the Law* only leads him into sin, indeed this effort itself in the end *is already sin*. It is the insight which Paul has achieved into the nature of sin that determines his teaching on the Law. This embraces two insights. One is the insight that sin is man's self-powered striving to undergird his own existence in forgetfulness of his creaturely existence, to procure his salvation by his own strength (§ 23, 1), that striving which finds its extreme expression in "boasting" and "trusting in the 'flesh'" (§ 23, 2). The other is the insight that man is always already a sinner, that, fallen into the power of sin (§ 23, 3), he is always already involved in a falsely oriented understanding of his existence (§§ 25, 26). The reason, then, that man shall not, must not, be "rightwised" by works of the Law is that he must not be allowed to imagine that he is able to procure his salvation by his own strength; for he can find his salvation only when he understands himself in his dependence upon God the Creator.

Simultaneously, this answers the question that arises in Rom. 7:7 after it has been established in 3:21–7:6 that "righteousness" is bestowed only upon the faith which appropriates the grace of God and not upon the works of the Law. This is the question: *What meaning does the Law still have?* The two questions belong together and each of the answers given interprets the other.

The answer given in Rom. 7:7ff. expands what had already been briefly said in 3:20: "through the law comes knowledge of sin." For this sentence (coming after vv. 10–19) does not, of course, mean that *through the Law* man is led to knowledge of what sin is, but does mean that by it he is *led into sinning*. What is meant is practical "knowledge," the "knowing how" to sin, just as "knowing sin" in Rom. 7:7 or II Cor. 5:21 is the practice of sin (*cf.* II Cor. 5:11 where "knowing the fear of the Lord" is not a theoretical knowledge about the fear of the Lord but means "being experienced in fearing the Lord"). This is just the idea that Rom. 7:7–11 develops:

"I would never have come to know sin except through the Law; for I would never have come to know desire, were it not that the

Law says, 'You shall not desire.' But sin took advantage of the commandment and thereby brought about in me every sort of desire.
For without the Law sin was dead, but I was once alive without the
Law. But when the commandment came, sin came to life and I
went to death. And the result was that the commandment which
was intended to lead men to life led me straight to death. For sin
took advantage of the commandment and deceived me and with its
help killed me"· (Blt.).

Thus, the Law brings to light that man is sinful, whether it be
that his sinful desire leads him to transgression of the Law or that
that desire disguises itself in zeal for keeping the Law. But what
appears in Rom. 7:7ff. as a wile of sin is actually God's intention:
"Law came in (*sc.* between Adam and Christ) to increase the trespass"; and the continuation shows what meaning that has: "but
where sin increased, grace abounded all the more" (Rom. 5:20).
Thus, the Law leads into sin the man who has forsaken his creaturely
relation to God and wants to procure life for and by himself; it does
this in order thereby to bring him back again to the right relation to
God. This it does by confronting him with the grace of God which
is to be appropriated in faith.

Gal. 3:19 says the same thing: "Why then the law? It was added
for the sake of transgressions (i.e. in order to evoke transgressions),
till the offspring should come to whom the promise had been made
(i.e. until Christ, in whom God's grace becomes effective)." It is
just by evoking sin that the Law must bring about the fulfilment of
the divine promises: "Is the Law then contrary to the promises (of
God)? By no means! For only if the Law had been given as one
that could make alive would righteousness actually have its origin
in the Law. But instead the scripture shut up all things under sin in
order that the promise might be bestowed on the basis of faith in
Jesus Christ upon those who have faith. Before faith came, however, we were confined under the Law, kept under restraint in prospect of the faith that was to be revealed. Hence, the Law became
our discipliner until Christ, in order that we might be rightwised on
the basis of faith. But since faith has come we are no longer under
the discipliner" (Gal. 3:21–25 Blt.).

Rom. 4:13–16, finally, has the same meaning: "The promise given
to Abraham or his descendants that he should be the heir of the
world was not founded upon the Law, but upon the righteousness of

faith. For if the right to the inheritance were founded upon the Law, faith would be done for (primarily faith in the promises is meant, but this is regarded as identical with Christian faith) and the promise would be void; for the Law only yields wrath. But where there is no Law, there is no transgression (and hence no wrath, either. What was the Law for, then? Why, it was intended to yield wrath; its purpose was to cause transgression!). 'On the basis of faith' holds true for just this reason: In order that 'on the principle of grace' may hold true, making the promise sure for every descendant . . ." (Blt.).

Though the purpose of the Law is, or was, that of being a *paidagogos to Christ*, it is not conceived in either the Greek sense or the modern sense as an educator who is to train man up to a higher level of mental (and especially of ethical) life. Is faith opening up to divine grace the product of education? Of course not. It does not even become possible except upon the basis of God's grace working in Christ. The "educating" done by the Law leads, on the contrary, into sin, and "educates" indirectly toward faith, it is true, because by it the sinner can understand the alternative—*either* works of the Law *or* faith—when grace confronts him. But the Law does this not by leading man into subjective despair, but by bringing him into an objectively desperate situation which he does not recognize as such until the message of grace hits its mark in him. Gal. 3:21-25 does not have the development of the individual in mind but the history of mankind, and Rom. 7:14-24 is not a confession of Paul describing his erstwhile inner division under the Law, but is that picture of the objective situation of man-under-the-Law which became visible to him only after he had attained the viewpoint of faith. The cry, "Wretched man that I am! Who will deliver me from this body of death" (v. 24) was not uttered by Saul-Paul struggling and groaning in time past under the Law—how *that* Paul regarded himself, Phil. 3:4-6 says. Not *that* Paul utters this cry, but Paul the Christian, who puts it into the mouth of the Jew and thereby exposes the situation of the Jew which is not visible to himself.

Nor does Paul elsewhere argue against the way of the Law with the argument that this way leads to subjective despair, and he never praises faith as the escape from an inner division caused by conscience, or as a release from an unbearable burden. His accusation against Jews and Judaizers is that the way of the Law is wrong not because in consequence of transgressions it does does not lead to the goal, but because its *direction* is wrong, for it is the way that is supposed to lead to "one's own righteousness" (Rom. 10:3, *cf.* Phil. 3:9). It is not merely evil deeds already committed that make a man reprehensible in God's sight, but man's intention of becoming righteous before God by keeping the Law and thereby having his "boast" is already sin.

To lead man into sin, therefore, is *the purpose of the Law in the history of salvation,* not only by arousing his desires to transgression but also by offering him the uttermost possibility of living as a sinner by perverting his resistance to the commandment into a striving after a "righteousness of his own" through keeping the commandment—a highly plausible perversion, for in the knowledge that transgression is sin (a knowledge that is directly given with the possession of the Law or is awakened by conscience; § 19, 4) and in the fear of transgressing, lies the foundation of a false supposition that Law-observance—which, as a conquering of desire, takes on the appearance of a good work—can procure "righteousness." That fear and this supposition show how deep in sin man lies ("in order that sin . . . through the commandment might become sinful beyond measure," Rom. 7:13); and bound up with this in the very nature of the case is man's ignorance of the situation he is in: It is hidden from him that his life is steering not toward life but toward death ("for what I am bringing about, I do not know," Rom. 7:15; see § 24, 2).

Then *the ultimate purpose of the Law is to lead man to death* and thereby to let God appear as God, for the Law gives sin its power; while sin is the "sting" of death (I Cor. 15:56); sin kills man by means of the commandment by dangling before him the deceptive promise of procuring him life (Rom. 7:11). So it can also be said, "The letter (i.e. the Law itself) kills" (II Cor. 3:6). The fruits of the "sinful passions" aroused by the Law ripen for death (Rom. 7:5; see § 24, 2). But by this process the Law leads man to God as the Creator who bestows life and from whom alone life can be given to man—this man who on the way to "his own righteousness," the way of "boasting," has blundered into death. It is as this God that he appears in the "grace" of the salvation-occurrence, and it is this God toward whom faith is directed. Abraham (Rom. 4:2), who has no "boast" (i.e. nothing to boast about), believes in "God who gives life to the dead and calls into existence the things that do not exist"

(Rom. 4:17). And for Paul, the upshot of the "affliction" he has experienced is that he has pronounced the sentence of death upon himself, "in order that we might not trust in ourselves but in God who raises the dead;" just that is also the upshot of the "educating" done by the Law (II Cor. 1:9).

3. At the end, then, it becomes apparent that even *the demand of God embodied in the Law* is grace only. It was already grace that God gave the Law "for life" (Rom. 7:10). And though this life-giving purpose was defeated by man's sinful desire, that still was not able to wipe out God's grace, for it is still God's grace that the Law factually led "to death," because by this route man is led to God, the "God who gives life to the dead." The Law is not "against the promises of God" (Gal. 3:21); the unity of the divine will is clear: It wills now nothing else than it always has, and God's law, the "spiritual law" (Rom. 7:14), remains in effect as the "law of Christ" (Gal. 6:2) and in *agape* (see above, p. 262) is kept by those who have faith. Now for the first time its real intention comes to fulfilment: God has removed the powerlessness of the Law ("what the law weakened by the flesh could not do") "in order that the just requirement of the law might be fulfilled in us, who walk not according to the flesh but according to the Spirit" (Rom. 8:3f.).

The difference between the Law as the eternal will of God and the Law that is abolished is expressed to a certain degree in Paul's terminology, in which frequently the Law as abolished by Christ figures as the *Law of Moses*. Thus, Christ and Moses are contrasted in Rom. 10:46f.; likewise, in II Cor. 3:7–18 in the comparison between the ministry of the old and the new covenant (*cf.* also I Cor. 10:2). The Law that intervened (Rom. 5:20) is identified by v. 14 as the Law of Moses. Especially significant is the fact that in the polemic of Gal. 3:19f., Paul can take up the Gnostic myth of the giving of the Law by angels in order to prove that the Law of Moses is not attributable to God Himself. Paul can do that only because he views the Law as a matter of course in the role in which the Jew lets it encounter him.

As the unity of the divine will is clear, so is the *unity of man's existence* clear as he moves from the situation under the Law to the situation under grace. No break takes place; no magical or mysterious transformation of man in regard to his substance, the basis of

his nature, takes place. Rather, his new existence stands in historical
continuity with the old—not, indeed, in a continuity of development
as understood within the Greek-idealistic picture of man. Compared with that kind of continuity we really do have to do here with
a break: A new understanding of one's self takes the place of the
old—it does so, nevertheless, in such a manner that historical continuity is preserved; indeed, it thereby becomes one's own true history, for the transition from the old existence to the new does not
take place as a mental development from sin to faith; rather, faith is
decision in regard to the grace which encounters a man in the proclaimed word. However much Paul's view of the history of salvation
is oriented toward mankind, and not the individual (see above, p.
266), it still is true that the situation of mankind is also that of the
individual. He, the sinner who is in death, is confronted by the gospel when it reaches him with the decision whether or not he is willing to understand himself anew and to receive his life from the hand
of God. The possibility of understanding is given him in the very
fact that he is a sinner, that he is in death. This rescue of man from
death does not take as its point of departure some higher spiritual
principle or faculty in him that is not under the power of sin, if there
were such; what it rescues is not—as the Gnostic myth maintains—a
fully inconceivable and only negatively describable self, the pre-
existent spark of light, but precisely the sinner, the innerly divided
and self-misunderstanding human self. Salvation is naught else than
the realization of that destined goal of "life" and selfhood which are
God's will for man and man's own real intention, but which were
perverted under sin (§ 23, 3).

CHAPTER V

Man under Faith

A. THE RIGHTEOUSNESS OF GOD

§ 28. The Concept of Righteousness

1. Since Paul regards *man's existence* prior to *faith* in the transparency it has gained to the eye of faith, therefore *man's existence under faith* has already been indirectly pre-sketched in the presentation of pre-faith existence. If pre-faith man is man fallen into the power of death, man under faith is man who receives life. If man's death has its cause in the fact that man in his striving to live out of his own resources loses his self (§ 23, 3), life arises out of surrendering one's self to God, thereby gaining one's self.

This is just what is expressed in Paul's manner of interpreting the *"righteousness,"* or the *"being rightwised"* * (KJ "justification"), which is the presupposition for receiving life. In the thesis that salvation, the receipt of life, is dependent upon and conditioned by a man's righteousness, Paul is only repeating at the outset what Jewish tradition takes for granted. But the way he understands the possibility and the actualization of righteousness or rightwising—even speaking of it as the very substance of salvation—indicates the basic contrast between him and Judaism and reveals his new grasp of man's existence before God.

Strictly speaking, *righteousness is the condition for receiving salvation or "life."* As Abraham's (faith-)righteousness was the presupposition for his receiving the promise (Rom. 4:13), so now he who is righteous (by faith) *will* receive life (Rom. 1:17; Gal. 3:11). It is to those who are rightwised ("justified therefore . . .") that salvation will be imparted (Rom. 5:1ff.). As sin led to death, so righteousness leads to life (Rom. 5:17, 21; 8:10). The goal ahead of

* See footnote p. 253.

him who has righteousness is the gain of life (Phil. 3:9f.); God's rightwising act is followed by His glorifying act (Rom. 8:30).

But since this connection between righteousness and salvation is so tight and inevitable, *righteousness itself can become the essence of salvation.* "Striving after righteousness," the concern of the Jews (Rom. 9:30f.; Gal. 2:16), is the same thing as "striving after salvation," for in the former, one has the latter. Though in Rom. 5:9, salvation ("being saved") lies in the future awaiting the "right-wised," yet in Rom. 10:10, "righteousness" and "salvation" are used in synonymous parallelism. As Christ's death brought it about that we are "alive," it is also said, meaning the same thing, that we in him are "the righteousness (of God)"—i.e. that we have the standing of righteous men (II Cor. 5:15, 21). The "ministry of righteousness" (whose opposite is the "ministry of condemnation," i.e. of condemnation to death) is identical with the "ministry of the Spirit" (whose opposite is the "ministry of death"—II Cor. 3:7–9). Further, "righteousness" can be joined with other terms that also denote the state of salvation (I Cor. 1:30: "righteousness and consecration and redemption"; *cf.* 6:11). That which was brought to light by the occurrence of salvation in Christ, and which is the content of "the gospel," is the new possibility of a "righteousness" which shall be a "righteousness of God" (Rom. 1:16f.; 3:21); just for that reason the office of apostle can be called the "ministry of righteousness" (II Cor. 3:9). But it is possible to speak so of "righteousness" not only because of the tight connection that exists between "righteousness" (as condition) and "life" (as result), but especially because *not merely salvation (the result) is the gift of God but even the condition for it is already the gift of God Himself.* For what, we must now ask, is meant by "righteousness" and especially by "righteousness of God"?

2. The word *dikaiosyne* (righteousness) is (like its Hebrew analogue, צְדָקָה) ambiguous. We must here disregard a number of meanings which the word can have in both Biblical and secular usage, for instance, the very important meaning of "distributive justice" dealt out by a judge, which occurs in Paul (Rom. 9:28), according to many manuscripts at any rate, in his quotation from Is. 10:22. Aside from such meanings, *dikaiosyne* (and likewise *dikaios*, "righteous") is used in both an ethical sense (then meaning "uprightness") and a forensic sense. When it denotes the condition

for (or the essence of) salvation, *dikaiosyne is a forensic term*. It does not mean the ethical quality of a person. It does not mean any quality at all, but a relationship. That is, *dikaiosyne* is not something a person has as his own; rather it is something he has in the verdict of the "forum" (= law-court—the sense of "forum" from which "forensic" as here used is derived) to which he is accountable. He has it in the opinion adjudicated to him by another. A man has' righteousness," or is "righteous," when he is acknowledged to be such, and that means, in case such acknowledgment of him is in dispute: when he is "rightwised," "pronounced righteous" (*cf.* the parallelism between "righteous before God" and δικαιωθήσονται— "be pronounced righteous"—in Rom. 2:13). Specifically, the "righteous" one is that one in a legal action (κρίνεσθαι; note the parallelism between "be justified" and "prevail"—win out—in Rom. 3:4), who wins his case or is acquitted. Normally, therefore, he is the "innocent" one—but he is "righteous" not to the extent that he may *be* innocent, but to the extent that he is *acknowledged* innocent. "Righteousness" then is the "favorable standing" that a person has in the eyes of others; it is that "right" which a man seeks to establish by process of law as "his rights." In this sense Michael Kohlhaas (in Kleist's story of the same name) is the type of the man who "demands righteousness"—viz. that he be acknowledged to be in the right.

This is in accord with Old Testament-Jewish usage. In exhorting men to trust Jahweh, the Psalmist says (Ps. 37:6):

"He brings forth thy righteousness (צְדָקָה,
LXX: δικαιοσύνη) as the light,
And thy judgment (מִשְׁפָּט, κρίμα) as the noonday."

Or he implores (Ps. 17:2, 15):

"Let my right (מִשְׁפָּט, κρίμα) come forth from thy presence . . . May I behold thy face in righteousness (צֶדֶק, δικαιοσύνη).

In this sense it may also be said of God that He is "declared righteous," in other words that He is acknowledged to be in the right. Thus, we read in the passage quoted at Rom. 3:4 (Ps. 51:4):

"Against thee, thee only, have I sinned and done this evil in thy sight

That thou mightest be justified (pronounced right, תִּצְדַּק,
δικαιωθῇς) when thou speakest
And be clear (תִּזְכֶּה, νικήσῃς) when thou judgest."

This use is also frequent in the Psalms of Solomon (2:16: "I
will justify thee [acknowledge thy righteousness] O God; 3:5;
4:9; 8:7, 27ff.); likewise, Lk. 7:29 ("and all the people and
the tax-collectors 'justified' God"); cf. Lk. 7:35 and its parallel,
Mt. 11:19).

The more Jewish piety came to be determined by eschatology—
i.e. the more the pious expected God's rightwising verdict to come
from His eschatological judgment—the more *the forensic term*
"righteousness" became an eschatological term. By those who
"hunger and thirst after righteousness," Mt. 5:6 obviously does not
mean those who "ever striving, endeavor" to attain ethical perfection, but those who long to have God pronounce the verdict
"righteous" as His decision over them in the judgment. What the
pious Jew endeavors to do, however, is to fulfill the conditions which
are the presupposition for this verdict of God; these conditions are,
of course, keeping the commandments of the Law and doing good
works. Hence, Paul can call the righteousness sought by the Jews
"righteousness from the Law" (Phil. 3:9), while his thesis is that
"righteousness" (as "God's righteousness") has been revealed "apart
from the Law" (Rom. 3:21).

But before we proceed further to clarify the contrast between
the Pauline and the Jewish conception, it must be clearly recognized that *there is complete agreement between them as to the*
formal meaning of DIKAIOSYNE: *It is a forensic-eschatological term.*
The forensic meaning of "righteous" and "be rightwised" is already
a clear implication of Rom. 2:13 (see above) as it also is of the
expressions modeled after Gen. 15:6 that speak of "being reckoned
(λογίζεσθαι) as righteousness" (Rom. 4:3, 5, 22; Gal. 3:6; cf. "to
reckon righteousness to . . ." Rom. 4:6), in which "reckon" has the
same forensic meaning as the Hebrew חָשַׁב (Lev. 7:18; II Sam.
19:19 [19:20 in Heb.]; Ps. 32:2), for which the LXX uses precisely
the same Greek verb (or its compound, διαλογίζειν). The eschatological meaning of *dikaiosyne* is clear as day in the passages that
speak of a future verdict of righteousness to come in the eschatological judgment; such are Rom. 2:13 again and also Gal. 5:5 ("we wait
for the hope of righteousness").

The future tenses in Rom. 3:20 ("no human being will be justified") and 3:30 ("he [God] will justify") are perhaps not genuine futures, but gnomic (or logical) futures. Rom. 5:19, "many will be made righteous," is evidently said as if uttered in Jesus' time (the dividing point of the ages); hence it is already true in the present in which Paul is speaking (cf. vv. 17, 21). On the other hand, neither is the present used in the present-tense statements of Gal. 2:16; 3:11; 5:4 a genuine present, but the timeless present of didactic statement and may therefore apply in spite of the tense to the decision of God in the coming judgment.

§ 29. Righteousness as a Present Reality

1. The first difference from Jewish usage is that Paul asserts of this forensic-eschatological righteousness that *it is already imputed to a man in the present* (on the presupposition that he "has faith"). After Rom. 3:21–4:25 has dealt with faith as the presupposition for being "rightwised," Rom. 5:1 begins: "Rightwised therefore by faith we have peace with God." * And in keeping with this v. 9 says: "Since therefore we are now rightwised . . . how much more shall we be saved . . ." For the present that exists since Christ the purpose expressed in v. 21: "that . . . grace might reign through righteousness to eternal life," is being fulfilled. Rom. 8:10 also applies to the present: "if Christ is in you, although your bodies are dead because of sin, your spirits are alive because of righteousness" (which is scarcely to be understood with Lietzmann as meaning: "because of the sin you have committed" and "because of the righteousness you will practice," but rather: "because sin is condemned [cf. v. 3]" and "because righteousness has been established," as Barth interprets). Though one may understand "those whom he called he also rightwised" (Rom. 8:30) as proleptic (like the following "he also glorified"), Paul, nevertheless, says to the Corinthians "you *were* rightwised" (I Cor. 6:11) and says of the Gentiles "who did not pursue righteousness," "they *have attained* righteousness" (Rom. 9:30). And Rom. 1:17 is to be understood in this same way when it says that in the preaching of the gospel the righteousness of God "is revealed." For this does not mean that the preached gospel expounds some teaching about righteousness, but that through it right-

* The variant reading ἔχωμεν (let us have) is not to be entertained.

eousness becomes a possibility (which in faith becomes reality) for the hearer of the gospel.

"Revealed" has the same meaning in Rom. 1:18: "the wrath of God is revealed from heaven"; i.e. God's wrathful judgment (see § 31, 1) appears, takes place—likewise in the present. The same meaning is also found in Gal. 3:23: "Now before faith came, we were confined under the law, kept under restraint until faith should be revealed"; this expected "revealing" has now become a thing of the present ("now that faith has come," v. 25); this does not mean that now a hitherto unknown teaching about faith is being expounded, but that it has now become a possibility and, in those who have faith, a reality—faith has made its appearance, for this is just what "*be revealed*" (ἀποκαλύπτεσθαι) or its noun "revelation" (ἀποκάλυψις), and also "be manifested" (φανεροῦσθαι, Rom. 3:21), mean when used as eschatological terms—appear on the scene, become possibility, or become operative. The awaited "revelation of the Lord Jesus Christ" (I Cor. 1:7 KJ mg.) is not some communication that he will impart, but his appearing in person at his parousia, just as the "revelation" of God's righteous judgment (Rom. 2:5) is the effective execution of it. And when I Cor. 3:13 says of the Day: "it will be revealed with fire," that means that the judgment day will fierily appear. "To appear on the scene" is also the meaning in Rom. 8:18f.: "I consider that the sufferings of this present time are not worth comparing with the glory *that will make its appearance in us.* For the creation waits with eager longing for the revealing (= the appearing) of the sons of God." The same usage occurs in II Thess. 1:7; 2:3, 6, 8; I Pet. 1:5, 7, 13; 4:13; 5:1; Lk. 17:30. Of course, both the verb and the noun can also mean the disclosing of something hitherto hidden, the divulging of a secret (I Cor. 14:6, 26, 30; II Cor. 12:1, 7; Gal. 1:12; 2:2; Phil. 3:15, and elsewhere).

This "appearing on the scene" or "becoming effective," since either is an event occurring to or for men, does, of course, *enable man to understand or perceive the event.* While that is true, it is not the perceiving of the event but the event itself that is denoted by "being revealed." The "revealing" of God's wrath (Rom. 1:18) takes place even though those concerned are not even aware of it themselves. In I Cor. 3:13 the clause "the Day will disclose it" does make a distinction between this informing function of revelation and revelation as actual occurrence (viz.

the occurrence of the judgment day meant in: "it will be 'revealed' with fire"), but this disclosure will take place not through any proclamation but in the event itself. (*Cf.* R. Bultmann, "Der Begriff der Offenbarung im NT" [1929] in *Glauben und Verstehen* [1933], pp. 153–187; the article: "Offenbarung" in *RGG*, 2nd ed.)

2. At this point it is of basic importance to comprehend that by his thesis that *righteousness is a present reality* Paul, nevertheless, does not rob it of its *forensic-eschatological meaning*. The paradoxicality of his assertion is this: God already pronounces His eschatological verdict (over the man of faith) in the present; the eschatological event is already present reality, or, rather, is beginning in the present. Therefore, the righteousness which God adjudicates to man (the man of faith) is not "sinlessness" in the sense of ethical perfection, but is "sinlessness" in the sense that God does not "count" man's sin against him (II Cor. 5:19).

That disposes of many questions that arise only from the fact that "righteousness" is not understood in its forensic-eschatological sense but is misunderstood as ethical perfection. When God rightwises the sinner, "makes him righteous" (Rom. 4:5), that man is not merely "regarded as if" he were righteous, but really is righteous—i.e. absolved from his sin by God's verdict. What consequences this has for his ethical conduct will be considered later (§ 38). That it must have such consequences is clear from the outset, for the "rightwised," being men who have been transplanted into eschatological existence, are also "saints" who can have no further contact with sin. Christ is "our righteousness and our consecration" (I Cor. 1:30); and side by side with "you were rightwised" stands "you were consecrated" (I Cor. 6:11). But that is not expressed by the term "righteousness" itself, and the relation between "righteousness" and "consecration" ("sanctification" KJ) is for the present unclear. Before it can be clarified the meaning of "rightwising" must first be clearly determined. Its meaning becomes apparent from such a sentence as Rom. 5:19:

> "For as by one man's disobedience
> many were made sinners,
> so by one man's obedience
> many will be made righteous."

Just as certainly as Adamitic men were not "merely regarded as if they were sinners," but really were sinners, so are the members of the humanity founded by Christ really righteous. II Cor. 5:21 indicates the same thing:

> "For our sake he made him to be sin who knew no sin,
> so that in him we might become the righteousness of God."

It would be an error to regard the main clause as meaning that God treated the (ethically) sinless Christ "as if" he were a sinner (which in itself would not be untrue). Rather, this clause intends to express the paradoxical fact that God made the (ethically) sinless Christ to be a sinner (in the forensic sense)—viz. by letting him die on the cross as one accursed (*cf.* Gal. 3:13). Correspondingly, the purpose clause says that we (through him) are to become righteous (in the forensic sense). Thus, the old debate over whether he who is rightwised is really righteous or is only regarded "as if" he were righteous, rests upon a misunderstanding. So does the question: How is it possible for him to be a truly righteous man? So does the temptation to supply an "as if." So, finally, does the problem how Paul can, nevertheless, proceed to place these truly righteous, and hence "sinless," men under the ethical imperative. These perplexities all rest upon the misunderstanding that "righteousness" denotes the ethical quality of a man, whereas in truth it means his relation to God.

If one takes Paul's statements as they stand, without a supplied "as if," and yet fails to recognize the forensic-eschatological meaning of "righteousness," two wrong tracks are easy to take: 1. the idealistic and 2. the Gnostic misunderstanding. According to 1. "rightwising" means that one takes into his consciousness a new principle, the principle of obedience to the idea of the good. When one has done this, a "qualitative fulfilment of the Law" has taken the place of a "merely quantitative" fulfilment; man is righteous since his will affirms the ethical law in its totality (F. C. Baur). Righteousness, then, denotes the "ideal" character of the man whose living tends toward the good; "striving toward not sinning" (Epictetus, Diss. IV 12, 19) is the characteristic of the man who is "progressing" (προκόπτων), to use Stoic terminology; by approaching in endless progress toward the ideal of ethical uprightness he can be regarded, *sub specie* of the idea, as righteous. He stands under the imperative," become what thou art" (viz. what thou, *sub specie* of the

[277]

idea, art). 2. The other misunderstanding is one related to Hellenistic Gnosticism, in which "righteousness" is considered a divine "power" (δύναμις) which flows into the initiate along with other divine powers in the mystery of re-birth and drives out the demonic powers which have hitherto reigned in him (Corp. Herm. 13:9 [Mead]: "We are made righteous, son, by the departure of Unrighteousness"). This is the sense R. Reitzenstein (*Hellenistische Mysterienreligionen*, 3rd ed., 257–261) professed to find in Rom. 6:7; 8:30; I Cor. 6:11. Even if it should turn out that Paul was influenced in these passages by the terminology of the mysteries, his conception of "righteousness" and "rightwising" would still not be explainable as a whole from the mystery terminology.

3. The *present reality* of righteousness rests upon its having been "revealed" by the occurring of salvation in Christ (Rom. 3:21–26; II Cor. 5:21; *cf.* I Cor. 1:30). This saving occurrence, however, is the *eschatological event* by which God ended the old course of the world and introduced the new aeon. For "when the time had fully come, God sent forth his son" (Gal. 4:4); so now "the old has passed away" and "the new has come" and whoever is "in Christ" is a "new creature" (II Cor. 5:17). The New Covenant (II Cor. 3:6ff.) predicted for the eschatological period by Jeremiah has taken the place of the Old Covenant, and the "acceptable time" prophesied by Isaiah has arrived (II Cor. 6:2).

The forensic-eschatological sense of "righteousness" is also corroborated, finally, by its parallelism with the term *"adoption to sonship"* (υἱοθεσία), which is also both a legal term (though not derived from the trial-court) and an eschatological term. Just as the salvation-occurrence can be described as having taken place "for our justification" (rightwising), Rom. 3:25f.; 4:25; 5:18; II Cor. 5:21), its purpose can also be given by the expression, "that we might receive adoption as sons" (Gal. 4:5). "Adoption" has the same peculiar double nature as "righteousness" has. On the one hand, it is a thing of the future, a longed-for goal (Rom. 8:23: "we wait for adoption as sons"); on the other hand, it is a present thing, as is attested by the fact that in the Spirit—that eschatological gift—we cry "Abba!" (Rom. 8:15f.; Gal. 4:6f.).

4. The contrast between Paul and Judaism, then, is not that each has a different conception of righteousness as a forensic-eschatolog-

ican entity. Rather, the immediate contrast is that what for the Jews is a *matter of hope* is for Paul a *present reality*—or, better, is also a present reality. But how can it be both? That can only be cleared up in the course of our further investigation of Paul's thinking. For the present, the problem itself must be pointed more sharply. It emerges clearly in the arrangement of Romans. After the section 1:18–3:20 has demonstrated that before the revealing of "God's righteousness" both Gentiles and Jews stood under the "wrath of God," the thesis of righteousness now established by the occurrence of salvation in Christ is presented in 3:21–31 and the Scripture proof of it is offered in 4:1–25. For the Jew, with whom Paul is debating in all these arguments, the assertion of the present reality of eschatological righteousness could only appear absurd; for where, he could ask, are the blessings that were to be given along with righteousness? Where is "life"? Are not death and sin still present realities?

Paul replies in chapters 5–8. In chapter 5 he endeavors to demonstrate that eschatological life, though a matter of hope, is, nevertheless, in a certain manner already a present reality. Further, he shows in 6:1–7:6 that even sin has lost its domination for the rightwised. Then, after a digression (7:7–25) has discussed the significance of the Law in the history of salvation, chapter 8 is the conclusion; it deals once more with freedom from sin (8:1–11) and from death (8:12–39), pointing out again the peculiar double character of salvation: future and yet already present.

§ 30. Righteousness as God's Righteousness

1. The contrast between Paul and Judaism consists not merely in his assertion of the present reality of righteousness, but also in a much more decisive thesis—the one which concerns the condition to which God's acquitting decision is tied. The Jew takes it for granted that this condition is keeping the Law, the accomplishing of "works" prescribed by the Law. In direct contrast to this view Paul's thesis runs—to consider its negative aspect first: "*without works of the Law.*" After the demonstration, Rom. 1:18–3:20, that Gentiles and Jews are fallen under sin has ended with "No human being will be justified ('rightwised') in his (God's) sight by works of the Law," the next verse enters like a new theme stating the thesis: "But now

the righteousness of God has been manifested apart from law," and after a short discussion v. 28 sums it up: "For we hold that a man is justified (rightwised) by faith apart from works of law" (in which by the context "by faith" certainly means *sola fide*—"by faith alone"). For this thesis, chapter 4 offers the Scripture proof: Even Abraham did not achieve his righteousness by his works. In the arguments about the fate of the Jewish people (chapters 9–11) this thought recurs at 9:31f.; 10:4–6; 11:6, particularly in the pithy sentence 10:4: "For Christ is the end of the law, that every one who has faith may be justified (rightwised)." The same assertion is defended in Galatians against the Judaizers who want to combine Christian faith with the acceptance of the Law (Gal. 2:16; 3:11, 21; 5:1); 2:21 in particular formulates the idea in utmost pointed form: "for if justification (rightwising) were through the law, then Christ died to no purpose." In his other letters, where Paul is not contending with Judaism and Judaizing Christians, such sentences are quite naturally missing except for one example in Philippians (3:9: "not having a righteousness of my own, based on law").

The negative aspect of Paul's thesis does not stand alone; a positive statement takes its place beside it: "*by, or from, faith.*" Right in the thematic sentences at Rom. 1:16f. where the "gospel" is described as "a power for salvation," the reason given for this description is: "For in it the righteousness of God is revealed through faith for faith," in support of which Hab. 2:4 is cited as Scripture proof. Accordingly, the negative sentence quoted above, Rom. 3:21, receives its positive complement in v. 22: "the righteousness of God through faith in Jesus Christ for all who believe." Similarly, in v. 28 (see above) "by faith" and "apart from works of the law" are brought together, and the catch-word "faith" appears in vv. 25 and 30. So Abraham in chapter 4 is the Scripture proof both for "apart from works of Law" and for "by faith" on the strength of Gen. 15:6. The new discussion beginning at 5:1 starts with "Therefore, since we are justified (rightwised) by faith . . ." and the catchword "faith" recurs again in 9:30–32, 10:4–6 (here "righteousness based on law" and "righteousness based on faith," both personified, are contrasted each with the other) and 10:10. Once again Galatians contains the same declarations (2:16; 3:6, 8, 11, 24; 5:5) and the same passage in Philippians (3:9) contrasts "righteousness based on law" with "righteousness from God that depends on faith."

2. What does this antithesis of Paul's to the Jewish view signify? Its full significance will emerge in our investigation of the structure of the concept "faith" (§§ 35ff.). But for the time being one thing is clear about it: *"faith" is the absolute contrary of "boasting."* The announcement of the thesis "by faith, apart from the Law," Rom. 3:21-26, is followed by a question addressed to Paul's Jewish opponent: "Then what becomes of boasting? It is excluded. On what principle? On the principle of works? No, but on the principle of faith" (Rom. 3:27). "Boasting (in the Law)" is the fundamental attitude of the Jew, the essence of his sin (Rom. 2:17, 23 and see § 23, 2), and the radical giving up of boasting is faith's attitude. Thus, Paul can say of Abraham, who was rightwised not by his works but by his faith, that he has no "boast" (4:2). Righteousness, then, cannot be won by human effort, nor does any human accomplishment establish a claim to it; it is sheer gift.

This may also be expressed by naming *"grace"* (with or without the specification *"God's"*) as the basis of rightwising. "Righteousness through faith" (Rom. 3:22) has an equivalent in v. 24: "justified (rightwised) by his grace as a gift," in which "as a gift" further emphasizes the gift-character of righteousness already stated in the term "grace." "Grace" and "gift" also appear in combination in Rom. 5:15, 17: ". . . how much more have the grace of God and the free gift in the grace . . . abounded." " . . . how much more will those who receive the abundance of grace and the free gift of righteousness reign . . ." (*cf.* v. 21 and the synonymous term χάρισμα in v. 15f. and 6:23).

Therefore, *"grace,"* like "faith" *can be placed in direct antithesis to "works of the Law."* "You are not under law but under grace" (Rom. 6:19), Paul reminds the rightwised. He speaks still more pointedly in Gal. 5:4: "You are severed from Christ, you who would be justified (rightwised) by the law; you have fallen away from grace." Paul declares of himself on the contrary, "I do not nullify the grace of God; for if justification (rightwising) were through the law, then Christ died to no purpose" (Gal. 2:21). While a remnant of the Jewish people has come to have faith, it did so "chosen by grace. But if it is by grace, it is no longer on the basis of works; otherwise, grace would no longer be grace" (Rom. 11:5f.). In the same way, "faith" and "grace" in conjunction are contrasted with the Law in the compressed and somewhat tortuous train of thought,

Rom. 4:14–16: verse 13 had established through scriptural proof that Abraham and his posterity had received the promise thanks not to the Law but thanks to his "faith-righteousness." Verse 14 then continues: "If it is the adherents of the law who are to be the heirs, faith is null and the promise is void." The promise, Paul assumes, makes sense only for "faith" (= those who have faith); under the Law this promise cannot come to fulfilment, "for the law brings wrath" (v. 15a). Then the thought turns from the negative to the positive significance of the Law. For when v. 15b goes on to say: "but where there is no law there is no transgression," this evidently means the Law is also intended to bring about transgression, for it is by doing just that that the Law confirms that the promise was given to faith: "the reason why it (righteousness) depends upon faith is: that it (righteousness) may depend upon grace" (v. 16, see § 27, 2, p. 265).

The paradox in "grace" is that it is precisely *the transgressor, the sinner,* to whom it applies, just as God in Rom. 4:5 is He "who justifies (rightwises) the ungodly." Rom. 3:23f. also says it: "all have sinned . . . they are justified (rightwised) by his grace as a gift," and so, especially, does Rom. 5:20: "Law came in to increase the trespass; but where sin increased, grace abounded all the more." Gal. 3:22, without explicitly mentioning "grace," says in substance the same thing: "the scripture consigned all men to sin that what was promised to faith in Jesus Christ might be given to those who believe" (tr.). Rom. 11:32 similarly: "For God consigned all men to disobedience, that he may have mercy upon all."

The term ἔλεος (mercy) used in Rom. 11:32 (here in verb-form) in place of the term "grace," means substantially the same thing, but more strongly emphasizes the eschatological character of God's act (when He rightwises). "Ἔλεος (or rather חֶסֶד, which the LXX as a rule renders ἔλεος) had taken on this eschatological emphasis in salvation-history (see *ThWB*, II 477, 4ff.; 478, 15ff.; 480, 8ff.). Paul speaks of God's "mercy" (except in the benediction, Gal. 6:16) only in his reflections on the history of salvation in Rom. 9–11, specifically 9:15–18 (after Ex. 33:19); 9:23; 11:30–32 and 15:8f. (We are naturally not concerned here with the passages that deal with his personal experience of God's "grace" and "mercy"—I Cor. 15:10; II Cor. 12:9 and I Cor. 7:25; II Cor. 4:1, respectively). Only rarely does he speak of God's "kindness" (χρηστότης, Rom. 2:4a, 11:22; or χρηστόν, Rom. 2:4b). In the Psalms of Solomon the reverse is true: "grace" does not occur, but (God's) "mercy" and "kindness" are frequently met. In the deutero-Pauline literature, "mercy" again becomes more frequent; here, too, "kindness" appears only a few times (Eph. 2:7; Tit. 3:4).

One readily understands, then, that just as "righteousness by faith" can designate the content of the gospel (see above, 1.), in the same way the content and significance of the message and the character of Christian existence can be denoted by the simple term "grace." Paul urges the Corinthians "not to accept the *grace* of God in vain" (II Cor. 6:1). To "nullify the grace of God" (Gal. 2:21) or to "fall away from grace" (Gal. 5:4; see § 32, 1) would mean to forsake the saving way of faith—the Christian faith itself.

It may serve to consolidate what has been said up to this point in § 30 if we pause to refute such a misinterpretation as that advocated by W. Mundle (*Der Glaubensbegriff des Paulus*, (1932), 99ff.). Mundle denies that the rejection of "works" as the condition for rightwising is to be understood to mean rejection of absolutely every accomplishment that can get or earn something for the doer. He maintains that when Paul rejects works, only the works demanded by the Mosaic Law are meant. And if faith, which appropriates God's grace, is an act of obedience, then "there is always a certain measure of activity on man's own part assumed in it." Against this interpretation must be said 1. Mundle does not ask himself *why* it is, according to Paul, that "works" do not rightwise. If the reason they do not is that man must not have any boast before God (Rom. 3:27; 4:2), then the "works *of the Law*," on which Paul naturally concentrates in this discussion with the Jew, represent works in general, any and all works as works-of-merit. 2. Paul explicitly emphasizes the contrariety of "working" and a "gift" (or "act of grace") and contrasts "grace" (or "gift") and "due (wage)" (Rom. 4:4f.); he therefore understands "work" in the fundamental sense—to earn claim to a reward. 3. Although according to Paul, the man of faith also is required—but from an entirely new point of view—to keep the Law (Rom. 13:8-10; Gal. 5:14), it is clear that the works of the Law not as to their content but as to the manner of their fulfilment are meant. 4. Mundle overlooks the parallelism between Paul's polemic against "one's own righteousness based on law" and his polemic against the "Greeks" (§ 23, 2). This parallelism shows that the former was aimed not against the accomplishment of specific acts—viz. those required by the Mosaic Law—but against the attitude of that man who wants to pass muster before God on his own strength. If Mundle protests that faith's act of obedience "involves a certain measure of activity on man's own part," it must be said that faith, as decision, is even preeminently the deed of man; but Mundle overlooks the distinction between "deed" and "work," with which the analysis of the term "faith" will deal (§ 35).

"Righteousness," then, has its origin in God's grace—i.e. in His act of grace accomplished in Christ. "Grace" can mean simply to be graciously disposed toward another. The extent to which "grace" surpasses this meaning and means a deed or event—eschatological in either case—will soon be discussed in greater detail (§ 32). But it is already apparent at this point that God in His grace acts as the absolutely free God who has not been brought into debt by any human claim and who acts, therefore, as "the gracious One" in a radical sense. To the extent that a man wishes by his own accomplishment to have a boast before God, he brings divine grace to naught for himself. The receipt of grace presupposes on the contrary that man be utterly brought to naught; it is just the sinner to whose lot it falls. This meaning of grace is clearly corroborated by the passages in which Paul speaks of the grace of God at work in his own person, I Cor. 15:9f.: he, "the least of the apostles," the erstwhile persecutor of God's Church, says of himself: "by the grace of God I am what I am, and his grace toward me was not in vain. On the contrary, I worked harder than any of them, though it was not I but the grace of God which is with me" that worked. Recall, further, II Cor. 12:9, where Paul reports a word that the Lord had imparted to him: "My grace is sufficient for you, for power is made perfect in weakness" (omitting "my" before "power" with Nestle).

God's grace, therefore, is not His kindliness and goodness which cause Him to take man's weakness into account and, in view of his endeavor toward the good, to excuse an occasional mistake, or even many, to forgive small sins, or even great ones. On the contrary, that endeavor is exactly what the grace of God repudiates—for in it is just where man's sin of sins lurks, his arrogance, his fooling himself that he can live on his own. And however much this man may be struggling, fighting with himself, pleadingly looking for divine help and redemption, even so the grace of God comes to him, not as approval of his striving and a prop for his failing strength, but as the decisive question: Will you surrender, utterly surrender, to God's dealing—will you know yourself to be a sinner before God?

3. The reason why "righteousness" is called *"God's righteousness"* is just this: Its one and only foundation is God's grace—it is God-given, God-adjudicated righteousness (Rom. 1:17; 3:21f., 26; 10:3). The meaning of this phrase (i.e. the classification of the genitive as a genitive of the author) is unequivocally determined by Rom. 10:3: "For, being ignorant of the righteousness *that comes from God*, and seeking to establish *their own,* they (the Jews) did not submit to *God's* righteousness," and Phil. 3:9: "not having a righteousness *of my own,* based on law, but that which is through faith in Christ, the righteousness *from God* that depends on faith." As "their own" or "my own" means the righteousness which man exerts himself to achieve by fulfilling the "works of the Law," so "God's righteousness" means the righteousness from God which is conferred upon him as a gift by God's free grace alone.

In the New Testament, outside of Paul, the expression "righteousness of God" occurs at Jas. 1:20 and II Pet. 1:1. In the former of the two it means "what is right in God's eyes." This is the meaning the rabbis gave to the "righteousness of Jahweh" at Deut. 33:21 (though some interpreted it as an act of beneficence such as Yahweh does). Here, then, the term is used in the ethical sense, not in the forensic one. In the other passage, the word is used in an indeterminate and formula-like fashion in the salutation-formula: "To those who have obtained a faith of equal standing with ours in the righteousness of our God and Savior Jesus Christ." Here *dikaiosyne* appears to be the "distributive justice" which apportions to each his due, and the genitives apparently are subjective genitives.

§ 31. Reconciliation

Another term can be substituted for the term "righteousness" (or the cognate verb) as the designation of the new situation which God Himself has opened up to man: "reconciliation" (or the cognate verb—καταλλαγή and καταλλαγῆναι). Examination of Paul's statements on "righteousness" and of those on "reconciliation" results in mutual corroboration. Since "we have peace with God" (Rom. 5:1) means the same as if Paul had said "we are reconciled," and is a result of "being rightwised," then strictly speaking "reconciliation" is a consequence of "righteousness." But in point of fact "we have peace" only unfolds the meaning of "righteousness": "as rightwised men we have peace with God." So in Rom. 5:9, "we are rightwised" from v. 1 is picked up again and in vv. 10f. is paraphrased in the words, "For if while we were enemies we were *reconciled* to God . . ." and "much more, now that we are *reconciled* . . ." Just as "rightwising" is effected through Christ (Rom. 3:24), Christ is he "through whom we have now received our *reconciliation*" (5:11). The winning of the heathen world to the gospel can be equally well described as "the reconciliation of the world" (11:15) or by saying: "the Gentiles . . . have attained . . . righteousness" (9:30). The gospel, through which the "righteousness of God" is revealed (Rom. 1:16f.) is also called "the message of reconciliation" (II Cor. 5:19), and the office of its proclaimer is called both "ministry of righteousness" (II Cor. 3:9 Blt.) and "ministry of reconciliation" (II Cor. 5:18). The man of faith "receives" reconciliation (Rom. 5:11) as he "receives" righteousness (5:17).

The use of the word "reconciliation" makes clear that a complete reversal of the relation between God and men has taken place. Hitherto, men had been "enemies" of God (Rom. 5:10), which can have either active meaning—"hostile" (Rom. 8:7), or passive— "hated" (Rom. 5:10; 11:28); the connection between the two meanings is indicated by Rom. 8:7f.: the latter is the consequence of the former. The reversal of this relation takes place, as II Cor. 5:19 indicates, by God's not counting men's sins against them; and this takes place—quite as being "rightwised" does—not because of any human deed or attitude, but on God's own initiative: "all this has its origin in God who through Christ reconciled us to himself" (II Cor. 5:18). We were reconciled with God "while we were (still) enemies" (Rom. 5:10; *cf.* v. 6)! That is, the "reconciliation" precedes any effort—indeed any knowledge—on man's part, and "reconciliation" does not mean a subjective process within man but an objective factual situation brought about by God. All man can do is to "receive" the reconciliation (Rom. 5:11); therefore, at the same time God set up reconciliation He also set up the "ministry" or the "message" of reconciliation, and men are invited henceforth on their side to accomplish the subjective alteration in themselves: "be reconciled to God" (II Cor. 5:20). The "word of reconciliation," then, is not the conciliatory and reconciling word but the proclamation of the already accomplished reconciliation, and "be reconciled" is the invitation to faith. God's "reconciling" is His restoration of peace by no longer letting His "wrath" (§ 32, 1) prevail. One might almost say that in using the term "reconciliation" Paul's intention to show man's radical dependence upon the grace of God is still more clearly expressed than when he uses the term "righteousness of God," for while the latter means that *without* our doing anything we arrive at "peace" with God (Rom. 5:1), the former means that *before* any effort of man God made an end of enmity (Rom. 5:10). But in substance, of course, there is no difference: both "without us" and "before us" intend to declare the absolute priority of God.

The old question, "How is God to be reconciled?" is wrongly put. Naturally all pagan notions that men must do something to reconcile (propitiate) God, are far from Paul's thought. It never occurs to him at all that *God* needed to be reconciled; it is *men* who receive the reconciliation which God has conferred —not by removing their subjective resentment toward Him but by removing the objective state of enmity which, in consequence of sins, existed between Him and men.

It is noteworthy that Paul hardly ever speaks of the "forgiveness of sins," which plays so large a role in the earliest Christian preaching (§ 13, 1) and soon reappears in deutero-Pauline literature (Col. 1:14; Eph. 1:7), though he does describe God the reconciler as "not counting their trespasses." Only in the quotation from Ps. 32:1 do we encounter: "Blessed are they whose iniquities are forgiven" (Rom. 4:7); and only in Rom. 3:25 does he speak of God's "passing over former sins," a phrase probably based on a traditional formula (§ 7, 3). His avoidance of the term "forgiveness of sins" (which is connected with his avoidance of the term "repentance," § 35, 1) is evidently due to the fact that "forgiveness of sin" is insofar ambiguous as it seems to declare only release from the guilt contracted by "former sins," whereas the important thing for Paul is release from *sinning*, release from the power of sin (§ 38).

B. GRACE

§ 32. Grace as Event

1. God's "grace" is not a quality, not His timeless kindliness (§ 30, 2), and what the gospel brings is not enlightenment as to God's hitherto misunderstood nature as if till now He had been wrongly conceived as wrathful and ought henceforth to be regarded as gracious. On the contrary! Now, as then, *"God's wrath"* pours out "against all ungodliness and wickedness of men" (Rom. 1:18). Paul warns the unrepentant: "you are storing up wrath for yourself on the day of wrath when God's righteous judgment will be revealed" (Rom. 2:5; *cf.* 2:8). "To inflict wrath" belongs inherently to God's "faithfulness," "truthfulness," and judicial "justice" (Rom. 3:3–6). God continues to be the Judge, and Christian faith in the grace of God does not consist in the conviction that God's wrath does not exist or that there is no threateningly impending judgment (II Cor. 5:10), but in the conviction of being rescued from God's wrath: "Since, therefore, we are now justified (rightwised) by his blood, much more shall we be saved by him from the wrath of God" (Rom. 5:9; I Thess. 1:10; 5:9).

That misunderstanding, however, is based upon the false notion that *God's wrath* is a quality, an emotion, wrathfulness—a notion against which the ancient Church, under the influence of Stoic thinking, though it had to defend God. In reality "wrath of God" means an occurrence, viz. *the judgment of God.* God is He who "inflicts wrath" (Rom. 3:5); when the "wrath of God" is said to be "revealed" (Rom. 1:18), that does not refer to a didactic communication about it but to its becoming effective (§ 29, 1). When the "wrath of God" is described (Rom. 1:18–32), it is shown to be identical with that which factually already takes place in the heathen world: abandonment to the "lusts of their hearts" (v. 24), to "dishonorable passions" (v. 26), to a "base mind" (i.e. corrupted intent, v. 28). The "day of wrath" is "the day when God's righteous judgment will be revealed," the future judgment day (Rom. 2:5). "Wrath" as the verdict of condemnation has its counterpart in the gift of "eternal life" (Rom. 2:7f.) or of "salvation" (I Thess. 5:9). The "wrath" of Rom. 5:9 and I Thess. 1:10 is likewise the punishment (soon) to take place. Though for the most part the future judgment is meant (*cf.* in addition Rom. 9:22), Rom. 1:18–32 means

[288]

the judgment that is constantly taking place; so does Rom. 13:4f. where governmental authority is called "the servant of God to execute wrath (= punishment) on the wrong-doer" and the Christian is exhorted to practice civil obedience not only "on account of wrath (i.e. punishment)." "Wrath" without temporal limitation means divine punishment: Rom. 4:15, "for the law brings wrath"; Rom. 12:19 probably has the same meaning: "leave it to the wrath (of God)" (rather than KJ: "give place unto wrath").

The above observations yield two insights for the understanding of "*grace*": 1. God's grace is not His hitherto unknown or misconceived graciousness, but is His now occurring act of grace. 2. This act of grace does not, as it might seem, take the place of God's previous judgeship, but is His gracious dealing precisely as the Judge. God's "wrath" continues to be at work and will soon take effect decisively and definitively on the "day of wrath" (Rom. 2:5) as certainly as God is the Judge who is to be feared (Rom. 11:20; II Cor. 5:10f.; Phil. 2:12; see § 35, 4). The "grace of God" is the grace of the judge who "rightwises" the guilty (§ 30, 2).

2. The grace of God, as His judicial act of grace, can be still more precisely defined: It is not a mode of dealing which God has decided henceforth to adopt, but is *a single deed* which takes effect for everyone who recognizes it as such and acknowledges it (in faith)—"grace" is God's *eschatological deed*.

When Rom. 3:24 says of "rightwised" men, "they are rightwised by his (God's) grace as a gift," the word δωρεάν (gratis, without price, in the manner of a gift) emphasizes the gift-character of grace; grace itself is the act of grace which is described in the following words: "the redemption which is in Christ Jesus, whom God put forward as an expiation by his blood, to be received by faith." That is, God's deed of grace consists in the fact that He gave Christ up to die—to die as a propitiatory sacrifice for the sins of men. The *deed of God* "who gave him (his Son) up for us all" (Rom. 8:32) has its analogue in the "obedience" of the Son "who gave himself for me" (Gal. 2:20) and was "obedient unto death" (Phil. 2:8). Therefore, just this *occurrence of Christ's obedience* (which Paul contrasts with Adam's "disobedience" or calls Christ's "act of righteousness" in contrast to Adam's "trespass," Rom. 5:15-21) can also be regarded as the "deed of grace." As the occurrence of Adam's fall brought death over mankind, so the occurrence of Christ's obedience brought life, and the latter occurrence constitutes "grace," which instead of the usual word (χάρις) can also be called χάρισμα (gift of grace) because it is for the benefit of men (Rom. 5:15f.). The divine deed of grace is, as such, a *gift* of grace—the gift which is the event that takes place in Christ's obedience. Therefore Paul can equate "the grace of God" and "the free gift in the grace of that one man Jesus Christ" (Rom. 5:15) or speak of "the abundance of grace and the free gift of righteousness . . . through the one man Jesus Christ" (Rom. 5:17).

In one passage the thing emphasized may be that "grace" is the deed of God or Christ, in another that it is the occurrence which is bestowed upon men as a gift, in a third both emphases may meet, but in every case the same deed, the identical occurrence is meant. In II Cor. 6:1 when Paul urges the reader "not to accept the grace of God in vain," what he means by "grace" is that deed of God (*cf.* 5.21) which is at the same time the deed of Christ (5:14f.: "he died for all"); but simultaneously "grace" here means the gift which man must "accept" as in Paul's expression (I Cor. 2:12) for God's saving deed: "the gifts bestowed on us by God." In II Cor. 8:9 he reminds his readers of the event of salvation as the deed of Christ: "For you know the grace (i.e. gracious *deed*) of our Lord Jesus Christ, that though he was rich, yet for your sake he became poor" (in which, of course, he has in mind all that is said in Phil. 2:6–8). And "God's (deed of) grace" which he declares he does not "nullify" (Gal. 2:21) consists of just that deed of Christ described in the preceding verse: "who loved me and gave himself for me."

Because this deed or occurrence is the decisive eschatological event in which the time of salvation, "the acceptable time" (II Cor. 6:1), has dawned, therefore grace may be spoken of as a personified power which works against the power of sin and takes over its lost command: "but where sin increased, grace abounded all the more, so that, as sin (had) reigned in death, grace also might reign through righteousness to eternal life through Jesus Christ our Lord" (Rom. 5:20f.). The meaning of "grace" approaches actual identity with that of "spirit" (see § 38, 2f. and *cf.* above § 14, 1). That is the reason that *the new situation* into which men of faith—they who have received the Spirit (Gal. 4:6, etc.)—are put can also be called "grace"; here "grace" means the territory of the divine deed's sway. The Christian is called "to grace" (Gal. 1:6) and "stands" in it

(Rom. 5:2); he must beware not to "fall out of grace" (Gal. 5:4). Thus, Paul can address the Philippians as "partakers with me of grace" (Phil. 1:7; i.e. my fellow-participants in grace—unless "grace" is here used in a narrower sense, meaning the shared grace of suffering bestowed upon both Paul and the Philippians. (*Cf.* v. 29.)

Even where "grace" does not mean the eschatological occurrence, it still means God's gracious deed or dealing which man experiences as a gift. Combined with "peace" (= salvation!) in the greetings at the beginning or end of the epistles, "grace" is that which God does and confers for salvation.

The apostle's office committed to Paul as a gift—but also as a commission to be fulfilled—can be called a "grace," i.e. a gift: Rom. 1:5; 12:3; 15:15; I Cor. 3:10 (see RSV!); Gal. 2:9. Gal. 2:8 ("for he who worked through Peter . . . worked through me also") shows how much the "grace" of the following verse denotes God's working through Paul; Rom. 15:18 ("For I will not venture to speak of anything except what Christ has wrought through me") is the same kind of commentary to Rom. 15:15. The exercise of the Christian obligation to love is likewise a "gift" of God, a "grace": II Cor. 8:1, 4, 6f., 19; and so, in the end, is every manifestation of Christian living: I Cor. 1:4; II Cor. 9:8 and 8:7. Special gifts given to individuals are called *charismata*: Rom. 12:6; I Cor. 7:7. *Charis* is contained in both the word and the idea; that this *charis* means the mighty working of God is abundantly attested by the synonymity of *charismata* (gifts of grace) and *pneumatika* (spiritual gifts; see § 14, 1) and by the remark which refers to the latter: "it is the same God who inspires (lit. effects) them all in every one" (I Cor. 12:6).

The following passages, especially, indicate that God's "grace" is a power that determines the life of the individual: I Cor. 15:10 ("by the grace of God I am what I am"), II Cor. 1:12; 12:9 ("My grace is sufficient for you"). I Cor. 15:10 and II Cor. 12:9 particularly show that "grace" and "power" (§ 14, 1) can be synonymous.

3. In the same way as Paul speaks of "grace" and with the same meaning, he can speak of (God's or Christ's) *agape* (love); therefore, a consideration of his statements about *agape* confirms our treatment of "grace." It may be that in *agape* the sentiment (of love) is emphasized more than in the case of "grace"; but Paul

speaks of *agape* as it reveals itself in a deed, *agape at work, in action.* When he says in Rom. 5:8, "God shows his love for us in that while we were yet sinners Christ died for us," *agape* certainly has, as part of its meaning, the sentiment of love, but Paul speaks of it only as God "shows" it—by letting Christ die for us. V. 5 must be interpreted similarly: ". . . because God's love (subjective genitive!) has been poured into our hearts through the Holy Spirit which has been given us": through the Holy Spirit, God's deed of love, which v. 6f. describes as being the deed of Christ, attains certainty and effectiveness for us. The question of Rom. 8:35: "Who shall separate us from the love of Christ?" refers in its word "love" to the salvation-occurrence named in the preceding verse—the death and resurrection of Christ. Christ is "he who loved us," and his "love" consisted in giving himself up to death (Rom. 8:35; Gal. 2:20). And the identity of God's deed with Christ's deed is expressed in Paul's assurance that nothing will be able to separate us from "God's love (i.e. deed of love) in Christ Jesus our Lord"—in other words, from the salvation which God brought about through Christ (Rom. 8:39). When II Cor. 5:14 says that we are "controlled" by the love of Christ (subjective genitive!), this love is paraphrased in the next clause as Christ's "dying for all." Here *agape*, like *charis*, is also represented as a personified power.

Like "grace," "love" also appears occasionally in formula-like expressions, sometimes taking the place of "grace" (II Cor. 13:11: "the God of love and peace will be with you"), sometimes combined with it (II Cor. 13:14: "the grace of the Lord Jesus Christ, and the love of God . . . be with you all"). In such cases, *agape* like *charis* means all that God has done or bestowed for salvation. The activity of the Holy Spirit for salvation is termed "love" when Paul makes an appeal (Rom. 15:30) "by our Lord Jesus Christ and by the love of the Spirit."

§ 33. Christ's Death and Resurrection as Salvation-occurrence

1. The deed of divine grace consists in the fact that God gave Christ up to die on the cross (§ 32, 2); Christ is preached as "the crucified" (I Cor. 1:23; 2:2; Gal. 3:1). Therefore, the gospel can be called the "word of the cross" (I Cor. 1:18), a "stumbling-block" (Gal. 5:11) to natural man, or a "stumbling-block and folly" (I Cor.

1:23). The enemies of the gospel are "enemies of the cross of Christ" (Phil. 3:18; *cf.* I Cor. 1:17; Gal. 6:12). But the death and the resurrection of Christ are bound together in the unity of one salvation-occurrence: "he who died" is also "he who was raised up" (Rom. 8:34; II Cor. 5:15; 13:4), and it may also happen that Paul refers to the resurrection alone without mentioning the cross (I Thess. 1:10; I Cor. 6:14; II Cor. 4:14; Rom. 1:4; 8:11; 10:9) and terms God accordingly "he who raised him from the dead" (see references in § 9, 4, p. 80f.)

The salvation-occurrence, then, includes the death and the resurrection of Jesus. Such was the tradition that Paul had received (I Cor. 15:1–4), and such was the tradition that he passed on. He is quoting or paraphrasing statements of tradition which were obviously more or less definitely formulated when he speaks of Jesus' death (Rom. 3:24f.; § 7, 3, p. 46) or his resurrection (Rom. 1:4; 10:9; § 7, 3, p. 49; § 9, 4, p. 80), or of both together (Rom. 4:25; I Cor. 15:3f.; § 7, 3, p. 46; § 9, 4, p. 82; § 7, 3, p. 44) also, of course, when he speaks of baptism (Rom. 6:2–5, § 13, 1, p. 140f.) or of the Lord's Supper (I Cor. 11:23–26), the celebration of which "proclaims" Christ's death (§ 13, 2, p. 148). Strictly speaking, the incarnation is also a part of that one salvation-process; for he who gave himself up to die is no other than the pre-existent Son of God (Phil. 2:6ff.; II Cor. 8:9; Rom. 15:3; § 12, 3, p. 128f., p. 131). Yet the incarnation is never accorded a meaning independent from the crucifixion; rather it and his death are bound together in Christ's total deed (active and passive) in which his "obedience" took place (Phil. 2:8; Rom. 5:19). It plays a separate role only in the hint (I Cor. 2:8; § 15, 4c) that the demonic cosmic powers were deceived by the redeemer's human disguise. However, this motif does not belong to the actual proclamation, the "word of the cross," but belongs in the area of a "wisdom" intended for the "perfect" (I Cor. 2:6 KJ).

Jesus' death-and-resurrection, then, is for Paul the decisive thing about the person of Jesus and his life experience, indeed, in the last analysis it is the sole thing of importance for him— implicitly included are the incarnation and the earthly life of Jesus as bare facts. That is, Paul is interested only in the *fact* that Jesus became man and lived on earth. *How* he was born or lived interests him only to the extent of knowing that Jesus was a definite, concrete man, a Jew, "being born in the likeness of man and being found in human form" (Phil. 2:7), "born of woman, born under the law" (Gal. 4:4). But beyond that, Jesus' manner of life, his ministry, his personality, his character play no role at all; neither does Jesus' message (§ 16). To Paul, Jesus is not the teacher and prophet. It is true that as the exalted Lord he is also the law-giver of the Church (I Cor. 7:10f., *cf.* v. 25, 9:14) and Paul accompanies his exhortations with appeals to the authority of "the Lord" (I Thess. 4:1f.; Rom. 15:30; I Cor. 1:10). But Paul is not thinking of the historical Jesus here. Nor is he when he refers to Christ's example (Phil. 2:5ff.; II Cor. 8:9; Rom. 15:3); for in these cases he means the pre-existent Christ, and his appeal to the "meekness and gentleness of Christ" (II Cor. 10:1) is precisely an appeal to him who "emptied himself," "humbled himself," "became poor," "did not please himself."

It is self-evident that neither for Paul nor for the earliest Jerusalem Church (§ 5, 3) did Jesus and his passion and death appear in a heroic light like the heroes of the hero-cults. Likewise, every sort of pietistic-edifying absorption in a contemplation of the passion is unknown to him; and when he says he has "publicly portrayed" Christ as crucified "before the eyes" of the Galatians (Gal. 3:1), he means nothing else than the preaching of the "word of the cross" as the fact of salvation. By human norms, the cross cannot be recognized as the fact of salvation, but remains a "stumbling-block" and "folly." Any "evaluation" of the historical person Jesus according to human categories would be a *kata sarka* (flesh-wise) regarding of Christ and hence would mean seeing him as a "*kata sarka* Christ" (§ 22, 3).

2. It is clear that the salvation-occurrence, viz. Christ's death and resurrection, is the deed of the prevenient grace of God; and that the various expressions which describe this deed intend to express its unprecedented nature and its might which so radically transformed the human situation. It is an occurrence purely by God's initiative; for man, pure gift; by accepting it he is released from his perverse striving to achieve life or self-hood by his own efforts—in which he does the very opposite—only to be given it as a gift in the "righteousness of God."

The question now is *how can this occurrence be recognized and experienced by man as the deed of grace?* For only then can it take effect as a compelling and transforming power, when it can be

understood as directed at man, reaching him, happening to him—
i.e. when the challenge to accept it as salvation-occurrence thrusts
him into genuine decision. So far as it is an event that God causes
to occur to the pre-existent son of God, it seems to take place in a
mythical sphere outside the realm of human experience.

Let it be granted that there is a difference between this and the
salvation-occurrences related by the myth of the mystery-religions
and by Gnosticism: Here the subject is an historical person, Jesus,
and his death on the cross only a few years earlier is at the center
of the salvation-occurrence. Still, how is one to recognize that this
death has such vast significance? Is it so important because a pre-
existent divine being died it? If so, then does not faith in the saving
significance of this death presuppose a previous faith that Jesus is
the incarnate son of God? And if faith in salvation by Jesus is only
made complete by faith in the resurrection, does that not also demand a previous faith? For the resurrection, of course, simply cannot be a visible fact in the realm of human history. When Paul is
pushed to do so by Gnosticizing objections to belief in any resurrection whatever, he does, I grant, think he can guarantee the resurrection of Christ as an objective fact by listing the witnesses who
had seen him risen (I Cor. 15:5-8, § 15, 2).° But is such a proof
convincing?

3a. In order to describe the significance of the salvation-occurrence, Paul uses a series of terms originating in a number of different
thought-complexes. One group is composed of the statements which
understand Jesus' death in terms of Jewish sacrificial practice—and
that also means in terms of the juristic thinking that dominated it—
regarding his death as a propitiatory sacrifice by which forgiveness
of sins is brought about; which is to say: by which the guilt contracted by sins is canceled. Jesus' death is the "*hilasterion* in his
blood," the means of reconciliation efficacious through his blood, by
which God, to prove that He is a righteous judge, made possible the
"passing over of previously committed sins" (Rom. 3:25f. tr.). The
same thought occurs tersely formulated in Rom. 5:9: "justified
(rightwised) now by his blood." The liturgy of the Lord's Supper

---

° It has been denied, I know, (by K. Barth) that the listing of the witnesses
has this meaning; the contention is that it only intends to guarantee the identity
of Paul's message with that of the earliest Jerusalem Church. Undoubtedly that
is one of its purposes (v. 11); nevertheless, its primary purpose is the one indicated above.

in I Cor. 11:24f. (§ 9, 4, p. 84) is likewise governed by the conception of Jesus' death as a propitiatory sacrifice merged with a conception of it as a covenant sacrifice. The propitiatory idea is also behind the passages in which Jesus is described as he who died "for our sins" (I Cor. 15:3; II Cor. 5:14) or simply died "for us" (Rom. 5:6, 8; 14:15; I Thess. 5:10; *cf.* I Cor. 1:13), or he who was "given up" or "gave himself up" for us (Rom. 4:25; 8:32; Gal. 1:4; 2:20).

In all these cases, Paul is following a tradition which probably originated in the earliest Church (§ 7, 3) and, at any rate, was widespread in Hellenistic Christianity (§ 9, 4); Paul is in part quoting or paraphrasing the crystallized formulations of this tradition (see above under 1). At any rate, the above passages do not contain Paul's characteristic view. Neither does the only once-suggested thought (I Cor. 5:7) that Jesus' death is a passover-sacrifice, in Jewish eyes a sin-removing sacrifice. The same is true of the covenant-sacrifice idea that we find woven into the eucharistic liturgy (I Cor. 11:25).

(b) Closely related to the idea of propitiatory sacrifice is that of *vicarious sacrifice,* which likewise has its origin in the field of cultic-juristic thinking (§ 7, 3). The same phrase (ὑπὲρ ἡμῶν) that is translated "for us" can also express this idea, meaning now: "instead of us," "in place of us." Thus: Gal. 3:13, "becoming a curse in our stead" (tr. *cf.* Goodspeed); II Cor. 5:21: "he made him who was unacquainted with sin to be sin in our stead" (tr. §29, 2). The idea is probably also present in Rom. 8:3: "having sent his own son (clad) in (our) self-same, sin-ruled flesh and (sent him) to take sin's place, God (in condemning Christ to die) condemned (our) sin (= Christ) in the flesh (he shared with us)" (tr.). The ideas of vicarious and propitiatory sacrifice merge in II Cor. 5:14f. V. 14b, "therefore all have died," interprets the phrase in 14a εἷς ὑπὲρ πάντων ἀπέθανεν (which could mean either "one died *for the sake of all*" or "one died *taking the place of all*") as having the vicarious meaning: "one died in the place of all, therefore all have (vicariously) died." But in v. 15 the ὑπέρ in "he died ὑπέρ all" means "for the sake of"—contains, in other words, the propitiatory idea. But still another conception of Christ's death plays a part here—the conception, soon to be treated (see "e" below), that it was a cosmic event, for within the conception of vicarious representation "all have died" can only mean "all *are regarded as dead,*" but by analogy with

Rom. 6:3, 5 this certainly also means in the mind of Paul: "all *are* dead."

(c) The vicarious death of Christ, according to Gal. 3:13, is the means by which men are *"redeemed"* (ransomed)—redeemed, that is, from the "curse of the Law"—and that evidently means from the punishment imposed upon sin (which is here equated with transgression of the Law). This view agrees with the statements containing the propitiatory sacrifice idea in this: the sacrifice cancels guilt or the punishment for guilt. Nevertheless, that is not the full extent of the thought, for it is scarcely permissible to isolate Gal. 3:13 from 4:4f. What the latter passage names as the means to "redemption" is not Jesus' death, it is true; yet it does name his humanity and his subjection to the Law—and in these his death is involved. But here, according to the context, the resulting freedom (here = "adoption as sons") is not considered to be freedom from the punishment contracted by transgressing the Law, but freedom from the Law itself. Into this same context one must probably bring, finally, Gal. 1:4; here the purpose attributed to Christ's death is: "to deliver us from the present evil age." The "present age" is subject to the Law and because of that is subject to the power of sin and death. Hence the freedom bought by Christ's death is not only freedom from punishment but freedom from those "powers" (sin and death) and thereby is freedom not only from the guilt of sin but above all from sin as a power—i.e. freedom from the compulsion to sin. This interpretation is confirmed by the statement in I Cor. 6:20 and 7:23: "you were bought with a price," which in the context of 6:12–20 means: to freedom from sin; and in the context of 7:17–24: to freedom from men—i.e. from the standards and evaluations which prevail in this sin-dominated age.

For Paul, that takes care of the question to whom the τιμή (price or payment) earned by Christ's death was paid: It was paid to those powers who lay claim to man who has fallen into their grasp, primarily the Law. The expression is figurative, and the mythological idea of a bargain with the Devil is far from Paul's thought.

The essential thing, then, is that here the categories of cultic-juristic thinking are broken through: *Christ's death* is not merely a sacrifice which cancels the guilt of sin (i.e. the punishment contracted by sinning), but is also *the means of release from the powers of this age: Law, Sin, and Death.*

(d) The question then arises how Christ's death can have such an effect. It finds an answer in the statements in which *Paul describes Christ's death in analogy with the death of a divinity of the mystery religions.* This view, too, which had attached itself to the initiation-sacrament of baptism and which lay behind the sacrament of the Lord's Supper (§ 13, 1 and 2, p. 140–142; 147f.), had already come down to Paul out of tradition. But he gave it a new, more comprehensive meaning. The original meaning is, as we have seen, that participation in the fate of the mystery-divinity through baptism and sacramental communion grants the *mystes* (initiate) participation in both the dying and the reviving of the divinity; such participation, that is, by leading the *mystes* into death delivers him from death. One could have a good statement of this general conception by altering the words of Rom. 6:10—and applying them both to the god and to his initiate—to read: "The death he died he died *to death* once for all." Only Paul says ". . . he died to sin . . ."! That applies primarily to Christ, but for that very reason (v. 11) it also applies to those who are baptized "into his death" (v. 3). To Paul, release from death is simultaneously—no, primarily—release from the power of sin. What is true of baptism is, of course, also true of the Lord's Supper, even though Paul—following the traditional liturgy—does not expressly say so, but only points out that the rite "proclaims" Christ's death—i.e. both proclaims it and grants the participants a share in Christ's death (I Cor. 11:26).

(e) But Paul expands the mystery idea. He does so by simultaneously interpreting Christ's death *in the categories of the Gnostic myth,* regarding his death as unified with his incarnation and resurrection or exaltation. In so doing he is again following a tradition that is to be inferred as having existed in Hellenistic Christianity before him, inasmuch as he cites the Christ-hymn (Phil. 2:6–11) in which that tradition had taken form (§ 15, 4c and d). The Gnostic myth, in itself, contains only the notion of the Redeemer's coming and going as his humiliation and exaltation, not necessarily implying that his departure from the earth is caused by a violent death. It is plausible to assume that that mystery-conception (d, above) readily combined with the Gnostic myth in certain Gnostic groups organized as mystery-cults. In one such group, for example, the mystery-god Attis had coalesced with the Gnostic Redeemer-figure. At any rate, such a combination is present in Paul.

Now, for the Gnostic view it is an essential presupposition that men (or, rather, the Gnostics among men) together with the Redeemer constitute a unity. This unity is conceived in terms of substance: they and he belong to *one soma* (body). Just as the Redeemer himself is a cosmic figure and not really an individual person, so is his *soma* a cosmic entity (§ 15, 1 and 4d, p. 166, 178). What happens to the Redeemer, or happened while he tarried in human form on earth, happens to his whole *soma*—i.e. not to him alone but to all who belong to that *soma*. So if he suffered death, the same is true of them (II Cor. 5:14). If he was raised from the dead, the same is true of them (I Cor. 15:20–22). And just as his return to the heavenly home as the "redeemed Redeemer" means his release from the sinister powers that rule this world below, likewise they who are bound up with him into one body share in this release or "redemption."

It is in this light that Paul sees baptism. According to I Cor. 12:13 it unites the baptized with Christ into one *soma*. By baptism into his death we who have faith are "grown together" with him (Rom. 6:5). That is why the believer's whole life is stamped by Christ's death, but also by his resurrection. As Jesus' dying continues to occur in the apostle's body, so Jesus' life also lives in it (II Cor. 4:7–12; *cf.* 1:5). But this is by no means true for the apostle only, but for all believers, as Phil. 3:10f. shows. Here Paul only takes himself as one example among the many when he describes the goal of faith to be "that I may know him and the power of his resurrection and may share his sufferings, becoming like him in his death, that if possible I may attain the resurrection from the dead."

Christ's death and resurrection, accordingly, are cosmic occurrences, not incidents that took place once upon a time in the past. By them the old aeon along with its powers has been basically stripped of power. Its powers are already "destroyed" (καταργού-μενοι, I Cor. 2:6), even though the life of the believer is not yet visible in the present but is hidden under the mask of death (II Cor. 4:7–12). For the present is only a short interval: "the time is short" (I Cor. 7:29 KJ; perhaps more literally: "the allotted time has shrunk together," tr.) . . . "for the form of this world (= this world

itself) is passing away" (I Cor. 7:31). Therefore, Paul can also triumphantly say: "the old has passed away, behold the new has come"
(II Cor. 5:17). As the first Adam ushered in the old mankind, so
Christ, the "last Adam," ushered in the new. As the old, Adamitic
mankind received its stamp from the transitory, earthly first parent
who had brought sin and death into the world, so the new received
its stamp from Christ, who, through his obedience (in becoming
man and dying) and his resurrection, brought life and freedom from
the annihilating powers (Rom. 5:12–19; I Cor. 15:21f., 44–49).

4. Clearly Paul found none of these thought-complexes and none
of their terminologies adequate to express his understanding of the
salvation-occurrence. Why did he not confine himself to presenting
the significance of Jesus' death in the categories of Jewish cultic and
juristic thinking? Because in them the meaning of the resurrection
had no chance to come into its rightful place. Why did he, rather,
also resort to the categories of the mysteries and the Gnostic myth?
He obviously did so because through them the salvation-occurrence
could be interpreted as happening actually to and for and in man.
But in regard to all his formulations must not the question be raised
whether the hearer of such a message must not have a preliminary
conviction that Jesus Christ is by nature the pre-existent Son of God,
that he became man and rose from the dead, if he is to believe in the
saving significance of these events—especially in the saving significance of the sole objectively tangible fact: his death? What justification is there for demanding such a preliminary faith to serve as
the necessary basis for actual salvation-faith?

If, simply copying, one reproduces the statements of Paul, it
becomes evident, therefore, that, in reality, *two acts of faith or
belief and consequently also two concepts of faith-belief* must be
distinguished. The first is belief (in the narrower popular use of the
English word): willingness to consider true (= believe) the facts
reported of the pre-existent Son of God—incarnation, crucifixion,
resurrection from the dead—and to see in them a demonstration of
the grace of God. The second is a faith which is self-surrender to
the grace of God and which signifies the utter reversal of a man's
previous understanding of himself—specifically, the radical surrender of his human "boasting."

A homogeneous concept of faith-belief and a single decisive act
of faith-belief would be detectable only if the decision-question

whether a man is willing to give up his old understanding of himself
and henceforth understand himself only from the grace of God and
the question whether he will acknowledge Jesus Christ as the Son
of God and Lord should turn out to be one and the same question.
That is just what they evidently are in the real intention of Paul.

5. At any rate, one thing is clear: Paul can speak of Christ as
"the Son of God who loved me and gave himself up for me" only as
the Paul who has waived his own righteousness and given up his self
(his ἐγώ) to die (Gal. 2:19f.; Phil. 3:4–11). He knows of that Christ
only by knowing himself anew in the same act of recognition. From
the outset, Paul, the "zealot" for the "traditions of the fathers" (Gal.
1:14), understood the proclamation of Christ the Son of God and
Lord when it reached him as the demand that he give up his former
sort of "zeal for God" (Rom. 10:2; § 16). It was as such a demand
that he passed on the proclamation of Christ, not as "wisdom-dis-
course" (σοφία λόγου, I Cor. 1:17)—instruction like that of the mysteries concerning mythical events and metaphysical entities—but as
the "word of the cross," which to natural man is a "scandal" and
"folly": "so that no human being might boast in the presence of God"
(I Cor. 1:18–31) and as the "word of reconciliation" (II Cor. 5:18–
6:2 KJ), face to face with which there can be no "boasting over
externals" (II Cor. 5:12, tr.).

It accords with the above that in Romans, where Paul is connectedly presenting the main ideas of his message to a hitherto
unknown congregation in order to legitimate himself as a genuine
apostle, he—unlike the Hermetic tractates with their initial cosmological teachings—does not first present the salvation-occurrence, the
credibility of which would first have to be acknowledged. Instead
he begins by exposing the plight of mankind, so that then the proclamation of God's salvation-deed becomes a decision-question. In
keeping with this is the train of thought in Rom. 7:7–8:11: after
man-under-the-Law has been made to see his situation under it as
that of the "miserable wretch" groaning for deliverance from the
"body of death," he can then see the salvation-occurrence as salva-
tion-bringing.

But if it is true that the proclamation of the salvation-occurrence
is not a preparatory instruction which precedes the actual demand
for faith, but is, in itself, the call for faith or the challenge to give up
one's previous self-understanding or the cry, "Be reconciled to God!"

—if that is so, then that means that *the salvation-occurrence is nowhere present except in the proclaiming, accosting, demanding, and promising word of preaching*. A merely "reminiscent" historical account referring to what happened in the past cannot make the salvation-occurrence visible. It means that the salvation-occurrence continues to take place in the proclamation of the word. The salvation-occurrence is eschatological occurrence just in this fact, that it does not become a fact of the past but constantly takes place anew in the present. It is present not in the after-effect of a significant fact of world-history but in the proclamation of the word, which, unlike world events, does not get absorbed into the evolution of the human mind. Paul expresses this by saying that at the same time that God instituted reconciliation He also instituted the "ministry of reconciliation" which is the "message (lit. "word," KJ) of reconciliation" (II Cor. 5:18f.). Consequently, in the proclamation Christ himself, indeed God Himself, encounters the hearer, and the "Now" in which the preachèd word sounds forth is the "Now" of the eschatological occurrence itself (II Cor. 6:2).

Here, then, the question asked above (2, p. 294) finds its answer: *How can the salvation-occurrence* be understood *as an occurrence directed at man, reaching him, and happening to him?* It takes place in the word, which accosts the hearer and compels him to decide for or against it. Moreover, this answer transposes the salvation-occurrence, which in the Gnostic myth remained in the dimension of cosmic-natural occurrence, into the dimension of genuine occurrence in man's actual life. The union of believers into one *soma* with Christ now has its basis not in their sharing the same supernatural substance, but in the fact that in the word of proclamation Christ's death-and-resurrection becomes a possibility of existence in regard to which a decision must be made, and in the fact that faith seizes this possibility and appropriates it as the power that determines the existence of the man of faith.

The transformation which the Gnostic categories have to undergo comes to light in Rom. 5:12–19. Since in mankind after Adam there was no choice but to be like Adam fallen under the power of sin and death, the logical consequence would be that after Christ, the second Adam, there is also no choice but to be like him under the power of "obedience" and "life." In point of fact, however, after Christ the necessity to decide between the two possibilities exists—and the reservation "those who receive" (v. 17) in the Christ-aeon has and can have no correlative limitation in the Adam-aeon (for the participle λαμβάνοντες implies a condition: if, or so far as, they receive). Likewise, in consistent logic the meaning of I Cor. 15:22, "For as in Adam all die, so also in Christ shall all be made alive," would have to be: all men will be made alive by (in) Christ. But in point of fact the meaning is: All receive the possibility of being made alive; but only for them "that are Christ's" (v. 23 KJ) will the possibility be realized.

6a. Also answered, then, is the question *by what sign the cross of Christ is recognizable as salvation-event.* Not by preparatory instruction concerning the Crucified. He cannot first be recognized in his divine quality in order that one may then advance to faith in the significance of the cross—for that would rob the "word of the cross" of its scandal-and-folly character. It gets that character by the fact that a crucified one is proclaimed as Lord; and only in the fact that this proclamation occurs is the cross recognizable as salvation-event. But that means such recognition takes place only as acknowledgment. This is the decision-question which the "word of the cross" thrusts upon the hearer: whether he will acknowledge that God has made a crucified one Lord; whether he will thereby acknowledge the demand to take up the cross by the surrender of his previous understanding of himself, making the cross the determining power of his life, letting himself be crucified with Christ (I Cor. 1:18-31; Gal. 6:14; *cf.* 5:24). The fact that this acknowledgment does take place demonstrates that Christ's death is a "cosmic" event; i.e. that it may no longer be considered as just the historical event of Jesus' crucifixion on Golgotha. For God made this event the eschatological occurrence, so that, lifted out of all temporal limitation, it continues to take place in any present moment, both in the proclaiming word and in the sacraments (§ 34, 3). The apostle bears about in his body the dying of Jesus and is stamped with the *"stigmata* of Jesus" (II Cor. 4:10f.; Gal. 6:17); the sufferings of Christ overflow abundantly upon him (II. Cor. 1:5).* But it is not only in the proclamation that the cross thus becomes present; it also

---

* A disciple of Paul so formulated this thought as to let the apostle say (Col. 1:24) he is completing through his own sufferings for the Church what is still lacking in the sufferings of Christ.

does so in all those who let it become the determining power of their lives, those who are united with Christ into one *soma*.

(b) To the extent that the statements about *Christ's pre-existence and incarnation* are of mythological nature, they neither have the character of direct challenge nor are they expressions of the faith that is surrender of "boasting." Yet in context within the proclamation they express a decisive fact: The origin and significance of Jesus' person and his fate are not within earthly occurrence, but God was acting in them and this action of His took place "when the fulness of time was come" (Gal. 4:4). That is, that it is the eschatological deed of God—a deed, furthermore, for the salvation of men, for whose sake He delivered Christ up (Rom. 8:32). The fact of Christ's pre-existence, so understood, does not make faith in the Crucified easier (as if the assertion of the cross's salvation-significance would be credible, once it were recognized that it was precisely the pre-existent Son of God who died on the cross) but itself becomes a "scandalous" and "foolish" matter of faith at one with the "word of the cross."

As to the assertion that *Christ's incarnation is also his own deed of obedience and love* (Phil. 2:8; Gal. 2:20; Rom. 8:35, 39), it must first be admitted that the "obedience" and "love" of the pre-existent Son are not visible data and cannot be experienced as directly aimed at the man who is challenged to believe. However, they are indirectly experienced in the fact that Christ is present in the "ministry" of the proclaimer. As he by his incarnation became a "servant to the circumcised" (Rom. 15:8), so the proclaimers are "servants of a new covenant" (II Cor. 3:6), "servants of God" (II Cor. 6:4) or "of Christ" (II Cor. 11:23; *cf.* I Cor. 3:5), "slaves" or "servants" of Christ (Rom. 1:1; Gal. 1:10; Phil. 1:1; I Cor. 4:1) and thereby are "servants" (δοῦλοι) of men" (II Cor. 4:5; I Cor. 9:19), in whom he who "took the form of a servant (δοῦλος)" (Phil. 2:7) is actively present. What is true of the pre-existent Son—he "did not please himself" but took all reproach upon himself (Rom. 15:3)—is also true of the apostle: "I please all in all things" (I Cor. 10:33), and he, too, travels his way through reproach and shame (I Cor. 4:9–13; II Cor. 6:8f.). As Christ gave himself up to die in order to obtain life for men, so death is at work in the apostle in order that life may be at work in the hearers of his preaching (II Cor. 4:12); the "love of Christ" (Rom. 8:35) dominates the apostle (II Cor. 5:14—subjective genitive!). Hence he can exhort men not only to imitate Christ (Phil. 2:5; Rom. 15:3; II Cor. 8:9) but, as the representative of Christ to his hearers (II Cor. 5:20), he can even urge them: "be imitators of me" (I Cor. 4:16; *cf.* Gal. 4:12; Phil. 3:17; 4:9) and may add as motivation for such exhortation: "as I am of Christ" (I Cor. 11:1; *cf.* I Thess. 1:6).

Therefore, the incarnation of the pre-existent Son also has "cosmic" dimension—i.e. in reality, *historic dimension* (a locus in the actual living of men, which is true "history"). The incarnation is present and active in the Christian proclamation. Differently formulated: There exists a divinely authorized proclamation of the prevenient grace and love of God; this is the fact that finds mythological expression in what is said of the pre-existence of Christ. What the hearer affirms when he believes the pre-existence of Christ is that what has encountered him is the word of God.

Even the role of mediator in the creation of the world is attributed to the pre-existent Christ ("through whom are all things," I Cor. 8:6 = through whom the universe exists; see § 12, 3, p. 132). But the next phrase ("and we through him"—supply: are what we are: men under grace) intimately binds this role with his role as mediator of salvation. This intimate connection by itself indicates that the cosmological and soteriological roles are to be understood in unity with each other. That is, what is said of the pre-existent Christ as the mediator of creation expresses the faith that creation and redemption constitute a unity: The love of God which encounters the hearer in the word of proclamation originated before all time.

(c) Nothing preceding the faith which acknowledges the risen Christ can give insight into the reality of *Christ's resurrection*. The resurrection cannot—in spite of I Cor. 15:3–8—be demonstrated or made plausible as an objectively ascertainable fact on the basis of which one could believe. But insofar as it or the risen Christ is present in the proclaiming word, it can be believed—and only so can it be believed. Belief in the resurrection and the faith that Christ himself, yes God Himself, speaks in the proclaimed word (II Cor. 5:20) are identical. For in the proclamation Christ is not in the same way present as a great historical person is present in his work and its historical after-effects. For what is here involved is not an influence that takes effect in the history of the human mind; what does take place is that a historical person and his fate are raised to the rank of the eschatological event. The word which makes this proclamation is itself a part of this event; and this word, in contrast to all other historical tradition, accosts the hearer as personal challenge. If he heeds it as the word spoken to him, adjudicating to him death and thereby life, then he believes in the risen Christ.

Any counter-questioning as to the proclamation's right to its claim means that it is already rejected. Such questioning must be transformed into the question which the questioner has to ask himself—whether he is willing to acknowledge the Lord-ship of Christ which is putting this decision-question to his self-understanding. The meaning of Jesus' resurrection is not that he is translated into the beyond, but that he is exalted to the status of Lord (Phil. 2:11), which status he has until he gives it back to the Father (I Cor. 15:24). That is, he has it now—the now that is made Now by the now-sounding proclamation. At his command, the proclamation is being made (Rom. 10:17). The apostles are his "ministers," "slaves," and "servants" (see above). In them he is speaking (II Cor. 5:20; 13:3) and through them he is working (Rom. 15:18). When the apostle comes, it is "with the fulness of Christ's blessing" (Rom. 15:29) that he comes. It is as the risen Christ that Christ is present in the apostle; for in bearing about in his body the dying of Jesus, Paul is manifesting in his body the life of Jesus (II Cor. 4:10f.); through the apostle, Christ is demonstrating his power to the hearers: "For as he was crucified out of weakness but lives out of the power of God, so we, too, are weak through him but we shall live out of the power of God toward you" (II Cor. 13:4 Blt.)—i.e. the risen Christ himself encounters the hearer in the apostle.

§ 34. The Word, the Church, the Sacraments

1. The salvation-occurrence is the *eschatological occurrence* which puts to end the old aeon. Though Paul still expects the end of the old world to come as a cosmic drama that will unfold with the imminent parousia of Christ (I Thess. 4:16; I Cor. 15:23, 51f., etc.), that can only be the completion and confirmation of the eschatological occurrence that has now already begun. For with the sending of Christ "when the fulness of time was come" (Gal. 4:4) it decisively began, so that it can already be said now: "the old has passed away, behold, the new has come" (II Cor. 5:17). Eschato-

logical "righteousness" and "adoption" are already present realities
(§ 29); the Spirit, that "first-fruit" (Rom. 8:23) or "guarantee" of
the coming consummation (II Co. 1:22; 5:5), has already been
given to the Church (Gal. 4:6; Rom. 8:15). Though Paul describes
the present actuality of the new Life in Gnostic terminology (§ 33,
3a), he nevertheless has lifted the present eschatological occurrence
out of the dimension of cosmic occurrence into that of historic
(§ 33, 5) by regarding it as taking place in the preaching of the
word which proclaims Jesus as the crucified and risen Lord. In this
proclamation the judgment already is taking place, for it spreads
abroad death for refusal of faith and life for faith (II Cor. 2:15f.).
Paul has historized the Jewish apocalyptic speculation of an inter-
mediate messianic reign preceding the new aeon by conceiving the
time of the Messiah's reign as the time between Christ's resurrection
and parousia—i.e. as the Now in which the proclamation is sounding
forth (I Cor. 15:23-28).

In the "word," then, the salvation-occurrence is present (§ 33, 5).
For the proclaimed word is neither an enlightening *Weltanschauung* flowing out in general truths, nor a merely historical account
which, like a reporter's story, reminds a public of important but
by-gone facts. Rather, it is *kerygma*—herald's service—in the literal
sense—authorized, plenipotent proclamation, edict from a sovereign.
Its promulgation requires authorized messengers, "heralds," "apostles" (= sent men) (Rom. 10:13-17). So it is, by nature, personal
address which accosts each individual, throwing the person himself
into question by rendering his self-understanding problematic, and
demanding a decision of him.

If the salvation-occurrence is present in the proclamation, then
the latter belongs to the former as a part of it; as "ministry" or
"word" of "reconciliation" (II Cor. 5:18f.; § 33, 5) it was instituted
at the same time. In it, therefore, the eschatological occurrence is
taking place; the eschatological "acceptable time," the "day of salvation" foretold by Is. 49:8, is present reality in the Now in which
the word encounters the hearer (II Cor. 6:2; § 33, 5).

Then the proclaimer, *the apostle,* who represents Christ and God
to his hearers (II Cor. 5:20; § 33, 6a and b), whose word is God's
word (I Thess. 2:13), belongs to the eschatological occurrence. He
spreads abroad the "fragrance of the knowledge of him (God)"
(II Cor. 2:14); and if, through his preaching, God causes the "light

of the knowledge of the glory of God in the face of Christ" to flare up, then He who once said, "Let light shine out of darkness," is thereby now accomplishing His new creation (II Cor. 4:6). Therefore the apostle must lay claim to the obedience of his congregations (II Cor. 2:9; 7:15; Phil. 2:12; Phlm. 21) exposing himself to being misunderstood as a tyrant over the believers (II Cor. 1:24), whereas, being himself a believer, he is under the same Lord as they, and, proclaiming him, makes himself the "slave" of the men to whom he preaches (II Cor. 4:5; I Cor. 9:19-23). Nevertheless, in the function of apostle he must demand that the congregation's "obedience to Christ" prove itself in obedience to him (II Cor. 10:5f.).

2. The preachèd word calls and gathers men into the *ecclesia*, the *Church*, the *Congregation* of those who are "called" and "saints" (§ 10, 3). It is the eschatological Congregation, and hence its existing belongs to the eschatological salvation-occurrence. As it was called into existence by the proclaimed word, its existence in turn is the foundation of preaching. Only in the *ecclesia* is there authorized preaching; the "ministry of reconciliation" is the "ministry of a new covenant" (II Cor. 3:6ff.)—i.e. apostolic preaching stands from the outset within the frame of the salvation-history of the People of God. The apostles, to whose missionary work the separate congregations owe their origin, are, nevertheless, themselves within the Congregation (I Cor. 12:28). If Paul could not be assured that his work has the approval of the Jerusalem Church—the original Congregation—he would have to believe he "had run in vain" (Gal. 2:2).

The fact that *ecclesia* sometimes means the total Church, sometimes the local congregation (§ 10, 1), reflects the peculiar double character of the eschatological Congregation. On the one hand, it is no phenomenon of the world but belongs to the new aeon; on the other hand, this eschatological Congregation, which as such is invisible, takes visible form in the individual congregations within the world. The *ecclesia* is just as ambiguous a phenomenon as the cross of Christ: visible as a worldly fact, invisible—yet to the eye of faith also visible—as a thing of the world to come.

The eschatological Congregation takes its purest form from time to time in the cultic gathering in which Christ is confessed as Lord (I Cor. 12:3; Phil. 2:11). In their "assembling as a congregation" (I Cor. 11:18) he is present and demonstrates his presence by the working of the Spirit in the various "spiritual gifts" (I Cor. 14).

Indeed, God himself, who "inspires them all (the gifts) in every one" (I Cor. 12:6), is present; and the outsider present as a guest when struck by the prophetic word has to confess: "truly God is among you" (I Cor. 14:25 tr.).

The eschatological holiness which takes form in the cultic gathering determines the structure of the Congregation and its life in general. Since the Congregation is withdrawn from the world, this world's distinctions have lost their meaning. Hence:

> "There is neither Jew nor Greek,
> there is neither slave nor free,
> there is neither male nor female;
> for you are all one in Christ Jesus."
>   (Gal. 3:28; *cf.* I Cor. 12:13)

The indifference of worldly distinctions also emerges in the admonition: "let each one remain in the state in which the call of God encountered him" (I Cor. 7:17–24 Blt.)—i.e. the negation of worldly differentiations does not mean a sociological program within this world; rather, it is an eschatological occurrence which takes place only within the eschatological Congregation.

From the surrounding world, the "outsiders" (I Cor. 5:12f.; I Thess. 4:12), the "unrighteous" (I Cor. 6:1), the Congregation is *set apart* as the temple of God (I Cor. 3:16f.), the Congregation of the "saints." Believers are to be "children of God without blemish in the midst of a crooked and perverse generation" and are to "shine as lights in the world" (Phil. 2:15). The Christian, it is taken for granted, does not take part in heathen worship (I Cor. 10:1–22; § 10, 3). Neither is he to go to law in the heathen courts (I Cor. 6:1–8), though he is expected conscientiously to fulfill his duties toward governmental authority (Rom. 13:1–7). It is not as if all intercourse with "unbelievers" were to be cut off, however (I Cor. 5:9f.; 10:27). Still, it is not only in its cultic gathering that the eschatological Congregation makes its appearance. From it as a center there develops a secular faith-determined community of living in which there is mutual obligation and mutual service: "assistances" and "administrations," the functions of "presiding" (προΐστασθαι), "laboring" (κοπιᾶν), and "ministering" (διακονεῖν) in various forms (I Cor. 12:28; 16:15f.; Rom. 12:7f.; I Thess. 5:12). As official representatives of a Congregation *episkopoi* and *diakonoi* ("administrators" and "assistants" rather than "bishops" and "deacons") appear for the first time in Phil. 1:1. I Cor. 6:1ff. also prepares the way for the development of a Christian court of arbitration.

Paul may designate the eschatological character of the Church in keeping with the general Christian view in terms of the Old Testament history of salvation. He does so when he connects it with the "new covenant" (II Cor. 3:6ff.; I Cor. 11:25) or calls it "the Israel of God" (Gal. 6:16), or speaks of Abraham as the father of those who have faith (§ 10, 2). Such designations characterize the Church as the end and goal of the history of salvation; in the Church all promises find their fulfilment (Rom. 15:4; I Cor. 10:11; cf. 9:10). But Paul may also express the supramundane, eschatological character of the Church in Gnostic terminology. He is doing so when he calls it the "body of Christ" (I Cor. 12:27) or "one body in Christ" (Rom. 12:5; § 15, 4e). These terms express both the unity of the Church and the foundation of this unity in an origin transcendent to the will and deed of individuals and hence express its transcendental nature. The ecclesia is not a club in which like-minded individuals have banded together, though seen from without it may seem so; it is not a conglomeration of the Spirit-endowed, each of whom has and enjoys his private relationship to Christ. It is just this misconception, which has emerged in Corinth, that Paul combats in I Cor. 12:12–30. In doing so, he secondarily designates the Church as an organism (soma), using this metaphor from the classic Greek tradition, which in the latter means an organically developed and compact community. But he uses that association only secondarily (v. 14–26). Primarily he is describing the Church as the "body of Christ." His guiding thought is not that the several members of the body, being various, constitute the whole and therefore, in their variety, are equally important for the body. His main thought is, rather, that the members are equal because they belong to Christ, and therefore their differences are unimportant (v. 12f.). It is not the members that constitute the body but Christ (Rom. 12:5 implies the same). Christ is there, not through and in the members, but before they are there and above them. Thus, the body of Christ is, to speak Gnostically, a cosmic thing; however, Paul's Gnostic terminology serves to express the comprehensive historic complex, instituted by the salvation-occurrence, into which the individual is

placed (§ 33, 5). But it is quite natural that cosmological speculations about the *ecclesia* soon arise in connection with the term "body
of Christ" (§ 10, 1; § 15, 4e).

3. The individual is taken into the "body of Christ" by the *sacrament of baptism;* "for by one Spirit we were all baptized into one
body" (I Cor. 12:13). Or it may be said instead, simply: "into
Christ" (Gal. 3:27; II Cor. 1:21) with the result that now Christian
existence can be called existence *"in Christ":* "for you are all one in
Christ Jesus" (Gal. 3:28). To belong to the Christian Church is to
be "in Christ" or "in the Lord" (Rom. 16:7, 11; I Cor. 1:30), and
Christian congregations may also be called congregations "in
Christ" (Gal. 1:22; I Thess. 2:14). "In Christ," far from being a
formula for mystic union, is primarily an *ecclesiological* formula. It
means the state of having been articulated into the "body of Christ"
by baptism, although baptism need not be directly implied in every
instance (such as Rom. 8:1; II Cor. 5:17; Gal. 2:17). It must also
be noted that from this basic meaning the formula took on an extension of meaning: It often expresses in a quite general way the state
of being determined by Christ whereby it supplies the lack of the
not yet coined adjective "Christian" or a corresponding adverb.
Since the Church, into which baptism incorporates the member, is
the *eschatological* Congregation, the formula "in Christ" has not
only ecclesiological but at the same time eschatological meaning:
"if anyone is in Christ, he is a new creation" (II Cor. 5:17). Similarly, the fact that "in Christ" can interchange with "in the Spirit"
also indicates the eschatological meaning of "in Christ" (Rom. 8:9;
14:17). But since the Spirit is conferred by baptism (I Cor. 12:13;
II Cor. 1:22; § 13, 1, p. 138), "in the Spirit" can also be regarded
vice versa as an ecclesiological formula, though it, like the other,
also underwent an extension of meaning.

But what is the relation between incorporation into the Church
by the sacrament of *baptism* and the dynamic process in which the
salvation-occurrence continues itself through the proclaimed *word*
(§ 33, 5 and 6)? If baptism grants participation in the death and
resurrection of Jesus, does it do so in another way than the word
proclaimed and heard in faith? Paul found baptism already conceived before his time as a sacrament of the mystery religions and
strove so to interpret it as purification from sin as to see in it the
founding of a new ethical life (§ 13, 1, p. 140). To be sure, it is

scarcely permissible to say that he completely freed himself of the mystery-conception of sacrament as having a magical effect; for he leaves vicarious baptism, which rests upon such a conception, at least uncontested (I Cor. 15:29) and also shows himself influenced by it in his view of the Lord's Supper (see below). Nevertheless, he by no means unconditionally attributes magic influence to baptism, as if receiving it guaranteed salvation. As the desert-generation of Israel, which once had received prototypes of the Christian sacraments, was not thereby preserved from destruction, so baptized Christians must be warned: "Therefore let any one who thinks that he stands take heed lest he fall" (I Cor. 10:1–12). When Paul emphatically says, "For Christ did not send me to baptize but to preach the gospel" (I Cor. 1:17), baptism obviously plays a subordinate role to the word. The baptizer does not have the character of priest as in the mysteries, and the act of baptizing does not, as was often the case in them, establish some mysterious relationship between the baptizer and the baptized.

Nevertheless, baptism is an objective occurrence which happens to the baptized, not simply a symbol for a subjective process within him. Whatever inward experiences the one being baptized may have, Paul does not reflect about them. As an event occurring objectively to the baptized, baptism certifies to him participation in the salvation-occurrence, the death and resurrection of Jesus. It, then, makes the salvation-occurrence present for him just as the proclaiming word also does, only this time with special reference to him, the one being baptized, as valid for him. But the appropriation on his part is the same as the appropriation of the salvation-occurrence when it comes through the preachèd word. For if, as can scarcely be doubted, Rom. 10:9 is a reference to the confession made at baptism—"if you confess with your lips that Jesus is Lord and believe in your heart that God raised him from the dead"—then baptism on the part of him who is being baptized is an act of faith confessing itself. And as acceptance of the word in faith is the acknowledgment of the Lord who is speaking in it, so baptism also brings a man under the domination of the Lord. To be "in Christ" is also to be "of Christ"—i.e. to belong to Christ as one's Lord (*cf.* Gal. 3:29 with 3:27f.; 5:24; II Cor. 10:7; Rom. 8:9; 14:8). As the acceptance of the "word of the cross" means willingness to let one's self-understanding and one's conduct be determined by the cross (§ 33, 6a), so baptism means crucifixion with Christ (Rom. 6:6). Consequently, the indicative (of Rom. 6:6 and 8, for example, which imply you already share Jesus' death and resurrection) now furnishes real justification for Paul's imperative: "yield yourselves to God as men who have been brought from death to life" (Rom. 6:13). Or, as another example, Gal. 3:27 says: "For as many of you as were baptized into Christ have put on Christ," which Paul can also say in the imperative: "Put on the Lord Jesus Christ" (Rom. 13:14).

Similarly, in Paul's conception of the *Lord's Supper* mystery-ideas unite with his own view of the salvation-occurrence. Paul took over from the Hellenistic Church (§ 13, 2) both the celebration of the Lord's Supper and a conception of it as a sacrament which effects communion with the crucified and risen Christ by means of bread and wine, eaten and drunk. Two facts indicate how little Paul consciously disavows the idea that the Supper has a magical effect. One is that he regards its effect as analogous to that of heathen cult-meals (I Cor. 10:20f.; p. 148). The other is his opinion that partaking in an unworthy manner results in damage to the partaker's body or even in his death (I Cor. 11:29f.). But when Paul formulates his thought of "communion" by saying that the participants become one "body" (the "body" of Christ, I Cor. 10:16f.), it is beyond doubt that his view of the "body of Christ" also determines his view of the Lord's Supper. And when he calls the process by which the Lord's Supper makes Christ's death a present reality a "proclaiming" (I Cor. 11:26)—using the same word that he otherwise uses for preaching (Rom. 1:8; I Cor. 2:1; 9:14; Phil. 1:17f.)—that indicates that the sacrament of the Lord's Supper like that of baptism is also coordinate with the word-proclamation and ultimately only a special mode of it. The particular effect of this sacrament, like that of baptism, is its special application of the salvation-occurrence just to those who here and now are celebrating it. Besides this, it has the additional effect of instituting fellowship among the celebrants (I Cor. 10:16f.), an effect not explicitly emphasized in the case of word-proclamation and baptism. Obviously, then, the efficacy of the sacrament—in spite of the influence of mystery ideas—does not really rest upon the elements, the bread and wine partaken, but rests upon the doing of this act as an act of "proclamation." In any case, the Lord's Supper is for Paul not a "medicine of immortality" (§ 13, 2, p. 147), the taking of which guarantees immortal life; his warning against supposed security (I Cor. 10:1–12) holds for the Lord's Supper just as for baptism. In the Lord's Supper, too—as the name κυριακὸν δεῖπνον itself implies—the lordship of the Lord is set up over believers and acknowledged by them.

C. FAITH

§ 35. The Structure of Faith

The attitude of man in which he receives the gift of "God's righteousness" and in which the divine deed of salvation accomplishes itself with him is *faith*. We inevitably caught sight of it in our earlier discussion of "God's righteousness" (§ 30), and its nature was indirectly clarified by our investigation of "grace" (§§ 32–34). Our present task is to set forth faith in its full structure and meaning.

At the outset, it may be simply said that "faith" is the condition for the receipt of "righteousness," taking the place of "works," which in the Jewish view constitute that condition. It may also be simply said at the outset that such "faith" is the acceptance of the Christian message (§ 9, 5)—following a usage that developed in the missionary enterprise of Hellenistic Christianity. An understanding of such acceptance, or a concept of "faith," was developed by several others besides Paul (p. 99), but by him it was given a characteristic and decisive stamp.

1. *Paul understands faith primarily as obedience;* he understands the act of faith as an act of obedience. This is shown by the parallelism of two passages in Romans: "because your faith is proclaimed in all the world" (1:8) and "for your obedience is known to all" (16:19). Thus, he can combine the two in the expression ὑπακοὴ πίστεως ("the obedience which faith is," Rom. 1:5) to designate that which it is the purpose of his apostleship to bring about.

Cf. further, I Thess. 1:8: "your faith in God has gone forth everywhere" and Rom. 15:18: "For I will not venture to speak of anything except what Christ has wrought through me to win obedience from the Gentiles." Further, he says of Jews who have not come to faith, Rom. 10:3: "they did not submit to (= obey) God's righteousness," and 10:16: "they have not all heeded (= obeyed) the gospel." Correspondingly, the Jews' refusal of faith is denoted by "disobey" and "disobedience" in

[314]

Rom. 11:30–32; *cf.* Rom. 15:31; Gal. 5:7. II Cor. 9:13 describes faith as "obedience in acknowledging the Gospel of Christ." Paul considers it his task, according to II Cor. 10:5f., to "take every thought captive to obey Christ," and warns the unruly Corinthians that he will "punish every disobedience when your *obedience* is complete" (for obedience rendered to the apostle is identical with obedience to Christ, § 34, 1). But he substitutes the word "faith" where we might expect to read "obedience" when he expresses the hope that he will become greater through them when their *faith* is increased (see II Cor. 10:15 KJ).

For Paul the acceptance of the message in faith takes the form of an act of obedience because of the fact that the message which demands acknowledgment of the crucified Jesus as Lord demands of man the surrender of his previous understanding of himself, the reversal of the direction his will has previously had (§ 33, 6a). "Faith's obedience" is the genuine obedience which God's Law had indeed demanded, but which had been refused by the Jews by their misuse of it to establish "their own righteousness," using it as a means for "boasting" (§ 23, 1 and 2). Faith's attitude is the radical opposite of the attitude of "boasting" (§ 30, 2); nor can faith take credit for itself—that would be "boasting." Accordingly, he warns even the man of faith, who is no longer under the Law, with a warning that corresponds to his opinion about Jewish boasting: "What have you that you have not been given? And if you have been given it, why do you boast as if you had not been given it" (I Cor. 4:7 tr.)? He exhorts the Gentile Christians who have been grafted into the cultivated olive tree as shoots from the wild olive: "Do not boast over the branches. If you do boast . . . it is not you that support the root, but the root that supports you" (Rom. 11:18). For the purpose of God's salvation-deed is: "that no flesh may boast before God" (I Cor. 1:29 tr.), and there is only one boast left: "Let him who boasts, boast of the Lord" (I Cor. 1:31; II Cor. 10:17). Accordingly, Paul thus describes the faith of Abraham: "he grew strong in his faith as he gave glory to God" (Rom. 4:20).

As true obedience, "faith" is freed from the suspicion of being an accomplishment, a "work" (§ 30, 2, p. 283). As an accomplishment it would not be obedience, since in an accomplishment the will does not surrender but asserts itself; in it, a merely formal renunciation takes place in that the will lets the content of its accomplishment be dictated by an authority lying outside of itself, but precisely in so doing thinks it has a right to be proud of its accomplishment. "Faith"—the radical renunciation of accomplishment, the obedient submission to the God-determined way of salvation, the taking over of the cross of Christ (§ 33, 6a)—is the free deed of obedience in which the new self constitutes itself in place of the old. As this sort of decision, it is a deed in the true sense: In a true deed the doer himself is inseparable from it, while in a "work" he stands side by side with what he does.

As free deed of decision, the obedience of faith is also insured against another misconception. "Faith" is not an "experience," not the "truly religious in religion," not a state of soul, not a διάθεσις (propensity, disposition) or an ἀρετή (virtue, excellence). It is not —as if it were the perfected state of the soul—salvation itself. Rather —as genuine obedience—it is the condition for receiving salvation.

The frequently made comparison with *Philo's* concept of "faith" is instructive (see Bousset, *Kyrios Christos*, 2nd ed., 145–149; *cf.* H. Windisch, *Die Frömmigkeit Philos* (1909); Schlatter, *op. cit.*, 66–86). Philo understands "faith" as a "propensity" (διάθεσις) of the soul, the soul's perfect state, an excellence (ἀρετή). In his thought, therefore, "faith" stands at the end "as the goal of life's movement toward God" (Schlatter), while for Paul it stands at the beginning furnishing the basis for the new life.

W. Michaelis (following Deissmann) attempts to escape the misconception of faith as an accomplishment which would be the condition for rightwising by altogether eliminating its condition-character and declaring that "righteousness by faith" (Rom. 1:17; 10:6) is only an antithetic formula to "righteousness from the Law." In reality, according to him, faith is the experience of being rightwised, fellowship with Christ. But he has overlooked, first, that "faith" equals "obedience" and, second, has ignored such expressions as "reckoned as righteousness" (Rom. 4:3, 5ff.; Gal. 3:6) and "believe unto righteousness" (Rom. 10:10 KJ), which clearly show that faith is not righteousness but the condition for it. The condition-character of "faith" is the clear implication of the passages that speak of rightwising or righteousness ἐκ ("from," "on the basis of") "faith": Rom. 3:30; 5:1; 9:30; 10:6 (*cf.* also 1:17; 3:26; 9:32), especially Gal. 2:16: "we have believed in Christ Jesus in order to be justified (rightwised) by (ἐϰ) faith in Christ," and also Gal. 3:7f., 11f., 24; 5:5. The same is true of the synonymous formulas using διὰ πίστεως ("through faith," Rom. 3:22, 30; Gal. 2:16; 3:14; Phil. 3:9), ἐπὶ τῇ πίστει ("that depends on faith," Phil. 3:9), or the simple dative (Rom. 3:28). Paul's position seems incomprehensible or contradictory only to those who can conceive the fulfilling of a condition only as an accomplishment, whereas for Paul "faith" is precisely the waiver of any accomplishment whatever and thereby is radical obedience.

Neither is it adequate to understand faith as trust, founded on repentance, in God's gracious forgiveness which brings the sinner back to the way of the Law which in his transgressions he had forsaken (Schlatter). The very rarity of the terms "forgiveness of sins" and "repentance" in Paul (§ 31) and the similar rarity of ἐπιστρέφειν ("turn to"—only at I Thess. 1:9 and II Cor. 3:16 in Paul; § 9, 3) indicate that the movement of will contained in "faith" is not primarily remorse and repentance. Of course, they are included in it; but it is primarily the obedience which waives righteousness of one's own. Phil. 3:7–9 is not the self-condemnation of Paul's previous life as one soiled by trespasses, not condemnation of that which even in existence under the Law and by one so existing could be and, as IV Ezra shows, was condemned. Rather, it describes his sacrifice of all that had been his pride and "gain" in existence under the Law. It is evident that "faith" has the character of obedience and is an act of decision.

2. "Faith" is further insured against such misconceptions by the fact that *it is simultaneously "confession."* "Faith" is "faith in . . ." That is, it always has reference to its object, God's saving deed in Christ.

Hence, "confess" and "believe" correspond to each other:
"If you confess with your lips that Jesus is Lord and
    believe in your heart that God raised him from the
    dead, you will be saved." (Rom. 10:9)

The object of belief or faith is expressed by a ὅτι-clause, as here, in I Thess. 4:14; Rom. 6:8. Equivalent locutions are "believe in" or "faith in" (εἰς in both cases with "Christ Jesus" as object) Gal. 2:16; Rom. 10:14; Phil. 1:29; πρός (faith toward) Phlm. 5; ἐν (in) Gal. 3:26; ἐπί ("on, in" quoted from Is. 28:16) Rom. 9:33; 10:11. An abbreviating substitute is the objective genitive (§9, 5) with "Jesus Christ" as object: Gal. 2:16; 3:22; Rom. 3:22, 26; Phil. 3:9; or other objects: Son of God (Gal. 2:20), the gospel (Phil. 1:27).

Faith, therefore, is not "piety" or trust-in-God in general. Rather, it has "dogmatic" character insofar as it is acceptance of a word: "the word of faith" (Rom. 10:8) or "the heard word" (ἀκοή, KJ: "the hearing") of faith (Gal. 3:2, 5). Hence, faith can also be called "faith of the gospel"—i.e. faith in the gospel (Phil. 1:27).

"Faith," which arises from "what is heard" (Rom. 10:17), consequently contains a *knowing*. That is why Paul can, at times, speak as if knowledge were the basis of faith. For instance, Rom. 6:8f.: since we *know* that death no longer has power over the risen Christ, we *believe* that if we have died with him we shall also live with him (*cf.* II Cor. 4:13f.). But since this knowledge can be appropriated only in obedient, comprehending faith, and hence contains an understanding of one's self, knowledge may also appear as arising out of faith. It is so in Rom. 5:3 where the knowledge "that suffering produces endurance" is just the knowledge of those who are "rightwised by faith." So also in II Cor. 1:7; 5:6. Thus, "we know" or "you know" sometimes makes an appeal to a "dogma"—i.e. a statement in the *kerygma* (I Thess. 5:2; Rom. 6:3; II Cor. 5:1; 8:9)—and sometimes to truths which "faith"-ful reflection must draw as consequences (Rom. 8:28; 13:11; 14:14; I Cor. 3:16; 6:2f., 9; 15:58). Ultimately "faith" and "knowledge" are identical as a new understanding of one's self, if Paul can give as the purpose of his apostleship both "to bring about the obedience of faith" (Rom. 1:5) and "to give the light of the knowledge of the glory of God in the face of Christ" (II Cor. 4:6; *cf.* 2:14: "God . . . who . . . through us spreads the fragrance of the knowledge of him"). The same conclusion is to be drawn from his saying that he has given up "confidence in the flesh" for the sake of "the surpassing worth of knowing Christ Jesus" and his then proceeding to develop the purpose of "righteousness from God that depends on faith" as this: "that I may know him and the power of his resurrection and may share his sufferings . . ." (Phil. 3:4–10). An additional clarification of the character of "knowledge" lies in the fact that human "knowing" has its basis in a "being known by God" (Gal. 4:9; I Cor. 13:12).

"Faith," that is, also has, on the other hand, "undogmatic" character insofar as the word of proclamation is no mere report about historical incidents: It is no teaching about external matters which could simply be regarded as true without any transformation of the hearer's own existence. For the word is *kerygma,* personal address, demand, and promise; it is the very act of divine grace (§ 34, 1). Hence its acceptance—faith—is obedience, acknowledgment, confession. That is the reason why "grace" as well as "faith" can likewise be named as the opposite of "works" to designate the basis for rightwising (§ 30, 2); for "faith" is what it is only with reference to the "grace" which is actively present in the word.

In his "confession" of faith, the believer turns away from himself, confessing that all he is and has, he is and has through that which God has done. Faith does not appeal to whatever it itself may be as act or attitude but to God's prevenient deed of grace which preceded faith (§ 31). That is why Paul (and the New Testament in general) never describes faith as a state of soul nor its genesis as a psychological process. Though Gal. 3:23–26 sketches the preparation and the "coming" of "faith," what is sketched is not the individual's development but the history of salvation. The attention of the believer does not turn reflectively inward upon himself, but is turned toward the object of his faith. "Faith," then, as "obedience," is also "confession."

3. This same thing, that the believer is turned away from himself, is also expressed by the fact that *"faith" is also "hope."* "Faith" is no self-contained condition of man's soul, but points toward the future: "he who by faith is righteous shall live" (Gal. 3:11; Rom. 1:17). "For if we have died with Christ, we believe that we shall also live with him" (Rom. 6:8; *cf.* I Thess. 4:14). "For with the heart man believeth unto righteousness and with the mouth confession is made unto salvation" (Rom. 10:10 KJ).

The "righteousness" which is the goal of "faith" is no quality which adheres to man, but is his relation to God (§ 28, 2). If it has become a present possibility (§ 29, 1), this "present-ness" is not a temporal and therefore a temporary state. Rather, its "present-ness" is that of the eschatological Now. That is, it is always both here and ahead of the already rightwised believer as future to him. That is why we can be said to be both "rightwised by faith" (Rom. 5:1) and "waiting for the hope of righteousness" "through the Spirit, by faith" (Gal. 5:5). That is why "righteousness" and "salvation" correspond to each other in Rom. 10:9f. Though men of faith may already be called the "saved" (I Cor. 1:18; II Cor. 2:15), still: "in this hope we were saved. Now hope that is seen is not hope. For who hopes for what he sees? But if we hope for what we do not see, we wait for it with patience" (Rom. 8:24f.).

This "hope" is the freedom for the future and the openness toward it which the man of faith has because he has turned over his anxiety about himself and his future to God in obedience. For the sin of unbelief is just this: The unbeliever insists upon living out of his own resources and so is anxious about his own future in the illusion of being able to dispose over it. Though the man without faith naturally has his hopes, too—just as those "who have no hope" (I Thess. 4:13), of course, also live with certain hopes—still they are no real hopes. The man who is concerned for himself factually lives in fear (§ 23, 2), shutting himself up against the future, which is not at his disposal. The man of faith is relieved of this fear because in faith he has let anxiety about himself go. He hopes where humanly there is nothing to hope, following the example of Abraham, who "hoping against hope believed" (Rom. 4:18 tr.). He lives, that is, in the true hope "which does not disappoint" (Rom. 5:5). It manifests itself in the patient waiting (Rom. 8:25; see above) or "patience," of which "rejoicing in our sufferings" (Rom. 5:3) is characteristic. Believers "rejoice in hope," are "patient in tribulation" (Rom. 12:12). "Hope," like "love" (see § 39, 3) is bound up with "faith" in a unity (I Cor. 13:13); the "work of faith," the "labor of love" and the "steadfastness of hope"—all three together belong to the totality of Christian existence (I Thess. 1:3; cf. 5:8). When Paul prays for the perfecting of Christian existence, he prays: "May the God of hope fill you with all joy and peace in believing so that . . . you may abound in hope" (Rom. 15:13).

4. Such "hope," nevertheless, has a peculiar correlative in "fear" (φόβος), which is an indispensable constitutive element in "faith," inasmuch as it guarantees the centering of the believer's attention upon God's "grace." How it does so is illustrated by Paul's description of his conduct on arriving at Corinth (I Cor. 2:1-5). He came to Corinth "in weakness and in much fear and trembling"—so far, that is, as he looked to himself. But since he waived any eloquence or wisdom of his own and determined to know one thing only, "Jesus Christ and him crucified," he was effective with a "demonstration of

Spirit and power" having as its purpose and result: "that your faith might not rest in the wisdom of men but in the power of God."

That this is the appropriate attitude of the man of faith is also declared in the warning directed to the Gentile Christians who want to boast of their faith, comparing themselves with unbelieving Jews (Rom. 11:20–22): "They were broken off because of their unbelief, but you stand fast (only) through faith. (So) do not become proud, but stand in awe (i.e. do not be haughty—toward them—but rather fear—for yourself) . . ." Faith would be cheated of its purpose if the believer were to consider himself insured by it. God's "kindness," in which faith takes comfort, is only valid "provided you continue in his kindness." The man of faith, who in view of God's "grace" is freed from fear, must not forget that the grace that emancipates him is the "grace" of a Judge. When the man of faith looks to himself, his faith must ever contain "fear" as the knowledge of his own insignificance and his constant dependence upon God's "grace." Thinking of the "judgment seat of Christ" before which we must all be arraigned (II Cor. 5:10), Paul says: "knowing the fear of the Lord . . ." (v. 11). This sentence runs parallel with "since we have such a hope" (3:12), demonstrating the unity of "hope" and "fear." This sentence also shows, however, that "fear" has not only the negative purpose of destroying false security and directing the believer's attention away from himself toward God's "grace" which alone supports him (as in Rom. 11:20), but also the positive purpose of making man conscious of his responsibility, which he can assume now that he is no longer under Law but under "grace" (Rom. 6:14). Just because he has been set free (§§ 38, 39), what he does—previously a thing of no account—now really matters, and he can be exhorted (Phil. 2:13f.): "work out your own salvation with fear and trembling; for God is at work in you, both to will and to work for his good pleasure."

As long as the believer lives "in the flesh," his is a constantly threatened existence exposed to temptations (§ 26, 3). Therefore, he is not to look down in a false security of faith upon one overtaken in some trespass, but is to look to himself, lest he, too, fall into temptation (Gal. 6:1). Satan lies in wait (II Cor. 2:11) to tempt believers (I Thess. 3:5; I Cor. 7:5). Hence the exhortation that a man is to "test" himself (πειράζειν) or "examine" himself (δοκιμάζειν) as to whether he truly stands fast in faith (II Cor. 13:5; I Cor. 11:28;

Gal. 6:4). Hence the warning: "let anyone who thinks that he stands take heed lest he fall" (I Cor. 10:12), and the exhortation: "stand firm in your faith" (I Cor. 16:13; *cf.* Gal. 5:1; Phil. 1:27; 4:1) and "be immovable" (I Cor. 15:58). Hence, also, Paul's petition in his prayers for the believers that God may establish or strengthen or sustain them (I Thess. 3:13; 5:23; *cf.* I Cor. 1:8; II Cor. 1:21).

Though "hope" and "fear" equally belong to the structure of "faith," that does not mean that Christian existence is a wavering between hope and fear; rather, hope and fear belong together as correlatives: Just because faith is "hope," it is also "fear" and vice versa. This fact makes clear the obedience aspect of faith: the man of faith utterly surrenders to God's care and power, waiving all care or power of his own and all security that might be at his own disposal. Paul is describing this aspect of faith in Phil. 3:12–14:

> "Not that I have already obtained this or am already perfect;
> but I press on to make it my own,
> because Christ Jesus has made me his own.
> Brethren, I do not consider that I have made it my own;
> but one thing I do, forgetting what lies behind
> and straining forward to what lies ahead,
> I press on toward the goal for the prize of the upward call . . ."

Existence in faith, then, is a movement between "no longer" and "not yet." "No longer": The decision of faith has done away with the past; nevertheless, as true decision, the decision must be maintained—that is, made again and again anew. As that which is overcome, the past is always with us, and faith must remember the past as that which constantly threatens. Paul's "forgetting" does not mean putting the past out of mind, but does mean constantly holding it down, not letting one's self be caught by it again. "Not yet": giving up that which is past, i.e. surrendering a possession which had given a supposed security, precludes taking a new possession in exchange for it. Viewed from man's side no one can say, "I have made it my own"; and yet in view of the fact that "Jesus Christ has made me his own," it can be said, "Nevertheless the hoped-for has already occurred."

5. To the extent that faith is "hope" which has its foundation in "grace" and hence "does not disappoint" (Rom. 5:5), faith is naturally also *confidence*; thus, "since we have such a hope" (II Cor.

3:12) corresponds to "such is the confidence that we have" (3:4). In fact, precisely as obedience, faith in the end is confidence, trust; for in the radical sense confidence in or trust in God is nothing else than complete surrender of one's own care and strength to God: In other words, the obedience of faith. In this sense, faith is trust in God—but not just trust-in-God in general; rather, that trust which, by accepting the cross, lays its foundation upon God's deed of salvation. Paul makes this unmistakably clear by never using πιστεύειν in the simple sense of "trust" and hence never construing it with the dative, which it takes in the Septuagint and often has in the rest of the New Testament (§ 9, 5), except in the Old Testament quotations about the "trust" of Abraham, Gal. 3:6; Rom. 4:3. Instead, Paul distinguishes between the trust-aspect and the obedience-aspect of faith by using for the former πεποιθέναι or πεποίθησις.

For the man of faith, "trusting in one's self" (II Cor. 1:9) or "in the flesh" (Phil. 3:3f.) has ceased and given place to "trusting in God who raises the dead" (II Cor. 1:9). Similarly, natural man's "boasting" (§ 23, 2), almost synonymous with "trusting," has been replaced by "boasting of the Lord" (see above: 1) and even by "boasting of sufferings" (Rom. 5:3), which is nothing else than "trusting in God who raises the dead." In such "trust" fear is overcome; out of it grows that "boldness" which has no fear of being "put to shame" (Phil. 1:20). Or it is synonymous with the "boldness" which is founded on "hope" (II Cor. 3:12, cf. 3:4). It is the opposite of ἐγκακεῖν ("losing heart" or "being cowardly," II Cor. 4:1, 16; cf. "fearlessly" in relation to "made confident" in Phil. 1:14).

Only in II Cor. 1:9 (and by implication Phil. 3:3f.) does πεποιθέναι ("trust") denote the trusting surrender to God that is contained in "faith" and characterizes Christian existence in general. More frequently, Paul speaks of that trust in God arising from faith that gives him his apostolic consciousness and supports him in his ministry as an apostle (II Cor. 3:4; 10:2). He trusts in God's guidance and assistance for himself and the Church (Phil. 1:6, 25; 2:24). The trust which he places in a Congregation (Gal. 5:10; II Cor. 1:15; 2:3; cf. 8:22) or a friend (Phlm. 21) is probably also to be understood as flowing out of his "faith," especially since he characterizes it as a confidence "in the Lord" (Gal. 5:10, though B omits ἐν κυρίῳ).

Paul does not speak of trust in God in the traditional Old

Testament sense (found especially in Psalms), since his message has for its theme not the lot of individuals but eschatological salvation. For the contrary, see I Pet. 5:7, for example.

§ 36. Life in Faith

1. "Faith" as man's relation to God also determines man's relation to himself; for human existence, as we have seen (§ 17), is an existence in which man has a relationship to himself. "Faith" is the acceptance of the *kerygma* not as mere cognizance of it and agreement with it but as that genuine obedience to it which includes a new understanding of one's self. Therefore, it cannot be an act that takes place once and then becomes a thing of the past. Neither is it a quality of man that mysteriously and imperishably clings to him like, for instance, the "incorruption" imparted in the mysteries. Still less is "faith" an "experience," mystical or otherwise, to which one might look back contentedly and which could either occasionally repeat itself, interrupting the course of everyday life, or else maintain itself as one's "life-feeling." Rather, *it determines one's living in its manifold historical reality,* and there is no moment in which the man of faith is released from the obedience of constantly living out of the "grace" of God. Therefore, "whatever does not proceed from faith is sin" (Rom. 14:23). The Christian must "continue in (God's) kindness" (Rom. 11:22), and "the life I now live in the flesh I live by faith in the Son of God" (Gal. 2:20). Hence, there are no special practices designated for the man of faith—"for in Christ Jesus neither circumcision nor uncircumcision is of any avail (and that also means: no specifically religious practices), but faith working through love" (Gal. 5:6). Accordingly, *"faith" both as to degree and to kind realizes itself in concrete living: in the individual acts of the man of faith.* As to degree: A weakness in faith (Rom. 14:1) exists, so do "lacks of faith" (I Thess. 3:10); there is also "progress" (Phil. 1:25) and "increase" (II Cor. 10:15) in faith. A believer may be overtaken in some "trespass" (Gal. 6:1) and the exhortation that one should "correct" or "restore to a proper condition" (καταρτίζειν and καταρτίζεσθαι) occurs again and again (Gal. 6:1; I Cor. 1:10; II Cor. 13:11); so does the prayer that God may establish, strengthen, sustain, or the like (II Cor. 13:9; Rom. 15:13; I Thess. 3:13; 5:23; *cf.* § 35, 4). The fact that the "weakness in faith" of

Rom. 14:1f. fully corresponds to the "weak conscience" of I Cor. 8:7–12 clearly indicates that "faith" realizes itself in knowledge of what one has to do or not to do in the specific instance (*cf.* § 19, 4). The Christian henceforth is to consider himself only as one who has faith; that is just the reason why "whatever does not proceed from faith is sin." The life of the believer, therefore, will be a continual movement in which that basic movement between "no longer" and "not yet" (§ 35, 4) takes concrete form, heeding the exhortation: "Let those of us who are mature be thus minded (i.e. "strain forward to what lies ahead"); and if in anything you are otherwise minded, God will reveal that also to you. Only let us hold true to what we have attained" (Phil. 3:15).

"Faith," however, is also individualized as to kind, viz. according to the "measure of faith" which God has assigned to each one (Rom. 12:3). This "measure of faith" is equivalent to one's share of the "gifts" which God or the Spirit bestows (§ 14, 1). For as "faith" is individualized in various concrete ways of acting, so divine "grace" is also individualized in various concrete "gifts of grace": "having gifts that differ according to the grace given to us" (Rom. 12:6). As Paul was given the "grace" of apostleship to the Gentiles (Rom. 1:5; 12:3; 15:15; I Cor. 3:10; Gal. 2:9) and the "gift" of celibacy, so others were given other things: "each has his own special gift from God, one of one kind and one of another" (I Cor. 7:7). Paul's lists of such "gifts" in Rom. 12:6ff.; I Cor. 12:4ff., 28ff. show that he considers as "gifts" not only striking phenomena that were generally so considered, such as ecstatic glossolalia, the gift of prophecy and the working of miracles, but also includes all demonstrations of brotherly love (§ 14, 1 and 3). Moreover, the modifiers "in liberality," "with cheerfulness," and "genuine" (unfeigned) attached to the gifts of contributing, acts of mercy, and love, and designating in each case the norm of the respective activity, are equivalent to the phrase "in proportion to our faith" which is appended to prophecy (Rom. 12:6, 8f.). We see, then, that by virtue of all such gifts Christian existence in faith takes concrete shape in individually varied forms. As "faith" founded upon "grace" is at work in "love" (Gal 5:6), love's activity itself can be called "grace" (II Cor. 8:1, 4, 6f. 19): "God is able to make every grace (= activity of love) abound in you, so that you may always have enough of everything and may provide in abundance for every good work" (II Cor. 9:8 tr.).

2. One eminent "gift" is *knowledge,* γνῶσις, and it already came to light in our analysis of the structure of "faith" that it contains a knowledge both capable of further development and requiring such (§ 35). The outward contradiction between I Cor. 8:1, "we know that all of us possess knowledge," and 8:7, "however, not all possess this knowledge," indicates that there are differences within that knowledge. The "weakness in faith" (Rom. 14:1) is a lack in knowledge (see 1, above), just as "not all possess this knowledge" is said in reference to the "weak." He who is "strong" is to be considerate of such "weak" ones and is not to judge them; for each one is responsible only to the Lord (Rom. 14:4, 22). When it is said: "let each one be fully convinced in his own mind" (v. 5), it is clear that each one is independent in his "faith" and is to achieve his own knowledge. So it is explicitly said: "Have the faith that you have by yourself before God . . ." (v. 22f., tr.).

This does not mean, however, that each is to insist upon his own standpoint. Just as Paul leaves no doubt but that he approves the knowledge of the "strong" (Rom. 14; I Cor. 8), he wishes for the Philippians: "that your love (here denoting the Christian attitude as a whole) may abound more and more with knowledge and all discernment so that you may approve what is excellent" (Phil. 1:9f.). Likewise Rom. 12:2: "be transformed by the renewal of your mind that you may prove what is the will of God . . ." In the meetings of the congregation the "word of wisdom" and the "word of knowledge" play an important role (I Cor. 12:8) and Paul is glad when he can boast that a congregation is rich in "understanding" (λόγος) and "knowledge" (I Cor. 1:5; II Cor. 8:7; Rom. 15:14), and he is proud that, though he is "unskilled in speech," he is not so in "knowledge" (II Cor. 11:6).

Such "knowledge" or "wisdom" develops the knowing that is contained in "faith" into ever clearer and more comprehensive knowledge. Paul stimulates his readers in this direction with his queries, "Are you ignorant?" "do you not know?" and the like (§ 35, 2). In Rom. 6:3, for example, he refers the Romans to a knowledge which he obviously presupposes them to have: "Do you not know that all of us who have been baptized into Christ Jesus were baptized into his death?" and then in v. 11 makes them aware of the consequence: "so you must consider yourselves dead to sin and alive to God . . ."

Knowledge as a special aspect of "faith" is a gift of the Spirit (see 1); this, nevertheless, does not mean that it is not to be conceived as a task or that it is not to be developed, as Phil. 1:9f. and Rom. 12:2 (see above) clearly show. Though here and probably in the majority of cases the knowledge meant is knowledge of the will of God—i.e. one's grasp of ethical duties—elsewhere it is knowledge of the mysteries of the history of salvation or of the eschatological occurrence (Rom. 11:25; I Cor. 2:7; 15:51). For by the power of the Spirit knowledge can soar aloft to a "wisdom" which lies beyond the paradoxical, foolish-seeming "wisdom" of the proclaimed cross; this higher "wisdom," however, is reserved for "mature" Christians (I Cor. 2:6). There is a Spirit-given "searching of the depths of God" (2:10). However great the danger is that *gnosis* may separate out of "faith" as speculation—a danger which has undoubtedly become reality in the Gnostics of Corinth—in Paul it retains its basic character of an existential knowledge in which faith unfolds itself. For Paul defines its purpose to be: "that we may understand the gifts bestowed on us by God" (2:12). To understand God's gift means to understand one's self as the receiver of it; hence, this highest "wisdom" and "knowledge" must simultaneously be the clearest understanding of one's self.

The restriction of this "wisdom" to those who have ethical maturity (I Cor. 3:1-3) likewise indicates that in Paul, knowledge has not been cut loose from its inner mooring to "faith" to become a free-floating speculation (or a neutrally investigating science). I Cor. 8, above all, indicates that Christian *gnosis* is the understanding of one's self under divine "grace." For "knowledge" is not genuine if it leads to getting "puffed up" and hence damages the "love" (ἀγάπη) in which "faith" ought to be working. So here, too, it becomes clear that "knowledge" in all its forms and degrees besides being an understanding of its object is simultaneously an existential understanding of one's self in "faith" (§ 35, 2). So far as this self-understanding unfolds as object-knowledge—i.e. as ever more penetrating knowledge of divine grace—it remains only partial knowledge, which will not be succeeded by clear comprehension without riddles until the consummation "when that which is perfect is come" (I Cor. 13:10-12); for now "we walk only by faith, not by sight" (II Cor. 5:7).

3. In this way the formula *"in Christ"* takes on a meaning beyond or in addition to its ecclesiological and eschatological meaning (§ 34,

3): It denotes not, to be sure, an individual mystical relationship to Christ, but the fact that the individual actual life of the believer, living not out of himself but out of the divine deed of salvation, is determined by Christ. It makes no difference whether Paul speaks of the believer's being in Christ or of Christ's being in the believer (Rom. 8:10; II Cor. 13:5; Gal. 2:20; *cf.* 4:19). Either one means nothing else than that conditioning of concrete life which Paul also calls the "law of Christ" (Gal. 6:2). Furthermore, as there is a "standing fast in faith" (§ 35, 4), there is also a "standing fast in the Lord" (I Thess. 3:8; Phil. 4:1). As there are degrees of "faith" (see 1 above), so there are degrees of existence in Christ, such as "babes in Christ" (I Cor. 3:1), "approved in Christ" (Rom. 16:10), or "wise in Christ" (I Cor. 4:10).

The believer's existence as a member of the "body" of Christ (§ 34, 2), eschatological existence, in other words, while he lives "in the flesh" realizes itself in his "walk," his conduct, which is no longer a "walking according to the flesh" (Rom. 8:4; II Cor. 10:2; § 38). For to have died with Christ—as the believer has—means "that our old self was crucified with him so that the sinful body might be destroyed, and we might no longer be enslaved to sin" (Rom. 6:6). Or "those who belong to Christ Jesus have crucified the flesh with its passions and desires" (Gal. 5:24). Thus, Paul confesses of himself: "far be it from me to glory (boast) except in the cross of our Lord Jesus Christ, by which the world has been crucified to me, and I to the world" (Gal. 6:14). Correspondingly, he describes "gaining Christ and being found in him" as the state of being completely determined by the salvation-occurrence; for that is the force of the words: "that I may know him and the power of his resurrection, and may share his sufferings, becoming like him in his death" (Phil. 3:10). His meaning is the same when he says, "I have been crucified with Christ; it is no longer I who live, but Christ who lives in me" (Gal. 2:19f.). Christ's sufferings overflow upon the apostle (II Cor. 1:5); in his body he carries about the dying of Jesus (II Cor. 4:10). But what is true of the apostle only exemplifies what is true of all Christian existence: "we suffer with him (Christ) in order that we may also be glorified with him" (Rom. 8:17).

How this basic determination of one's life by the deed of salvation (or by faith) extends even to details is indicated by the manifold use of the formula "in Christ" or "in the Lord. These phrases fill the place of an adjective or adverb which the linguistic process had not yet developed: "Christian" or "as a Christian," "in a Christian manner." They are used to characterize all sorts of conduct and attitudes: speech (II Cor. 2:17; 12:19) and exhortation (Phil. 2:1), boldness (Phlm. 8) and greetings (Rom. 16:22; I Cor. 16:19), concord (Phil. 4:2), brotherly love (Rom. 16:8; I Cor. 16:24), and friendly reception (Rom. 16:2), as well as effort and concern for the congregation (I Thess. 5:12; Rom. 16:12). Not only what the believer does but also what happens to him has taken on the new stamp denoted by the phrase "in Christ": "in Christ" Paul's imprisonment has become known (Phil. 1:13); for the believer to die is to "fall asleep in Christ" (I Cor. 15:18), and the Church's dead are "the dead in Christ" (I Thess. 4:16). For "whether we live or whether we die, we are the Lord's" (Rom. 14:7-9).

§ 37. Faith as Eschatological Occurrence

Faith as response to the proclaimed word (which is called ἀκοή πίστεως, "preaching of faith"), like that word itself, is part of the salvation-occurrence, the eschatological occurrence. As new *possibility* faith is the newly opened way of salvation. It is in this sense that the "principle of faith" can be contrasted with the "principle of works" (Rom. 3:27). Faith can also be said to "come" and "to be revealed" (Gal. 3:23, 25).

This, of course, does not take from the concrete "faith" of the individual that decision-character which belongs to its very nature as "obedience" (§ 35, 1). Nevertheless the concrete realization of the possibility of faith in the individual's decision of faith is itself eschatological occurrence. Since the believer experiences the possibility of the faith-decision as grace, it is only as a gift of grace that he can understand his decision—his own decision! And because he knows that it is God who accomplishes his willing and doing—his concrete, historical existing in "faith"—he is conscious not of being relieved of responsibility for it but on the contrary of being made responsible for it (Phil. 2:13f.; § 35, 4).

Thus, Paul can say that faith in Christ is "granted" as a gift (Phil. 1:29). In fact, he can speak of it in downright predestinarian terms (Rom. 8:29; 9:6-29). If such statements about God's "foreknowing" and "predestining" or His "electing" and "hardening" be taken literally, an insoluble contradiction results, for a faith brought about by God outside of man's decision would obviously not be genuine obedience. Faith is God-wrought to the extent that prevenient grace first made the human decision possible, with the result that he who has made the decision can only understand it as God's gift; but that does not take its decision-character away from it. Only so does the imperative, "be reconciled to God" (II Cor. 5:20; § 31) make sense. The predestinarian statements express the fact that the decision of faith does not, like other decisions, go back to this-worldly motives of any sort whatever—that, on the contrary, such motives lose all power of motivation in the presence of the encountered proclamation.

The eschatological nature of faith is testified, lastly, by the fact that Paul does not describe faith as inspired, attributable to the "Spirit." * Just the opposite: The Spirit is the gift which faith receives (Gal. 3:2, 5, 14) and in which the grace of God appropriated by faith becomes effective in concrete living (§ 38, 3). Therefore, Paul calls the "love" (ἀγάπη) in which "faith" is operating the "fruit of the Spirit," just as he regards the Christian "virtues" as a whole to be such fruit (Gal. 5:22). A comparison between the parallel sentences Gal. 5:6 and 6:15: in Christ neither circumcision nor uncircumcision has any meaning, but (in the first case) "faith working through love" or (in the other case) "a new creation," reveals that the existing of a Christian in the faith that operates in love is eschatological occurrence: a being created anew.

D. FREEDOM

§ 38. Freedom from Sin and Walking in the Spirit

1. Faith's obedient submission to God's "grace," the acceptance of the cross of Christ, is the surrender of man's old understanding of himself, in which he lives "unto himself," tries to achieve life by his own strength, and by that very fact falls victim to the powers of sin

---

* In II Cor. 4:13 "Since we have the same spirit of faith . . . (so we speak)," "spirit of faith" does not mean the Spirit which bestows faith, but the spirit that is typical of faith. Ultimately "spirit of faith" here means "kind or sort of faith." When I Cor. 12:3 gives the cry, "Lord Jesus" as the criterion for possession by the Spirit, this does not intend to attribute the confession of faith to the Spirit, but to state the means by which spiritual and demonic ecstasy are to be distinguished.

and death and loses himself (§§ 23, 24). Therefore, "faith"—as "obedience of faith"—is also released from these powers. The new self-understanding which is bestowed with "faith" is that of *freedom,* in which the believer gains life and thereby his own self.

This freedom arises from the very fact that *the believer,* as one "ransomed," *no longer "belongs to himself"* (I Cor. 6:19). He no longer bears the care for himself, for his own life, but lets this care go, yielding himself entirely to the grace of God; he recognizes himself to be the property of God (or of the Lord) and lives for Him:

> "None of us lives to himself
> and none of us dies to himself.
> If we live, we live to the Lord,
> And if we die, we die to the Lord;
> So then, whether we live or whether we die,
> We are the Lord's."
> (Rom. 14:7f.; *cf.* 7:4; Gal. 2:19f.; II Cor. 5:14f.)

The mightiest expression of freedom is I Cor. 3:21-23:

> "For all things are yours . . .
> whether the world or life or death
> or the present or the future,
> all are yours."

But the concluding clauses are "and you are Christ's; and Christ is God's."

The life of him who is released from the power of death is no phenomenon of nature, either, but is the life of the striving, willing self which is always after something and is always faced with its various possibilities, but it is constantly faced with those two basic possibilities: to live "according to the flesh" or to live "according to the Spirit"—to and for one's self or to and for God or the Lord (§ 18, 4). This alternative also presents itself to the man of faith (Gal. 6:7f.; Rom. 8:12f.), and *the freedom to which he is set free* is not a "freedom (to be offered) as a base of operations to the flesh" (Gal. 5:13 tr.)—i.e. not a release from all binding norms, from the law of God, but rather a new servitude (Rom. 7:6), the service of the "living God" (I Thess. 1:9) or of Christ (Rom. 14:18; 16:18), an enslavement not to "sin" any longer, but to "righteousness" (Rom. 6:16-18). A paradoxical servitude! For the "slave of Christ" is, at the same time, "a freedman of Christ" (I Cor. 7:22). It will presently appear that this servitude is also a "serving of one another" (Gal. 5:13) and can demand that one make himself "a slave to all" (I Cor. 9:19). At any rate, the "obedience of faith" proves itself genuine when the believer places himself at God's disposal to obey Him (Rom. 6:16), and his members as "instruments of righteousness" (Rom. 6:12ff.); for "God condemned sin in the flesh, in order that the just requirement of the Law might be fulfilled" in the "walking according to the Spirit" which our "walking" has become (Rom. 8:3f.).

Neither is this freedom a mysterious emancipation from sin and death considered as powers of nature. It is not a decisionless capacity henceforth to do the good only—which would itself be a capacity of nature and hence also a supranatural compulsion. "Sinlessness" is not a magical guarantee against the *possibility* of sin—the believer, too, must beware of the "tempter" (I Thess. 3:5; I Cor. 7:5; II Cor. 2:11; § 26, 3)—but release from the *compulsion* of sin. Freedom from sin consists in the possibility, once flung away, of realizing the commandment's intent to bestow life (§ 27). That which to man is good—"life"—both before and after his emancipation is also that which is required of him (§ 19, 1; § 21, 1; § 27, 1). Therefore, freedom from death means possessing genuine future, whereas man under the power of death, as he formerly was, had no future (§ 24, 2).

Therefore, the *imperative*, "walk according to the Spirit," not only does not contradict the *indicative* of justification (the believer is rightwised) but results from it: "Cleanse out the old leaven that you may be fresh dough, as you really are unleavened" (I Cor. 5:7f.). In a certain sense, then, "Become what thou art!" is valid—but not in the sense of idealism, according to which the "idea" of the perfect man is more and more closely realized in endless progress. In this idealistic sense the transcendence of "perfection" is conceived as the "idea's" transcendence, and man's relation to it is regarded (Stoically expressed) as a "progressing" or a "tending" toward it. Rather, "sinlessness"—i.e. freedom from the power of sin —is already realized in the "righteousness of God" (§ 29, 2); its transcendence is that of the divine verdict, and man's relation to it is that of "obedience of faith." The way the believer becomes what he already is consists therefore in the constant appropriation of grace by faith, which also means, in the concrete, "obedience," which is henceforth possible in his "walking": "for sin will have no dominion over you, since you are not under law but under grace" (Rom. 6:14). Likewise, the indicatives "you were washed, you were consecrated" (I Cor. 6:11) are the motivation for the preceding exhortation. In Rom. 6, Paul develops this idea on a broad scale. He is opposing a purely sacramental understanding of baptism as the means by which one achieves assurance of a future life. He does so by showing that the life conferred by baptism must prove itself in the present by its freedom from the power of sin (§ 13, 1; p. 140; § 34, 3): "so you also must consider yourselves dead to sin and alive to God in Jesus Christ" (v. 11). Likewise, the imperative "walk by the Spirit" (Gal. 5:16ff.) concludes with the paradoxical statement, "If we live by the Spirit, let us also walk by the Spirit" (v. 25)—a sentence open to misunderstanding so far as it seems to imply that there could be a "living by the Spirit" without a "walking by the Spirit." But the purpose of this formulation is to avoid the opposite misunderstanding that there must first be a "walking by the Spirit" which would then establish this "living by the Spirit." The meaning is clear: the faith-bestowed possibility of "living by the Spirit" must be explicitly laid hold of by "walking by the Spirit." The indicative is the foundation for the imperative.

2. The believer has been given (in baptism) the *gift of the Spirit.* What that means is just this: He has been given freedom—freedom from the power of sin and death.

Paul, as a matter of course, shares the general Christian view that the Spirit is conferred by baptism (I Cor. 6:11; 12:13; II Cor. 1:22; § 13, 1, p. 139) and also the conception of the Spirit as a miraculous, divine power (Rom. 15:19; I Cor. 2:4, etc.; § 14, 1). In speaking of the Spirit, he uses animistic and dynamistic terminology promiscuously (p. 155), a fact which in itself indicates that he is unconcerned with any speculative interest in the idea of Spirit. Corresponding to a mode of thinking that is undeveloped in the direction of abstraction, locutions occur in which the Spirit is conceived as a non-worldly *material* or as borne by such. At least Paul can speak of the Spirit as a something that can take residence in a man (Rom. 8:9, 11; I Cor. 6:19), and therefore is bound to a locality. But such a locution is scarcely to be taken strictly, since it can also be used in reference to the congregation (I Cor. 3:16), in which case a conception strictly corresponding to the literal wording is inconceivable. Nevertheless, Paul's term "spiritual body" (I Cor. 15:44, 46) strongly suggests that Paul conceived of the Spirit as a material, just as the term "glory" (§ 14, 1; p. 156), closely related to that of Spirit, undoubtedly denotes a (heavenly) substance in I Cor. 15:40f. Moreover, though II Cor. 3:7 naively speaks of the externally visible brightness of "glory," still Paul's contrasting of the glory of the old and the new "covenant" (3:7ff.) indicates by itself that he does not stick to this conception; for the "greater splendor" of the "new covenant" is not visible at all, but is a power which demonstrates itself in its effect—and that is that it produces freedom. When Paul says of those who along with the Spirit of the Lord have received freedom: "we are being transformed from glory into glory . . ." (v. 18), it is clear that this present glory is no shining material. It is nothing other than the power by means of which the "inward self" (§ 18, 1) is renewed day by day (4:16); recall that "glory" and "power" can be synonymous (§ 14, 1; p. 156).

We may accordingly say that the sporadically occurring notion of the Spirit *as a material* is not one that is really determinative for Paul's concept of the Spirit. That is sufficiently indicated by Paul's characterization of the Law as "spiritual" (Rom. 7:14), where the notion of materiality is out of the question, but also by such constructions as "spiritual gift" (Rom. 1:11) and "to share in spiritual blessings" (Rom. 15:27; *cf.* I Cor. 9:11) or the contrast of "letter" to "Spirit" (Rom. 2:29; 7:6; II Cor. 3:6), or the description of mature Christians as being "spiritual" (I Cor. 2:13, 15; 3:1; Gal. 6:1). Then the true meaning of Paul's Spirit-concept must be reached in some other way.

The Spirit is the opposite of "flesh" (Gal. 5:16; 6:8; Rom. 8:4ff., etc.). As "flesh" is the quintessence of the worldly, visible, controllable, and transitory sphere which becomes the controlling power over the man who lives "according to the flesh" (§ 22), so "Spirit" is the quintessence of the non-worldly, invisible, uncontrollable, eternal sphere (p. 234) which becomes the controlling power for and in him who orients his life "according to the Spirit." And as the power of "flesh" is manifested in the fact that it binds man to the transitory, to that which in reality is always already past, binds him to death, so the power of the Spirit is manifested in the fact that it gives the believer freedom, opens up the future, the eternal, life.

For freedom is nothing else than being open for the genuine future, letting one's self be determined by the future. So Spirit may be called the power of futurity.

The expression of this conception is the fact that the Spirit is the eschatological gift: the "first-fruit" (Rom. 8:23), or the "guarantee" (II Cor. 1:22; 5:5). For such statements declare that the believer's life is determined by that future which is his origin and his strength as well as his norm—just as "glory" is ultimately the power that flows out of the opened future and determines the present (II Cor. 3:18). Therefore, the Spirit is also called "the Spirit of adoption to sonship" (Rom. 8:15; *cf.* Gal. 4:6; § 29, 3); by its receipt in baptism we are "rightwised" (I Cor. 6:11) and incorporated into the "body of Christ" (I Cor. 12:13; *cf.* Gal. 3:27f.). As the eschatological existence can be called a "being in Christ" (§ 34, 3), so it can also be called a "being in the Spirit" (Rom. 8:9), and the locutions "to have the spirit of Christ" or "Christ in you" (v. 9f.) can take its place with no difference in meaning. What Paul has done "in the power of the Spirit" Christ has wrought through him (Rom. 15:18), and "being minded according to Christ Jesus" (Rom. 15:5) corresponds antithetically to "being minded according to the flesh." The believer has freedom "in Christ" (Gal. 2:4); Christ has freed us for freedom (Gal. 5:1). On the other hand, commenting on "to the Lord" from Ex. 34:34, Paul can say, "now the Lord is the Spirit" and add "and where the Spirit of the Lord is, there is freedom" (II Cor. 3:17). As to the last phrase of v. 18, καθάπερ ἀπὸ κυρίου πνεύματος, it is hard to decide whether it means "from the Lord of the Spirit" or "from the Lord who is the Spirit"—not to mention other possibilities.

"To be in the Spirit" no more denotes the state of ecstasy than "to be in Christ" is a formula of mysticism. Though Paul is familiar with ecstatic experience as a rare exception (II Cor. 12:1-4; v. 2: "fourteen years ago"), the Spirit, nevertheless, does not mean to him the capacity for mystical experiences. Rather, everything indicates that by the term "Spirit" he means the eschatological existence into which the believer is placed by having appropriated the salvation deed that occurred in Christ. To have received the Spirit means to be standing in grace (Rom. 5:2); when II Cor. 1:12 contrasts behavior "in fleshly wisdom" with behavior in "the grace of God," the latter phrase is synonymous with "according to the Spirit." Hence, Paul can say to describe rhetorically the whole of the salvation-occurrence: "the grace of the Lord Jesus Christ and the love of God and the fellowship of the Holy Spirit" (II Cor. 13:13). Again, the fact that the future has been opened up by the Spirit on the basis of the divine deed of salvation is expressed in the reason given for the certainty of Christian hope: "because God's love (§ 32, 3) has been poured into our hearts through the Holy Spirit which has been given to us" (Rom. 5:5).

3. There is a peculiar double meaning about the term "Spirit," because it can denote both the miraculous power that is bestowed upon the man of faith and is the source of his new life, and also the norm of his earthly "walk." This is the same paradox as in that utterance of Gal. 5:25: "If we live by the Spirit, let us also walk by the Spirit"—in which the first "Spirit" means the power, the second the norm, for it stands in place of a κατὰ πνεῦμα ("according to the Spirit," as in 5:16). The primary idea is that of the miraculous power of God; then, since it has the effect of emancipating from the power of sin and death (Rom. 8:2)—i.e. it grants freedom of action and opens up the possibility of "reaping eternal life" (Gal. 6:8)—it is also the norm for "walking." The newly opened possibility of laying hold of "life" by its very nature contains the ethical imperative (see 1, above). Freedom and demand constitute a unity: Freedom is the reason for the demand, and the demand actualizes the freedom. Only when this unity is understood, is Paul's thought of the Spirit understood aright—and that means: when the Spirit is conceived of not as a mysterious power working with magical compulsion but as the new possibility of genuine, human life which opens up to him who has surrendered his old understanding of himself, letting himself be crucified with Christ, in order to experience the "power of his resurrection" (Phil. 3:10). For it is clear that to be "led by the Spirit" (Rom. 8:14; Gal. 5:18) does not mean to be dragged along willy-nilly (cf. I Cor. 12:2) but directly presupposes decision in the alternative: "flesh" or "Spirit" (Rom. 8:12–14; Gal. 5:16–18). That unity of power and demand is likewise hidden in those seemingly mythological expressions, "the mind of the Spirit" (Rom. 8:6, 27) and the "desires of the Spirit" (Gal. 5:17; § 18, 3), for these expressions mean that the Spirit founds a new will, whose origin is not within man but within the salvation-deed of God—a will that has definite direction, free from the "flesh" and in battle against it, guided by the demand of God. Therein lies the solution of the con-

tradition that the Spirit is, on the one hand, the gift conferred upon all Christians at baptism and that, on the other hand, it shows its operation in special deeds (§ 14, 3). For, on the one hand, along with faith the possibility of eschatological existence is given to all, and, on the other hand, this possibility must actualize itself in the concrete deed from case to case.

In the view that the "Spirit" is miraculous power, Paul, it must first be said, simply shares without reflection popular notions, according to which "miraculous" events—i.e. strange phenomena that fall outside the frame of normal life—are regarded as spirit-wrought: glossolalia, prophecy, miracles of healing, etc. (§ 14, 1). Indirectly, however, he is already contesting the allegedly obvious meaning of such phenomena when he only so far recognizes them to be caused by the Spirit of God as they produce unity in the congregation—having themselves ·unity of origin in "the same Spirit" (I Cor. 12:4–6)—and serve for the "edification" of the congregation (I Cor. 12 and 14). The really characteristic feature of his conception of the Spirit, however, is the fact that he reckons the ministrations of love within the congregation among the Spirit's workings, an idea evidently foreign to the popular view (§ 14, 1 and 3; § 36, 1), and the further fact that he attributes ethical conduct to the Spirit (Rom. 8:4–9). The Spirit is at war with the "flesh" (Gal. 5:17), and the "virtues" (Gal. 5:22; *cf.* Rom. 14:17) are the "fruit" of the Spirit. This is no spiritualizing, ethicizing re-interpretation of the "Spirit" concept. It means that free, ethical obedience can have its origin only in miracle—quite in keeping with the view that from the fetters of flesh and sin man must be freed to obedience by the deed of God.

In respect to its meaning freedom from death and the source and power of the life to come, "Spirit" will come up for further discussion. So far as it produces freedom from sin and is the source and power as well as the norm of present conduct, those statements are characteristic in which *conduct* is described by such locutions as: "serve . . . in the newness (καινότητι) of the Spirit" (Rom. 7:6), "walk by the Spirit" (Gal. 5:16) or "be guided" (στοιχεῖν) (Gal. 5:25) by it, or "walk according to the Spirit" (Rom. 8:4), "be in the Spirit" (Rom. 8:5), "set the mind on the things of the Spirit" (Rom. 8:5); likewise the expression "Spirit of gentleness" (I Cor. 4:21; Gal. 6:1—semitizing for: the gentle Spirit) and "the love of the Spirit" (Rom. 15:30). Since λογικός ("reasonable," KJ Rom. 12:1f.), following Hellenistic usage, has for Paul the meaning "spiritual," the λογική λατρεία ("spiritual worship" RSV) which has its foundation in the renewal of the νοῦς—i.e. of one's "character" (§ 19, 1)—and results in "proving what is the good and acceptable and perfect will of God," is only another expression for the same thing. Also characteristic, lastly, is the fact that the Spirit is received by the "heart" (Gal. 4:6; II Cor. 1:22; Rom. 5:5; *cf.* 8:27), i.e. is taken up into the will of man (§ 20); and also the fact that Paul describes his "conscience" as speaking "in the Holy Spirit" (Rom. 9:1).

Other descriptions of the Christian "walk," though not explicitly using the word "spirit," express substantially the same thing: the power and the obligation given when one is brought into eschatological existence—the Christian must walk "becomingly as in the day" (Rom. 13:13), "worthily of God who calls you into his own kingdom and glory" (I Thess. 2:12), "according to love" (Rom. 14:15). Where such conduct has its origin is betrayed by the characterization of the opposite kind as a "walking according to man," which is coordinate with being "of the flesh" (I Cor. 3:3).

The Spirit is the "Holy Spirit," πνεῦμα ἅγιον, and the use of the holiness-concept is likewise significant for the unity of the indicative and the imperative—i.e. of power and obligation. Believers are ἅγιοι, ἡγιασμένοι ("holy," "made holy"—though English translations through the influence of the Vulgate conventionally render the first "saints" and the second "sanctified" or "consecrated"—§ 10, 3), which means in the first place those who have been taken out of the world and transplanted into the eschatological existence by Christ's salvation-deed (I Cor. 1:2: as those "made holy in Christ Jesus") which in baptism was carried over to them (I Cor. 6:11: "but you were washed, you were made holy," etc.). Christ is to us "righteousness and consecration and redemption" (abstract expression for the concrete: "he who makes us righteous and holy and redeemed" I Cor. 1:30). But from this very fact arises our obligation to the active "holiness" which God demands of us (I Thess. 4:3; Rom. 6:19, 22); whoever disregards this demand disregards God who gave us His Holy Spirit (I Thess. 4:8). Our body is the Holy Spirit's temple, which must be kept clean (I Cor. 6:19). The congregation also is the holy temple of God, and God will destroy the destroyer of this temple (I Cor. 3:16f.). Similar are

Paul's wishes that God, or the Lord, may establish believers' hearts "unblamable in holiness" and utterly sanctify them (I Thess. 3:13; 5:23). The bestowal of holiness through baptism can be called "putting on Christ"; but in addition to the indicative, "you have put on Christ" (Gal. 3:27), we also find the imperative: "put on the Lord Jesus Christ" (Rom. 13:14).

4. It may seem strange that in the list of virtues at Gal. 5:22f. "joy" appears as a fruit of the Spirit second only to "love." But "joy" actually is one of the qualities of the eschatological existence founded by the Spirit, for the nature of the Reign of God is "righteousness and joy and peace in the Holy Spirit" (Rom. 14:17). The combination of "joy" and "peace" occurring here and elsewhere (Gal. 5:22; Rom. 15:13) permits us to recognize "joy," too, as an eschatological phenomenon, for "peace" here means "salvation" in the eschatological sense, as Rom. 2:10; 8:6 (joined with "life"!) indicate, or the wish at Phil. 4:7, or the formula "the God of peace" (Rom. 15:33; 16:20; Phil. 4:9; I Thess. 5:23).*

The believer's existence, being eschatological, is an existence in joy. Paul hopes that he may yet work for the congregation in Philippi "for your progress and joy in the faith" (Phil. 1:25); to the Corinthian congregation he wants to be only a "fellow-worker for your joy" (II Cor. 1:24); his wish for the Romans is: "May the God of hope fill you with all joy and peace in believing" (Rom. 15:13). When God is called "the God of hope" in this wish, it is clear that the joy of the present is based upon the reference of Christian existence to the future; "rejoicing in hope" is one of the characteristics of believers (Rom. 12:12). Indeed, this joy, which is not a joy over anything within this world, is itself the Christian's relatedness to the future, insofar as it is consciously realized. And he *should* be conscious of it: hence, Paul's exhortations to be joyful (I Thess. 5:16; II Cor. 13:11 [English tradition here renders it "farewell"; but do ancient letters confirm this as a *closing* formula?] Phil. 3:1; 4:4). This is a joy that wells up in the midst of worldly tribulation (II Cor. 6:10) as a "joy inspired by the Holy Spirit" (I Thess. 1:6).

Such eschatological joy actualizes itself furthermore in the fel-

---

* Of course, εἰρήνη can retain its root-meaning, "peace." This specific meaning is demanded by the context in II Cor. 13:11; it also occurs at Rom. 5:1; I Cor. 14:33. The succession of Rom. 14:19 upon 14:17 indicates how closely related these two meanings are.

lowship and mutual helpfulness of those whom it binds together. It is right and proper that the apostle or the congregation should cause the other joy or rejoice in the other (II Cor. 1:15?; 2:3; Rom. 15:32; 16:19; Phil. 2:2, 17f.; 4:1, 10; I Thess. 2:19; 3:9) or give each other reciprocal joy (II Cor. 8:2) or rejoice with each other (Rom. 12:15).

§ 39. Freedom from the Law and the Christian's Attitude toward Men

1. The "power of sin" is "the Law" (I Cor. 15:56; § 27, 2)—or rather, for believers: it was. For to them Christ is the "end of the law" (Rom. 10:4); "in him" or "through him" we have freedom from the Law (Gal. 2:4). For freedom he set us free (Gal. 5:1); to it we were "called" (Gal. 5:13). The Christian Church is the Congregation of the free, while Judaism is under bondage to the Law, as the Sarah-Hagar allegory (Gal. 4:21–31) sets forth. The old period of the "custodian's" restraint lies in the past; the man who once held the position of a slave under the Law has been set free, to be no longer a ward; now he has the rights of a son (Gal. 3:23–4:7). The "old covenant" and the "ministration of death" and "of condemnation" which "faded away" have been replaced by the "new covenant" and the "ministration of the Spirit" and "of righteousness" which is "permanent" (II Cor. 3:6–11).

Since "flesh" has been condemned by the salvation-occurrence, sin has been condemned with it, for God "condemned sin in the flesh" (Rom. 8:3). For it is in the "flesh" that sin had its origin (§ 22, 3; § 23) and it was awakened in the flesh by the Law (§ 27, 2). Since the power of sin is destroyed for those who share in the salvation-deed of the cross (Gal. 5:24), for them the Law, and hence also sin, have both lost their power: "for sin will have no dominion over you, since you are not under law but under grace" (Rom. 6:14). "When we were living in the flesh, there worked in our members the sinful passions aroused by the law, so that we bore fruit for death. But now we are free of the law, dead to that by which we were fettered, so that we serve in the new Spirit and not in the old letter" (Rom. 7:5f.). As those who are "led by the Spirit" (Gal. 5:18), believers are no longer under the Law, and so far as they produce the fruit of the Spirit Paul says: "against such people there is no law" (Gal. 5:23). That is the reason for Paul's struggle against the Judaizers in Galatia and for his exhortation to those freed by Christ: "stand fast, therefore, and do not submit again to a yoke of slavery" (Gal. 5:1).

It is clear that Christ is the end of the Law so far as it claimed to be the way to salvation or was understood by man as the means of establishing "his own righteousness" (§ 23, 1; § 27, 2), for *so far as it contains God's demand* (§ 27, 2), *it retains its validity.* Of course, it is self-evident that so far as the νόμος of God is represented to Paul's mind by the Old Testament Torah with all its cultic and ritual rules (§ 27, 1), it cannot be valid in its whole extent. Paul's struggle in Galatia against the Law as the way to salvation is simultaneously a struggle against the ritual and cultic rules, particularly against circumcision and the Jewish festivals (Gal. 4:10). Where Paul calls the Law "holy" and "spiritual" (Rom. 7:12, 14) he is thinking only of the ethical commandments summarized in the formula, "you shall not desire" (v. 7)—likewise where he calls "love" the fulfilment of the Law (Gal. 5:14; Rom. 13:9f.; *cf.* § 27, 1). Then, however, freedom from the Law also actualizes itself in the freedom to differentiate between the valid and the non-valid, according to its content, within the Law as it has been handed down. Paul did not work out this problem in detail, but the obligation to practice such criticism is contained in the capacity of "proving what is the good and acceptable and perfect will of God" (Rom. 12:2) or of "approving what is excellent" (i.e. "distinguishing what is important"—Phil. 1:10).

2. Freedom from the Law, therefore, has a dialectic or paradoxical character: freedom from its demand and obligation to it nonetheless—depending upon the sense in which the demand is understood. This freedom can find expression in the formula, "All things are lawful for me" (I Cor. 6:12; 10:23), which was evidently a slogan of the Gnosticizing Christians in Corinth (§ 15, 4f.). Paul approves of it, but when he adds: "but not all things are wholesome (tr.) . . . but I will not be enslaved by anything," the ambiguity of the formula becomes apparent: It is to be rejected so far as it asserts that man is released from all obligations and that his subjective caprice is given free rein. If this were true, then this principle would have the consequence hinted at in the words, "but I will not be enslaved by anything," viz.: that man would fall into

subjection to whatever exercises motivating power upon his personal choice. "All things are lawful for me" in its true sense has for its presupposition inner freedom from the world, a freedom in which all claims from within the world have lost their motivating power and all worldly things and situations have sunk down into indifference. This freedom, however, arises precisely out of the believer's binding obligation to the Lord or to God: "for you are not your own" (I Cor. 6:19; § 38, 1). The sense, then, in which the reservation "not all things are wholesome" limits the principle that "all things are lawful for me" is not that within the field of "all things" there is this or that which is "not wholesome," for "nothing is unclean in itself" (Rom. 14:14) and "all things are clean" (14:20). It does assert, however, that the whole field of "all things" becomes "an unwholesome thing" as soon as I lose my freedom to anything whatever in which that field encounters me. The indifference of everything worldly disappears in the concrete situation of personal responsibility.

But this situation receives its stamp not alone from the demands that apply to the individual by himself, such as that of chastity (I Cor. 6:12ff.), but especially from the obligations that arise from human fellowship. In this respect "all things are lawful for me" is restricted by the limitation (I Cor. 10:23b): "but not all things build up"—some things do not contribute to building up fellowship. This limitation is also given in positive form: "let no one seek his own good, but the good of his neighbor" (I Cor. 10:24). Neither does that mean a quantitative diminution of "all things"; it does mean that this basic freedom may at any moment take on the form of *renunciation*—seemingly a renunciation of freedom itself, but in reality it is a paradoxical exercise of that very freedom, such as is expressed in Paul's declaration, "for though I am free from all men, I have made myself a slave to all" (I Cor. 9:19). Out of Christian "freedom" flows *"authorization"* (ἐξουσία), which is expressed in "all things are lawful for me" (which could just as well be translated: "for me all things are authorized"). This authorization is the Christian's independence from all worldly claims, among which are the ritual and cultic rules of the Torah. It is the authorization, or the right, to find for one's self, by that independent "proving," what the "good" is—and hence, is also independence from the judgment of any other person's conscience (I Cor. 10:29b; *cf.* Rom. 14:5). In this respect, of course, there can be no waiving of "authorization"; for in this respect it is "freedom" itself. But so far as "authorization" is regarded as a personal right to inconsiderate exercise of "freedom," Paul distinguishes between it and "freedom": the latter manifests itself, in case consideration for one's brother demands it, precisely in waiving "authorization" as a personal right. As a personal right it would no longer be Christian freedom but a legal claim, which higher purposes naturally may demand that one give up, as Paul makes clear by his own waiver of the apostle's right to support by the churches (I Cor. 9:1–23). Exercise of freedom in this sense is just what is being demanded when Paul urges: "take care lest this liberty (authorization) of yours somehow become a stumbling-block to the weak" (I Cor. 8:9; *cf.* Rom. 14:13). He is perfectly willing to give up what in principle is completely permissible to him, if enjoyment of it would be a cause of offense to his brother (I Cor. 8:13; *cf.* Rom. 14:21). However, it is clear, as the letter to the Galatians shows, that this consideration must be dropped in the situation of witness-bearing to one's faith—whenever, that is, it would expose itself to being misunderstood as the surrender of "freedom." Only as the exercise of freedom for a brother's sake does consideration have validity, but as that it is demanded of the Christian.

Consideration for one's brother does not mean dependence upon his judgment (I Cor. 10:29b; Rom. 14:5). On the contrary, Christian freedom is *freedom from all human conventions and norms of value*. The social distinctions of freedom and slavery as well as those of sex and race have lost their significance "in Christ" (Gal. 3:28; I Cor. 12:13) and "do not become slaves of men" (I Cor. 7:23) applies to all desires for emancipation, for they stem from human evaluations. The Christian, then, is free from all men, and yet there is a proper subjection of himself as "slave to all" (I Cor. 9:19) and the imperative, "be servants of one another" (Gal. 5:13) still stands. Here again, however, this is no surrender of freedom, but precisely the exercise of it.

3. "Be servants of one another" does not stand alone but has the modifier "through love," which gives it its character. For the believer has the freedom that is his as a "slave" of the "Lord" (§ 38, 1), and he who is "not under the law himself" has become a slave "to those under the law" and "to those outside the law" as "one outside the law" because he is within "the law of Christ" (I Cor. 9:20f.). And

the "law of Christ" (Gal. 6:2) is *the demand that one love.* The "bearing" of "one another's burdens" which Paul terms the fulfilling of this "law," is nothing else than a manifestation of being "servants of one another through love." It is love (ἀγάπη) which builds up the congregation and hence requires the waiving of one's "authorization" or "right" (I Cor. 8:1; Rom. 14:15). It is love that requires the Christian not to "seek his own good, but the good of his neighbor" (I Cor. 10:24; 13:5). Love is the fulfilment of the Law. whose demands are summed up in "You shall love your neighbor as yourself" (Rom. 13:8-10; Gal. 5:14).

Such fulfilling of the law, however, is no "work" in the sense of meritorious accomplishment, but is a deed done in freedom. To perform this deed of love believers are "God-taught" (ϑεοδίδακτοι, I Thess. 4:9). Love, then, is an eschatological phenomenon; in it the faith which transplants men into eschatological existence is at work (Gal. 5:6). Love, as sheer existence for one's neighbor, is possible only to him who is free from himself—i.e. to him who has died with Christ, to live no longer for himself but for him who for his sake died and was raised (II Cor. 5:15) and hence is obedient to the "law of Christ," the love commandment. Placing the parallel statements of I Cor. 7:19; Gal. 5:6; and 6:15 side by side makes clear the nature of "love": for the man of faith the characteristics "circumcision" and "uncircumcision," which once determined a man's classification, have sunk into insignificance; all that now matters is "keeping the commandments of God" (I Cor. 7:19)—or, in the second case, "faith working through love"—or, in the third case, "a new creation." That is, God's demand is for love; it becomes real as the manifestation of faith in living, and it is just in this that eschatological existence becomes reality; this existence, moreover—the "new creation"—is to be found only "in Christ" (II Cor. 5:17). Love is also designated as an eschatological phenomenon by the fact that it is the primary fruit of the Spirit (Gal. 5:22). Though Paul lists other fruits after it, I Cor. 13 shows that love really cannot be regarded as just one of the Spirit's gifts by the side of others. This chapter calls it the "still more excellent way," the way that exceeds all other "gifts" and without which all the others are nothing. Though all the Spirit's other gifts will disappear when "that which is perfect" comes, yet love, like faith and hope, will abide—and not only abide, but will be the greatest of the three. It can be called nothing less because in it the possibility opened up by "faith" and "hope" becomes reality in concrete existence.

A special phase of *agape* is *"humility"* (ταπεινοφροσύνη). Phil. 2:3, representing Christ as the example of it, is an exhortation to it. It is described as "each counting the other better than himself," a parallel formulation to Rom. 12:10: "in honor preferring one another" (KJ). This "humility" does not mean a "disposition" of soul nor man's relation to God, as II Cor. 7:6, for instance, does, but means man's relation to men. Humility pays heed to their claim and does not insist upon pushing through one's own claims: "looking not to one's own interests, but each one looking to the interests of others" (Phil. 2:4; *cf.* I Cor. 10:24; 13:5). Humility, therefore, is a form of love. Its special character is indicated by the fact that it is placed in contrast with ἐριθεία (self-seeking, egoism) and κενοδοξία (conceit, egotism). Its opposite is "haughtiness," which looks down upon others and "boasts"—the attitude against which Gal. 6:3 warns: "For if anyone thinks he is something, when he is nothing, he deceives himself. But let each one test his own work, and then his reason to boast will be in himself alone and not in his neighbor." All such comparing of one's self with others and all judging of one's neighbor (II Cor. 10:12–18; Rom. 14:4, 10, 12f., 22) has ceased in "love."

§ 40. Freedom from Death

1. Freedom from the Law and sin is also freedom from death, for death is the "wage" and the "fruit" of sin (Rom. 6:23; 7:5; etc.; § 24). The believer, having died with Christ, also shares in his resurrection. Paul expresses this in language that stems from the mystery religions and Gnosticism (§ 33, 3d, e) in order to say: By faith in the word in which the risen Christ himself speaks to him, man lets the resurrection of Christ, like his cross, become the power that henceforth determines his life (§ 33, 6c). He now no longer lives—so Paul can paradoxically say—but in him Christ lives (Gal. 2:19).

However, Paul differs from the view prevalent in the mysteries and Gnosticism in not understanding the "life" thus mediated by Christ as a power, like those of nature, infused into man, a power of immortality which has become the property of the soul (or of the innermost self), and by means of which, after the death of the body, the soul soars into the sphere of divine blessedness, the heavenly world of light. Instead, he holds fast to the traditional Jewish-Christian teaching of *the resurrection of the dead*, and in so doing he also retains the apocalyptic expectation of the last judgment and of the cosmic drama which will end the old world and introduce the new world of salvation, "that which is perfect" (I Cor. 13:10). He expects the "day" (or the "coming"—*parousia*) of the "Lord" (I Cor. 1:8; 5:5; 15:23; II Cor. 1:14; Phil. 1:6, 10; 2:16; I Thess. 2:19; 3:13; 4:15; 5:2, 23) which will also be the end of his reign, which began with the resurrection, and the dawn of the period of salvation, in which God will be all in all (I Cor. 15: 24-27).

The form of imagery in which Paul expresses the view that "life" has a future beyond the death of the body is that of the Jewish-Christian tradition (§9, 3; p. 77): *the resurrection of the dead*. Paul presents this teaching, strange to Hellenistic ears, in I Thess. 4:13-17 and defends it at length in I Cor. 15. The details in his picture of the cosmic drama have no theological importance. But it is important that Paul, in contrast to Jewish apocalypticism and Gnostic mythology, refrains from depicting the condition of the resurrection life, for a complex of future conditions could only be painted on analogy with earthly life, as an ideal picture of earthly life, and that would directly contradict the character of the future as that which is "not seen" (II Cor. 4:18). So Paul goes no further than to speak generally of the "glory" that is to be revealed (Rom. 8:18; II Cor. 4:17) or of "being with Christ," which will then begin (I Thess. 4:17; 5:10; Phil. 1:23; II Cor. 5:7f.). "Walking by sight" (II Cor. 5:7) will then take the place of "walking by faith." What we now behold is only a mirrored image full of riddles; then we shall see "face to face." "Now I know in part; then I shall understand fully, even as I have been fully understood" (I Cor. 13:12). Indeed, Paul actually gets into contradiction with the resurrection doctrine when he hopes in Phil. 1:23 that his "being with Christ" will begin immediately after his death. (As to II Cor. 5:1ff., where many interpreters find the same view expressed, see §17, 3). This contradiction betrays how little difference it makes what images are used to express the fact that "life" has a future beyond life in the "flesh."

As resurrection-life beyond bodily death, "life," then, is a future thing yet to come. In Rom. 5:1–11, Paul has to defend his thesis that eschatological righteousness is already present, against the objection that the other signs of eschatological salvation are not yet to be seen. Hence, he also has to point out that "life" is already bestowed upon the rightwised (§ 29, 4). When he does this, he first does it by speaking of "life" as a thing of the future which determines the present as only a "hope of the glory of God"—but such a hope, be it noted, as "does not disappoint," for its foundation is the Spirit-given knowledge of God's "love."

This present time in which we "live" and "walk in the flesh" (§ 22, 3) is, of course, no "glory"-present yet, but one of "tribulations" and "sufferings"; the resurrection life with its "eternal weight of glory" is yet to come (II Cor. 4:17; Rom. 8:18). Even believers still groan in "bondage to decay" (Rom. 8:21), in the earthly body (II Cor. 5:1ff.) and long for their heavenly one, "the spiritual body" or "the glory-body" (I Cor. 15:44; Phil. 3:21). "In hope we were saved" (Rom. 8:24; § 35, 3), and we now lead our lives only "by faith", not yet "by sight" (II Cor. 5:7; cf. I Cor. 13:12); being far from the Lord, we long to be united with him (II Cor. 5:6, 8; Phil. 1:21, 23). The cosmic drama which will bring "redemption of the body" (Rom. 8:23) has, nevertheless, already begun with the resurrection of Christ, and the consummation lies near ahead (I Thess. 4:15; I Cor. 15:51; cf. Rom. 13:11f.). Christ is the "first fruit of them that sleep" and those who believe in him will follow him, but "each in his own order," and not until the coming of Christ at the end of the world will death be destroyed as the "last enemy" (I Cor. 15:20–27).

Nevertheless, it is to be noted that Paul's recourse to the Gnostic proto-man idea (Rom. 5:12–21; § 15, 4d), in order to prove that "life" is bestowed upon the rightwised, shows that the futurity of "life" and "glory" is not conceived simply according to the scheme of Jewish eschatology as a mere contrast between Now and Then. As Adam brought death upon Adamitic mankind, so Christ brought life for the new mankind; in him it is already present even though it will not actualize itself for the believer until the future (v. 17, 21). Life is already here; for Christ's resurrection is conceived not just as the first case of rising from the dead, but as the origin of the resurrection life of all believers, which necessarily proceeds from it and hence can be regarded as already present in its origin. Also in I Cor. 15:12–16 the logic of the argument is not that the possibility of any resurrection is proved by *one* case of resurrection such as demonstrably occurred with Christ; rather, the resurrection of all believers is comprised in that of Christ, which is the origin of theirs, as v. 21f. clearly shows. A disciple of Paul discovered a fitting formulation for this idea: "for you have died, and your life is hid with Christ in God . . ." (Col. 3:3f.). Paul himself formulates it more paradoxically when he says: "it is no longer I who live, but Christ who lives in me" (Gal. 2:20).

2. Thus, in a certain sense, *"life" is a present thing after all*—present to hoping faith, though not as an "experience" in the life of the soul. For in baptism, too, which also brings participation in Christ's death and resurrection, the important thing is not what takes place in the soul. What it really is, is the bestowal of the salvation-occurrence and the appropriation of it by the faith of him who in it confesses his faith (§ 34, 3); accordingly, Rom. 6:8 characterizes the "life" mediated by that sacrament as a life to come: "but if we have died with Christ, we believe that we shall also live with him." Nevertheless, "life" already actualizes itself in the present, for he who is baptized has received the gift of the Spirit as the "firstfruit" or "guarantee" of future salvation (Rom. 8:23; II Cor. 1:22; 5:5). Thanks to this gift his hope will not disappoint him (Rom. 5:5); thanks to this gift—and here Paul approaches the manner of thinking found in the mysteries and Gnosticism—our future resurrection is certain (Rom. 8:11). The Spirit proves itself the ruling power of the present, however, in the fact that the latter is determined by the future. The Spirit is both the norm and the source and power of the Christian's new "walk" (§ 38, 2–3). "Life" is a present reality in the Christian's openness for the future and in his being determined by it. For the person one used to be is crucified with Christ; his *"soma* of sin" (his sin-ruled self) is destroyed, the "world" for him no longer exists (Rom. 6:6; 7:4–6; Gal. 5:24; 6:14); he is a "new creation," for "the old has passed away, behold, the new has come" (II Cor. 5:17). Hence, the exhortation: "consider yourselves dead to sin and alive to God in Christ Jesus . . . yield yourselves to God as men who have been brought from death to life" (Rom. 6:11, 13). Like "life," so is "glory" a thing of the present, so that Paul can say of God in bold anticipation: "and those whom he justified (right-

wised) he also glorified" (Rom. 8:30). Hence, the believer's life can be described not only as a daily renewal of our inner nature (II Cor. 4:16) but also as a transformation "from glory to glory" (II Cor. 3:18; § 38, 2).

Not alone in "walking" by the power and according to the norm of the Spirit does that future "life" make itself known as present— it also does so powerfully in *triumph over suffering*. Paul is as little concerned with theodicy as the rest of the New Testament is. Suffering in its implications for the present condition of this world does not need to be justified or defended, because this world is the old aeon hastening toward its end and under the dominion of death; therefore one of its essential qualities is suffering, in which death, ever future, is, nevertheless, always at work in the present, for it is the power behind transitoriness. So the real problem for early Christian thinking is not suffering but death. But for the believer this problem is solved by Christ's victory over death, which the believer, having died with 'Christ, shares. Therein he has won a new understanding of suffering, by which he becomes master over it—but since it flows out of his new understanding of himself it does not, of course, lay bare to him the cosmic meaning of suffering in general, but in the suffering that strikes his own person he finds a question addressed to himself and a new possibility of his life. The dominion of death which makes itself known in suffering (II Cor. 4:12), the transitoriness of everything earthly—"for the things that are seen are transient" (II Cor. 4:18)—all this warns him not to let himself get bound to the world by desire and care—"for the *schema* of this world (= this world itself) is passing away" (I Cor. 7:31)—and compels him to focus his gaze on the "things that are unseen, eternal" (II Cor. 4:18).

Suffering, which makes man aware of his weakness and insignificance, becomes a compulsion, indeed a help, to the believer, who, in the "obedience of faith" (§ 35, 1), has basically renounced his own strength to make real this renunciation and his radical surrender to "grace" in concrete living. In the face of threatening death, Paul learns to pronounce the death-verdict over himself, "in order that we should not rely upon ourselves but on God who raises the dead" (II Cor. 1:9 tr.). The treasure of grace bestowed upon him he carries in an earthen vessel, "in order that the transcendent power may be from God and not from us" (II Cor. 4:7); and lest he should

get haughty, he was struck with a bodily ailment (II Cor. 12:7).
Though at first he struggled against it, he was permitted to hear
the voice of the Lord saying: "My grace is sufficient for you; for
power comes in weakness to perfection" (II Cor. 12:8 Blt.). So he
wants to boast of his very weaknesses in order that the power of
Christ may come over him; so, for Christ's sake, he accepts whatever
sort of sufferings may strike him, "for when I am weak, then I am
strong" (II Cor. 12:9f.). This strength Paul illustrates in the following antitheses:

> "When reviled, we bless;
> when persecuted, we endure;
> when slandered, we try to conciliate." (I Cor. 4:12f.)
> ". . . as impostors, and yet true;
> as unknown, and yet well known;
> as dying, and behold we live;
> as punished, and yet not killed;
> as sorrowful, yet always rejoicing;
> as poor, yet making many rich;
> as having nothing, and yet possessing everything."
>   (II Cor. 6:9f.)

In such acceptance of sufferings, the believer, as one "who is
made like him (Christ) in his death," concretely experiences the
"fellowship of his sufferings" (Phil. 3:10). The traces of past sufferings which he bears on his body are to him the "marks of Jesus"
(Gal. 6:17). To stand with such an understanding in the storm of
sufferings means nothing else than to bear about in one's own body
the dying of Jesus in order that the life of Jesus may be manifested
in one's own body (II Cor. 4:10f.). As Christ was "crucified in
weakness," so it is true of Paul: "we are weak in him." As Christ
"lives by the power of God," so the apostle: "we live with him by
the power of God"—and so live "for you" (II Cor. 13:4); for "fellowship" with Christ is also "fellowship" with all who belong to his
soma (I Cor. 12:25f.)—which means, thinking gnostically, all who
are related to Christ by having a common origin with him. To Paul,
though, it is a relationship of concretely living for each other, in
which what happens to one cannot but be full of consequence to the
other. Through the "fellowship of suffering," the sufferer is released

from the loneliness of his suffering. The sufferings of Christ overflow abundantly upon Paul, in order that he, comforted by Christ, may also comfort others (II Cor. 1:5–7). If death is at work in him, it is in order that life may be at work in others (II Cor. 4:12–13).

It is clear that the "fellowship of suffering" does not mean simply the historical relationship of follower and master which leads the follower of Jesus into suffering. It means the bond with Christ which takes place in faith, conceived in the cosmological terminology of Gnosticism (§ 33, 3e), but factually accomplished by the decision of faith. Nor is this "fellowship" artificially induced by an *imitatio Christi*—furthermore, it is by no means restricted to those sufferings into which one is led by following Christ, whether one's specific following be that of the apostolic office or simply that of confessing faith. Rather, it comprises all the sufferings which strike man, such as the physical affliction of Paul (II Cor. 12:7). Paul's dictum "for power comes in weakness to perfection" (II Cor. 12:9) is spoken as a basic principle and holds true for any "weakness." Moreover, it is mistaken to speak of this as "passion-mysticism." For this "fellowship" or "sharing" does not take place in absorbed meditation on the passion or in the soulful appropriation of Christ's suffering in mystical experience (the "marks of Jesus" are visible on Paul's body—his battle-scars as a soldier of Christ!). It does take place in the understanding of suffering learned beneath the cross. In that understanding, sufferings are overcome and become things to boast of. The believer's sufferings have become transparent to him as the process in which that "crucifixion" takes place by which the "world" sinks into insignificance for him.

Given freedom from death, *freedom from the world and its powers* (§ 26) are also given. The man of faith is freed from the care of one who relies upon himself, has the world (supposedly) at his disposal, and yet is its victim (§ 23, 3). He knows only one care, "how he may please the Lord" (I Cor. 7:32) and only one ambition: "to please the Lord" (II Cor. 5:9). Free from the world's care which binds one to perishing things, free from "worldly grief" which produces death (II Cor. 7:10), he faces the world free, as one who rejoices with those who rejoice and weeps with those who weep (Rom. 12:15), one who participates in the tumult of the world but does so with an inner aloofness—"as if (he did it) not":

"let those who have wives be as if they had not,
and those who mourn as if they mourned not,
and those who rejoice as if they rejoiced not,
and those who buy as if they possessed not,
and those who have to do with the world as if they
　　　had nothing to do with it."
　　　　　　　　　(I Cor. 7:29–31 tr.)

—in other words, as a free man. So Paul can boast: "for I have learned in whatever state I am to be content. I know both how to be abased and how to abound; to any and all circumstances I am initiate: to be full and to hunger, to have abundance and to be in want. I can endure anything in him who is my inward power" (Phil. 4:11–13 tr.).

Since neither life nor death can separate us from the love of God in Christ (Rom. 8:38), since in life as in death we belong to Christ (Rom. 14:7–9), then life and death as we know them as men "in the flesh" have lost their charm and terror, respectively (*cf.* II Cor. 5:9). He who belongs to Christ, and through him to God, has become master of everything:

"For all things are yours . . .
whether the world or life or death,
or things present or things future,
all are yours;
but you are Christ's, and Christ is God's."
　　　　　　　　　(I Cor. 3:21–23)

In God, freedom, righteousness, and life have their cause, and it is in them that the glory of God as ultimate meaning and ultimate goal comes to its own. To the glory of God, Christ is confessed as Lord (Phil. 2:11). To the glory of God, prayers of praise and thanksgiving are to sound forth in the congregation (Rom. 15:6; II Cor. 1:20; 9:12–15). Our eating and drinking and our every undertaking it to be done to His glory (I Cor. 10:31) as well as the work of the apostle (II Cor. 4:15). To His glory, Christ accomplished his work (Rom. 15:7) and to Him he will resign his reign "in order that God may be all in all" (I Cor. 15:28 KJ).

Table of Abbreviations

Anglican Theol. Rev. = Anglican Theological Review

Ap, *see* Justin Ap.

AT (in German titles) = Altes Testament (Old Testament)

B = codex Vaticanus of the Bible

Barn. = Epistle of Barnabas (in Apostolic Fathers)

Blass-Debrunner = *Grammatik des neutestamentlichen Griechisch* by Friedrich Blass, revised by Albert Debrunner, 5th ed. (1921)

Blt. after a Biblical reference = Bultmann, signifying that the German text offered Bultmann's rendering of the Greek text into German, of which the wording here offered is a faithful English equivalent

c. Cels., *see* Origen

I Clem. = First Epistle of Clement (in Apostolic Fathers)

II Clem. = Second Epistle of Clement (in Apostolic Fathers)

Corp. Herm. = Corpus Hermeticum (edition by W. Scott, 1924)

D = Codex Bezae of the New Testament

D° = the original hand of the above MS

Dial., *see* Justin

Did. = Didache (in Apostolic Fathers)

Diogn. = The Epistle to Diognetus (in Apostolic Fathers)

ed. = edition

Epictetus, Diss. = Epictetus' "Dissertationes"

Ev. Theol. = *Evangelische Theologie*

IV Ez. = IV Ezra or IV Esdras (Latin numeration) = II Esdras (KJ numeration)

Expos. Times = *Expository Times*

f = and the following verse

ff = and the following verses

G = codex Boernerianus of Paul's epistles

Gesch. d. synopt. Trad., 2nd ed. = Rudolf Bultmann, *Geschichte der synoptischen Tradition*, 2nd ed. (1931)

Harnack, *Mission u. Ausbreitung* = Adolf von Harnack, *Die Mission und Ausbreitung des Christentums in den drei ersten Jahrhunderten*, 3rd ed. (1915) (English translation by James Moffatt, 1908: *The Mission and Expansion of Christianity in the First Three Centuries*—translates the second German edition)

[353]

Herm. mand. = Shepherd of Hermas (in Apostolic Fathers), mandata

Herm. sim. = Shepherd of Hermas (in Apostolic Fathers), similitudines

Herm. vis. = Shepherd of Hermas (in Apostolic Fathers), visiones

HUCA = *Hebrew Union College Annual*

Ign. = Epistles of Ignatius (in Apostolic Fathers)

Ign. Eph. = his epistle to the Ephesians

Ign. Mg. = his epistle to the Magnesians

Ign. Tr. = his epistle to the Trallians

Ign. Rom. = his epistle to the Romans

Ign. Phld. = his epistle to the Philadelphians

Ign. Sm. = his epistle to the Smyrneans

Ign. Pol. = his epistle to Polycarp

Iren. = Irenaeus, "Against Heresies"

it = itala, the pre-Vulgate Old Latin translations of the NT taken as a whole

J. Theol. Stud. = *Journal of Theological Studies*

Jahrb. d. theol. Schule Bethel = *Jahrbuch der theologischen Schule Bethel*

JBL = *Journal of Biblicial Literature*

Joh.-Ev. = Rudolf Bultmann, *Das Evangelium des Johannes* (1941), (2nd ed., 1950)

Justin Ap. = Justin Martyr, "Apology"

Justin Dial. = Justin Martyr, "Dialogue with Trypho"

Kerygma Pet. = Kerygma Petri, fragments of a second century writing

I–IV Kingdoms = I and II Samuel and I and II Kings in the nomenclature of the Septuagint

KJ = the King James translation of the Bible (1611)

l.c. = loco citato

LXX = the Septuagint translation of the Old Testament

Marb. Theol. Stud. = *Marburger Theologische Studien*

Mart. Pol. = Martyrdom of Polycarp (in Apostolic Fathers)

mg = marginal reading

n.d. = no date

op. cit. = opere citato

Origen, c. Cels. = Origen, "Contra Celsum"

par in references to the Synoptics = parallel (i.e., see the parallel "Q"-passage in Mt. or Lk.)

Past. = the Pastoral Epistles in the New Testament

Pol. (or Polyc) Phil. = the Epistle of Polycarp to the Philippians (in Apostolic Fathers) pr. = proemium (the unnumbered introductions in the Apostolic Fathers)

Princeton Theol. Rev. = *Princeton Theological Review*

Ps.-Aristeas = Pseudo-Aristeas, the so-called "Letter of Aristeas" in the Old Testament Pseudepigrapha

Ps.-Clem. hom. = Pseudo-Clementine Homilies

Q = the hypothetical second source (Quelle) common to Matthew and Luke

Realenzykl. der Klass. Altertumswiss. = *Realenzyklopädie der Klassischen Altertumswissenschaft,* Pauly-Wissowa-Kroll

RGG = *Religion in Geschichte und Gegenwart,* 2nd ed. (1927)

RSV = Revised Standard Version of the NT (exactly: The New Covenant commonly called the New Testament of our Lord and Savior Jesus Christ, Revised Standard Version, 1946)

see above, see below = these references always refer to something which precedes or follows *within the same section* (§)

Sitzungsb. d. Heidelb. Akad. d. Wiss., Phil.-hist. Kl. = *Sitzungsbericht der Heidelberger Akademie der Wissenschaften, philosophisch-historische Klasse*

Sitzungsb. d. Preuss. Akad. d. Wiss., Phil.-hist. Kl. = *Sitzungsbericht der Preussischen Akademie der Wissenschaften, Philosophisch-historische Klasse*

Str.-B. = Strack-Billerbeck, *Kommentar zum NT aus Talmud und Midrasch*

Symb. Bibl. Upsal. = Symbolae Biblicae Upsalienses

Theol. Bl. = *Theologische Blätter*

ThR, NF = *Theologische Rundschau,* Neue Folge (New Series)

ThStKr. = *Theologische Studien und Kritiken*

ThWB. = *Theologisches Wörterbuch zum Neuen Testament,* G. Kittel, editor

tr. in bibliographies = translated

tr. after a Biblical reference = translator, signifying that the translator of this book felt it necessary to translate the Greek text quoted by Bultmann in the latter's sense where this was not identical with a common English translation

Trajan ep. = Epistles of the Emperor Trajan (to and from Trajan)

ZNW = *Zeitschrift für die neutestamentliche Wissenschaft*

ZsystTh = *Zeitschrift für systematische Theologie*

ZThK = *Zeitschrift für Theologie und Kirche*

Bibliographies

[As in the original, the bibliographies are given not for the work as a whole but for the sections (§§) and chapters to which they pertain. Wherever possible, two bibliographies are given, one wholly in English, the other covering non-English languages. Each English bibliography contains, first, English works cited by Bultmann along with English translations of works cited by him from the original languages, and, second, pertinent works in English added by the translator at the author's request. The second bibliography (non-English) may be assumed to be Bultmann's (with some additions made by him since the publication of the German edition) except that it has not been felt necessary to give the original titles of works translated into English and already included in the English bibliography.]

For Chapter I as a whole. *English:* Wilhelm Bousset: *Jesus,* tr. by Janet P. Trevelyan, 1906; Rudolf Bultmann: *Jesus and the Word,* tr. by Louise P. Smith and Erminie Huntress, 1934; F. C. Burkitt: *Jesus Christ,* 1932; Maurice Goguel: *The Life of Jesus,* tr. by Olive Wyon, 1933; A. C. Headlam: *Jesus Christ in History and Faith,* 1925; T. W. Manson: *The Teaching of Jesus,* 1935; Rudolf Otto: *The Kingdom of God and the Son of Man,* tr. by Floyd Filson and B. L. Woolf (1938 and 1943 from 2nd German ed., on which see R. Bultmann in *ThR* NF 9, 1937); Albert Schweitzer: *The Quest of the Historical Jesus* (1910 and 1931; 2nd English ed. 1911, often reprinted, most recently 1948, of the first German ed.: *Von Reimarus zu Wrede*); Henry J. Cadbury: *Jesus, What Manner of Man?*, 1947; Martin Dibelius: *Jesus,* tr. by Charles B. Hedrick and Frederick C. Grant, 1949.

Catholic: Karl Adam: *The Son of God,* tr. by Philip Hereford, 1934; August Reatz: *Jesus Christ,* tr. by G. Brinkworth, 1933.

Non-English: Ad. Jülicher: *Die Religion Jesu und die Anfänge des Chistentums bis zum Nicaenum* (Die Kultur der Gegenwart I, 4, 2nd ed., 1922); Paul Wernle: *Jesus,* 2nd ed., 1916; Wilhelm Heitmüller: *Jesus,* 1913; Ad. Schlatter: *Die Geschichte des Christus,* 2nd ed., 1923; Karl Bornhäuser: *Das Wirken des Christus durch Taten und Worte,* 2nd ed., 1924; Karl L. Schmidt: "Jesus Christus," (*RGG,* 2nd ed., III. 110–151); Walt. Grundmann: *Jesus der Galiläer und das Judentum,* 1940; Rudolf Meyer: *Der Prophet aus Galiläa,* 1940.

[357]

BIBLIOGRAPHIES

§1. *English:* E. C. Hoskyns and F. N. Davey: *The Riddle of the New Testament,* 1938.

Non-English: Joh. Weiss: *Die Predigt Jesu vom Reiche Gottes,* 2nd ed., 1900; H. D. Wendland: *Die Eschatologie des Reiches Gottes bei Jesus,* 1931. For the presuppositions in the field of comparative religion: Wilh. Bousset: *Die Religion des Judentums in der späthellenistischen Zeit,* 3rd ed., 1926; also the literature cited for Chapter I.

§2: *English:* See the literature for §1. Also: B. D. T. Smith: *The Parables in the Synoptic Gospels,* 1937; C. G. Montefiore: "The Originality of Jesus," *Hibbert Journal,* XXVIII (Oct. 1929), 98–111; the same: *Rabbinic Literature and Gospel Teachings,* 1930; A. Lukyn Williams: *Talmudic Judaism and Christianity,* 1933; E. F. Scott: "The Originality of Jesus' Ethical Teaching," *JBL,* XLVIII (1929), 109–115; A. N. Wilder: *Eschatology and Ethics in the Teaching of Jesus,* 1939; Henry J. Cadbury: *The Peril of Modernizing Jesus,* 1937; G. F. Moore: *Judaism in the First Centuries of the Christian Era,* I. II., 1927.

Non-English: Joh. Weiss (as in §1): E. Grimm: *Die Ethik Jesu,* 2nd ed., 1917; E. Klostermann: *Jesu Stellung zum AT,* 1904; Fr. K. Karner: *Der Vergeltungsgedanke in der Ethik Jesu,* 1927; H. Windisch: *Der Sinn der Bergpredigt,* 1929; E. Lohmeyer: *Kultus und Evangelium,* 1942; on Jewish ethics, besides Bousset (§1) and Moore, above: Reinh. Sander: *Furcht und Liebe im palästinischen Judentum,* 1935; Erik Sjöberg: *Gott und die Sünder im palästinischen Judentum,* 1939.

§3: See the literature for Chapter I. Also: Joh. Leipoldt: *Das Gotteserlebnis im Lichte der vergleichenden Religionsgeschichte,* 1927; Rich. Ad. Hoffmann: *Das Gottesbild Jesu,* 1935; Walt. Grundmann: *Die Gotteskindschaft in der Geschichte Jesu und ihre religionsgeschichtlichen Voraussetzungen,* 1938.

§4: *English:* Edwin A. Abbott: *The Son of Man,* 1910; Vincent Taylor: *Jesus and his Sacrifice,* 1933; R. H. Lightfoot: *History and Interpretation in the Gospels,* 1934; Rud. Otto: *The Kingdom of God and the Son of Man,* tr. by Floyd Filson and B. L. Woolf [1938 and 1943, 2nd German ed., on which cf. R. Bultmann *ThR* NF 9 (1937), 1–35]; Gustav Dalman: *The Words of Jesus Considered in the Light of Post-Biblical Jewish Writings and the Aramaic Language,* tr. D. M. Kay, 1902; see also: *Jesus-Jeschua: Studies in the Gospels,* tr. by Paul Levertoff, 1929; C. H. Kraeling: *Anthropos and Son of Man,* 1927.

Non-English: Wm. Wrede: *Das Messiasgeheimnis in den Evangelien,* 1901; H. J. Holtzmann, *Das messianische Bewusstsein Jesu,* 1907; Ad. Schlatter: *Der Zweifel an der Messianität Jesu,* 1907; A. Frövig: *Das Selbstbewusstsein Jesu als Lehrer und Wundertäter,* 1918; the same: *Das Sendungsbewusstsein Jesu und der Geist,* 1924; the same: *Der Kyriosglaube des NT und der Geist,* 1928; R. Bultmann: *ZNW* 19 (1919–20), 165–74; the same: *Gesch. d. synopt. Trad.,* 2nd ed., 1931, 263–281, also 147–150; Hans Jurg. Ebeling: *Das Messiasgeheimnis und die Botschaft des Marcus-Evangelisten,* 1939 (Beiheft 19 of ZNW); specifically on the Son of Man question :ee H. Lietzmann: *Der Menschensohn,* 1896 (whose thesis, however, Lietzmann later retracted); Arn. Meyer: *Jesu Muttersprache*, 1896, 91–100, 140–149; Paul Fiebig: *Der Menschensohn*, 1901; Jul. Wellhausen: *Einleitung in die drei ersten Evangelien*, 2nd ed., 1911, 123–130; Wilh. Bousset: *Kyrios Christos*, 2nd ed., 1931, 5–13; Joach. Jeremias: *Erlösung und Erlöser im Urchristentum*, 1929.

For Chapter II as a whole. *English:* Carl Weizsäcker: *The Apostolic Age of the Christian Church*, tr. from 2nd German ed. by James Miller, 1894–99; Paul Wernle: *The Beginnings of Christianity*, tr. by G. A. Bienemann, 1903–4; F. J. Foakes Jackson and Kirsopp Lake: *The Beginnings of Christianity*, I–IV, 1920–1933; Joh. Weiss: *The History of Primitive Christianity*, ed. by F. C. Grant, 1937; C. H. Dodd: *The Apostolic Preaching and its Developments*, 1936.

Non-English: Ernst V. Dobschütz: *Probleme des apostolischen Zeitalters*, 1904; Rud. Knopf: *Das nachapostolische Zeitalter*, 1905; Ad. Jülicher: see Chapter I; Wilh. Bousset: *Kyrios Christos*, 2nd ed., 1921; Hans Achelis: *Das Christentum in den ersten drei Jahrhunderten*, 2nd ed., 1925; Rol. Schütz: *Apostel und Jünger*, 1921; Wilh. Michaelis: *Täufer, Jesus, Urgemeinde*, 1928; Ed. Meyer: *Ursprung und Anfänge des Christentums* III, 1923; Karl Kundsin: *Das Urchristentum im Lichte der Evangelien-forschung*, 1929; Ernst Lohmeyer: *Galiläa und Jerusalem*, 1936; W. G. Kümmel: *Kirchenbegriff und Geschichtsbewusstsein in der Urgemeinde und bei Jesus*, 1943.

§5: See the literature for Chapter II. Also C. H. Dodd: "The Gospels as History: A Reconsideration," *Bull. of the John Rylands Library*, Vol. 22, No. 1, 1938; the same: *History and the Gospels*, 1938.

Non-English: Joh. Weiss: *Jesus im Glauben des Urchristentums*, 1910.

§6: *English:* See the literature given in §1, 3, p. 10. Also: George Johnston: *The Church in the New Testament*, 1943.

§7: See the literature for Chapter II, especially W. Bousset: *Kyrios Christos;* and for §5. Also: W. Staerk: *Soter* I, 1933; Paul Volz: *Die Eschatologie der jüdischen Gemeinde*, 1934.

§8: *English:* See the literature for Chapter II. Also: Floyd V. Filson: "The Separation of Christianity from Judaism," *Anglican Theol. Rev.*, 21 (1939), 171–185; B. H. Streeter: *The Primitive Church*, Chap. III, 1929; A. C. McGiffert: *History of Christianity in the Apostolic Age*, Chap. V, VI, 1897; A. B. Macdonald: *Christian Worship in the Primitive Church*, 1934. Ernst Troeltsch: *The Social Teaching of the Christian Churches*, tr. by Olive Wyon, 1931.

Non-English: Lyder Brun and Anton Fridrichsen: *Paulus und die Urgemeinde*, 1921; Walter Bauer: *Der Wortgottesdienst der ältesten Christen*, 1930; Jos. Mar. Nielen: *Gebet und Gottesdienst im NT*, 1937; Ernst Lohmeyer: *Kultus und Evangelium*, 1942; Oscar Cullmann: *Urchristentum und Gottesdienst*, 1944.

For Chapter III as a whole. See the literature for Chapter II. Also: *English:* B. H. Streeter: *The Rise of Christianity* (The Cambridge Ancient History XI), 1936.

Non-English: Walter Bauer: *Rechtgläubigkeit und Ketzerei im ältesten*

Christentum, 1934; the relevant sections in histories of the primitive church are, of course, also pertinent here.

§9: Ad. v. Harnack: *The Mission and Expansion of Christianity in the First Three Centuries*, tr. by James Moffatt, 2nd ed., 1908; M. Dibelius: *From Tradition to Gospel*, tr. by B. L. Woolf, 1934. Also: *Gospel Criticism and Christology*, 1935.

Non-English: K. Axenfeld: "Die jüdische Propaganda als Vorläuferin und Wegbereiterin der urchristlichen Mission," in *Missionswissenschaftliche Studien* (Festschrift für G. Warneck), 1904, 1–102; Albr. Oepke: *Die Missionspredigt des Apostels Paulus*, 1920; Ed. Norden: *Agnostos Theos*, 1913; Mart. Dibelius: *Paulus auf dem Areopag* (Sitzungsber. d. Heidelb. Akad. d. Wiss., Phil,-hist. Kl. 1938–39, 2. Abh.), 1939; Wilh. Schmid: "Die Rede des Apostels Paulus vor den Philosophen und Areopagiten," *Philologus*, 95 (1942), 79–102; Max Pohlenz: "Paulus und die Stoa," *ZNW*, 42 (1949), 69–104. Here the various investigations of Alfr. Seeberg should be named; they show the stock of traditional formulations which gradually crystallize out of missionary preaching and from which ultimately the creed (in various forms) develops. Only Seeberg makes the mistake of placing a more or less definitely formulated "catechism" at the beginning of the development. Read from the standpoint of tradition-history (Bultmann's paraphrase of and improvement upon Dibelius' term "form-history") these investigations, which also reveal the connection of Christian preaching with Jewish tradition, have a high value: *Der Katechismus der Urchristenheit*, 1903; *Das Evangelium Christi*, 1905; *Die beiden Wege und das Aposteldekret*, 1906; *Die Didache des Judentums und der Urchristenheit*, 1908; *Christi Person und Werk nach der Lehre seiner Jünger*, 1910; on sub-section 5: Jul. Schniewind: *Euangelion*, Lieferung 1 und 2, 1927–31; Einar Molland: *Das Paulinische Euangelion*, 1934; Ad. Schlatter: *Der Glaube im NT*, 4th ed., 1927; R. Gyllenberg: *Pistis* (in Swedish), 1922.

§10: *English:* Ernst v. Dobschütz: *Christian Life in the Primitive Church*, tr. by Geo. Bremner, 1904; the same: *The Apostolic Age*, tr. by F. L. Pogson, 1910.

Non-English: N. A. Dahl: *Das Volk Gottes*, 1941; Ed. Grafe: *Das Urchristentum und das AT*, 1907; O. Michel: *Paulus und seine Bibel*, 1929; H. Jacoby: *Neutestamentliche Ethik*, 1899; Mart. Dibelius: Excursus on Herm. sim. II 5 in the supplement volume of Lietzmann's *Handbuch zum NT*, IV, 555f.

§11: See the literature for §8 and the works listed in §8, 2. Also: Rud. Knopf: *Das nachapostolische Zeitalter*, 1905, 346–369; Hans Wenschkewitz: *Die Spiritualisierung der Kultusbegriffe. Tempel, Priester und Opfer im NT*, 1932.

§12: *English:* See the literature for Chapter II. Also: Martin Dibelius: *Gospel Criticism and Christology*, 1935; Joh. Weiss: *Christ, the Beginnings of Dogma*, tr. by V. D. Davis, 1911.

Non-English: W. Bousset: *Kyrios Christos*; M. Dibelius: "Christologie des Urchristentums," in *RGG* I, 1592–1607. On 1. see W. Bauer, J. M.

Nielen, O. Cullmann as listed in §8. Also: R. Knopf: *Das nachapostolische Zeitalter*, 1905, 222–252; Andr. Duhm: *Gottesdienst im ältesten Christentum*, 1928. On 2. see §7, 5 and W. Graf Baudissin: *Kyrios*, II, 257–301; Ed. v. d. Goltz: *Das Gebet in der ältesten Christenheit*, 1901; A. Klawek: *Das Gebet zu Jesus*, 1921; On 3 see: G. P. Wetter: *Der Sohn Gottes*, 1916; Ludw. Bieler: ΘΕΙΟΣ ΑΝΗΡ I, 1935, 134–140; M. Dibelius: Excursus on Col. 1:17 in Lietzmann's *Handbuch zum NT*, 12, 2nd ed., 1927, 9–12.

§13: *English:* J. C. Lambert: "The Passover and the Lord's Supper," *J. Theol. Studies*, IV, 1903, 184–193; H. E. D. Blakiston: "The Lucan Account of the Institution of the Lord's Supper," *J. Theol. Studies*, IV, 1903, 548–555; Jacob Mann: "The Last Supper as a Paschal Meal," *HUCA*, I, 1924, 177; C. C. Richardson: "Early Patristic Evidence for the Synoptic Chronology of the Passion," *Anglican. Theol. Rev.*, 22, 1942, 299–308; G. H. Box: "The Jewish Antecedents of the Eucharist," *J. Theol. Stud.* 3, 1902, 357–367 and 10, p. 106; F. C. Burkitt: "St. Luke 22:15,6: What is the General Meaning?" *J. Theol. Stud.*, 9, 1908, 569–571; the same: "The Lord's Supper and the Paschal Meal," *J. Theol. Stud.*, 17, 1916, 291–297; R. H. Kennett: *The Last Supper, its Significance in the Upper Room*, 1921; W. O. E. Oesterley: *The Jewish Background of the Christian Liturgy*, 1925; G. H. C. Macgregor: *Eucharistic Origins*, 1928; F. Gavin: *The Jewish Antecedents of the Christian Sacraments*, 1928, 1933; T. W. H. Marfield: *The Words of Institution*, 1933; V. Taylor: *Jesus and His Sacrifice*, 1937, 1943; F. L. Cirlot: *The Early Eucharist*, 1939; L. S. Thornton: *The Common Life in the Body of Christ*, 1941; G. Dix: *The Shape of the Liturgy*, 1944; K. Barth: *The Teaching of the Church Regarding Baptism*, tr. SCM Press, 1948.

Non-English: On 1: R. Knopf: *Das nachapostolische Zeitalter*, 271–290; W. Heitmüller: *Im Namen Jesu*, 1903; the same: *Taufe und Abendmahl im Urchristentum*, 1911; Joh. Leipoldt: *Die urchristliche Taufe im Lichte der Religionsgeschichte*, 1928; Rich. Reitzenstein: *Die Vorgeschichte der christlichen Taufe*, 1929; Jos. Thomas: *Le mouvement baptiste en Palestine et Syrie*, 1935; Eth. Stauffer: "Taufe im Urchristentum," in *RGG*, 2nd ed., V, 1002–1010. On 2: Lietzmann, Cullmann, Lohmeyer as given in §8, 3. Also: R. Knopf: *op. cit.*, 253–271; W. Heitmüller: see above at §13, 1; Maur. Goguel: *L'Eucharistie des origines à Justin Martyr*, 1910.

§14: *English:* H. B. Swete: *The Holy Spirit in the New Testament*, 1910; E. F. Scott: *The Spirit in the New Testament*, 1923; W. R. Shoemaker: "The Use of Ruach in the OT and of Pneuma in the New Testament," *JBL*, XXIII (1904); Vincent Taylor: *The Holy Spirit* (Headingley Lectures), 1937; H. Wheeler Robinson: *The Christian Experience of the Holy Spirit*, 1928.

Non-English: Paul Volz: *Der Geist Gottes und die verwandten Erscheinungen im AT und im anschliessenden Judentum*, 1910; Herm. Gunkel: *Die Wirkungen des Heil. Geistes nach der populären Anschauung der apostolischen Zeit und der Lehre des Apostels Paulus*, 3rd ed., 1909; Heinr. Weinel: *Die Wirkungen des Geistes und der Geister im nachapos-*

tolischen Zeitalter bis auf Irenäus, 1899; Friedr. Büchsel: *Der Geist Gottes im NT*, 1926; Mart. Dibelius: Excursus on Herm. mand V 2, 7 in the supplement volume to the *Handbuch zum NT*, IV, 517–519.

§15: *English:* Carl H. Kraeling: *Anthropos and Son of Man*, 1927; F. C. Burkitt: *Church and Gnosis* (written against Bultmann among others, though he is never named. Nevertheless it contains information on Gnosticism not elsewhere available in English), 1932.

Non-English: Wilh. Bousset: *Hauptprobleme der Gnosis*, 1907; Paul Wendland: *Die hellenistisch-römische Kultur in ihren Beziehungen zu Judentum und Christentum* (*Handbuch zum NT* I, 2, 2nd and 3rd ed.), 1912, 163–187; Rich, Reitzenstein: *Die hellenistischen Mysterienreligionen*, 3rd ed., 1927; Hans Jonas: *Gnosis und spätantiker Geist*, I. *Die mythologische Gnosis*, 1934; Heinr. Schlier: *Religionsgeschichtlichen Untersuchungen zu den Ignatiusbriefen*, 1929; the same: *Christus und die Kirche im Epheserbrief*, 1930; Ernst Käsemann: *Leib und Leib Christi*, 1933; the same: *Das wandernde Gottesvolk*, 1939; Hans-Werner Bartsch: *Gnostisches Gut und Gemeindetradition bei Ignatius von Antiochien*, 1940; Walter Bauer: *Rechtgläubigkeit und Ketzerei im ältesten Christentum*, 1934.

Part II as a whole. *English:* Alb. Schweitzer: *Paul and His Interpreters*, tr. by W. Montgomery, 1912; Ferd. Chr. Baur: *Paul, the Apostle of Jesus Christ*, tr. by A. Menzies, 1876; Otto Pfleiderer: *Paulinism*, tr. by Edward Peters from 2nd German ed., 1890; cf. by same author: *The Influence of the Apostle Paul on the Development of Christianity*, tr. by Fred Smith, 1885; Wm. Wrede: *Paul*, tr. by Edward Lummis, 1908; Ad. Deissmann: *Paul, a Study in Social and Religious History*, tr. by Wm. E. Wilson from 2nd German ed., 1926; Alb. Schweitzer: *The Mysticism of Paul the Apostle*, tr. by Wm. Montgomery, 1931; Wilfred L. Knox: *St. Paul and the Church of Jerusalem*, 1930; the same: *St. Paul and the Church of the Gentiles*, 1939.

Non-English: Ernest Renan: *St. Paul*, 1869; Carl Holsten: *Das Evangelium des Paulus*, I, II, 1880, 1898; Ernst Lohmeyer: *Grundlagen paulinischer Theologie*, 1929; Rud. Bultmann: "Paulus," (*RGG*, 2nd ed., IV, 1019–1045).

§16: *English:* On the problem "Paul and Jesus": Arnold Meyer: *Jesus or Paul?* 1907; C. A. A. Scott: "Jesus and Paul" (in *Essays on Some Biblical Questions of the Day*, ed. by H. B. Swete), 1909; B. W. Bacon: *Jesus and Paul*, 1920; Joh. Weiss: *Paul and Jesus*, tr. by H. J. Chaytor, 1909.

Non-English: On the conversion of Paul: W. G. Kümmel: *Römer 7 und die Bekehrung des Paulus*, 1929; Robert Steiger: *Die Dialektik der paulinischen Existenz*, 1931; Ottfried Kietzig: *Die Bekehrung des Paulus*, 1932; R. Bultmann: "Kritischer Bericht über einzelne neuere Untersuchungen zum Werdegang und zur Bekehrung des Paulus," *ThR*, NF 6 (1934), 229–246.

On the problem "Paul and Jesus": Maurice Goguel: *L'apôtre Paul et Jésus Christ*, 1904; Ad. Jülicher: *Paulus und Jesus*, 1907; Arnold Meyer:

Wer hat das Christentum gegründet, Jesus oder Paulus?, 1907; Wilh. Heitmüller: "Zum Problem Paulus und Jesus," *ZNW*, 13 (1912), 320–337; the same: "Jesus und Paulus," *ZThK*, 25 (1915), 156–179; Paul Wernle: "Jesus und Paulus," *ZThK*, 25 (1915), 1–82; R. Bultmann: "Die Bedeutung des historischen Jesus für die Theologie des Paulus," (in *Glauben und Verstehen*, 1933, 188–213); the same: "Jesus und Paulus," (in *Jesus Christus im Zeugnis der Heiligen Schrift und der Kirche*, 1936, 68–90).

On I Pet. 3:18–22 see R. Bultmann: *Coniectanea Neotestamentica* XI (1949), 1–14; on Col. 1:15–20 see E. Käsemann: *Bultmann-Festschrift*, 1949, 133–148.

Chapter IV A: *English*: Franz Delitsch: *A System of Biblical Psychology*, tr. by A. E. Wallis, 1867; John Laidlaw: *Bible Doctrine of Man*, 2nd ed., 1895; W. P. Dickson: *St. Paul's Use of the Terms Flesh and Spirit*, 1883; H. Wheeler Robinson: "Hebrew Psychology in relation to Pauline Anthropology" in *Mansfield College Essays*; the same: *The Christian Doctrine of Man*, 3rd ed., 1926.

Non-English: Herm. Lüdemann: *Die Anthropologie des Apostels Paulus*, 1872; Walter Gutbrod: *Die paulinische Anthropologie*, 1934.

§17: *English*: E. de Witt Burton: *Spirit, Soul, and·Flesh*, 1918; M. Scott Fletcher: *The Psychology of the NT*, n.d.; H. Wheeler Robinson: *The Christian Doctrine of Man*, (Chapter II, "The New Testament Doctrine of Man"), 3rd ed. 1926; A. B. D. Alexander: *The Ethics of St. Paul*, (Chapter III, "The Psychology of Paul"), 1910.

Non-English: Ernst Käsemann: *Leib und Leib Christi*, 1933; P. Torge: *Seelenglaube und Unsterblichkeitshoffnung im AT*, 1909; W. Georg Kümmel: *Das Bild des Menschen im NT*, 1948.

§18: F. C. Porter: "The Pre-existence of the Soul in the Book of Wisdom and in the Rabbinical Writings," in *Old Testament and Semitic Studies in Memory of Wm. Rainey Harper*, 1908; F. C. Burkitt: "Life, Zoe, Hayyim," *ZNW*, 12, 1911, 228–230.

Chapter IV B, §21: Günther Bornkamm: "Die Offenbarung des Zornes Gottes," *ZNW*, 34 (1935), 239–252; Heinr. Schlier: "Über die Erkenntnis Gottes bei den Heiden.," *Ev. Theol.*, 1935, 9–26.

§22: H. Lüdemann and W. Gutbrod: (for titles see the literature for Chapter IV A); E. Käsemann: (See the literature for §17); Wilh. Schauf: *Sarx*, 1924.

§24: Werner Georg Kümmel: *Römer 7 und die Bekehrung des Paulus*, 1929; Rud. Bultmann: "Römer 7 und die Anthropologie des Paulus," (in *Imago Dei, Festschrift für G. Krüger*, 53–62), 1932; Paul Althaus: *Paulus und Luther über den Menschen*, 1938.

§27: *English*: Wilfred L. Knox: *St. Paul and the Church of Jerusalem.* *Non-English*: Ed. Grafe: *Die paulinische Lehre vom Gesetz*, 2nd ed., 1893; the same: *Das Urchristentum und das AT*, 1907; Otto Michel: *Paulus und seine Bibel*, 1929; Ad. Schlatter: *Der Glaube im NT*, 4th ed., 1927, 323–399; Käte Oltmanns: *Theol. Bl.* 8 (1929), 110–116; R. Bultmann: see literature for §24.

For Chapter V A as a whole. *English:* Th. Häring: *The Christian Faith,* tr. by John Dickie and George Ferries, 1913; Floyd V. Filson: *St. Paul's Conception of Recompense,* 1931.

Non-English: H. Cremer: *Die paulinische Rechtfertigungslehre im Zusammenhang ihrer geschichtlichen Voraussetzungen,* 2nd ed., 1910. The abundant recent literature is given in the article δικαιοσύνη in Bauer's *Wörterbuch zum NT;* see especially: E. von Dobschütz: "Uber die paulinische Rechtfertigungslehre," *ThStKr,* 85 (1912), 38–87; W. Michaelis: "Rechtfertigung aus Glauben bei Paulus," *Festgabe für Ad. Deissmann:* 1927, 116–138; Herb. Braun: *Gerichtsgedanke und Rechtfertigungslehre bei Paulus,* 1930; Wilh. Mundle: *Der Glaubensbegriff des Paulus,* 1932; R. Gyllenberg: "Die paulinische Rechtfertigungslehre und das AT," *Studia Theologica* I (1935), 35–52; Hans-Wolfgang Heidland: *Die Anrechnung des Glaubens zur Gerechtigkeit,* 1936.

§28: J. H. Ropes: "Righteousness in the OT and in St. Paul," *JBL,* XXII, 1903, 211–227; F. B. Westcott: *St. Paul and Justification,* 1913.

For Chapter V B as a whole. *English:* J. Moffatt: *Grace in the NT,* 1931; W. T. Whitley: *The Doctrine of Grace,* 1932.

Non-English: G. P. Wetter: *Charis,* 1913; J. Wobbe: *Der Charisgedanke bei Paulus,* 1932.

§32: G. Bornkamm: "Die Offenbarung des Zornes Gottes," *ZNW,* 34 (1935), 239–262.

§33: *English:* W. E. Wilson: "The Development of Paul's Doctrine of Dying and Rising again with Christ," *Expos. Times,* 42 (1930–32), 562 ff.

Non-English: A. Seeberg: *Der Tod Christi in seiner Bedeutung für die Erlösung,* 1895; Theod. Hoppe: *Die Idee der Heilsgeschichte bei Paulus,* 1926; Joh. Schneider: *Die Passionsmystik des Paulus,* 1929; Karl Mittring: *Heilswirklichkeit bei Paulus,* 1929; Emil Weber: *Eschatologie und Mystik im NT,* 1930; Gustav Wiencke: *Paulus über Jesu Tod,* 1939; on 6b, Heinr. Schumacher: *Christus in seiner Präexistenz und Kenose,* 1914; Ernst Barnikol: *Philipper 2,* 1932; the same: *Mensch und Messias,* 1932.

§34: *English:* A. B. Macdonald: *Christian Worship in the Primitive Church,* 1934.

Non-English: On 1: Otto Schmitz: *Die Bedeutung des Wortes bei Paulus,* 1927; R. Bultmann: *Glauben und Verstehen,* 1933, 153–187; Einar Molland: *Das paulinische Euangelion,* 1934; On 2: Traug. Schmidt: *Der Leib Christi,* 1919; Wilh. Koester: *Die Idee der Kirche beim Apostel Paulus,* 1928; Gerh. Gloege: *Reich Gottes und Kirche im NT,* 1929; Heinr. Schlier: *Christus und die Kirche im Epheserbrief,* 1930; Ernst Käsemann: *Leib und Leib Christi,* 1933; Alfred Wickenhauser: *Die Kirche als der mystische Leib Christi nach dem Apostel Paulus,* 1940; Franz-J. Leenhardt: *Etudes sur l'Eglise dans le NT,* 1940; Otto Michel: *Das Zeugnis des NT von der Gemeinde,* 1941; Nils A. Dahl: *Das Volk Gottes,* 1941; Ernst Percy: *Der Leib Christi,* 1942. On 3: see literature for §13; also: Ad. Deissmann: *Die neutestamentliche Formel "in Christo Jesu,"* 1892; Otto Schmitz: *Die Christusgemeinschaft des Paulus im Lichte seines Genetivgebrauchs,* 1924; Wilh. Weber: *Christusmystik,* 1924;

BIBLIOGRAPHIES

Erwin Wissmann: *Das Verhältnis von* Πίστις *und Christusmystik bei Paulus*, 1926; Alfr. Wickenhauser: *Die Christusmystik des heiligen Paulus*, 1928; Wilh. Mundle: *Der Glaubensbegriff des Paulus*, 1932; Werner Schmauch: *In Christus*, 1935; M. Dibelius: *Paulus und die Mystik*, 1941. For Chapter V C as a whole. *Non-English:* Ad. Schlatter: *Der Glaube im NT*, 4th ed., 1927; Raf. Gyllenberg: *Pistis*, 1922 (in Swedish). In addition to the works by Schmitz, Wissmann, Mundle and Wilh. Michaelis, named for §34, see Wilh. Michaelis: "Rechtfertigung aus Glauben bei Paulus," *Festgabe für Ad. Deissmann*, 1927, 116–138.

§35: W. Morgan: *The Religion and Theology of Paul*, 1917; W. H. P. Hatch: *The Pauline Idea of Faith in its relation to Jewish and Hellenistic Religion*, 1917.

§36: A. B. D. Alexander: *The Ethics of St. Paul* (Chapter V, "The Dynamics of the New Life"), 1910. *Non-English:* See the literature for §34, 3; also: Ernst Sommerlath: *Der Ursprung des neuen Lebens nach Paulus*, 1923. For Chapter V D as a whole. Joh. Weiss: *Die christliche Freiheit nach der Verkündigung des Paulus*, 1902; Otto Schmitz: *Der Freiheitsgedanke bei Epiktet und das Freiheitszeugnis des Paulus*, 1923; Mich. Müller: "Freiheit," *ZNW*, 25 (1926), 177–236; Hans Jonas: *Augustin und das paulinische Freiheitsproblem*, 1930; K. Deissner: *Autorität und Freiheit im ältesten Christentum*, 1931; W. Brandt: *Freiheit im NT*, 1932; Heinr. Schlier: the article, "ἐλεύθερος," *ThWB* II, 484–500.

§38: *English:* Albert Schweitzer: *The Mysticism of Paul the Apostle*, tr. by Wm. Montgomery, 1931; J. E. Frame: "Paul's Idea of Deliverance," *JBL*, 49, 1930, 1–12; M. S. Enslin: *The Ethics of Paul*, 1930; H. R. Hoyle: *The Holy Spirit in St. Paul*, 1918.

Non-English: Paul Wernle: *Der Christ und die Sünde bei Paulus*, 1897; Rud. Bultmann: "Das Problem der Ethik bei Paulus," *ZNW*, 23 (1924), 123–140; Hans Windisch: "Das Problem des paulinischen Imperativs," *ZNW*, 23 (1924), 265–281; Wilh. Mundle: "Religion und Sittlichkeit bei Paulus," *ZsystTh*, 4 (1927), 456–482; Hans v. Soden: *Sakrament und Ethik bei Paulus* (*Marb. Theol. Stud.* I), 1931; On 2 and 3: H. Gunkel und Fr. Büchsel: (see literature given in §14); E. Sokolowski: *Die Begriffe Geist und Leben bei Paulus*, 1903; Alfr. Juncker: *Die Ethik des Apostels Paulus*, I, II, 1904, 1919; K. Deissner: *Auferstehungshoffnung und Pneumagedanke bei Paulus*, 1912; H. Bertrams: *Das Wesen des Geistes nach der Anschauung des Apostels Paulus*, 1913; W. Reinhard: *Das Wirken des Heiligen Geistes im Menschen nach den Briefen des Apostels Paulus*, 1918; Otto Schmitz: "Der Begriff δύναμις bei Paulus," *Festgabe für Ad. Deissmann*, 1927, 139–167; Herb. Preisker: *Geist und Leben*, 1933; On 3: E. G. Gulin: *Die Freude im NT*, I, 1932.

§39: *English:* James Moffatt: *Love in the NT*, 1925. *Non-English:* See the literature for Chapter V D. Also: on 3: Wilh. Lütgert: *Die Liebe im NT*, 1905; Herb. Preisker: "Die Liebe im Urchristentum und in der alten Kirche," *ThStKr*, 95 (1924), 272–294; the same:

Die urchristliche Botschaft von der Liebe Gottes, 1930; Günther Born-kamm: "Der Köstliche Weg (1. Kr 13)," *Jahrb. d. theol. Schule Bethel*, 1937, 131–150.

§40: *English*: G. Vos: "The Pauline Doctrine of the Resurrection," *Princeton Theol. Rev.* 27 (1929), 1–35, 193–226; F. C. Burkitt: "Life, Zoe, Hayyim," *ZNW*, 12 (1911), 228–230.

Non-English: See the literature for §38. Also: K. L. Schmidt: "Escha-tologie und Mystik im Urchristentum," *ZNW*, 21 (1922), 277–291; Hans Emil Weber: *"Eschatologie"* und *"Mystik" im NT*, 1930; On 1: Rich. Kabisch: *Die Eschatologie des Paulus*, 1893; E. Teichmann: *Die pauli-nischen Vorstellungen von Auferstehung und Gericht*, 1896; On 2: Arn. Steubing: *Der paulinische Begriff "Christusleiden,"* Heidelberg disserta-tion, 1905; Ernst Lohmeyer: Σὺν Χριστῷ (*Festgabe für Ad. Deissmann*, 1927, 218–258); Joh. Schneider: *Die Passionsmystik des Paulus*, 1929; M. Dibelius: *Paulus und die Mystik*, 1941.

SUBJECT INDEX

261, 268, 341, 344; for good, 228; legal, 260, 262; for love, 18, 19; ritual, 260

Demonic, being, 238; hordes, 172; powers, 165, 166, 172, 174, 257; world rulers, 166, 173, 176, 177, 244

Demons, 7, 32, 41, 48, 100, 120, 127, 138, 139, 148, 155, 167

Descent of Jesus, 175, 176; from David, 49

Deutero-Pauline literature, 74, 76, 88, 118, 136

Devil, 105, 113, 174, 258, 297

Dikaios, Dikaiosyne, 271, 272, 273, 285

Disciples of Jesus, 10, 26, 37, 38, 39, 44, 45, 58, 148, 187, 188

Disobedience, 97, 282; of Adam, 251, 276, 289; of Christians, 112, 213, 228, 241; of Israel, 112

Divinity of Christ, *128-133*

Divorce, 13, 15, 113

Dualism, 106, 107, 163, 164, 170, 172, 173, 199, 201, 202, 203

Dynamis, Dynamistic thinking, *155-157*

EBIONITES, Gospel of the, 134

Ecclesia, 93 f., 308, 310, 311

Ecclesiastical forms (development), 53 ff.

Ecclesiology, 132 f.

Ecstasy, 41, 152, 154, 157, 158, 161, 163, 164, 166, 180, 202, 211, 325, 335; demonic, 330; spiritual, 330

Elders, 59, 61, 95, 113

Elect, the, Election, 38, 39, 59, 97, 193

Elemental spirits, 141, 254, 257, 258

End, doctrine of the, 9, 20, 25, 29, 38, 41, 42, 43, 58, 75, 77, 92, 120; of days, 41, 42, 44, 93, 155; of the world, 4, 20, 22, 23, 62, 103, 106, 152

Epiclesis, 137

Epiphanius, 39

Eschatological, act, 3; appearing, 79; concept, 256; condemnation, 75; congregation, 37 ff , 53, 54, 55, 57, 58, 59, 62, 93, 97, 99, 100, 108, 117, 118, 124, 133, 152, 161, 308, 309, 311; consciousness, 37, 40, 42, 53, 101, 106; consummation, 198; deed, 289, 304; delimitation, 106; divine power, 163; drama, 36, 74, 92; dualism, 106, 163, 164, 172; end, 5, 7; entity, 54; ethic, 19; events, 25, 93, 155, 278, 284, 290, 306; existence, 144, 328, 335, 337, 338, 339, 344; expectation, 34; faith, 92; fulfilment, 41; gift, 155, 278, 335; holiness, 309; hour of decision, 44; joy, 40, 339; judge, 78; judgment, 74, 75, 76, 79, 273; *kerygma,* 78; life, 279; meaning, 164, 276, 277, 327; message, 4 ff., 19, 20, 22, 23, 92, 164; mood, 41; occurrence, 36, 37, 43, 53, 92, 97, 98, 118, 152, 181, 182, 291, 302, 303, 306, 307, 309, 327, 329, 330; period, 278; phenomenon, 339, 344; prayer, 51; preaching, 20, 22, 35, 42, 72, 93; proclamation, 20, 21, 74; regents, 37; righteousness, 274, 347; role, 80, 83; ruler, 27; sacrament, 40; salvation, 34, 49, 52, 54, 124, 155, 163; salvation occurrence, 308, 324; saviour, 78, 124; sect, 42; temper of God, 155; terms, 38, 275, 278; theme, 78; titles, 38; verdict, 75

Eschatology, 25, 39, 97, 106, 166, 168, 169, 172, 176, 178, 228, 257, 273, 282, 310, 330, 347; Jewish, 37

Eternal, 75, 77; life, 16, 157, 158, 162, 204, 262, 274, 288, 290, 334, 336

Ethics, 11, 13, 19, 95, 110, 112, 113, 115, 118, 119, 141

Eucharist, 116, 122, 133, 135, 144, 145, 147, 148, 149, 150, 151, 158, 296

Evil, 138, 198, 202, 209, 213, 216,

Rejection of Jesus by Israel, 97

Relation, Relationship, between Christ and God, 129, 191; of Church to Judaism, 108 f.; between cult and eschatology, 152; between cult and everyday life, 152; between deed and faith, 120; between God and man, 25, 34, 89, 90, 133, 190, 191, 192, 198, 231, 265, 277, 286, 319, 324, 345; between God's will and His grace, 119; human, 255; of Law, 254; of man to himself, 195, 196, 197, 198, 199, 202, 209, 216, 227, 324; mystical, 328; to world (Christian), 92

Release, 298, 299; from flesh, 200, 201, 203; of self, 201; from sin, 85

Religion, 13, 152, 170, 316; and ritualism, 21

Remission of sin, 114, 119, 137, 143

Renewal, 104, 138, 143, 211, 326, 338, 349

Renunciation, 11, 103, 104, 106, 210, 240, 243, 315, 316, 342, 349

Repentance, 21, 22, 24, 34, 39, 42, 73, 74, 83, 103, 104, 112, 114, 120, 134, 158, 188, 214, 287, 317

Responsibility, 181, 191, 219, 253, 258, 321, 329, 342

Resurrection, 5, 6, 26, 27, 29, 30, 32, 36, 37, 43, 45, 49, 50, 60, 71, 74, 77, 78, 80, 81, 82, 83, 86, 92, 123, 127, 130, 140, 141, 142, 143, 144, 145, 147, 157, 162, 168, 169, 172, 177, 178, 180, 188, 192, 198, 201, *292-306*, 298, 299, 300, 302, 305, 306, 307, 308, 309, 310, 311, 312, 313, 318, 328, 336, 345, 346, 348; body, 197, 198; of Christ, 292 ff.; life, 199, 201

Return of Jesus, 29, 33, 111

Revelation, 48, 73, 75, 102, 109, 118, 120, 123, 154, 160, 189, 191, 241, 262, 275; of Faith, Ch. IV *passim*; of God, 25, 36, 43, 118, 150

Reward and punishment, 12, 14, 15, 282

Righteousness, 19, 22, 46, 73, 78, 105, 113, 133, 136, 187, 189, 194, 208, 225, 226, 240, 242, 243, 244, 248, 250, 253, 261, 262, 263, 264, 265, 267, *270-285*, 286, 287, 290, 294, 301, 307, 314, 315, 316, 317, 318, 319, 331, 332, 338, 339, 340, 341, 347, 352; concept of, 270 ff.; of God, 270 ff., 279 ff.; as a present reality, 274 ff.

Right-wise, Right-wised, Right-wising, 253, 262, 263, 264, 265, 270, 271, 272, 273, 274, 277, 278, 280, 281, 282, 286, 288, 289, 316, 318, 319, 332, 335, 347, 348

Ritual, 11, 25, 39, 54, 112, 113, 114, 115, 123, 134, 139, 260; commandment, 110; prescriptions, 17; regulations, 13, 102, 114, 141, 152

Risen One, 3, 37, 48, 60, 81, 129, 187

Rome, Romans, 7, 108, 109, 112

SACRAMENTS, 57, 59, 62, 64, 85, 86, 133 ff., 167, 168, 298, 303, *306-314*, 348

Sacrifice, 17, 46, 47, 53, 84, 85, 98, 111, 114, 115, 116, 121, 122, 123, 143, 146, 148, 149, 150, 152, 188, 192, 194, 219, 253, 289, 295, 296, 297; propitiatory, 295 ff.; vicarious, 296, 297

" Saints," members of Church as 38, 39, 99, 276, 308, 309, 338

Salvation, 3, 4, 5, 7, 9, 20, 21, 22, 23, 25, 28, 34, 46, 47, 49, 52, 53, 54, 55, 56, 59, 60, 61, 62, 73, 79, 83, 84, 86, 88, 89, 93, 95, 97, 101, 106, 107, 108, 111, 113, 115, 119, 123, 128, 129, 131, 139, 140, 144, 151, 152, 153, 158, 163, 164, 165, 172, 175, 176, 179, 181, 189, 191, 211, 227, 232, 262, 264, 267, 269, 271, 272, 274, 278, 279, 280, 282, 288, 290, 291, *292-300*, 307, 310, 311, 312, 313, 314, 315, 316, 319, 321, 323, 324, 327, 328, 329, 335,

SCRIPTURE INDEX

OLD TESTAMENT

NEW TESTAMENT

PATRISTIC REFERENCES

EPISTLE OF BARNABAS
1.2 f...155, 159, 160. 1.3
...156. 1.6...75. 1.7...
155. 1.8...162. 2.1...111,
119. 2.6...111, 119.
3.6...98. 4.6-8...98, 110.
4.8...91. 4.9...90, 162.
4.10...103, 104. 4.11...
115, 160. 4.12...75.
4.13...76, 78, 99, 103.
Chs. 5-8...111. 5.1...85.
5.2...31, 5.5...125. 5.6 f.
...81. 5.7...78, 98. 5.9
...88. 6.4...76. 6.11...
101, 142, 143. 6.13...
101. 6.14...101. 6.15
...115. 6.16 ff...111. 7.2
...78. 7.3...85. 7.5...85,
98. 7.9...76, 111. 7.11...
78, 94. 8.1...85. 8.3...
85, 88, 111. 8.5 f...78.
Ch. 9...110. 9.3...89.
9.4...110. 9.6...138.
9.8...111. Ch. 10...110.
10.7...71. 10.9...110.
10.11...111, 119. 11.9-
11...139. 11.11...133,
137, 158. 12.10...80, 82.
Chs. 13-14...98, 110. 13.
1...98. 13.7...95. 14.1 ff.
...98. 14.4...98. 14.5...
89. 14.5 f...85, 173.
14.6...98. 14.9...88. 15.
5...78. 15.9...82, 123,
145. 16.1...70. 16.5 ff.
...155. 16.7...99, 100.
16.7 f...138. 16.7-10...
115. 16.8 f...137. 16.9
...73, 89. 16.18...143.
17.1...72. 18.1...173.
19.2...70. 19.10...76,

89, 99. 19.12...72. 20.1
...99, 100. 21.1...76,
111, 119. 21.3...103.
21.5...70. 21.6...76.

FIRST EPISTLE OF
CLEMENT, 64, 112
Proemium...94, 99, 100.
1.3...72. 2.2...156, 160.
2.3...70. 2.8...112, 119.
3.4...72. 6.4...98. 7.2...
104, 105. 7.3...70. 7.4
...73, 85. 8.2...70. 8.5
...70. 9.1...104, 105.
10.7...112. 12.1...112.
12.7...85, 91, 112. 13.1
...105. 13.2...75. 14.3
...70. 16.3-14...31. 19.2
...70. Ch. 20...69, 71.
20.11...70. 20.12...126.
Chs. 20-23...78. 21.1
...75. 21.6...85. Chs.
23-25...169. Ch. 23...
8, 103. 23.1...70. Chs.
24-26...77. Ch. 24-28...
78. 24.1...81. 24.5...71.
26.1...70, 90, 91. Ch. 28
...104. 28.1...75, 105.
29.1...70. 30.1...105.
32.4...70. 33.2...70. 35.2
...90, 91. 35.3...70.
35.5...72. 36.1...115.
36.2...173. 36.5...82.
38.1...154. 38.2...103.
38.3...70. Chs. 40-42...
116. Ch. 40...112, 150.
40.1...112. Ch. 41...112.
41.3...72. 41.4...112.
42.1...88. 42.3...76, 81,
88, 161. 42.4...88. 43.6
...69. 44.4...122. 45.1

...72. 46.6...69, 156.
47.2...88. 48.5...103.
49.6...85. 50.3...78. 50.
6 f...112. 50.7...126.
52.1...70, 72, 112. 56.1
...99. 57.2...105. 58.1
...90. 58.2...112, 119,
128. Chs. 59-61...124.
59.2 ff...51, 67, 70. 59.3
...69, 85. 59.4...98.
60.1...69, 90. 60.4...70.
61.3...115, 124, 128. 62.
1...72. 62.2...70. Ch.
64...85, 115, 128. 65.2...
99, 126, 128.

SECOND EPISTLE OF
CLEMENT, 84
1.1...78. 1.4...173. 1.4 ff
...68. 1.6...105. 1.6 ff...
73, 106. 1.7...66. 1.8...
69. 2.1...94. 3.1...67,
69. 5.1...100, 102, 105.
5.5...76. 5.6...102, 106.
6.3-5...102. 6.4 f...105.
6.9...76, 101. 7.6...101,
137. 8.4...107. 8.5...88.
8.6...101, 107, 137. 9.1
...77, 169. 9.3...115.
9.6...76. Chs. 10-12...
169. 10.1...72, 105, 118.
Ch. 11 f...103. 11.1...91.
11.7...76. Ch. 12...103.
12.1...79. 12.1 ff...76.
13.1...76, 175. Ch. 14
...94. 14.1...70. 14.1 f...
179. 14.1-4...94. 14.3...
103. 14.3-5...107. 14.4
...160. 14.5...77, 158.
15.1...107. 16.2...105.
16.3...76. 17.1...67, 99.

86. 3. 31

李孝三